PEARSON CUSTOM
ANTHROPOLOGY

The Human Experience
An Introduction to Anthropology
2011 Edition for Vanier College

Managing Editor
Jeffrey H. Cohen
Ohio State University

Contributing Editors
Lee Cronk
Rutgers University (New Brunswick)

Martha Rees
Agnes Scott College

Donald C. Wood
Akita University Medical School

Randal Allison
Blinn College

Pearson Learning Solutions

New York   Boston   San Francisco
London   Toronto   Sydney   Tokyo   Singapore   Madrid
Mexico City   Munich   Paris   Cape Town   Hong Kong   Montreal

Senior Vice President, Editorial and Marketing: Patrick F. Boles
Editor: Ana Díaz-Caneja
Development Editor: Abbey Lee Briggs
Operations Manager: Eric M. Kenney
Production Manager: Jennifer Berry
Rights Manager: Jillian Santos
Art Director: Renée Sartell
Cover Designer: Kristen Kiley

Cover Art: Art Wolfe, "Karo Tribesman and Child" Courtesy of Corbis Photography/Veer Incorporated. "Tattooed Man Holding Baby" Courtesy of Art Wolfe/Veer Incorporated. "Cheering Fans" Courtesy of Corbis Photography/Veer Incorporated. "Alaska Native Eskimo Woman in Fur Parka" Courtesy of Canopy Photography/Veer Incorporated. "Portrait of an Asian woman holding up the palm of her hand which has henna patterns on it." Courtesy of Alloy Photography/Veer Incorporated. J. Rufenach, "Close up of man's face with lip ring" Courtesy of J. Rufenach/Veer Incorporated. Malcolm S. Kirk, "Mendi woman, New Guinea" Courtesy of Malcolm S. Kirk/Veer Incorporated. Grant Faint, "Karo tribe woman, portrait, close up" Courtesy of Grant Faint/Getty Images, Inc.

Please visit our website at *www.pearsoncustom.com*.

Attention Bookstores: For permission to return any unsold stock, contact us at *pe-uscustomreturns@pearson.com*.

Pearson Learning Solutions, 501 Boylston Street, Suite 900, Boston, MA 02116
A Pearson Education Company
www.pearsoned.com

ISBN 10: 0-558-88559-4
ISBN 13: 978-0-558-88559-5

Contents

CHAPTER 1

ANTHROPOLOGY AND THE STUDY OF CULTURE

Young boys on an outrigger canoe near one of the islands of New Ireland province in the northeastern part of Papua New Guinea. A preferred food source is shark, and some men are adept at "shark calling," which draws the shark near the boat so it can be speared and netted.

ANTHROPOLOGY AND THE STUDY OF CULTURE

the BIG questions

- ◆ What is anthropology?
- ◆ What is cultural anthropology?
- ◆ How is cultural anthropology relevant to a career?

A member of the Dani people, Irian Jaya, New Guinea, holding a stone adze, photographed in the 1990s.

Old bones, *Jurassic Park*, cannibalism, hidden treasure, *Indiana Jones and the Temple of Doom*. The popular impression of anthropology is based mainly on movies and television shows that depict anthropologists as adventurers and heroes. Many anthropologists do have adventures and discover

---

anthropology   the study of humanity, including prehistoric origins and contemporary human diversity.

biological anthropology or **physical anthropology** the study of humans as biological organisms, including evolution and contemporary variation.

archaeology or **prehistory**   the study of past human cultures through their material remains.

linguistic anthropology   the study of human communication, including its origins, history, and contemporary variation and change.

cultural anthropology or **social anthropology**   the study of living peoples and their cultures, including variation and change.

culture   people's learned and shared behavior and beliefs.

applied anthropology or **practicing anthropology** or **practical anthropology**   the use of anthropological knowledge to prevent or solve problems or to shape and achieve policy goals.

treasures such as ancient pottery, medicinal plants, and jade carvings. But most of their research is not glamorous. Some anthropologists spend years in difficult physical conditions searching for the earliest fossils of our ancestors. Others live among people in Silicon Valley, California, and study first-hand how they work and organize family life in a setting permeated by modern technology. Some anthropologists conduct laboratory analyses of the contents of tooth enamel to reveal where an individual once lived. Others study designs on prehistoric pottery to learn what the symbols mean, or observe nonhuman primates such as chimpanzees or orangutans in the wild to learn how they live.

Anthropology is the study of humanity, including prehistoric origins and contemporary human diversity. Compared to other disciplines that study humanity (such as history, psychology, economics, political science, and sociology), anthropology is broader in scope. Anthropology covers a much greater span of time than these disciplines and it encompasses a broader range of topics.

◆◆◆

Introducing Anthropology

In North America, anthropology is divided into four fields (see Figure 1) that focus on separate, but connected, subject matter related to humanity:

- **Biological anthropology** (or physical anthropology)—the study of humans as biological organisms, including evolution and contemporary variation.
- **Archaeology** (or prehistory)—the study of past human cultures through their material remains.

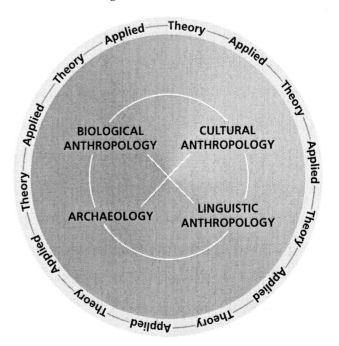

FIGURE 1   The Four Fields of Anthropology

A team of anthropologists and students discuss their research project on Silicon Valley culture.

▶ *If you were given a grant to conduct anthropological research, where would you go and what would you study?*

J. A. English-Lueck, Cofounder Silicon Valley Cultures Project

- **Linguistic anthropology**—the study of human communication, including its origins, history, and contemporary variation and change.
- **Cultural anthropology** (or social anthropology)—the study of living peoples and their cultures, including variation and change. **Culture** refers to people's learned and shared behaviors and beliefs.

Some anthropologists argue that a fifth field, applied anthropology, should be added. **Applied anthropology** (also called *practicing anthropology* or *practical anthropology*) is the use of anthropological knowledge to prevent or solve problems or to shape and achieve policy goals. The author of this book takes the position that the application of knowledge, just like theory, is an integral part of each of the four fields and should be integrated within each of them.

BIOLOGICAL OR PHYSICAL ANTHROPOLOGY

Biological anthropology encompasses three subfields. The first, *primatology*, is the study of the nonhuman members of the order of mammals called primates, which includes a wide range of animals from very small, nocturnal creatures to gorillas, the largest members. Primatologists study nonhuman primates in the wild and in captivity. They record and analyze how the animals spend their time, collect and share food, form social groups, rear offspring, develop leadership patterns, and experience conflict and conflict resolution. Primatologists are alarmed about the decline in numbers, and even extinction, of nonhuman primates. Many apply their knowledge to nonhuman primate conservation.

The second subfield is *paleoanthropology*, the study of human evolution on the basis of the fossil record. One important activity is the search for fossils to increase the amount and quality of the evidence related to the way human evolution occurred. Discoveries of new fossils provide "aha!" moments and arresting photographs for the covers of popular magazines. A less glamorous but equally important activity in paleoanthropology is dating and classifying new fossils.

The third subfield is the study of *contemporary human biological variation*. Anthropologists working in this area define, measure, and seek to explain differences in the biological makeup and behavior of contemporary humans. They study such biological factors as DNA within and across populations, body size and shape, human nutrition and disease, and human growth and development.

ARCHAEOLOGY

Archaeology means, literally, the "study of the old," but "the old" is limited to human culture. Therefore, the time-depth of archaeology goes back only to the beginnings of *Homo sapiens*, between 300,000–160,000 years ago when they first emerged in Africa. Archaeology encompasses two major areas: *prehistoric archaeology*, which concerns the human past before written records, and *historical archaeology*, which deals with the human

THINKING OUTSIDE THE BOX

What are your impressions of anthropology? How did you acquire them? Make notes of these impressions and review them at the end of the course.

past in societies that have written documents. Prehistoric archaeologists often identify themselves with broad geographic regions, studying, for example, Old World archaeology (Africa, Europe, and Asia) or New World archaeology (North, Central, and South Americas).

Another set of specialties within archaeology is based on the context in which the archaeology takes place. For example, *underwater archaeology* is the study of submerged archaeological sites. Underwater archaeological sites may be from either prehistoric or historic times. Some prehistoric sites include early human settlements in parts of Europe, such as household sites discovered in Switzerland that were once near lakes but are now submerged.

The archaeology of the recent past is another important research direction. *Industrial archaeology* focuses on changes in material culture and society during and since the Industrial Revolution. It is especially active in Great Britain, home of the Industrial Revolution. There, industrial archaeologists study such topics as the design of iron bridges, the growth and distribution of china potteries, miners' housing, and cotton mills. An important role of industrial archaeology is the conservation of industrial sites, which are more likely to be neglected or destroyed than are sites that have natural beauty or cultural glamour attached to them.

An example of what could be called the *archaeology of contemporary life* is the "Garbage Project" conducted by archaeologists at the University of Arizona at Tucson (Rathje and Murphy 1992). They have excavated part of the Fresh Kills landfill on Staten Island, near New York City. Its mass is estimated at 100 million tons and its volume at 2.9 billion cubic feet. Thus, it is one of the largest human-made

Maya people watch as forensic anthropologist Francisco de Leon conducts an exhumation of more than 50 bodies in a highland Guatemalan village in 1997.

▶ *Are courses in forensic anthropology offered at your school?*

Stephen Lubkemann, trained as a cultural anthropologist and an underwater archaeologist, documents the remains of the hull of DRTO-036, a vessel that wrecked in the Dry Tortugas in the midnineteenth century. The vessel lies within Dry Tortugas National Park in the Florida Keys.

▶ *You can access UNESCO's Convention on the Protection of Underwater Heritage on the Internet.*

Iron Bridge, England, is an important site of industrial archaeology. Considered the "birthplace of industry," the site includes the world's first iron bridge and remains of factories, furnaces, and canals.

▶ *Take a virtual tour of the site by going to http://www.ironbridge .org.uk/.*

structures in North America. Excavation of pop-top can tabs, disposable diapers, cosmetics containers, and telephone books reveals much about recent consumption patterns and how they affect the environment. One surprising finding is that the kinds of garbage people often blame for filling up land-fills, such as fast-food packaging and disposable diapers, cause less serious problems than paper. Newspaper, especially, is a major culprit because of sheer quantity. This information can improve recycling efforts worldwide. The Fresh Kills landfill continues to grow rapidly due to everyday trash accumulation and other, less common sources of debris, such as the remains from the World Trade Center in Manhattan following the 9/11 attack.

LINGUISTIC ANTHROPOLOGY

Linguistic anthropology is devoted to the study of communication, mainly (but not exclusively) among humans. Linguistic anthropology has three subfields: *historical linguistics*, the study of language change over time and how languages are related; *descriptive linguistics*, or structural linguistics, the study of how contemporary languages differ in terms of their formal structure; and *sociolinguistics*, the study of the relationships among social variation, social context, and linguistic variation, including nonverbal communication.

New directions in linguistic anthropology are connected to important current issues. First is a trend to study language in everyday use, or *discourse*, and how it relates to power structures at local, regional, and international levels (Duranti 1997a). In some contexts, powerful people speak more than less powerful people, whereas sometimes the more powerful people speak less. Power relations may also be expressed through intonation, word choice, and such nonverbal forms of communication as posture and dress. Second is increased attention to the role of information technology in communication,

especially the Internet and cell phones. Third is attention to the increasingly rapid extinction of indigenous languages and what can be done about it.

CULTURAL ANTHROPOLOGY

Cultural anthropology is the study of contemporary people and their cultures. It considers variations and similarities across cultures and how cultures change over time. Cultural anthropologists learn about culture by spending extended periods of time living with the people they study.

Prominent areas of specialization in cultural anthropology include economic anthropology, psychological anthropology, medical anthropology, political anthropology, and international development anthropology (the study of the effects and patterns of international development policies and plans in cross-cultural perspective). The rest of this book covers these and other topics.

APPLIED ANTHROPOLOGY: SEPARATE FIELD OR CROSS-CUTTING FOCUS?

In the United States, applied anthropology emerged during and after World War II. Its first concern was with improving the lives of contemporary peoples and their needs, and so it was more closely associated with cultural anthropology than with the other three fields.

Many anthropologists feel that applied anthropology should be considered a fifth field of anthropology, standing on its own. An alternative position is that the application of knowledge to solve problems, just like theory, should be part of each field (see Figure 1). This is the author's position, and

LESSONS applied

Orangutan Research Leads to Orangutan Advocacy

Primatologist Biruté Galdikas (beer-OOH-tay GAL-dee-kas) first went to Indonesia to study orangutans in 1971 (Galdikas 1995). She soon became aware of the threat to the orangutans from local people who, as a way of making money, capture them for sale to zoos around the world. The poachers separate the young from their mothers, often killing the mothers in the process.

Orangutan juveniles are highly dependent on their mothers, maintaining close bodily contact with them for at least two years and nursing until they are around 8 years old. Because of this long period of orangutans' need for maternal contact, Galdikas set up her camp to serve as a way station for orphans. She became the maternal figure. Her first "infant" was an orphaned orangutan, Sugito, who clung to her as though she were his own mother for years.

The survival of orangutans on Borneo and Sumatra (their only habitats worldwide) is critically endangered by massive commercial and illegal logging, population resettlement programs, plantations, and other pressures on the rainforests where the orangutans live. A **rainforest** is an environment found at mid-latitudes,

MAP 1 Orangutan Regions in Malaysia and Indonesia. Orangutans are the only great apes living outside Africa. Fossil evidence indicates that their habitats in the past extended throughout Southeast Asia and southern China. They are now limited to pockets of rainforest on the islands of Sumatra and Borneo.

of tall, broad-leaf evergreen trees, with annual rainfall of 400 centimeters (or 60 inches) and no dry season.

Galdikas is focusing her efforts on orangutan preservation. She says, "I feel like I'm viewing an animal holocaust and holocaust is not a word I use lightly. . . . The destruction of the tropical rainforest is accelerating daily" (Dreifus 2000:D3). Across all ranges, it is estimated that during the twentieth century the orangutan population experienced a huge decrease, from 315,000 in 1900 to 44,000 in 2000 (IUCN/SSC Conservation Breeding

Specialist Group 2004). Aerial surveys (Ancrenaz et al. 2005) and DNA analysis of living orangutans (Goossens et al. 2006) confirm recent and dramatic declines that, if not halted, will lead to extinction in the next few decades.

Galdikas has studied orangutans longer than anyone else. She links her knowledge of and love for the orangutans with applied anthropology and advocacy on their behalf. Since the beginning of her fieldwork in Borneo, she has maintained and expanded the Camp Leakey field site and research center (named after her mentor, Lewis

---

therefore many examples of applied anthropology appear throughout this book.

Applied anthropology is an important thread that weaves through all four fields of anthropology:

- Archaeologists are employed in *cultural resource management (CRM)*, assessing the presence of possible archaeological remains before construction projects such as roads and buildings can proceed.
- Biological anthropologists are employed as *forensic anthropologists*, participating in criminal investigations

through laboratory work identifying bodily remains. Others work in the area of primate conservation (see Lessons Applied box).

- Linguistic anthropologists consult with educational institutions about how to improve standardized tests for bilingual populations and conduct policy research for governments.
- Cultural anthropologists apply their knowledge to improve policies and programs in every domain of life, including education, health care, business, poverty reduction, and conflict prevention and resolution.

Applied roles of anthropologists are illustrated in the Anthropology Works profiles at the beginning of each of the five parts of this book and in the Lessons Applied boxes.

---

rainforest an environment, found at mid-latitudes, of tall, broad-leaf evergreen trees, with annual rainfall of 400 centimeters (or 60 inches) and no dry season.

(LEFT) Lowland rainforest in Borneo in the morning mist. (RIGHT) Biruté Galdikas has been studying orangutans in Borneo, Indonesia, for over three decades and is an active supporter of conservation of their habitat.

▶ *Learn about her work and the status of wild orangutans by searching on the Web.*

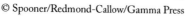

Leakey, who inspired her research on orangutans). In 1986, she co-founded the Orangutan Foundation International (OFI), which now has several chapters worldwide. She has published scholarly articles and given public talks around the world on her research. Educating the public about the imminent danger to the orangutans is an important part of her activism. Galdikas and other orangutan experts are lobbying international institutions such as the World Bank to promote forest conservation as part of their loan agreements.

Camp Leakey employs many local people in diverse roles, including anti-poaching guards. The OFI sponsors study tours to Borneo for international students and opportunities for them to contribute to conservation efforts.

The success of Galdikas's activism depends on her deep knowledge of orangutans. Over the decades, she has filled thousands of notebooks with her observations of orangutan behavior, along with such details about their habitat as the fruiting times of different species of trees. A donor recently gave software and funding for staff to

analyze the raw data (Hawn 2002). The findings will indicate how much territory is needed to support a viable orangutan population. In turn, these findings will facilitate conservation policy and planning.

◆ **FOOD FOR THOUGHT**

* Some people claim that science should not be linked with advocacy because it will create biases in research. Others say that scientists have an obligation to use their knowledge for good causes. Where do you stand in this debate and why?

◆◆◆
Introducing Cultural Anthropology

Cultural anthropology is devoted to studying human cultures worldwide, both their similarities and differences. Cultural anthropology makes "the strange familiar and the familiar strange" (Spiro 1990). Therefore, it teaches us to look at ourselves from the "outside" as a somewhat "strange" culture. A good example of making the familiar strange is the case of the Nacirema, a culture first described in 1956:

> The Nacirema are a North American group living in the territory between the Canadian Cree, the Yaqui and the Tarahumara of Mexico, and the Carib and the Arawak of

the Antilles. Little is known of their origin, though tradition states that they came from the east. According to Nacirema mythology, their nation was originated by a culture hero, Notgnihsaw, who is otherwise known for two great feats of strength—the throwing of a piece of wampum across the river Pa-To-Mac and the chopping down of a cherry tree in which the Spirit of Truth resided. (Miner 1965 [1956]:415)

The anthropologist goes on to describe the Nacirema's intense focus on the human body and their many private rituals. He provides a detailed account of a daily ritual performed within the home in a specially constructed shrine area:

> The focal point of the shrine is a box or chest which is built into the wall. In this chest are kept the many charms

and magical potions without which no native believes he could live. These preparations are secured from a variety of specialized practitioners. The most powerful of these are the medicine men, whose assistance must be rewarded with substantial gifts. . . . Beneath the charm box is a small font. Each day every member of the family, in succession, enters the shrine room, bows his head before the charm-box, mingles different sorts of holy water in the font, and proceeds with a brief rite of ablution. (1965:415–416)

If you do not recognize this tribe, try spelling its name backwards. (*Note:* Please forgive Miner for his use of the masculine pronoun in describing Nacirema society in general; his writings are several decades old.)

This section provides an overview of cultural anthropology's history and theoretical foundations. It also introduces the concept of culture, important cultural categories, distinctive features of cultural anthropology, and three major debates in cultural anthropology.

A BRIEF HISTORY OF CULTURAL ANTHROPOLOGY

The beginning of cultural anthropology goes back to writers such as Herodotus (fifth century BCE; note: BCE stands for "Before the Common Era," a secular transformation of BC, or "Before Christ"), Marco Polo (thirteenth to fourteenth centuries), and Ibn Khaldun (fourteenth century), who traveled extensively and wrote reports about cultures they encountered. More recent conceptual roots are found in writers of the French Enlightenment, such as philosopher Charles Montesquieu, who wrote in the first half of the eighteenth century. His book *The Spirit of the Laws,* published in 1748 [1949], discussed the temperament, appearance, and government of various people around the world. He explained cultural differences as due to the different climates in which people lived (Barnard 2000: 22ff). European colonial expansion prompted Enlightenment thinkers to question the accuracy of the biblical narrative of human origins. The Bible does not, for example, mention the existence of people in the New World.

FIGURE 2 Key Contributors to Cultural Anthropology

Late Nineteenth Century	
Sir Edward Tylor	Armchair anthropology, first definition of culture
Sir James Frazer	Armchair anthropology, comparative study of religion
Lewis Henry Morgan	Insider's view, cultural evolution, comparative method
Early Twentieth Century	
Bronislaw Malinowski	Functionalism, holism, participant observation
Franz Boas	Cultural relativism, historical particularism, advocacy
Margaret Mead	Personality and culture, cultural constructionism, public anthropology
Ruth Benedict	Personality and culture, national character studies
Zora Neale Hurston	Black culture, women's roles, ethnographic novels
Mid- and Late Twentieth Century and Early Twenty-First Century	
Claude Lévi-Strauss	Symbolic analysis, French structuralism
Beatrice Medicine	Native American anthropology
Eleanor Leacock	Anthropology of colonialism and indigenous peoples
Marvin Harris	Cultural materialism, comparison, theory building
Mary Douglas	Symbolic anthropology
Michelle Rosaldo	Feminist anthropology
Clifford Geertz	Interpretive anthropology, thick description of local culture
Laura Nader	Legal anthropology, "studying up"
George Marcus	Critique of culture, critique of cultural anthropology
Gilbert Herdt	Gay anthropology
Nancy Scheper-Hughes	Critical medical anthropology
Leith Mullings	Anti-racist anthropology
Sally Engle Merry	Globalization and human rights

Two giants in the history of anthropology. (LEFT) Franz Boas emphasized the four-field approach and the principle of cultural relativism. (RIGHT) Margaret Mead, a student of Boas at Columbia University, moved the Boasian legacy forward by her pioneering research on the cultural construction of personality and gender.

In the second half of the nineteenth century, the discovery of the principles of biological evolution by Charles Darwin and others offered for the first time a scientific explanation for human origins. Biological *evolution* says that early forms evolve into later forms through the process of natural selection, whereby the most biologically fit organisms survive to reproduce while those that are less fit die out. Darwin's model is thus one of continuous progress of increasing fitness through struggle among competing organisms. The concept of evolution was important in the thinking of early cultural anthropologists.

The most important founding figures of cultural anthropology in the late eighteenth and early nineteenth centuries were Sir Edward Tylor and Sir James Frazer in England and Lewis Henry Morgan in the United States. Inspired by the concept of biological evolution, they developed a model of cultural evolution whereby all cultures evolve from lower to higher forms over time. This view placed non-Western peoples at a "primitive" stage and Euro-American culture as "civilization" and assumed that non-Western cultures would either catch up to the level of Western civilization or die out.

Polish-born Bronislaw Malinowski is a major figure in modern cultural anthropology. In the first half of the twentieth century, he established a theoretical approach called **functionalism**: the view that a culture is similar to a biological organism, in which parts work to support the operation and maintenance of the whole. Religion and family

organization, for example, contribute to the functioning of the whole culture. Functionalism is linked to the concept of **holism**, the view that one must study all aspects of a culture in order to understand it.

Franz Boas is considered the founder of North American cultural anthropology. Born in Germany and educated in physics and geography, he came to the United States in 1887 (Patterson 2001:46ff). He brought with him a skepticism toward Western science gained from a year's study with the Inuit, the indigenous people of Baffin Island. He learned from the Inuit that people in different cultures may have different perceptions of even basic physical substances, such as "water." Boas came to recognize the individuality and validity of different cultures. He introduced the now widely known concept of **cultural relativism,** or the view that each culture must be understood in terms of the values and ideas of that culture and not be judged by the standards of

---

functionalism   the theory that a culture is similar to a biological organism, in which parts work to support the operation and maintenance of the whole.

holism   the perspective in anthropology that cultures are complex systems that cannot be fully understood without paying attention to their different components, including economics, social organization, and ideology.

cultural relativism   the perspective that each culture must be understood in terms of the values and ideas of that culture and should not be judged by the standards of another.

another. According to Boas, no culture is more advanced than another. His position thus contrasted markedly with that of the nineteenth-century cultural evolutionists.

Margaret Mead is Boas's most famous student. She contributed to knowledge of South Pacific cultures, gender roles, and the impact of child-rearing practices on personality. Her scholarly works as well as her columns in popular magazines had wide influence on U.S. child-care patterns in the 1950s. Mead was thus an early *public anthropologist* who took seriously the importance of bringing cultural anthropology knowledge to the general public in order to create positive social change.

Following World War II, cultural anthropology in the United States expanded substantially in terms of the number of trained anthropologists and departments of anthropology in colleges and universities. Along with this growth came increased theoretical diversity. Several anthropologists developed theories of culture based on environmental factors. They suggested that similar environments (for example, deserts or tropical rainforests or mountains) would predictably lead to the emergence of similar cultures.

At the same time, French anthropologist Claude Lévi-Strauss was developing a quite different theoretical perspective, known as *French structuralism*. He maintained that the best way to understand a culture is to collect its myths and stories and analyze the underlying themes in them. French structuralism inspired the development of *symbolic anthropology*, or the study of culture as a system of meanings, which was especially prominent in the United States in the latter part of the twentieth century.

In the 1960s, Marxist theory emerged in anthropology, stating the importance of people's access to the means of production. It inspired the emergence of a new theoretical school in the United States called **cultural materialism**. Cultural materialism is an approach to studying culture by emphasizing the material aspects of life, especially the natural environment and how people make a living. Also arising in the 1960s was the theoretical position referred to as **interpretive anthropology**, or intepretivism. This perspective developed from both U.S. symbolic anthropology and French structural anthropology. It says that understanding culture should focus on what people think about, their ideas, and the symbols and meanings that are important to them. These two positions will be discussed further later in this section.

Since the 1990s, two other theoretical directions have gained prominence. Both are influenced by *postmodernism,* an intellectual pursuit that asks whether modernity is truly progress and that questions such aspects of modernism as the scientific method, urbanization, technological change, and mass communication. The first theory is termed **structurism** (the author coined this term), the view that powerful structures such as economics, politics, and media shape cultures, influencing how people behave and think, even when they don't realize it. The second theory emphasizes human **agency**, or free will, and the power of individuals to create and change culture by acting against structures. These two positions are revisited at the end of this section.

Cultural anthropology continues to be rethought and refashioned. Over the past few decades, several new theoretical perspectives have transformed and enriched the field. *Feminist anthropology* is a perspective that emphasizes the need to study female roles and gender-based inequality. In the 1970s, early feminist anthropologists realized that anthropology had overlooked women. To address this gap, feminist anthropologists undertook research that explicitly focused on women and girls, that is, half of the world's people. A related area is *gay and lesbian anthropology,* or *queer anthropology,* a perspective that emphasizes the need to study gay people's cultures and discrimination based on sexual identity and preferences. Findings from both these areas are presented in this book.

In North American anthropology, African American, Latino, and Native American anthropologists are increasing in number and visibility. Yet anthropology in North America and Europe remains one of the "whitest" professions (Shanklin 2000). Some steps for moving the discipline toward *anti-racist anthropology* include these (Mullings 2005):

- Examine and recognize anthropology's history of and implications with racism.
- Work to increase diversity of professors, researchers, staff, and students in the discipline.
- Teach about racism in anthropology classes and textbooks.

Worldwide, non-Western anthropologists are increasingly questioning the dominance of Euro-American anthropology and offering new perspectives (Kuwayama 2004). Their work provides useful critiques of anthropology as a largely Western-defined discipline and promises to lead it in new directions in the future.

---

cultural materialism   a theoretical position that takes material features of life, such as the environment, natural resources, and mode of production, as the bases for explaining social organization and ideology.

interpretive anthropology or **interpretivism**   the view that cultures can be understood by studying what people think about, their ideas, and the meanings that are important to them.

structurism   a theoretical position concerning human behavior and ideas that says large forces such as the economy, social and political organization, and the media shape what people do and think.

agency   the ability of humans to make choices and exercise free will even within dominating structures.

microculture   a distinct pattern of learned and shared behavior and thinking found within larger cultures.

Colombian anthropologist Patricia Tovar (center) at an anthropology conference in Colombia. In Central and South America, applied anthropology is an integral part of cultural anthropology.

Patricia Tovar

THE CONCEPT OF CULTURE

Although cultural anthropologists are united in the study of culture, the question of how to define it has been debated for decades. This section discusses definitions of culture today, characteristics of culture, and bases for cultural identity.

DEFINITIONS OF CULTURE Culture is the core concept in cultural anthropology, so it might seem likely that cultural anthropologists would agree about what it is. In the 1950s, an effort to collect definitions of culture produced 164 different ones (Kroeber and Kluckhohn 1952). Since then, no one has tried to count the number of definitions of culture used by anthropologists.

British anthropologist Sir Edward Tylor proposed the first definition in 1871. He stated, "Culture, or civilization . . . is that complex whole which includes knowledge, belief, art, law, morals, custom, and any other capabilities and habits acquired by man as a member of society" (Kroeber and Kluckhohn 1952:81). The phrase "that complex whole" has been the most durable feature of his definition. Two other features of Tylor's definition have not stood the test of time. First, most anthropologists now avoid using the word man to refer to all humans; instead, they use generic words such as *people* and humans. One may argue that the word man can be used generically according to its linguistic roots, but this usage can be ambiguous. Second, most anthropologists no longer equate culture with civilization. The word *civilization* implies a sense of "highness" versus noncivilized "lowness" and sets up a distinction placing "us" (people of the so-called civilized regions) in a superior position to "them."

In contemporary cultural anthropology, the cultural materialists and the interpretive anthropologists support two different definitions of culture. Cultural materialist Marvin Harris says, "A culture is the total socially acquired life-way or life-style of a group of people. It consists of the patterned repetitive ways of thinking, feeling, and acting that are characteristic of the members of a particular society or segment of society" (1975:144). In contrast, Clifford Geertz, speaking for the interpretivists, believes that culture consists of symbols, motivations, moods, and thoughts. This definition focuses on people's perceptions, thoughts, and ideas and does not include behavior as a part of culture. The definition of culture used in this book is that culture is learned and shared behavior and beliefs, and thus is broader than Geertz's definition.

Culture exists among all human beings. It is something that all humans have. Some anthropologists refer to this universal concept of culture as *Culture* with a capital *C*. Culture also exists in a more specific way. The term **microculture**, or local culture, refers to distinct patterns of learned and shared behavior and ideas found in local regions and among particular groups. Microcultures are based on ethnicity, gender, age, and more.

THINKING
OUTSIDE
THE BOX

This brief history of cultural anthropology describes early contributions by anthropologists, most of whom were white, European or Euro-American, and male. Compare this pattern with the history of some other discipline you have studied. What are some similarities and differences?

Two prominent American cultural anthropologists of the twentieth century anthropology in North America. (LEFT) Marvin Harris argued for a cultural materialist/political economy perspective on understanding culture and an emphasis on deductive methods. Throughout the later twentieth century, Harris had frequent debates with Clifford Geertz (RIGHT), who championed a perspective on understanding culture informed by symbolic anthropology and an emphasis on meaning, text, and narrative and an inductive method.

CHARACTERISTICS OF CULTURE Understanding of the complex concept of culture can be gained by looking at its characteristics.

CULTURE IS NOT THE SAME AS NATURE The relationship between nature and culture is of great interest to cultural anthropologists in their quest to understand people's behavior and thinking. This book emphasizes the importance of culture.

Obviously, culture and nature are intertwined and often difficult to separate in terms of their effects. For example, certain aspects of biology affect people's behavior and lifestyle, such as being HIV-positive. But it is impossible to predict how a person who is HIV-positive will fare in Culture A versus Culture B. Different cultural contexts shape matters such as labeling and negative stereotypes and access to care and support. A good way to see how culture diverges from, and shapes, nature is to consider basic natural demands of life within different cultural contexts. Universal human functions that everyone must perform to stay alive are

- Eating
- Drinking
- Sleeping
- Eliminating

You may wonder about requirements for shelter and clothing. They vary, depending on the climate, so they are not included on this list. You may also wonder about sexual intercourse. It is not necessary for individual survival, so it is not included on this list, but it is discussed elsewhere in this book. Given the primary importance of these four functions in supporting a human being's life, it seems logical that people would fulfill them in similar ways everywhere. But that is not the case.

Eating Culture shapes what people eat, how they eat, when they eat, and the meanings of food and eating. Culture also defines foods that are acceptable and unacceptable. In China, most people think that cheese is disgusting, but in France, most people love cheese. Throughout China, pork is a widely favored meat. The religions of Judaism and Islam, in contrast, forbid consumption of pork. In many cultures where gathering wild plant foods, hunting, and fishing are important, people value the freshness of food. They would consider a package of frozen food on a grocery store shelf as way past its time.

Perceptions of taste vary dramatically. Western researchers have defined four supposedly universal taste categories: sweet, sour, bitter, and salty. Cross-cultural research disproves these as universals. For example, the Weyéwa people of the highlands of Sumba, Indonesia (see Map 2), define seven categories of flavor: sour, sweet, salty, bitter, tart, bland, and pungent (Kuipers 1991).

How to eat is also an important aspect of food behavior. Rules about proper ways to eat are one of the first things

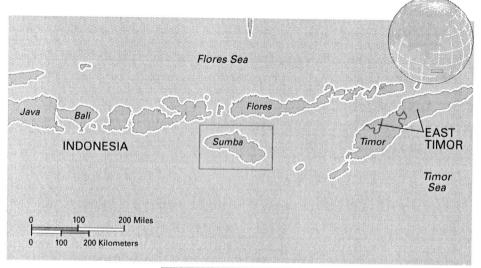

MAP 2 Weyéwa Region in Indonesia.
Sumba, one of Indonesia's many islands, is 75 miles long. The Weyéwa people number about 85,000 and live in small settlements on grassy plateaus in the western part of the island. They grow rice, maize, and millet, and they raise water buffaloes and pigs.

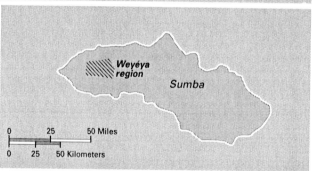

a person needs to learn when living in another culture. Dining rules in India require using only the right hand. The left hand is considered polluted because it is used for personal cleansing after elimination. A person's clean right hand is the preferred eating utensil. Silverware that has been touched by others, even though it has been washed, is considered unclean. In some cultures, it is important to eat only from one's own plate, whereas in others, eating from a shared central platter is considered proper.

Another area of cultural variation involves who is responsible for cooking and serving food. In many cultures, domestic cooking is women's responsibility, but cooking for public feasts is more often something that men do. Power issues may arise about who cooks what for whom (see Everyday Anthropology).

Drinking Cross-cultural variations related to drinking are also complex. Every culture defines the appropriate substances to drink, when to drink and with whom, and the meanings of the beverages and drinking occasions. French culture allows for consumption of relatively large amounts of table wine with family meals, including lunch. In the United States, water is generally served and consumed during family meals. In India, water is served and consumed at the end of the meal. Around the world, different categories of people drink different beverages. In cultures where alcoholic beverages are consumed, men tend to consume more than women.

Culture often defines the meaning of particular drinks and the style of drinking and serving them. Social drinking—whether the beverage is coffee, beer, or vodka—creates and reinforces bonds. Beer-drinking rituals in U.S. college fraternities

© Michael Newman/PhotoEdit

Ethiopian women dining at an Ethiopian restaurant. The main meal consists of several meat and vegetable dishes, cooked with special spices and laid out on injera bread, a soft flat bread that is torn into small pieces and used to wrap bite-sized bits of meat and vegetables. The entire meal can be eaten without utensils.

▶ *How does this dining scene resemble or differ from a recent meal that you have had in a restaurant?*

everyday ANTHROPOLOGY

Latina Power in the Kitchen

Within a family, cooking food for other members can be a sign of love and devotion. It may carry a message that love and devotion are expected in return.

Among Tejano migrant farm workers in the United States, preparing tamales is a symbol of a woman's commitment to her family and thus of the "good wife" (Williams 1984). The Tejanos are people of Mexican descent who live in Texas. Some of them move to Illinois in the summer, where they are employed as migrant workers.

For Tejanos, tamales are a central cultural identity marker. Tamales contain a rich inner mash of pig's head meat wrapped in corn husks. Making tamales is extremely time consuming, and it is women's work. Typically, several women work together over a few days to do the necessary tasks: buying the pigs' heads, stripping the meat, preparing the stuffing, wrapping the stuffing with the corn husks, and baking or boiling the tamale.

Tamales symbolize and emphasize women's nurturance of their husbands. One elderly woman, at home in Texas for Christmas, made 200 tamales with her daughters-in-law, nieces, and god-daughter. They distributed the tamales to friends, relatives, and local taverns. The effort and expense involved were enormous. But for the women, it was worth it. Through their tamale making, they celebrate the holiday, build ties with people whom they may need to call on for support, and maintain communication with tavern owners so they will watch over male kin who drink at their bars.

Tejano woman also use tamale making as a statement of domestic protest. A woman who is dissatisfied with her husband's behavior will refuse

Philip Gould/CORBIS

Tamales consist of fried meat and peppers in a cornmeal dough that is encased in cornhusks.

▶ *What is a similarly important food item in your cultural world?*

to make tamales, a serious statement on her part. The link between being a good wife and making tamales is strong, and so a husband can take his wife's unwillingness to make tamales as grounds for divorce. One young Tejano sued his wife for divorce in Illinois on the grounds that she refused to cook tamales for him, in addition to

dancing with other men at fiestas. The judge refused to grant a divorce.

◆ FOOD FOR THOUGHT

- Provide an example from your microcultural experience about food being used as a way of expressing social solidarity or social protest.

are a good example. In an ethnographic film entitled *Salamanders,* filmed at a large university in the northeastern United States, the fraternity brothers run to various "stations" in the fraternity house, downing a beer at each (Hornbein and Hornbein 1992). At one point, a brother chugs a beer, turns

with a stagger toward the next station, falls flat on his face, and passes out. The movie documents another drinking ritual in which both young men and women at fraternity parties swallow live salamanders, sometimes two or three at a time, with large gulps of beer (this practice is now forbidden by law).

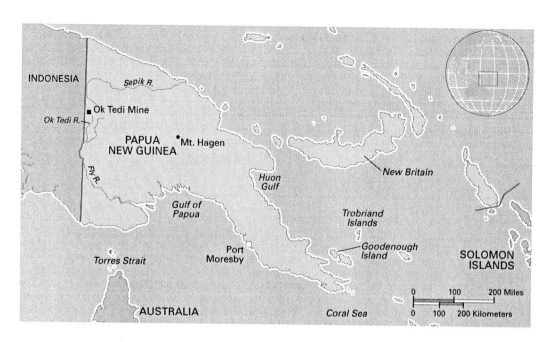

MAP 3 Papua New Guinea.
The Independent State of Papua New Guinea gained its autonomy from Australia in 1975. Mostly mountainous with coastal lowlands, PNG is richly endowed with gold, copper, silver, natural gas, timber, oil, and fisheries. Its population is around 5,700,000. Port Moresby, the capital, has a high rate of HIV/AIDS infection among the working-age population.

Sleeping Common sense might say that sleep is the one natural function that is not shaped by culture, because people tend to do it at least once every 24 hours, everyone shuts their eyes to do it, everyone lies down to do it, and most people sleep at night. Going without sleep for an extended period can lead to insanity and even death.

Sleep, however, is at least as much culturally shaped as it is biologically determined. Cultural influences on sleep include the questions of who sleeps with whom, how much sleep a person should have, and why some people have insomnia or what are called sleep disorders. Across cultures, marked variation exists in rules about where infants and children should sleep: with the mother, with both parents, or by themselves in a separate room? Among indigenous peoples of the Amazon region of South America, mothers and babies share the same hammock for many months, and breastfeeding occurs whenever the baby is hungry.

Culture shapes the amount of time a person sleeps. In rural India, women sleep fewer hours than men because they have to get up early to start the fire for the morning meal. In fast-track, corporate North America, "type A" males sleep relatively few hours and are proud of that fact—to sleep too much is to be a wimp. A disorder in Japan called *excessive daytime sleepiness* (EDS) is common in Tokyo and other large cities (Doi and Minowa 2003). Excessive sleepiness is correlated with more accidents on the job, more absenteeism, decreased productivity, deteriorated personal and professional relationships, and increased rates of illness and death. Women are almost twice as likely as men to experience EDS, and married women are especially vulnerable.

Eliminating Given its basic importance in cross-cultural experience, it is ironic that elimination receives little attention (in print) from anthropologists. Anyone who has traveled internationally knows that there is much to learn about elimination when in an unfamiliar context.

The first question is where to eliminate. Differences emerge in the degree to which elimination is a private act or can be done in more or less public areas. In many European cities, public options include street urinals for males but not for females. In most villages in India, houses do not have interior bathrooms. Instead, early in the morning, groups of women and girls leave the house and head for a certain field where they squat and chat. Men go to a different area. Everyone carries, in their left hand, a small brass pot full of water with which they splash themselves clean. Think about the ecological advantages: This system adds fertilizer to the fields and leaves no paper litter. Westerners may consider the village practice unclean and unpleasant, but village-dwelling people in India would think that the Western system is unsanitary because using toilet paper does not clean one as well as water, and they would find the practice of sitting on a toilet less comfortable than squatting.

In many cultures, the products of elimination (urine and feces) are considered polluting and disgusting. Among some groups in Papua New Guinea (see Map 3), people take great care to bury or otherwise hide their fecal matter for fear that someone will find it and use it for magic against them.

A negative assessment of the products of elimination is not universal, however. Among some Native American cultures of the Pacific Northwest region of Canada and the United States, urine, especially women's urine, was believed to have medicinal and cleansing properties and was considered the "water of life" (Furst 1989). In some death rituals, it was sprinkled over the corpse in the hope that it might rejuvenate the deceased. People stored urine in special wooden boxes for ritual use, including for a baby's first bath (the urine was mixed with water).

CULTURE IS BASED ON SYMBOLS   Our entire lives—from eating breakfast to greeting our friends, making money, creating art, and practicing religion—are based on and organized through symbols. A **symbol** is an object, word, or action with a culturally defined meaning that stands for something else with which it has no necessary or natural relationship. Symbols are arbitrary (bearing no necessary relationship to that which is symbolized), unpredictable, and diverse. Because symbols are arbitrary, it is impossible to predict how a particular culture will symbolize something. Although one might assume that people who are hungry would have an expression for hunger involving their stomach, no one could predict that in Hindi, the language of northern India, a colloquial expression for being hungry is saying that "rats are jumping in my stomach." The linguistic history of *Barbara*—the name of the author of this book—reveals that originally, in the Greek, it referred to people who were outsiders, "barbarians," and, by extension, uncivilized and savage. On top of that, the Greek term referred to such people as "bearded." The symbolic content of the American name Barbara does not immediately convey a sense of beardedness in its current context because symbolic meaning can change. It is through symbols, arbitrary and amazingly rich in their attributions, that culture is shared, stored, and transmitted over time.

CULTURE IS LEARNED   Because culture is based on symbols that are arbitrary, culture must be learned anew in each context. Cultural learning begins from the moment of birth, if not before (some people think that an unborn baby takes in and stores information through sounds heard from

Barbara Miller

In India, a white sari (women's garment) symbolizes widowhood.
▶ *What might these women think about the Western custom of a bride wearing white?*

the outside world). A large but unknown amount of people's cultural learning is unconscious, occurring as a normal part of life through observation. Schools, in contrast, are a formal way to learn culture. Not all cultures throughout history have been exposed to formal schooling. Instead, children learn appropriate cultural patterns through guidance from elders and by observation and practice. Hearing stories and seeing performances of rituals and dramas are other long-standing forms of learning.

CULTURES ARE INTEGRATED   To state that cultures are internally integrated is to assert the principle of holism. Thus, studying only one or two aspects of culture provides understanding so limited that it is more likely to be misleading or wrong than more comprehensive approaches.

Consider what would happen if a researcher were to study intertribal warfare in highland Papua New Guinea (see Map 3) and focused only on the actual practice of warfare without examining other aspects of culture. A key feature of highland culture is the exchange of pigs at political feasts. To become a political leader, a man must acquire many pigs. Pigs eat yams, which men grow, but pigs are cared for by women. This division of labor means that a man with more than one wife will be able to maintain more pigs and rise politically by giving more feasts. Such feasting enhances an aspiring leader's status and makes his guests indebted to him. With more followers attracted through feasting, a leader can gather forces and wage war on neighboring villages. Success in war brings gains in territory. So far, this example pays attention mainly to economics, politics, and marriage systems. But other aspects

symbol   an object, word, or action with culturally defined meaning that stands for something else; most symbols are arbitrary.

globalization   increased and intensified international ties related to the spread of Western, especially United States, capitalism that affects all world cultures.

localization   the transformation of global culture by local cultures into something new.

class   a way of categorizing people on the basis of their economic position in society, usually measured in terms of income or wealth.

Clash of civilizations	Conflict model
McDonaldization	Takeover and homogenization model
Hybridization	Blending model
Localization	Local cultural remaking and transformation of global culture

FIGURE 3 Four Models of Cultural Interaction

of culture are involved, too. Supernatural powers affect the success of warfare. Painting spears and shields with particular designs is believed to increase their power. At feasts and marriages, body decoration (including paint, shell ornaments, and elaborate feather headdresses) is an important expression of identity and status. Looking at warfare without attention to its wider cultural context yields an extremely narrow view.

Cultural integration is relevant to applied anthropologists interested in proposing ways to promote positive change. Years of experience show that introducing programs for change in one aspect of culture without considering their effects in other domains is often detrimental to the welfare and survival of a culture. For example, Western missionaries and colonialists in parts of Southeast Asia banned the practice of head-hunting. This practice was connected to many other aspects of the people's culture, including politics, religion, and psychology (a man's sense of identity as a man sometimes depended on the taking of a head). Stopping head-hunting might seem like a good thing, but its cessation had disastrous consequences for the cultures in which it was practiced.

CULTURES INTERACT AND CHANGE   Cultures interact with each other and change each other through contact such as trade networks, international development projects, telecommunications, education, migration, and tourism. **Globalization**, the process of intense global interconnectedness and movement of goods, information, and people, is a major force of contemporary cultural change. It has gained momentum through recent technological change, especially the boom in information and communications technologies.

Globalization does not spread evenly, and its interactions with and effects on local cultures vary substantially from positive change to cultural destruction and extinction. Four models of cultural interaction capture some of the variation (see Figure 3).

The *clash of civilizations* argument says that the spread of Euro-American capitalism and lifeways throughout the world has created disenchantment, alienation, and resentment among other cultural systems. This model divides the world into the "West and the rest."

The *McDonaldization* model says that, under the powerful influence of U.S.-dominated corporate culture, the world is becoming culturally homogeneous. "Fast-food culture," with its principles of mass production, speed, standardization, and impersonal service, is taken to be at the center of this new global culture.

Hybridization, also called *syncretism* and *creolization*, occurs when aspects of two or more cultures combine to form something new—a blend. In Japan, for instance, a grandmother might bow in gratitude to an automated banking machine. In the Amazon region and in the Arctic, indigenous people use satellite imagery to map and protect the boundaries of their ancestral lands.

A fourth pattern is **localization**, the transformation of global culture by local microcultures into something new. Consider the example of McDonald's restaurants. In many Asian settings, people resist the pattern of eating quickly and insist on leisurely family gatherings (Watson 1997). The McDonald's managers accommodate and alter the pace of service to allow for a slower turnover of tables. In Riyadh, Saudi Arabia, McDonald's provides separate areas for families and for heterosexual couples. Many other examples of cultural localization exist, throwing into question the notion that a form of Western "mono-culture" is taking over the entire world and erasing cultural diversity.

MULTIPLE CULTURAL WORLDS

Within large cultures, a variety of microcultures exist, as discussed in this section (see Figure 4). A particular individual in such a complex situation is likely to be a member of several microcultures. Microcultures may overlap or may be related to each other hierarchically in terms of power, status, and rights.

In discussing microcultures, the contrast between *difference* and *hierarchy* is important. People and groups can be considered different from each other in terms of a particular characteristic, but they may or may not be unequal on the basis of it. For example, people with blue or brown eyes might be recognized as different, but this difference does not entail unequal treatment or status. In other instances, such differences do become the basis for inequality.

CLASS   **Class** is a category based on people's economic position in society, usually measured in terms of income or wealth and exhibited in terms of lifestyle. Class societies may be divided into upper, middle, and lower classes. Separate classes are, for example, the working class (people who trade their labor for wages) and the landowning class (people who

Class	Gender and sexuality
"Race"	Age
Ethnicity and indigeneity	Institution

FIGURE 4   Some Bases of Microcultures

A view into the yard of a house in a low-income neighborhood of Kingston, Jamaica. People in these neighborhoods prefer the term "low-income" to "poor."

own land on which they or others labor). Classes are related in a hierarchical system, with upper classes dominating lower classes. Class struggle, in the classic Marxist view, is inevitable as those at the top seek to maintain their position while those at the bottom seek to improve theirs. People at the bottom may attempt to improve their class position by gaining access to resources and by adopting aspects of upper-class symbolic behavior, such as speech, dress, and leisure and recreation.

Class is a recent social development in human history, extending back in time for only about 10,000 years, and still not found in some remote local cultures. Among the few relatively undisturbed groups of indigenous peoples, everyone has equal wealth, and sharing food and other resources among the group is expected.

"RACE," ETHNICITY, AND INDIGENOUS PEOPLES
"Race" refers to groups of people with supposedly homogeneous biological traits. The term "race" is extremely complicated

---

"race" a classification of people into groups on the basis of supposedly homogeneous and largely superficial biological traits such as skin color or hair characteristics.

ethnicity a shared sense of identity among a group based on a heritage, language, or culture.

indigenous people groups who have a long-standing connection with their home territory that predates colonial or outside societies that prevail in that territory.

gender culturally constructed and learned behaviors and ideas attributed to males, females, or blended genders.

as it is used in diverse ways in different parts of the world and among different groups of people. Therefore, it makes sense to put the word in quotation marks in order to highlight its multiple meanings. In South Africa, as in the United States, "race" is mainly defined on the basis of skin color. In pre–twentieth-century China, body hair was the key biological basis for racial classification (Dikötter 1998). The "barbarian" races had more body hair than the "civilized" Chinese people. Chinese writers referred to bearded, male missionaries from Europe as "hairy barbarians." Into the twentieth century, some Chinese anthropologists divided humans into evolutionary stages on the basis of amounts of body hair.

Anthropological and other scientific research demonstrates that biological features do not explain or account for a person's behavior or lifestyle. Rather than being a biological category, racial classifications are cultural constructions. They are often associated with discrimination against and cruelty toward those "races" considered less worthy by those in power.

Ethnicity refers to a shared sense of identity among a group based on a heritage, language, or culture. Examples include African Americans and Italian Americans in the United States, the Croats of Eastern Europe, the Han of China, and the Hutu and Tutsi of Rwanda. This sense of identity may be expressed through political movements to gain or protect group rights and recognition or more quietly stated in how one lives one's daily life. Compared to the term "race," "ethnicity" appears to be a more neutral, less stigmatizing term. But it, too, has been, and still is, a basis for discrimination, segregation, and oppression. The "ethnic cleansing" campaigns conducted in the early 1990s by the Serbs against Muslims in the former Yugoslavia are an extreme case of ethnic discrimination. In China, Han ethnic domination over minority ethnic groups has been a reality for centuries. Han political repression of the Tibetan people prompted thousands of Tibetans to flee their homeland. Living in exile, they struggle to keep their ethnic heritage alive.

Indigenous people, following guidelines laid down by the United Nations, are defined as groups who have a long-standing connection with their home territory predating colonial or other societies that prevail in their territory (Sanders 1999). They are typically a numerical minority and often have lost the rights to their original territory. The United Nations distinguishes between indigenous peoples and *minority ethnic groups* such as the Roma, the Tamils of Sri Lanka, and African Americans. The San peoples of Southern Africa, and their several subgroups, are an important example of indigenous peoples whose way of life was dramatically affected first by colonialism and now by globalization (see Culturama).

GENDER Gender refers to culturally constructed and learned behaviors and ideas attributed to males, females, or sometimes a blended or "third" gender. Gender differs from

CULTURAMA

San Peoples of Southern Africa

San is a cluster name for many groups of people in southern Africa who speak related languages that have glottal click sounds. Around 2000 years ago, the San were the only people living in southern Africa, but today they are restricted to scattered locations throughout the region. European colonialists referred to San people as "Bushmen," a derogatory term at the time but one that San people now prefer over what some locals call them. Some San also refer to themselves with the English term "First People."

For many centuries, the San supported themselves through collecting food such as roots and birds' eggs and by hunting eland, giraffe, and other animals. Now, pressure from African governments, farmers, ranchers, game reserves, diamond companies, and international tourism have greatly reduced the San's access to their ancestral land and their ability to

survive. Some have been arrested for hunting on what they consider their land.

The Ju/'hoansi ("True People") are a subgroup of San who live in a region crossing the borders of Namibia and Botswana, and numbering between 10,000 and 15,000 people. As described by Richard Lee in the early 1960s, they were highly mobile food collectors and quite healthy (1979). Today, most have been forced from their homeland and live as poor, urban squatters or in government-built resettlement camps. Many work as farm laborers or in the international tourist industry, serving as guides and producing and selling crafts. Others are unemployed.

The specifics of the San people's situation depends on government policy toward indigenous people in the particular country where they live. Conditions are most difficult for San

peoples, at this time, in Botswana due to forced sedentarization.

Transnational advocacy organizations, including Working Group of Indigenous Minorities in Southern Africa (WIMSA) and First People of the Kalahari (FPK), are making progress in protecting the rights of San peoples. Recently, WIMSA waged an international legal case with a large pharmaceutical company and succeeded in ensuring that the San receive a portion of the profits from the commercial development of hoodia (*Hoodia gordonia*). Hoodia is extracted from a cactus indigenous to the Kalahari region. An effective appetite suppressant, it is now widely available in North America and on the Internet as diet pills.

Thanks to Alison Brooks, George Washington University, for reviewing this material.

Stan Washburn/AnthroPhoto

Louise Gubb/CORBIS

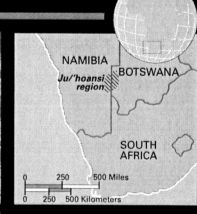

NAMIBIA
Ju/'hoansi region
BOTSWANA
SOUTH AFRICA

0   250   500 Miles
0   250   500 Kilometers

(LEFT) Richard Lee (wearing a shirt) asks Ju/'hoansi men about food plants of the Kalahari desert. This photograph was taken in 1968. Lee, and many other researchers affiliated with the Harvard Kalahari research project, learned to speak the Ju/'hoansi language.
(CENTER) San peoples have long consumed parts of the hoodia plant to suppress hunger and thirst when on long trips in the desert. (CENTER) Now they cultivate it for commercial use in a diet pill.

MAP 4 Ju/'hoansi Region in Namibia and Botswana. Before country boundaries were drawn, the Ju/'hoansi freely ranged across their traditional territory (shaded area), depending on the seasonal availability of food and water. Now they must show a passport when crossing from

Huli men of the Mount Hagen region of highland Papua New Guinea in festive attire for a dance performance.

sex, which is based on biological markers such as genitals and hormones to define categories of male and female. Cultural anthropology shows that a person's biological makeup does not necessarily correspond to gender. Biology directly determines only a few roles and tasks, such as giving birth and nursing infants.

Cross-culturally, gender differences vary from societies in which male and female roles and worlds are similar or overlapping, to those in which genders are sharply differentiated. In much of rural Thailand, men and women are about the same size, their clothing is similar, and their agricultural tasks are complementary and often interchangeable (Potter 1977). In contrast, among many groups in highland Papua New Guinea, extreme gender segregation exists in most aspects of life, including the kinds of food men and women eat (Meigs 1984). The men's house physically and symbolically separates the worlds of men and women. Men engage in rituals that purge them of female substances: nose or penis bleeding, vomiting, tongue scraping, sweating, and eye washing. Men possess sacred flutes, which they parade though the village from time to time. If women dare to look at the flutes, men traditionally had the right to kill them.

AGE   The human life cycle, from birth to old age, takes people through cultural stages for which appropriate behavior and thinking must be learned anew. In many African herding societies, elaborate age categories for males define their roles and status as they move from being boys with few responsibilities and little status, to young men who are warriors and live apart from the rest of the group, to adult men who are allowed

---

ethnocentrism   judging other cultures by the standards of one's own culture rather than by the standards of that particular culture.

to marry, have children, and become respected elders. "The Hill," or the collective members of the United States Senate and the House of Representatives, is a highly age-graded microculture (Weatherford 1981). The Hill is a *gerontocracy* (a group ruled by senior members) in which the older politicians dominate younger politicians in terms of amount of time they speak and how much attention their words receive. It may take a junior member between 10 and 20 years to become as effective and powerful as a senior member.

INSTITUTIONS   *Institutions,* or enduring group settings formed for a particular purpose, have their own characteristic microcultures. Institutions include hospitals, schools and universities, and prisons. Anyone who has entered such an institution has experienced a feeling of strangeness. Until you gain familiarity with the often unwritten cultural rules, you may do things that offend or puzzle people, that fail to get you what you want, and that make you feel marginalized and insecure.

Anthropologists who study educational institutions show that schools often replicate and reinforce stereotypes, power relations, and inequalities of the wider society. A study of middle schools in the southwestern Rocky Mountain region of the United States found a situation in which teachers marginalized Mexican immigrant girls (Meador 2005). In this school, Mexican immigrant students are labeled as ESL (English as a second language) students because they are not fluent in English and take special courses designed to improve their English. In addition, the teachers' mental model of a "good student" is a student who is:

- Motivated to do well in school and gets good grades
- An athlete
- Popular and has good students as friends
- Comes from a stable family

It is impossible for Mexican immigrant children to conform to this image. Mexicana girls are especially disadvantaged because most are not interested in, or good at, sports. The few Mexicana girls who are motivated to try to get good grades are consistently overlooked by the teachers, who instead call on students who are confident, bright, and popular, and who sit in front of the classroom and raise their hands eagerly.

DISTINCTIVE FEATURES OF CULTURAL ANTHROPOLOGY

Cultural anthropology has two distinct research goals and two distinct guiding concepts. Researchers and teachers in other disciplines have begun to adopt these goals and concepts in recent decades, so they are now found beyond cultural anthropology. Such cross-discipline contributions are something of which cultural anthropology can be proud.

CULTURAL RELATIVISM Most people grow up thinking that their culture is *the* way of life and that other ways of life are strange and inferior. Cultural anthropologists label this attitude **ethnocentrism**: judging other cultures by the standards of one's own culture rather than by the standards of other cultures. Ethnocentrism has fueled centuries of efforts to change "other" people in the world, sometimes through religious missionary work, sometimes in the form of colonial domination.

The opposite of ethnocentrism is **cultural relativism**, the idea that each culture must be understood in terms of its own values and beliefs and not by the standards of another culture. Cultural relativism assumes that no culture is better than any other. How does a person gain a sense of cultural relativism? The best way is to be able to spend substantial amounts of time living with people outside your own culture. Studying abroad and socially engaged travel help.

You can also experience aspects of other cultures by reading about them, learning about them in anthropology classes, doing Internet research, preparing and eating "foreign" foods, listening to "world music," reading novels by authors from other cultures, and making friends who are "different" from you.

One way that some anthropologists have interpreted cultural relativism is *absolute cultural relativism,* which says that whatever goes on in a particular culture must not be questioned or changed because it would be ethnocentric to question any behavior or idea anywhere (see Figure 5). The position of absolute cultural relativism, however, can lead in dangerous directions. Consider the example of the Holocaust during World War II in which millions of Jews, Roma, and other minorities in much of Eastern and Western Europe were killed as part of the German Nazis' Aryan supremacy campaign. The absolute cultural relativist position becomes boxed in, logically, to saying that because the Holocaust was undertaken according to the values of the culture, outsiders have no business questioning it. Can anyone feel comfortable with such a position?

Critical cultural relativism offers an alternative view that poses questions about cultural practices and ideas in terms of who accepts them and why, and who they might be harming or helping. In terms of the Nazi Holocaust, a critical cultural relativist would ask, "Whose culture supported the values that killed millions of people on the grounds of racial purity?" Not the cultures of the Jews, Roma, and other victims. It was the culture of Aryan supremacists, who were just one group among many. In other words, the situation was far more complex than a simple absolute cultural relativist statement suggests. Rather, it was a case of *cultural imperialism*, in which one dominant group claimed supremacy over minority cultures and took actions in its own interests and at the expense of the subjugated cultures. Critical cultural relativism avoids the trap of adopting a homogenized view. It recognizes internal cultural differences and winners/losers, oppressors/victims. It pays attention to the interests of various power groups. It can illuminate the causes and consequences of recent and contemporary conflict situations, such as those in Rwanda, Iraq, and Kenya.

Many cultural anthropologists seek to *critique* (which means to probe underlying power interests, not just to offer negative comments as in the general usage of the term "criticism") the behavior and values of groups from the standpoint of a set of generally agreed-on human rights and values. Two issues emerge in this endeavor. First, it is difficult if not impossible to generate a universal list of what all cultures would agree to as good and right. Second, as Claude Lévi-Strauss said, "No society is perfect" (1968:385), and so we have no perfect model of the best society.

VALUING AND SUSTAINING DIVERSITY Anthropologists value and are committed to maintaining cultural diversity throughout the world, as part of humanity's rich heritage. Many cultural anthropologists share their expertise and knowledge to support the survival of indigenous peoples and other small-scale groups worldwide.

In the United States, an organization called Cultural Survival helps indigenous peoples and ethnic minorities deal as equals in their interactions with outsiders. Cultural Survival's guiding principle is printed on the inside cover of this book. Cultural Survival sponsors programs to help indigenous peoples and ethnic minorities protect and manage their natural environment, claim land rights, and protect their cultural heritage.

Absolute Cultural Relativism	Whatever goes on within a particular culture cannot be questioned or changed by outsiders as that would be ethnocentric.
Critical Cultural Relativism	Anyone can pose questions about what goes on in various cultures, including their own culture, in terms of how particular practices or beliefs may harm certain members; follows Lévi-Strauss's comment that no society is perfect and that, therefore, all societies may be able to learn from others and improve.

FIGURE 5 Cultural Relativism: Two Views

Native American dancers perform at the annual Gateway Pow Wow in Brooklyn, New York.

▶ *Think of possible examples in your microculture of attempts to revitalize aspects of the culture.*

© CRDPHOTO/CORBIS

THREE THEORETICAL DEBATES IN CULTURAL ANTHROPOLOGY

Transitioning to theory, this section describes three debates in cultural anthropology that go to the heart of its basic questions about *how* people behave and think cross-culturally and *why* people behave and think the way they do. Introduced briefly here, they reappear throughout the book.

BIOLOGICAL DETERMINISM VERSUS CULTURAL CONSTRUCTIONISM **Biological determinism** seeks to explain why people do and think what they do by considering biological factors such as people's genes and hormones. Thus, biological determinists search for the gene or hormone that contributes to behavior such as homicide, alcoholism, or adolescent stress. They also examine cultural practices in terms of how they contribute to the "reproductive success of the species," or how they contribute to the gene pool of subsequent generations by boosting the number of surviving offspring produced in a particular population. In this view, behaviors and ideas that have reproductive advantages are more likely than others to be passed on to future generations. Biological determinists, for example, have provided an explanation for why human males apparently have "better" spatial skills than females. They say that these differences are the result of evolutionary selection because males with "better"

---

biological determinism   a theory that explains human behavior and ideas mainly as shaped by biological features such as genes and hormones.

cultural constructionism   a theory that explains human behavior and ideas mainly as shaped by learning.

---

spatial skills would have an advantage in securing both food and mates. Males with "better" spatial skills impregnate more females and have more offspring with "better" spatial skills.

Cultural constructionism, in contrast, maintains that human behavior and ideas are best explained as products of culturally shaped learning. In terms of the example of "better" male spatial skills, cultural constructionists would provide evidence that such skills are passed on culturally through learning, not genes. They would say that parents and teachers socialize boys and girls differently in spatial skills and are more likely to promote learning of certain kinds of spatial skills among boys. Though recognizing the role of biological factors such as genes and hormones, anthropologists who favor cultural construction and learning as an explanation for behaviors such as homicide and alcoholism point to childhood experiences and family roles as being perhaps even more important than genes or hormones. Most cultural anthropologists are cultural constructionists, but some connect biology and culture in their work.

INTERPRETIVE ANTHROPOLOGY VERSUS CULTURAL MATERIALISM Interpretive anthropology, or interpretivism, focuses on understanding culture by studying what people think about, their explanations of their lives, and the symbols that are important to them. For example, in understanding the eating habits of Hindus, interpretivists ask why Hindus do not eat beef. Hindus point to their religious beliefs, according to which cows are sacred and it is a sin to kill and eat them. Interpretivists accept this explanation as sufficient.

Cultural materialism attempts to learn about culture by first examining the material aspects of life: the natural

(TOP) Traffic in the city of Varanasi (Banaras), northern India. Foreign visitors to India often comment that the presence of so many wandering cows is a sign of wastefulness and inefficiency. (BOTTOM) SUVs, trucks, and buses share the road in Los Angeles. SUVs are still popular in the United States in spite of their poor gas mileage.

▶ *If you were an energy policy maker, what lessons would you draw from this pair of photographs?*

environment and how people make a living within particular environments. Cultural materialists believe that these basic facts of life shape culture, even though people may not realize it. They use a three-level model to explain culture. The bottom level is *infrastructure,* a term that refers to basic material factors such as natural resources, the economy, and population. According to this model, infrastructure tends to shape the other two domains of culture: *structure* (social organization, kinship, and political organization) and *superstructure* (ideas, values, and beliefs). This book's chapters are organized roughly in terms of these three categories, but with recognition that the layers are not neat and tidy but rather have interconnections.

A cultural materialist explanation for the taboo on killing cows and eating beef involves the fact that cattle in India play a more important role alive than dead or carved into steaks (Harris 1974). The many cattle wandering the streets of Indian cities and villages look useless to Westerners. Closer analysis shows that the seemingly useless population of bovines serves many useful functions. Ambling along, they eat paper trash and other edible refuse. Their excrement is "brown gold," useful as fertilizer or, when mixed with straw and formed into dried patties, as cooking fuel. Most important, farmers use cattle to plow fields. Cultural materialists take into account Hindu beliefs about the sacred meaning of cattle, but they see its relationship to the material value of cattle, as symbolic protection keeping these extremely useful animals out of the meat factory.

Some cultural anthropologists are strong interpretivists, whereas some are strong cultural materialists. Many combine the best of both views.

INDIVIDUAL AGENCY VERSUS STRUCTURISM This debate concerns the question of how much individual will, or agency, affects the way people behave and think, compared with the power of forces, or *structures,* that are beyond individual control. Western philosophical thought gives much emphasis to the role of agency, the ability of individuals to make choices and exercise free will. In contrast, structurism emphasizes that free choice is an illusion because choices are structured by larger forces such as the economy, social and political organization, and ideological systems.

A prime example is the study of poverty. Those who emphasize agency focus their research on how individuals attempt to act as agents, even in situations of extreme poverty, in order to change their situation as best they can. Structurists would emphasize that the poor are trapped by large and powerful forces. They would describe how the political economy and other forces provide little room for agency for those at the bottom. An increasing number of cultural anthropologists seek to blend a structural perspective with attention to agency.

◆◆◆

Cultural Anthropology and Careers

Some of you reading this book may take only one anthropology course to satisfy a requirement. Others may become interested in the subject matter and take a few more. Some will decide to major or minor in anthropology. Just one course in anthropology may change your way of thinking about the world and your place in it. More than that, anthropology coursework may enhance your ability to get a job. Take a look at the inside of the back cover of this book for specific résumé builders.

MAJORING IN ANTHROPOLOGY

An anthropology B.A. is a liberal arts degree. It is not, however, a professional degree, such as a business degree or a degree in physical therapy. It provides a solid education relevant to many career directions that are likely to require further study, such as law, criminal justice, medicine and health services, social services, education, humanitarian assistance, international development programs, and business. Students interested in pursuing a B.A. major in anthropology should know that anthropology is at least as useful as other liberal arts majors for either graduate study or a professional career.

Anthropology has several clear advantages over other liberal arts majors, and employers and graduate schools are increasingly recognizing these features. Cultural anthropology provides knowledge about the world's people and diversity. It offers insights about a variety of specialized research methods. Cross-cultural awareness and communication skills are valuable assets sought by business, government, health-care providers, and nongovernmental organizations.

The recurrent question is this: Will it be possible to get a good job related to anthropology with a B.A. in anthropology? The answer is yes, but it takes planning and hard work. Do the following: Gain expertise in at least one foreign language, study abroad, do service learning during your undergraduate years, and conduct an independent research project and write up the results as a professional report or conference paper. Package these skills on your résumé so that they appear relevant to employers. Do not give up. Good jobs are out there, and coursework and skills in anthropology are increasingly valued.

Anthropology is also an excellent minor. It complements almost any other area of study by adding a cross-cultural perspective. For example, if you are majoring in music, courses about world music will enrich your primary interest. The same applies to subjects such as interior design, psychology, criminal justice, international affairs, economics, political science, and more.

GRADUATE STUDY IN ANTHROPOLOGY

Some of you may go on to pursue a master's degree (M.A.) or doctorate degree (Ph.D.) in anthropology. If you do, here is some advice. Be passionate about your interest but also be aware that full-time jobs as a professor or as a professional anthropologist are not easy to get. To expand possibilities of a good job, it is wise to consider combining a professional skill with your degree program in anthropology, such as a law degree, an M.A. degree in project management, a Master's of Public Health (M.P.H.), a certificate in disaster relief, or participation in a training program in conflict prevention and resolution.

Useful skills will make your anthropology degree more powerful. In biological anthropology, it may be coursework in anatomy that helps you get a job working in a forensics lab or teaching anatomy in a medical school. In archaeology, it may be your experience on a summer dig that helps you get a job with a firm in your home state that investigates building sites before construction begins, to check for the presence of fossils or artifacts. In cultural anthropology, cross-cultural experiences or knowledge of a foreign language may get you a position with an international aid organization. In linguistic anthropology, your knowledge of bilingualism means that you can help design a more effective program for teaching English to refugees.

LIVING AN ANTHROPOLOGICAL LIFE

Studying cultural anthropology makes for smart people and people with breadth and flexibility. In North America, college graduates are likely to change careers (not just jobs, but careers) several times in their lives. Because you never know where you are going to end up working, or in what endeavor, it pays to be broadly informed about the world. Cultural anthropology prompts you to ask original and important questions about the world's people and their relationships with one another, and it helps provide some useful answers.

Beyond career value, cultural anthroplogy will enrich your daily life by increasing your exposure to the world's cultures. When you pick up a newspaper, you will find several articles that connect with what you have learned in your anthropology classes. You will be able to view your own everyday life as culturally constructed in interesting and meaningful ways. You will be a different person, and you will live a richer life.

the BIG questions REVISITED

◆ What is anthropology?

Anthropology is an academic discipline, like history or economics. It comprises four interrelated fields in its attempt to explore all facets of humanity from its origins through the present. Biological or physical anthropology is the study of humans as biological organisms, including their evolution and contemporary variation. Archaeology is the study of past human cultures through their material remains. Linguistic anthropology is the study of human communication, including its origins, history, and contemporary variation and change. Cultural anthropology is the study of living peoples and their cultures, including variation and change. Culture refers to people's learned and shared behaviors and beliefs.

Each field makes both theoretical and applied contributions. The perspective of this book is that applied anthropology, just like theoretical anthropology, should be an integrated and important part of all four fields, rather than a separate, fifth field. Examples of applied anthropology in the four fields include forensic anthropology, nonhuman primate conservation, assisting in literacy programs for refugees, and advising businesses about people's preferences.

◆ What is cultural anthropology?

Cultural anthropology is the field within general anthropology that focuses on the study of contemporary humans. Culture is defined as learned and shared ways of behaving and thinking. It has several distinctive features that set it apart from the other fields of general anthropology and from other academic disciplines. Its two basic goals are ethnography and ethnology. Cultural relativism, attributed to Franz Boas, is a guiding principle that other disciplines have widely adopted. Cultural anthropology values and works to sustain cultural diversity.

Culture is the key concept of cultural anthropology. Some anthropologists define culture as learned and shared behavior and ideas, whereas others equate culture with ideas alone and exclude behavior as a part of culture. It is easier to understand culture by considering its characteristics: Culture is related to nature but is not the same as nature; it is based on symbols and it is learned; cultures are integrated within themselves; and cultures interact with other cultures and change. Four models of cultural interaction involve varying degrees of conflict, blending, and resistance. People participate in cultures of different levels, including local microcultures shaped by such factors as class, "race"/ethnicity/indigeneity, gender, age, and institutions.

Cultural anthropology has a rich history of theoretical approaches and changing topical focuses. Three important theoretical debates are biological determinism versus cultural constructionism, interpretive anthropology versus cultural materialism, and individual agency versus structurism. Each, in its own way, attempts to understand and explain why people behave and think the way they do and to account for differences and similarities across cultures.

◆ How is cultural anthropology relevant to a career?

Taking just one course in cultural anthropology expands awareness of the diversity of the world's cultures and the importance of cross-cultural understanding. Employers in many fields—such as public health, humanitarian aid, law enforcement, business, and education—increasingly value a degree in cultural anthropology. In today's diverse and connected world, being culturally informed and culturally sensitive is essential.

Graduate degrees in cultural anthropology, either at the M.A. or Ph.D. level, are even more likely to lead to professional positions that directly use your anthropological education and skills. Combining graduate coursework in anthropology with a professional degree, such as a master's degree in public health or public administration, or a law degree, is a successful route to a meaningful career outside academia. Cultural anthropology, beyond its career relevance, will enrich your everyday life with its insights.

KEY CONCEPTS

agency
anthropology
applied anthropology
  or **practicing anthropology**
  or **practical anthropology**
archaeology or **prehistory**
biological anthropology
  or **physical anthropology**
biological determinism
class
cultural anthropology
  or **social anthropology**

cultural constructionism
cultural materialism
cultural relativism
culture
ethnicity
ethnocentrism
functionalism
gender
globalization
holism
indigenous people

interpretive anthropology, or
  interpretivism
linguistic anthropology
localization
microculture
"race"
rainforest
structurism
symbol

SUGGESTED READINGS

Thomas J. Barfield, ed. *The Dictionary of Anthropology*. Malden, MA: Blackwell Publishing, 1997. This reference work contains hundreds of brief essays on concepts in anthropology, such as evolution, myth, functionalism, and applied anthropology, and on important anthropologists.

Stanley R. Barrett. *Anthropology: A Student's Guide to Theory and Method*. Toronto: University of Toronto Press, 2000. This book organizes the theoretical history of cultural anthropology into three phases and summarizes trends in each. The author discusses how to do research in cultural anthropology.

Mario Blaser, Harvey A. Feit, and Glenn McRae, eds. *In the Way of Development: Indigenous Peoples, Life Projects and Globalization*. New York: Zed Books, in association with the International Development Research Centre, 2004. Twenty chapters contributed by indigenous leaders, social activists, and cultural anthropologists address indigenous peoples' responses to capitalism and indigenous ideas about future change that is positive for them and for the environment.

Ira E. Harrison and Faye V. Harrison, eds. *African-American Pioneers in Anthropology*. Chicago: University of Illinois Press, 1999. This collection of intellectual biographies highlights the contributions of 13 African American anthropologists to the development of cultural anthropology in the United States.

Takami Kuwayama, ed. *Native Anthropology: The Japanese Challenge to Western Academic Hegemony*. Melbourne: Trans Pacific Press, 2004. The chapters in this book discuss various topics in Japanese anthropology, including "native anthropology," the marginalization of Asian anthropologists, folklore studies, and how U.S. anthropology textbooks present Japan.

James H. McDonald, ed. *The Applied Anthropology Reader*. Boston: Allyn and Bacon, 2002. This collection of over 50 brief essays explores topics in applied cultural anthropology, including ethics, methods, urban settings, health, international development, the environment, education, and business.

R. Bruce Morrison and C. Roderick Wilson, eds. *Native Peoples: The Canadian Experience*, 3rd ed. Oxford, Ontario: Oxford University Press, 2004. This sourcebook on Northern Peoples contains 26 chapters with sections divided by region. Chapters about various cultural groups provide historical context and updates on the current situation.

Thomas C. Patterson. *A Social History of Anthropology in the United States*. New York: Berg, 2001. This history of anthropology in the United States emphasizes the social and political context of the discipline and how that context shaped theories and methods.

Richard J. Perry. *Five Key Concepts in Anthropological Thinking*. Upper Saddle River, NJ: Prentice-Hall, 2003. The five key concepts are evolution, culture, structure, function, and relativism. The author raises thought-provoking questions about anthropology as being Eurocentric and about the appropriation of the culture concept beyond anthropology.

Pat Shipman. *The Evolution of Racism: Human Differences and the Use and Abuse of Science*. Cambridge, MA: Harvard University Press, 1994. This book offers a history of the "race" concept in Western thought from Darwin to contemporary DNA studies. The author addresses thorny issues such as racism in the United States and Nazi Germany's use of Darwinism.

CHAPTER 2

THE EVOLUTION
OF HUMANITY AND CULTURE

Hominin footprints preserved at Laetoli, Tanzania, are about 3.6 million years old. These individuals were between 3 and 4 feet tall when standing upright. For a close-up view of one of the footprints and further information, go to the human origins section of the website of the Smithsonian Institution's National Museum of Natural History, www.mnh.si.edu/anthro/humanorigins/ha/laetoli.htm.

THE EVOLUTION OF HUMANITY AND CULTURE

the BIG questions

- What do living nonhuman primates tell us about human culture?

- What role did culture play during hominin evolution?

- How has modern human culture changed in the past 12,000 years?

Substantial scientific evidence indicates that modern humans have evolved from a shared lineage with primate ancestors between 4 and 8 million years ago. The mid-nineteenth century was a turning point in European thinking about human origins as scientific thinking challenged the biblical narrative of human origins. Two British thinkers, Charles Darwin and Alfred Russel Wallace, independently discovered the principle of **natural selection**, the process by which organisms better adapted to the environment reproduce more effectively compared to less well-adapted forms. This principle, in turn, supported the acceptance of the concept of **evolution**, or inherited and cumulative change in the characteristics of a species, population, or culture. This scientific view conflicts with some religious perspectives, including Christian *creationism*, based on a literal understanding of biblical writings, that all animal species, including humans, date from the Day of Creation and have always existed in the physical form that they do now. The scientific view of human origins, however, does not conflict with all religious perspectives, including nonliteralist Christians and Buddhists.

Fossils (the preserved remains of a plant or animal of the past), **artifacts** (portable objects made or modified by humans), and new genetic analyses provide strong evidence that modern humans existed before the Christian Day of Creation, estimated to be 4004 BCE. The evidence also shows that human anatomy evolved over time from more ape-like to more human-like, and human cultural capabilities have changed dramatically. Many anthropologists, like other scientists, find ways to reconcile the scientific evidence with their personal religious beliefs.

This chapter accepts the scientific perspective on human evolution. It therefore begins with a discussion of the primates closest to humans and describes how they provide insights into what the lives of the earliest human ancestors might have been like. It then turns to a description of the main stages in evolution to modern humans. The last section covers the development of settled life, agriculture, and cities and states.

◆◆◆

Nonhuman Primates and the Roots of Human Culture

According to abundant evidence from genetics, anatomy, physiology, and behavior, humans are primates. This section describes primate characteristics in general and then situates humans within the group of primate with whom we are most closely related in order to provide some comparisons.

PRIMATE CHARACTERISTICS

The **primates** are an order of mammals that includes modern humans. Primates vary in size from several ounces to over 400 pounds. Some inhabit limited areas, and others range more widely. In defining primate characteristics, *morphology,* or physical form, is a basic consideration because it is related to behavior. Compared to the faces of other mammals such as dogs or cows, primate faces tend to be flat with reduced snouts. Relatedly, primates differ from other mammals in terms of being highly reliant on vision for dealing with their environment and social interactions. Primates have five digits on their hands and feet, opposable thumbs, and they can grasp with both their hands and feet. Primate brains are large in relation to body size. Because of their large brain size, primates take longer to mature than other mammals do. This extended

Members of a group of Hanuman langurs in India involved in social behavior. Most primates are highly social and interact with their group-mates in complex ways.

© Cyril Ruoso/Minden Pictures

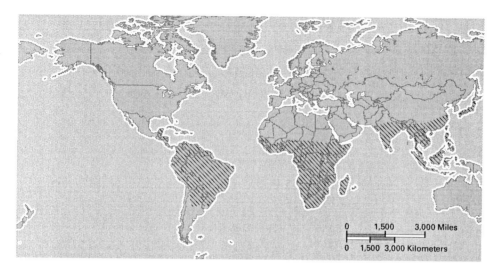

MAP 1 Where Nonhuman Primates Live Today. The habitats of nonhuman primates are greatly reduced from what they were in prehistory, and they are increasingly threatened by human encroachment and environmental change.

developmental period, combined with the fact that most primate species are highly social, provides a context for the social molding of primate behavior.

In terms of environmental adaptations, most nonhuman primate species live in low-altitude areas of the tropics or subtropics (see Map 1). A few live in high altitudes in Africa, Nepal, and Japan. Most primate species are *arboreal* (tree-dwelling), *quadrupedal* (moving on all fours), and *diurnal* (active during the day), and most, like humans, have a high degree of **sociality**, or a preference for living in groups and interacting regularly with members of the same species.

All nonhuman primates in the wild provide for their food needs by **foraging**, or obtaining food available in nature through gathering, hunting, or scavenging. Species vary, however, in terms of the kinds of foods they prefer (Strier 2007). Five major dietary patterns of primates are based on their primary food sources:

- *Frugivores* eat mainly fruit. They have large front teeth, or incisors, to allow them to puncture the flesh of large fruits and transfer pieces into their mouths, like when you bite into an apple. Digestion of fruits occurs in the small intestine, so frugivores have a long small intestine.

- *Folivores* eat primarily leaves. Leaves are difficult to digest because of the chemicals, such as cellulose, in their walls. Folivores' chewing teeth are designed to help them break leaves into small pieces, and bacteria in their digestive systems break down the cell walls of leaves. Some folivores have an expanded large intestine (Milton 1984).

- *Insectivores* eat mainly insects. They have high, sharp cusps on their molar teeth to puncture and break up the insects' hard covering. The contents of insects are quite easy to digest, so insectivores have short and simple guts. Insects are difficult to catch, so the limited food sources mean that insectivores are small-bodied.

- *Gummivores* have a diet that relies on the gums and saps of trees. Some have protruding lower incisors that they use to gouge the outer layer of trees to start the flow of gums and saps. Many have large intestines to help them digest these food sources.

- *Omnivores* are generalists: many kinds of foods make up their diet. Therefore, they lack specialized dental or gut morphology. Humans are omnivores.

Most primates live in a *social group,* or collection of animals that interact regularly. Group life has advantages in terms of information sharing about food sources and protection against threats from other groups. The details of group organization vary. The most common social group among nonhuman primates, by far, is the *multi-male/multi-female (MM/MF) group.* This type of group contains adults of both sexes and the females' offspring. Females make up the core of the group and often have strong alliances with each other. Male membership in these groups is less stable. A rare subvariety is called a *fission-fusion group,* a large group of 50 or more individuals that regularly breaks up into much smaller subgroups for foraging. Although rare among nonhuman primate species overall, the fission-fusion pattern is important because it is found in chimpanzees and bonobos, the nonhuman primates most like humans. Thus it is possible that the early human ancestors may have had a fission-fusion form of social organization.

natural selection   the process by which organisms better adapted to the environment reproduce more effectively compared with less well-adapted forms.

evolution   inherited and cumulative change in the characteristics of a species, population, or culture.

fossil   the preserved remains of a plant or animal of the past.

artifact   a portable object made or modified by humans.

primates   an order of mammals that includes modern humans.

sociality   the preference for living in groups and interacting regularly with members of the same species.

foraging   obtaining food available in nature through gathering, hunting, or scavenging.

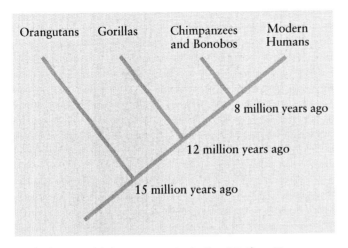

FIGURE 1 The Great Apes, Including Modern Humans.

Complex communication and signaling systems are another key feature of nonhuman primate behavior that enables individuals to exist in stable groups. Primates communicate through smell, touch, visual, and vocal channels. The facial muscles of most primates allow for a wider range of expressions compared to other mammals. Primates use facial expressions to communicate threats and fear and to facilitate courtship, play, grooming, and post-conflict reconciliation.

THE GREAT APES

According to genetic data, modern humans are closely related to the living great apes with whom we shared a *common ancestor* between 4 and 8 million years ago (see Figure 1). The term **great apes** refers to a category of large, tailless primates that includes the orangutans, gorillas, chimpanzees, bonobos, and humans All great ape species are considered to be endangered in the wild.

Since our last common ancestor with the other great apes, the human line diverged in two significant ways:

- Human anatomy evolved with an emphasis on habitual locomotion on two legs and much larger brains.

- Humans developed culture, including verbal language, to a more complex degree.

In spite of the many differences between humans and the other great apes, the great apes provide insights into what the lives and behavior of early human ancestors might have been like.

Apes differ from other primates in the absence of a tail, larger brains relative to body size, and the tendency to travel by brachiation. All apes, including humans, are capable of **brachiation**, a form of arboreal travel, using the forelimbs to swing from branch to branch, related to changes in the shoulder anatomy and distinct to apes (see Figure 2). Apes are typically frugivores but they eat a variety of other foods, including insects such as termites. Mountain gorillas eat mainly leaves and stalks.

Orangutans are the only Asian great ape. They live on the islands of Borneo and Sumatra. *Sexual dimorphism* in body size (difference in size between males and females) is marked, with the weight of an adult male (175–200 pounds) roughly double that of an adult female (73–99 pounds). In spite of their large size, however, orangutans are mainly arboreal and are known for their "four-handed" mode of movement in the tree canopy. Orangutans are frugivorous and spend substantial amounts of time each day locating and consuming food. They are the least social, and by implication, the most solitary of the great apes. When ripe fruit is abundant, however, orangutans will congregate temporarily. The only constant social unit is that of a mother and her offspring. Mothers and offspring forage together, and mothers often transfer food to immature offspring who solicit food, especially food that is difficult to process (Jaeggi, van Noordwijk, and van Schaik 2008). In this way, offspring gain nutrition and also knowledge about food processing. Orangutans in Sumatra make simple tools from branches that they use for termite and ant fishing and to access seeds. An adult male's territory overlaps the home ranges of several females and is defended from other males. Adult males use large air sacs on their necks to make loud bellowing noises so that they can locate, and usually avoid, each other. The primate line leading to humans split with the orangutans about 15 million years ago.

Gorillas, the largest of the living primates, live in sub-Saharan Africa. Gorillas eat a wide variety of plants, up to 200 species, and supplement their plant diet with termites and ants. Like orangutans, gorillas have a high degree of sexual dimorphism in body size. In the wild, adult male gorillas weigh

FIGURE 2 Brachiation in Action.

between 350 and 400 pounds, whereas adult females weigh between 150 and 200 pounds. Gorillas often live in social groups composed of a single male and multiple females with the females' dependent offspring. Males compete with each other intensely for access to the females. Although they live primarily in dense forests, gorillas are largely terrestrial, adult males especially so because of their large body size. They are quadrupedal and travel using a locomotor pattern called **knuckle-walking**. Knuckle-walking is a form of terrestrial travel that involves walking flat-footed while supporting the upper body on the front of fingers bent beyond the knuckle. The human line split with the gorillas about 12 million years ago.

Chimpanzees and bonobos, who live in sub-Saharan Africa, are the great apes most closely related to humans. Chimpanzees are found in several locations in West, Central, and East Africa. Bonobos live only in the Democratic

An adult male silverback gorilla knuckle-walking.

▶ *Practice knuckle-walking across a room and consider the role of arm-to-leg length in this form of locomotion.*

Republic of Congo. Several chimpanzee populations in conservation areas are somewhat protected from human hunting. Because no bonobo population has such protection, they are more heavily hunted and even more endangered.

Compared to orangutans and gorillas, chimpanzees and bonobos are smaller and exhibit less sexual dimorphism in body size. In the wild, adult males weigh between 75 and 150 pounds, adult females between 60 and 100 pounds. Chimpanzees and bonobos are more arboreal than gorillas, but like gorillas, they are knuckle-walkers when on the ground. They are frugivores

Orangutan mother and juvenile in Tanjung Puting National Park on the island of Borneo, Indonesia. Many thousands of years ago, their habitat included mainland Asia and Southeast Asia. DNA evidence suggests that, if the continued loss of their habitat persists, orangutans may be extinct 50 years from now. The most immediate threats include the expansion of palm oil agriculture, illegal logging, and poaching.

great apes   a category of large and tailless primates that includes orangutans, gorillas, chimpanzees, bonobos, and humans.

brachiation   arboreal travel, using the forelimbs to swing from branch to branch, that is distinct to apes.

knuckle-walking   a form of terrestrial travel that involves walking flat-footed while supporting the upper body on the front of fingers bent beyond the knuckle.

(LEFT) A chimpanzee using a stone hammer to crack open a nut. (RIGHT) A bonobo mother and her offspring show that leisure time and play are not limited to humans.

but occasionally eat other food, including insects, vegetation, and small animals such as monkeys. Chimpanzees in Senegal, for example, consume termites year round and derive substantial calories and nutrients from them (Bogart and Pruetz 2008), a finding that suggests the possibility of termites as an important part of the diet of early human ancestors.

Chimpanzees and bonobos spend 25 percent of their time in social interactions, compared with 10 percent for the other great apes, except for humans (Sussman and Garber 2004). Grooming is the major form of social interaction, with most of the interactions occurring between mothers and offspring.

Although chimpanzees and bonobos are alike in many ways, primatologists are also interested in the differences between them and which is the better model for the early human ancestors (see Figure 3). Bonobos are similar in size to chimpanzees, but they have less sexual dimorphism in body size, so they are more like humans in this respect. Bonobos use two-legged, upright locomotion more than chimpanzees, again appearing more like humans. In terms of diet, both chimpanzees and bonobos hunt and eat small animals, though bonobos hunt less frequently than chimpanzees. Given the diversity in human dietary preferences, which range from veganism to eating meat, it is impossible to speculate on which animal is the better model for early humans on this dimension. Evidence of animal carcass butchery during several stages of hominin evolution suggests that animal protein was an important part of the diet.

Chimpanzees live in large, fluid groups of 50 to 60 individuals, but the entire group is rarely, if ever, together in one area. Subgroups form, dissolve, and reform, sometimes with different members. Adult males often travel together, whereas adult females travel with their offspring. In contrast to many other primate species, chimpanzees are *patrilocal*, a residence pattern in which males stay in their birth group throughout their lives. Females leave their birth group at reproductive age, between 10 and 15 years, to join a new group. Therefore, the core of the large social group is biologically related males. Males often form "gangs" that, as a group, seek food or defend territory. In some instances, these males go beyond their home range to seek out and kill members of a neighboring group.

Like chimpanzees, bonobos are patrilocal, but a difference is that migrant bonobo females develop strong alliances with females in their new group, forming *matrifocal* social groups centered on one or more adult female. In contrast to chimpanzees, adult female bonobos dominate the control of food distribution, and males solicit their attention by offering them choice food items. Bonobo social organization is related to the fact that they eat more vegetation, which is common and abundant, than chimpanzees do. Females spend less time foraging and have more time to establish and maintain social ties.

Bonobos have the highest rates of sexual contact of all non-human primates. Sexual contact occurs among all possible sex and age combinations, although rarely between close relatives. Bonobo reproductive rates, nonetheless, are similar to those found among chimpanzees. Bonobos thus have high rates of social or recreational sex, and this pattern is related to lower rates of conflict compared to chimpanzees. Bonobos use sexual contact to prevent conflict and to resolve post-conflict situations.

THE EVOLUTION OF HUMANITY AND CULTURE

FIGURE 3 Chimpanzee/Bonobo
Differences.

Source: derived from Stanford 1998 and comments
by Frans B. M. de Waal, Barbara Fruth, Kano
Takayoshi, and William C. McGrew

Chimpanzees	Bonobos
Terrestrial and arboreal	Terrestrial, more erect posture
Frequent tool users	Little observed tool use
More hunting and meat-eating	Occasional hunting and meat-eating
Hunting by males	Hunting by males and females
Male dominance over females	Female dominance over males
Males share meat only	Females share fruit and sometimes meat
Infanticide documented	No infanticide observed
Frequent intergroup aggression	Infrequent intergroup aggression
Less frequent sexual behavior	Frequent sexual behavior
Male–female sexual interactions	Prolific sexual interactions between and among males and females

Attractive food, or almost anything of interest to more than one bonobo, sparks sexual interest. The two bonobos will suspend potential competition for the item of interest and briefly mount each other or participate in what primatologists refer to as *G-G rubbing,* or genital–genital rubbing (de Waal and Lanting 1997:109). G-G rubbing is unique to bonobos and may qualify as a cultural innovation. This activity appears to distract the two parties and reframe the relationship as one of alliance and cooperation rather than competition and conflict. In one example of conflict prevention, when one mother struck another mother's infant, the two females participated in intense G-G rubbing rather than hostility, and peace was the outcome.

The current genetic evidence indicates that chimpanzees and bonobos are equally close to modern humans. Considering behavioral evidence, some scholars argue that chimpanzees are the better model given human patterns of male dominance and high levels of intergroup violence (Wrangham and Peterson 1996). The bonobo model suggests, in contrast, that humanity's biological heritage includes a propensity for being sexually active, female-centric, and relatively peaceful. Neither the chimpanzee nor bonobo model applies neatly to all modern human cultures, no doubt because our lineages split between 4 and 8 million years ago, and much has happened since then in terms of human evolution.

NONHUMAN PRIMATE CULTURE

Culture has long been thought to be unique to humans and their recent ancestors. Increasing evidence, however, indicates that animals other than humans have aspects of culture. In primatology, *culture* is defined as behavior that is learned (not innate) and shared (not individual).

In the 1950s, Japanese primatologists first raised the possibility of nonhuman primate culture (Kawamura 1959). Their findings emerged from a long-term study of macaques, a variety of Old World monkeys, on the island of Koshima, Japan. In order to lure the macaques into areas where they could be observed easily, the researchers

provided sweet potatoes on the beach. Soon, an adult female monkey, whom they named Imo, began carrying the potatoes from the beach to a pool of fresh water to wash the sand from the potatoes before eating them. Some of Imo's relatives began to do the same thing, and the behavior spread throughout much of her group.

Later, the primatologists provisioned the monkeys with rice in order to keep them in open areas for longer periods of

A Japanese macaque washing a sweet potato. Sweet-potato-washing is an early example of a nonhuman primate cultural behavior studied by primatologists.

THINKING OUTSIDE THE BOX

What are the main forms of social groups in your microculture? What social groups do you belong to, how did you join, and what holds the group together?

time. They thought it would take the monkeys a long time to work out how to sort rice grains from beach sand. But Imo promptly started dropping handfuls of sandy rice into the fresh water pools. The sand sank and the rice floated, making it possible for her to collect sand-free rice grains. This practice, too, spread throughout much of the group, especially among younger individuals. The behaviors of Imo and her group, being learned and shared, conform to part of the definition of nonhuman primate culture. (Note that primatologists can study only behavior, not beliefs or symbol systems, so that part of the definition of culture is still reserved for humans.)

Comparative studies shed more light on the question of primate culture. Primatologists look for behavioral differences among primates of the same species at different field sites with similar environmental conditions. Comparison of data from seven chimpanzee research sites in East and West Africa revealed 39 differences in tool use, grooming, and other social behaviors that can be explained only as the result of cultural differences and social learning (Whiten et al. 1999). The tools include hammers and anvils for cracking open nuts, probes for ant-fishing, leaves to sit on, and sticks to fan away flies. Male chimpanzees in some groups in Uganda regularly use leaves to clean their penis after sexual intercourse (O'Hara and Lee 2006). Cultural variation in social interaction and communication includes the *grooming hand clasp*, or holding the arm of another individual over his or her head during grooming (McGrew 2004), and doing a slow bodily display, or "rain-dance," at the start of rain.

All great apes build sleeping nests. Comparison of nest-building patterns among chimpanzees in two sites in southeastern Senegal, West Africa, reveals that this behavior is an adaptation to predator pressures (Pruetz et al. 2008). The natural environment in both study sites is similar, but the degree of threat from animal predators differs. In the site where the threat from predators is higher, the chimpanzees build tree nests at higher levels than in the area where predation is a lesser threat. Building a nest several feet high in a tree requires planning and dealing with problems such as finding materials, transporting them to the nest site, and making sure the nest structure will hold. Furthermore, it is prompted by risk-assessment that is informed by degrees of predation.

Young primates learn various cultural behaviors by watching adults. Beyond learning, however, invention also

---

hominins a category of primates that includes modern humans and extinct species of early human ancestors that are more closely related to humans than to living chimpanzees and bonobos.

bipedalism upright locomotion on two feet.

australopithecines a category of several extinct hominin species found in East and Central Africa that lived between 4.5 and 3 million years ago.

occurs. For 27 years, Japanese primatologists have been observing chimpanzees using tools in Bossou, Guinea, West Africa (Yamamoto et al. 2008). But it was only in 2003 that they saw one youthful male, named JJ, transfer his considerable skills at using a stick to retrieve ants on the ground to obtaining them in trees. For the new activity, JJ had to adapt his tools by using a shorter stick. No immigrant chimpanzees had come into the area, so JJ came up with this new approach on his own. Future research is needed to show whether JJ's innovation will spread to others in his group.

These intriguing examples suggest how the earliest human ancestors began to develop culture, through invention and sharing, as a key form of adaptation to various environments. In addition to a fruit-based diet, they may have regularly eaten insects such as termites. They may have developed the technique of building nests high in trees to protect themselves from predators. They probably lived in flexible social groups and experienced occasional within-group and across-group conflict.

◆ ◆ ◆

Hominin Evolution to Modern Humans

This section provides an overview of the several extinct species of early humans with attention to changes in anatomy (physical structure of the body) and culture. **Hominins** is a category of primates that includes modern humans and extinct species of early human ancestors that are more closely related to humans than to living chimpanzees and bonobos. The main hominin evidence includes fossils, artifacts, and new evidence from the growing field of DNA analysis.

THE EARLY HOMININS

In the first stage of separation from the other great apes, lasting from 8 million years ago until 3 million years ago, all the early hominins lived in Africa. These hominins are distinct from other apes in changes to the pelvis and lower limbs for habitual bipedalism, larger brains, and smaller teeth. **Bipedalism** is upright locomotion on two feet. These three anatomical characteristics were probably associated with other important changes including culture.

TWO EARLIEST SPECIES The oldest known hominin fossil is *Sahelanthropus tchadensis* (Brunet et al. 2002). Dated to between 7 and 6 million years ago, this fossil, discovered in Toros-Menalla in Chad, is important because it dramatically extends the regional pattern of fossil evidence for the early era beyond eastern and southern Africa into central/western Africa (see Map 2). The discovery of *S. tchadensis* means that the early hominins most likely occupied a much wider area of Africa than paleoanthropologists previously thought.

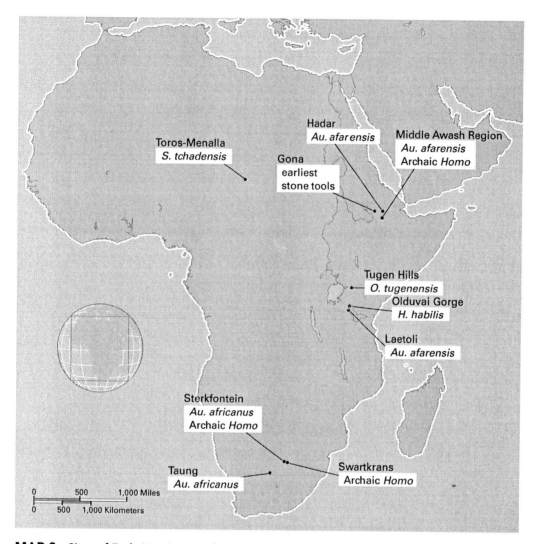

MAP 2 Sites of Early Hominins and Archaic *Homo* in Africa Mentioned in This Chapter.

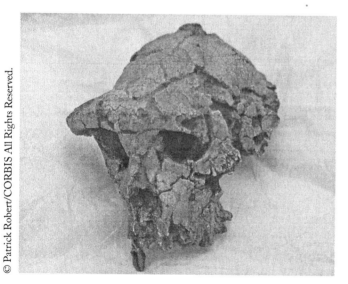

This fossil, discovered by a Chad-French team of paleoanthropologists, is nicknamed Toumaï, which means "a much-wanted child born after a long wait." The cranium of Toumaï is a mixture of features. Its dimensions suggest a chimpanzee-sized brain, but it has heavy brow ridges like hominins.

The second oldest primitive hominin species is *Orrorin tugenensis,* named for some fossils found in the Tugen Hills of Kenya that date to 6 million years ago (Senut et al. 2001). Although only a few fossils have been found for this species, the collection includes a femur (thighbone). Analysis of its shape and strength indicates bipedalism (Richmond and Jungers 2008).

THE AUSTRALOPITHECINES Australopithecines refers to a category of several extinct species of hominins found in East and Central Africa that lived between roughly 4 million and 2 million years ago. Abundant fossil evidence exists for this group. "Lucy," the most famous hominin fossil in the world, was found in Hadar, Ethiopia (Johanson 2004). She belongs to the species *Australopithecus afarensis,* which lived from 4.3 million to 3 million years ago. The 1974 discovery of Lucy made headlines because so much of her skeleton was preserved (see Figure 4).

The australopithecine era also provides the first artifacts, in the form of stone tools. The oldest stone tools, dating to 2.6 million years ago, are from Gona, Ethiopia (Semaw et al. 2003).

SUMMARY OF THE EARLY HOMININS The anatomy of these early species exhibits evolution away from ape-like characteristics to more human-like characteristics. Most would have been around 4 feet tall when standing upright and would have weighed around 100 pounds. Their arms were slightly longer than those of modern humans, and the shortness of their lower limbs would have made them look more like apes than like humans.

Orrorin tugenensis is the earliest fossil evidence for bipedalism, and later fossils such as Lucy confirm the trend, as do the footprints at Laetoli. It is less clear, however, when the early hominins abandoned knuckle-walking or brachiation for complete bipedalism. Although early hominins such as Lucy had a lower body that was fully designed for bipedalism, they retained some aspects of shoulder

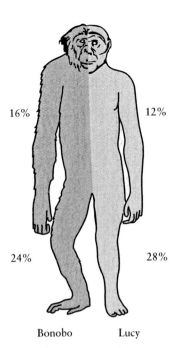

16%   12%

24%   28%

Bonobo   Lucy

FIGURE 4 Lucy's Body Weight Proportions Compared to a Bonobo. Primatologist Adrienne Zihlman found that living bonobos are similar to Lucy in body weight proportions. Lucy's arms are 12 percent of her body weight and her legs are 28 percent. In bonobos, arms are 16 percent of body weight and legs, 24 percent. This pattern of weight distribution indicates partial bipedal locomotion.

Source: Adapted from an original drawing by Carla Simmons in Sussman 1984:197

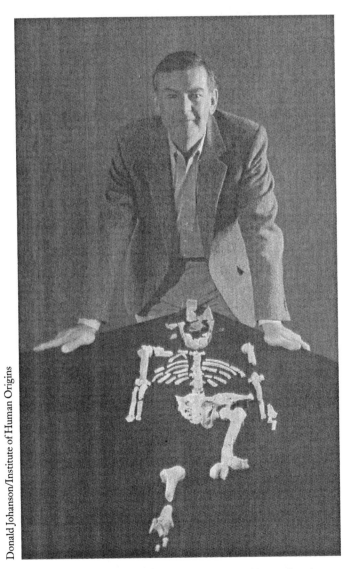

Donald Johanson/Institute of Human Origins

Lucy and Don Johanson, the paleoanthropologist who discovered her. Because they have fossils of about 40 percent of Lucy's skeleton, researchers can make fairly accurate estimates about her stature, body weight, and other characteristics.

and upper limb anatomy suggesting that they also brachiated to seek protection in trees. This combination could have given them a decisive advantage over other animals.

Why did bipedalism and upright posture evolve among early hominins? Scholars have proposed many theories for the emergence of upright posture and bipedalism (O'Higgins and Elton 2007, Thorpe et al. 2007). One prominent theory holds that upright posture and bipedalism evolved because they enabled hominins to see other animals over the tall grasses in the more open areas, or savanna, compared to dense rain forests. A **savanna** environment consists of open plains with tall grasses and patches of trees; during this period of hominin evolution, the extent of rainforests was declining and savannas were increasing due to climate change.

The general pattern of early hominin food acquisition was foraging. The diet of the early hominins was mixed, not specialized, and included a wide variety of fruits, insects, nuts, tubers (fleshy roots of plants), and some animal meat which was probably scavenged rather than hunted.

The evidence of stone tools is an indication of culture. Some early hominins made and used simple stone tools. Given that stone tool-making traditions were likely to be learned and shared, the early hominins therefore possessed some elements of culture.

© 2004 Frans Lanting

When the early hominins were evolving in Africa, the environment was changing from dense forest to patches of woodland interspersed with open grasslands.

▷ *How might this type of environment be related to the evolution of bipedalism?*

ARCHAIC *HOMO*

Archaic *Homo* is a category of extinct hominin species that lived from 2.4 million years to 19,000 years ago. Compared to the early hominins, these species have a more modern human-like body shape, larger brains, and smaller jaws and teeth. Stone tools are prominent in the culture of all archaic *Homo* species. These hominins migrated into much of the Old World. Paleoanthropologists argue about whether they are ancestors to modern humans. Some say they all died out whereas others say they interbred with later species. There is no conclusive proof to support either position at this time.

Homo habilis In Olduvai Gorge, Tanzania, in 1960, Louis and Mary Leakey discovered fossils representing a form they thought was human-like. They argued that the Olduvai evidence should be included in the genus *Homo* because it satisfied the accepted functional criteria of manual dexterity, upright posture, and fully bipedal locomotion. They argued for naming a new species called *Homo habilis* (literally "Handy Human") (Leakey et al. 1964). Associated with *H. habilis* are distinctive stone tools that are named Oldowan because they were first found in Olduvai Gorge. The **Oldowan tradition** is characterized by *core tools* and *flake tools*. Core tools are made

from rounded stones that have had flakes chipped off them, either at one end or along one side. Flake tools are more numerous than core tools. Flake tools are the sharp pieces of stone that break off a core when it is struck. It is unlikely that Oldowan stone tools were the only tools used by their makers. Rather, they were the tools that survived in the archaeological record because they were made of hard stone (see the Critical Thinking box).

Homo erectus *Homo erectus* ("Upright Human") is the first hominin species that was widely distributed across the Old World. Although *H. erectus* was a highly successful species in terms of duration, around 2 million years, and in terms of its colonization of much of the Old World, if you met an *H. erectus* individual in the street, you would not mistake him for a modern human. His head would be smaller, his forehead lower, and no modern human would have such a pronounced brow ridge. The average brain size of *H. erectus* was about 1000 centimeters, or two-thirds the size of the average modern human brain.

H. erectus is associated with the emergence, around 1.7 million years ago, of a new stone tool tradition called the **Acheulian tradition**, characterized by the prevalence of handaxes (Toth and Schick 1993). A *handaxe* is a bifacial (two-sided) stone tool that is flat, pear-shaped, and flaked on all its edges and on both surfaces. The Acheulian tradition is named after a site in St. Acheul, France, where European archaeologists first discovered handaxes. The oldest Acheulian stone tools are from Ethiopia and Kenya. Acheulian tools, in contrast to Oldowan tools, were worked on both sides, more finely crafted, more consistently shaped, and therefore indicate more planning, skill, and manual dexterity.

ARCHAIC *HOMO* MOVES OUT OF AFRICA Around 2 million years ago, archaic *Homo* began to migrate out of Africa. The question of why archaic *Homo* left Africa remains unanswered. Three major hypotheses exist:

- Hominins had become meat-eaters, and their preference for meat led them to follow herds of animals as these moved out of Africa to new areas.

---

savanna an environment that consists of open plains with tall grasses and patches of trees.

archaic *Homo* a category of several extinct hominin species that lived from 2.4 million years to 19,000 years ago and is characterized by different stone tool traditions, depending on the species.

Oldowan tradition the oldest hominin toolkit, characterized by core tools and flake tools.

Acheulian tradition the toolkit of *H. erectus*, used from 1.7 million years ago to 300,000 years ago, and characterized by handaxes.

CRITICAL thinking

What Is Really in the Toolbox?

It is reasonable to assume that stone tools were not the only tools that archaic *Homo* used, given that it is likely that other materials were available for tools and that a wider variety of uses existed than the probable functions of core tools, flakes, and scrapers. This exercise asks you to do a mini-experimental study by imagining that you are living in an open woodland environment like that of archaic *Homo*. Imagine your daily life, including how you obtain food and where you sleep at night.

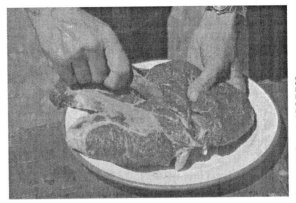

An experimental archaeologist uses a newly made stone tool to cut raw meat.

© Lowell Georgia/CORBIS

◆ CRITICAL THINKING QUESTIONS

- Make a list of the activities you would perform over a 24-hour period and what tools you might need for those activities.

- What materials in the savanna would provide useful tools for performing these activities?
- Assume you have 10 tools in your tool kit. Three of them are made from stone: one core tool

and two flake tools. What are the other seven tools? What is the likelihood that these other seven tools would be preserved in the archaeological record available to future ages?

Werner Forman/Art Resource, NY

Acheulian handaxe from Tanzania.

▶ *Imagine that you are gripping the widest part in your hand, with the narrow part pointing horizontal or downward, cutting through tree bark or striking at an attacking hyena.*

- They were attracted by the cool and arid northern climate, where their ability to adapt to varied conditions gave them an advantage over other species.
- Humans are "natural" migrants—they just have to keep moving.

No matter what the reason for leaving Africa, the general direction of migration was north and east, out of Africa toward the Middle East and then on into Asia. The earliest fossil evidence of hominins outside Africa, dated at 1.8 million years ago, comes from the site of Dmanisi in the Caucasus region of the country of Georgia (Vekua et al. 2002) (see Map 3). Dmanisi hominins are small in stature, and their brains are also small, around 600 centimeters, or not much larger than the average brain size of the Australopithecines. Yet their limb proportions are more modern, and they obviously had the capacity for long-distance travel. The stone tools at Dmanisi are core and flake tools, similar to the Oldowan toolkit.

From Dmanisi, there is a large geographical gap as to where *H. erectus* went. Some evidence indicates that *H. erectus* reached Java, in Southeast Asia, as early as 1.8 million years ago (Swisher et al. 1994). How they got to Java is a mystery, because no evidence exists to explain their migration (see Map 4).

Homo floresiensis Another Asian puzzle is the recent discovery of a dwarf-sized species of hominins, nicknamed "the Hobbit," found on the island of Flores in Southeast Asia (see Map 4). The fossil evidence for this species consists of a

MAP 3 Dmanisi, Georgia.
The country of Georgia has the distinction of being the site of 1.7 million-year-old hominin fossils found at Dmanisi. Many thousands of years later, during the Neolithic era, modern humans first domesticated grapes and produced wine in this region. Given its location on the Black Sea, Georgia has long been involved in trade.

found with the fossils, however, are like those of modern humans who had much larger brains. Scientists continue to debate whether the Hobbit is a separate species of archaic *Homo* or whether it is a pathologically dwarfed modern human from the recent past. Ongoing research and more fossil and archaeological evidence will help resolve this debate. If the Hobbit proves to be a legitimate archaic *Homo* species, then these questions remain: How did a hominin with such a small brain get to Flores? How did it produce modern-style stone tools? How did it survive until recent times?

THE NEANDERTHALS *Homo neanderthalensis*, informally referred to as Neanderthals, was first discovered in a site in Germany called Neanderthal. It is known from over a hundred sites spread across most of Europe, into what is now Israel and Iraq, and all the way into Siberia (see Map 5). The oldest Neanderthal sites are in Western Europe, where Neanderthal

well-preserved skeleton from one individual, dated at 18,000 years ago, and a single tooth from another individual, dated at 40,000 years ago (Morwood et al. 2004, Brown et al. 2004). This hominin was just over 3 feet tall, stood upright, and was probably bipedal. Its brain size was small. Stone tools

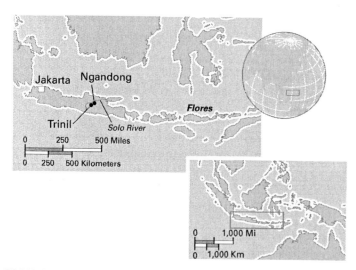

MAP 4 Hominin Sites on Islands of Indonesia.
Since the early twentieth century, paleoanthropologists and archaeologists have made important hominin discoveries at several island sites in Indonesia, including Java and Flores. This research demonstrates that early human ancestors were living in this part of the world earlier than anyone had suspected and had sophisticated nautical abilities.

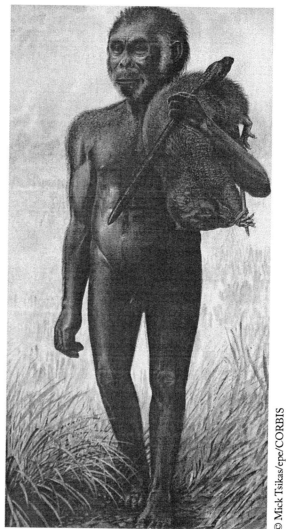

Artist's impression, based on fossil remains, of *H. floresiensis*, nicknamed "the Hobbit."

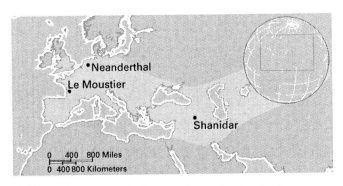

MAP 5 **Neanderthal Sites and Distribution in the Old World.**
The discovery of many Neanderthal sites across the Old World indicates that they occupied an extensive area. During their later period, they overlapped with modern humans in the Middle East and Europe. Whether Neanderthals and modern humans interbred is debated.

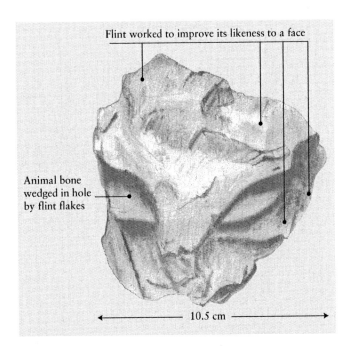

Flint worked to improve its likeness to a face

Animal bone wedged in hole by flint flakes

10.5 cm

FIGURE 5 **Worked Flint Found by the Loire River in Northern France. Dated to 35,000 years ago, this object was made by Neanderthals and is one of the earliest examples of sculpture.**

remains are found mainly in rock shelters and caves. The Neanderthals survived from 400,000 to 30,000 years ago.

The Neanderthals are highly distinctive in terms of their morphology. Compared to modern humans, they had heavier limb bones, larger brains, and distinctive facial skeletons. Neanderthals were the only hominin species able to tolerate, over thousands of years, the cold temperatures that intermittently affected Europe and northern Asia. Although the distinctive morphology of the Neanderthals may be the result of biological adaptations to a very cold climate, it is likely that they may also have developed cultural adaptations to the cold, including clothing (see Eye on the Environment). Another cultural feature is that Neanderthals were the first hominins to bury their dead regularly, so the quality and quantity of their fossil records are better than for other archaic *Homo* species.

Most Neanderthal fossils are found in association with a stone tool kit referred to as the **Mousterian tradition**, named after the site of Le Moustier, France, where such tools were first described. Mousterian tool kits, compared to the Acheulian, are characterized by smaller, lighter, and more specialized flake tools such as points, scrapers, and awls. Neanderthals created material items other than tools that demonstrate their relatively advanced way of thinking and behaving. This book's definition of *expressive culture*, is behavior and beliefs related to art and leisure.

Mousterian tradition   the toolkit of the Neanderthals characterized by the predominance of small, light, and more specialized flake tools such as points, scrapers, and awls.

Anatomically Modern Humans (AMH) or *Homo sapiens* or **modern humans**   the species to which modern humans belong and also referred to by that term; first emerged in Africa between 300,000–160,000 years ago and then spread throughout the Old and New Worlds.

The Neanderthals had elements of expressive culture including portable art, though of a simple sort (see Figure 5), and flutes. They may have had the capacity for verbal language, though this issue is debated. Another debated issue is whether the Neanderthals went extinct, perhaps wiped out by the incoming modern humans, or whether they interbred with modern humans and can be considered part of our direct lineage.

SUMMARY OF ARCHAIC *HOMO*   Compared to the early hominins, the smaller chewing teeth and the smaller and more slender jaws of archaic *Homo* suggest that these species either ate different kinds of food or ate the same food but processed it outside the mouth, possibly by cooking. One way to improve dietary quality was to eat more animal meat, birds, or fish, because these food sources provide large amounts of energy-rich protein and fat. Food sources such as eggs, worms, and insects can also provide protein and fat, but in smaller quantities per mouthful. Evidence that these species probably ate meat comes from an unlikely source: tapeworms (Hoberg et al. 2001). The first evidence of tapeworm infection in hominins coincides with the emergence of archaic *Homo* in Africa, a finding that points to the likelihood that they ate substantial amounts of meat. No one knows for sure how such meat was obtained, but most thinking leans toward the view that it was scavenged from animals killed by other predators.

Archaic *Homo* species inhabited a wide variety of habitats including those with temperate climates and those with cold climates. An increasingly complex culture was key to surviving in such varied environments. Evidence that *H. erectus*

Clothing as a Thermal Adaptation to Cold and Wind

During the many thousands of years in which Neanderthals lived in Eurasia, the climate was mainly cold, and winds were likely strong. Neanderthals' biological and cultural adaptations allowed them to survive in latitudes up to 55 degrees N (Gilligan 2007). Their biological adaptations include a short, wide body with short limbs, a body type that allows for conservation of heat. Neanderthal cultural adaptations include cave dwelling and the use of fire to provide heat and light inside the caves. Their Mousterian toolkit, which includes scrapers, points, and awls, strongly suggests the likelihood that they made and wore clothing.

Among the many theories about the fate of the Neanderthals, Australian archaeologist Ian Gilligan offers a novel theory. His explanation for Neanderthal extinction involves climate change, Neanderthal morphology, and Neanderthal culture. Gilligan argues that the Neanderthals' biological and cultural adaptations were sufficient under normal and consistent cold regimes but insufficient during severe cold weather spikes that occurred near the end of their time on earth. Most importantly, he differentiates between two types of clothing: simple and complex, and their thermal effectiveness in situations of extreme cold.

- *Simple clothing* is loosely draped around the body and has only one layer.
- *Complex clothing* has multiple layers and the first layer, at least, is fitted to the body.

Simple clothing provides limited protection against cold and wind, whereas complex clothing can protect against severe cold and wind in polar environments.

No surviving remains of clothing from the Neanderthals exist, so archaeologists can only make inferences about the type of clothing they wore from their tools. Given the reasonable assumption that the basic material for Neanderthal clothing was animal hides, these would have required cleaning and scraping in order to make them usable as simple clothing. The Neanderthal Mousterian toolkit was able to perform these tasks, and thus it is likely that they had simple clothing.

Complex clothing, however, requires more careful preparation of the various layers and stitching pieces together to form a fitted layer. More specialized tools such as borers and needles are necessary. The Neanderthals did not possess such tools, but the modern humans who arrived in Eurasia did.

Gilligan's working hypothesis is that the biological adaptation of Neanderthals, along with their cultural ability to produce simple clothing, was effective over many thousands of years. But, in later times, cold temperatures spiked, and the Neanderthals lacked the ability to protect themselves with complex clothing and therefore succumbed to hypothermia. In contrast, the in-coming modern humans lacked biological adaptations to the extreme cold, but they did have the technology to produce complex clothing which allowed them to survive spikes of cold weather better than the Neanderthals could.

Using knowledge of temperature changes during the later Neanderthal era and inferences from the Neanderthal and modern human toolkits, it is possible to generate a reasonable scenario that Neanderthals died out because of their inability to survive extreme cold stress. Although Neanderthals survived for thousands of years in cold conditions, they did not extend their territory from inner Siberia further to Alaska and on into the New World, as did their modern human successors. Complex clothing could have made all the difference.

◆ FOOD FOR THOUGHT

- What is your experience, in extremely cold weather, with the effectiveness of close-fitting and layered clothing versus loose-fitting and nonlayered clothing?

---

had reached islands in Southeast Asia over 1 million years ago means that the species had devised a way to travel by water, presumably using some sort of raft or boat, and could cross substantial distances, at least 15 miles from island to island, on open sea. This achievement marks a major locomotive advance, enabling archaic *Homo* to migrate to and settle in a far wider range of places than are available by foot.

Archaic *Homo* species had some aspects of culture including stone tools. Neanderthal artifacts document the beginning of art and music. Neanderthals buried their dead and may have had a sense of supernaturalism or a belief in life after death. They may have had verbal language.

MODERN HUMANS

The term **anatomically modern humans (AMH)** refers to *Homo sapiens*, the species to which modern humans belong; this book uses the term "modern humans." This era is the

THINKING
OUTSIDE
THE BOX

Listen to the interview on the Web with French paleoanthropologist Jean-Jacques Hublin about Neanderthals and their fate: www.pbs.org/wgbh/evolution/library/07/3/text_pop/1_073_02.htm. What is Hublin's position?

Blades from Kapthurin, Kenya, dated at 300,000 years ago. Many archaeologists say that these blades, and other early tools, indicate that humans had aspects of modern behavior far in advance of modern anatomy.

last period during which any evidence exists of significant morphological change. Compared to the Neanderthals, modern humans have steeper foreheads with smaller brow ridges, smaller faces, smaller incisor teeth, and thinner limb bones. Culture, in contrast, continues to become more elaborate and complex, as people alter how they interact with nature and with each other. In this relatively short period, the number of human species was reduced to one, and modern humans emerged as the only form of human life on the earth.

MODERN HUMAN ORIGINS IN AFRICA No one knows which, if any, of the earlier species may be a direct ancestor to modern humans. At this point, the fossil evidence does not indicate a clear line from any archaic *Homo* species to modern humans. Future fossil evidence may help fill in the gaps. The earliest fossil evidence for modern humans is from a site in Ethiopia and dates to 160,000 years ago. Archaeological evidence also supports the African origins theory of modern humans. Modern tools such as blades that may have been used on the tips of spears and arrows have been found in African sites dated to 300,000 years ago. Given the early date of the archaeological evidence for modernity, it is likely that future - fossil discoveries in Africa will be from that time, too. Or, modern behavior may have preceded modern biological evolution.

Upper Paleolithic the period of modern human occupation in Europe and Eurasia (including the Middle East) from 45,000–40,000 years ago to 12,000 years ago, characterized by microlithic tools and prolific cave art and portable art.

Cro-Magnons the first modern humans in Europe, dating from 40,000 years ago.

Clovis culture New World population characterized by the Clovis point with the earliest site dated to 11,000 years ago in the Southwest United States.

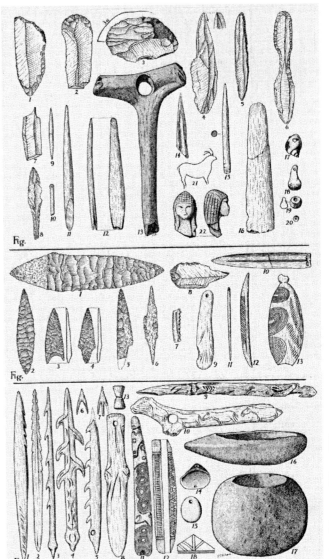

Upper Paleolithic artifacts. These artifacts were made by the earliest modern humans in Europe.

Genetic analysis indicates that all modern humans are descended from a common ancestral population that lived in Africa at least 200,000 years ago (Ingman et al. 2000, Quintana-Murci et al. 1999). There are more different versions of genes in contemporary modern human populations in Africa than in all the rest of the world put together (Tishkoff and Verrelli 2003). This finding is consistent with the view that Africa has been the dominant source of the novel genes and gene combinations of modern humans. Many novel versions of genes originated in African populations and then spread into the Middle East, Asia, and Europe (Pääbo 2003).

MODERN HUMANS DURING THE UPPER PALEOLITHIC IN THE OLD WORLD The **Upper Paleolithic** is the period of modern human occupation in Europe and Eurasia (including the Middle East) 45,000 years ago to 12,000 years ago. During this period, *microliths* and other small, finely made stone and bone tools are the defining elements of technology. Modern humans also made and used tools crafted from organic materials, such as nets and baskets. In many places, they created impressive works of art.

Modern humans, like *Homo erectus* before them, first migrated out of Africa by land to the Middle East, where the oldest modern human fossils outside Africa are found, dated at around 100,000 years ago (Hublin 2000). From there, modern humans probably took a coastal route around the Arabian peninsula, along the coastline of what is now India, and then on to Southeast Asia and the Pacific (Stringer 2000). Modern humans reached Australia around 50,000 years ago. Like the modern humans who later arrived in Europe, modern humans in Australia were prolific artists. Rock paintings in Australia are as old as many of the world-famous Paleolithic cave paintings of Europe.

Other modern humans moved north to Turkey and from there into Eastern and Central Europe. Yet others travelled into Central Asia, Siberia, and eventually the New World.

The arrival of modern humans in Europe marks the beginning of a period of rapidly increasing cultural complexity, often referred to as a cultural revolution or "Golden Age." The first evidence of modern humans in Europe comes from sites in Central Europe, around 40,000 years ago. By around 36,000 years ago, modern humans reached Western Europe. Cultural changes during the European Upper Paleolithic (see Map 6) include more complex and specialized tool kits. A major leap forward in symbolic thinking is also indicated by many examples of cave art and portable sculpture.

Archaeologists first discovered fossil evidence for modern humans at Cro-Magnon, a rock shelter site in Les Eyzies, France. This site provides the name for the first modern humans in Europe, the **Cro-Magnon** people, who arrived in Europe around 40,000 years ago. Although early Cro-Magnons overlapped in time with Neanderthals, the evidence is unclear as to whether there was interbreeding or cultural exchange.

The Cro-Magnons had a more sophisticated toolkit than the Neanderthals. They also left behind an impressive legacy of art including cave art and portable art. Given their many achievements, some scholars argue that they must have had verbal language. The many cultural accomplishments of the Upper Paleolithic provided the basis for the developments described in the next section of this chapter.

MODERN HUMAN MIGRATIONS INTO THE NEW WORLD
By 30,000 years ago, modern humans were migrating from Siberia into present-day Alaska. Two routes are possible: an *ice-free corridor* in Alaska and western Canada, which led them into the rest of North America, and a coastal route. Whichever path they followed, and it may have been both, in just a few thousand years, modern humans had spread throughout most of the unglaciated regions of North America and into Central and South America.

The major body of archaeological evidence about the first modern humans in the New World is that of the **Clovis culture**, a population characterized by the *Clovis point* (Haynes 2002). First discovered in New Mexico (see Map 7), a Clovis point is distinct in that it is bifacial and *fluted*, meaning that it has a long, vertical flake chipped from its base. The oldest Clovis sites are dated to slightly before 11,000 years ago, and shortly thereafter Clovis people spread over most of the unglaciated regions of North America (Waters and Stafford 2001, Haynes 2002). Clovis culture, however, lasted only a short while.

For a long time, archaeologists accepted Clovis sites as the earliest human sites in the New World, a position that left a large gap in time between then and when migrants were likely to have begun arriving and settling in the New World, given archaeological data from Siberia. Recently, several claims for pre-Clovis sites have been made. Monte Verde, in Chile, is the most definite of the earliest possible pre-Clovis sites in the New World. It suggests a human presence in South America by 12,500 years ago and raises the possibility of coastal migration and settlements (Dillehay 2000). Recovery of genetic data from *coprolites* (fossilized feces) in a site called Paisley Caves in Oregon proves the existence of modern humans in North America around 12,300 years ago (Gilbert et al. 2008). Such discoveries, with their implications for overthrowing the

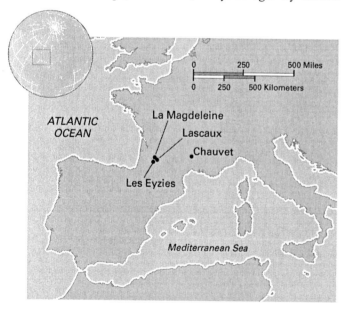

MAP 6 Upper Paleolithic Sites in Europe.
This map shows only a small number of the many sites in Europe from the Upper Paleolithic era. Les Eyzies (pronounced lay-zay-zee) is the first site where evidence of Cro Magnons was discovered. Lascaux (pronounced lah-SKOH) and Chauvet (pronounced shoh-VAY) are two of the most important cave art sites in Europe. La Magdeleine (pronounced la-mahd-LEN) is the site for the fourth and last cultural stage of the Upper Paleolithic. At French Magdalenian sites, the main food source of modern humans was reindeer. At Magdalenian sites in Germany and Russia, evidence exists that people had domesticated dogs, perhaps for hunting.

(LEFT) An Upper Paleolithic wall painting at Lascaux, France, depicting a variety of animals. Of the hundreds of figures painted in Lascaux's several galleries, only one depicts a human form, and it has a bird head. (CENTER) A so-called Venus figurine, found at Willendorf, Austria, is carved from fine limestone and is 11 centimeters tall (4 inches). This figurine is 25,000 years old. (RIGHT) A human head carved in mammoth ivory, called the Venus of Brassempouy, is 3.6 centimeters high (an inch and a half). Found in France, it is dated to between 30,000 and 26,000 years ago. Its stratigraphic position was not carefully documented at the time of its discovery. Because of the lack of details about its discovery and its lack of surface corrosion, some archaeologists question its authenticity.

Clovis points are large (11 centimeters long, or about 5 inches), bifacially flaked spear points. So far no evidence of hafting exists, and given the elegant flaking, some archaeologists therefore think that Clovis points were status items. Because many are found near water sources, another theory is that they were made to be used for sacred offerings.

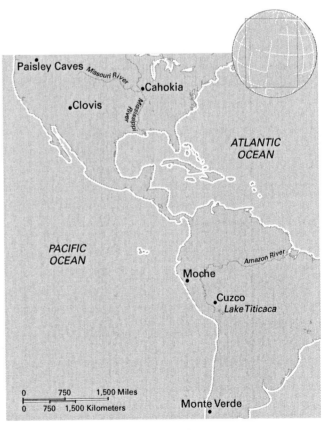

MAP 7 New World Sites Mentioned in This Chapter.

Clovis-first theory, create controversy but also open the way for new models of how the New World was occupied.

It is likely there were several migrant streams of modern humans into the New World. Different groups arrived and settled over different periods, and each made its own contribution to the genetic and cultural diversity of New World populations. No matter when, where, and how modern humans arrived in the New World, they spread rapidly over a diverse range of environments and left their enduring mark in settlement sites, artifacts, and fossils.

SUMMARY OF MODERN HUMANS Starting around 300,000 years ago in Africa, modern humans have since then colonized the entire world. Their technological knowledge advanced to include spears and microlithic tools. Plant and animal domestication provided a new degree of control over food sources as well as the ability to follow a more settled life.

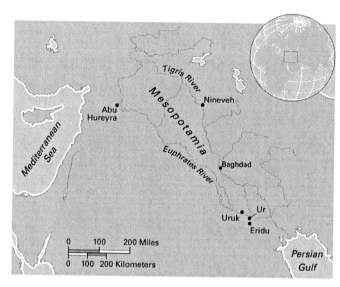

MAP 8 Neolithic Sites in the Middle East.
Archaeologists have excavated many important Neolithic sites in the Middle East including those mentioned in this chapter, shown here. In Iraq, archaeological sites and artifacts are endangered due to the war and looting.

The Neolithic Revolution and the Emergence of Cities and States

Around 12,000 years ago, people in many places across the world started changing their lives in ways that differed fundamentally from previous times. Many began to live in small, permanent settlements, called **sedentism**. Along with sedentism, people turned to plant and animal domestication instead of relying only on wild foods. Sedentism and plant and animal domestication, along with bipedalism, tool-making, and symbolic communication, are among the most important developments in human evolution (Zeder 2006).

Domestication is the process by which human selection causes changes in the genetic material of plants and animals. Through human selection, new species emerge. The earliest methods of selection could have been as simple as removing undesired plants from around desired plants. Later, more intensive kinds of selection took place, with intentional relocation of desired plants into garden areas. Concerning animal domestication, people may have kept preferred animals and promoted their reproduction while culling less desirable ones. Plant and animal domestication is a major defining feature of humanity's last several thousand years. It supported a new level of food production that promoted the growth of cities and states.

THE NEOLITHIC REVOLUTION

The **Neolithic Revolution** refers to a time of rapid transformation in technology related to plant and animal domestication, including tools such as sickle blades and grinding stones. The story of the Neolithic begins in the Old World in

Mesopotamia, especially the region called the *Fertile Crescent* between the Tigris and Euphrates Rivers in present day Iraq (see Map 8). Rye, wheat, and barley were first domesticated here, along with animals such as sheep, goats, cattle, and pigs (see Figure 6). Domestication of other plants and animals occurred in the Middle East, Africa, North America, Central America, and South America. Some of these events resulted from independent invention, or the creation of a new idea, behavior, or object. In others, diffusion, or the spread of culture through contact, was responsible for the Neolithic transition.

The stages of plant and animal domestication are revealed at several sites in the Middle East. One such site, Abu Hureyra (ah-boo hoo-RYUH-rah) is located near the Euphrates River (Moore et al. 2000). At the time, the region was rich in forest resources and wild grasses, and the climate was warmer and wetter than today. Abu Hureyra, like many Neolithic sites in the region, is a **tell**, a human-made mound resulting from the accumulation of successive generations of

sedentism   a lifestyle associated with residence in permanent villages, towns, and cities, generally linked with the emergence of farming.

domestication   a process by which human selection causes changes in the genetic material of plants and animals.

Neolithic Revolution   a time of rapid transformation in technology, related to plant and animal domestication, which includes tools such as sickle blades and grinding stones.

tell   a human-made mound resulting from the accumulation of successive generations of house construction, reconstruction, and trash.

FIGURE 6 The Origins
of Selected Plant and Animal
Domesticates.

Source: From *The Human Impact on the
Natural Enviroments*, 5th Edition, by
Andrew Goudie. Copyright © 2004.
Blackwell Publishers Ltd. Reproduced
with permission of Blackwell Publishers
& Andrew Goudie.

Plants	Region	Approximate Date BCE
Barley, wheat	Middle East	8000–7000
Squash, gourd, maize	Central America	7000–6000
White potato, chile pepper	South America	7000–6000
Rice, millet, water chestnut	East Asia	6000–5000
Pearl millet, sorghum	Africa	3000
African rice	Africa	3000
Animals		
Dog	Russia, Eastern Europe	10,000
Sheep, goat	Middle East	7000
Pig, cattle	Middle East	6000
Chicken	China	6000
Horse	Central Asia	4000
Llama, alpaca	South America	4000
Donkey	Middle East	3500
Bactrian camel	Central Asia	2000
Dromedary camel	Middle East	2000
Turkey	Central America	Unknown

house construction, reconstruction, and trash. Over thousands of years, tells gradually rose above the surrounding plain. The tell at Abu Hureyra is 8 meters high (about 25 feet), and it was occupied from 10,500 to 6000 BCE. The *stratigraphy* (study of the layers over time) of the tell provides the story of change during the Neolithic. The first occupants lived in a village of between 200 and 300 people. They were *sedentary foragers,* whose livelihood depended on hunting and gathering but who lived in a permanent settlement rather than in temporary camps. This residence pattern suggests that the environment could provide adequate food and water, within a fairly narrow region. They hunted gazelle and collected wild plants, including cereals, lentils, fruits, nuts, and berries.

The next levels at the site show the stages in the transition to plant domestication. By 10,000 BCE, the occupants had domesticated rye. After 9000 BCE, they had domesticated wheat and barley. The first domestic grains were probably produced on a small scale through gardening or *horticulture,* defined as the growing of domesticated plants by using hand-held tools and relying on natural sources of moisture and soil enrichment. Hunting gazelle was still important, and gazelle constituted 80 percent of the animal food that people ate. Later levels provide evidence of a fully Neolithic lifestyle combining sedentism and domesticated plants and animals, including two herd animals: goats and sheep. Perhaps because of an increasingly arid environment and human over-hunting, the gazelle population had declined, and domesticated animals gradually took their place as sources of animal meat. The scarcity of wild animals may have prompted people to domesticate replacements.

The village grew to 6000 inhabitants by 7000 BCE, when sedentary life was combined with a more intensive form of domesticated grain production called *agriculture* or *farming,* defined as the growing of crops on permanent plots of land by using the plow, irrigation, and fertilizer. The series of sequential transitions at Abu Hureyra is typical of those at other sites in the Middle East.

A different pattern of domesticates emerged in Africa's *Sahel,* the grassland regions south of the Sahara desert. For thousands of years, foragers had occupied this region of rich lakesides and abundant wild grasses. Their economy combined

British archaeologists discovered the important Neolithic site of Çatalhöyük (shah-tall-hoy-yuck) in 1958. It is located in south-central Turkey and dates to around 7000 BCE. So far, only a small portion of the tell has been excavated.

© Yann Arthus-Bertrand/CORBIS

Stonehenge, in southern England, is the most well-known late Neolithic monumental site. Many similar, though smaller, henge monuments exist in the British Isles and elsewhere in Europe and northern Africa. A henge monument is a construction in the shape of a circular enclosure with an opening at one point in the circle. They are generally interpreted as ceremonial sites. The latest evidence about Stonehenge indicates that it was also a burial ground.

fishing, hunting herd animals, and harvesting wild grasses such as millet, sorghum, and African rice. The domestication of cattle was the first step in the transition to the Neolithic in Africa (Marshall and Hildebrand 2002). The domestication of wild cattle supported the emergence of *pastoralism,* defined as an economic strategy in which people depend on domesticated animals for most of their food and which continues to be an important mode of livelihood in the region today.

The transition to the Neolithic in Europe relied on the introduction of plant and animal domesticates from the Middle East. The first plant and animal domesticates appeared in southeastern Europe around 6000 BCE (Richards 2003). By 4000 BCE, the combination of farming and keeping animals had spread across most of Europe. Archaeological evidence for the later Neolithic in Europe documents social status differences, group ceremonies and feasts, and religious sites that drew thousands of pilgrims from wide areas.

PLANT AND ANIMAL DOMESTICATION IN THE NEW WORLD Plant domestication in the New World first began in Middle America (or *Mesoamerica*), the region between North and South America. Later transitions in South America and North America occurred partly through independent invention and partly through the spread of *maize* (corn). Three features distinguish the pattern of plant and animal domestication and sedentism in Middle America:

- The first experiments with domesticated plants took place long before sedentism.
- The first domesticated plants were gourds, squash, beans, and maize, and the first animal domesticates were dogs, turkeys, and honey bees.

- The transition to an entirely agricultural way of life was slower than in the Middle East, extending from 8000 to 2000 BCE.

By 5000 BCE, three domesticated plant species were the most important parts of the diet in Mexico, the so-called *Mesoamerican triad:* maize (corn), squash, and beans. People in the Andes Mountains first domesticated the potato, a member of the tuber family of root crops (Ochoa 1991). Tubers are difficult to find archaeologically because they spread by sending out shoots underground rather than by seeds. Thus the date of 5000 BCE for potato domestication is conjectural, based on the assumption that it occurred around the time of other Andean domesticates, including beans, quinoa (a seed), llamas, alpacas, and guinea pigs. Gourds and squash were domesticated in Ecuador by 10,000 BCE.

By 4000 BCE, people in eastern North America were experimenting with various plants as part of a mixed economic strategy of hunting, collecting wild plants, and cultivating a few domesticated species of seed crops (Smith 1998). The most important indigenous domesticates were seed crops such as goosefoot (similar to spinach, but also grown for its seeds and related to quinoa of South America), sunflowers, and possibly squash. None of these plants, however, could support a sedentary farming population. Between the first and third centuries of the present era, it was the introduction of maize that led to the emergence of farming communities throughout North America.

CITIES AND STATES

The word *civilization* literally means "living in cities." A *city* is distinguished from a village or town by having a larger population (more than 10,000 people as a rough guide) and by having more occupational specialization, more elaborate architecture, and central services such as temples, government agencies, and trade organizations. Along with urbanization came the growth of the political institution of the state. A *state* is a centralized political organization encompassing many communities. States are typically bureaucratic; that is, they have specialized units with authority over limited areas of governance, with trained personnel and usually written records. States have the power to levy taxes, keep the peace through use of legitimate force, and wage war.

Cities and states first emerged in the Old World, once again in what is now Iraq. Mesopotamia, which means "the land between two rivers," referring to the Tigris and the Euphrates, is the home of the world's earliest cities, dated to 3500 BCE. Important early cities in Mesopotamia include Uruk, Ur, Eridu, and Nineveh, all of which were preeminent at different times (see Map 8).

Uruk is a well-studied Mesopotamian city. By 3500 BCE, its population was around 10,000 people and it grew to a peak of 50,000 (Adams 1981). People lived in houses, made of dried mud-brick, which were packed tightly together and interspersed with narrow, winding streets (Pollock 1999). Surrounding Uruk was a massive brick wall 7 meters (23 feet) high, its numerous gates and guard towers suggesting the need for defense. Monumental architecture included a prominent feature called a *ziggurat*, a massive stepped platform that supported temples and administrative buildings. Government and religion were closely connected, so temples served both sacred and secular purposes, including storage and redistribution of agricultural surpluses, craft production, and economic management and recordkeeping. Commoner laborers and slaves built and maintained the monumental buildings in which state rule and commerce were managed; they wove the fine linen garments that elite men and women wore; and they pressed the high-quality oils consumed at royal feasts.

Early Mesopotamian cities were centers of regional trade, a feature that some archaeologists view as the primary catalyst for the urban revolution (Algaze 2001). Trade is also probably the catalyst for the development of the world's earliest money and writing. Writing was first invented between 3500 and 3000 BCE in Mesopotamia, for financial recordkeeping (Lawler 2001). Mesopotamian writing, or *cuneiform*, used around 1500 signs, many of which referred to specific goods such as bread and oil. Specially trained scribes worked in administrative roles in what was an early sort of *bureaucracy*, a form of administration that is hierarchical and specialized and relies heavily on recordkeeping. The hundreds of thousands of cuneiform tablets that archaeologists have found in early Mesopotamian cities provide a wealth of information about life at the time.

In the New World, cities and states formed later than in the Old World. Another distinct feature is that some New World states, though powerful and extensive, did not have writing. They did, however, have elaborately constructed capital cities, lavish political feasting, competitive sports, and plentiful gold and other wealth.

The Moche or Mochica civilization emerged around 200 BCE in the deserts of Peru's north coast. Rivers descending from the Andes Mountains fed irrigation works that supported agricultural production to supply dense urban populations (Billman 2002). The Moche civilization is known for distinctive artistic styles and craftwork, especially mold-made portrait vessels and copper, silver, and gold metalwork (Quilter 2002). Warfare was an important component of state formation in the Andes, and Moche ceramics often depict warfare and human sacrifice. Moche civilization reached its

(LEFT) The remains of Uruk in southern Mesopotamia. Occupied starting around 5000 BCE, Uruk had the earliest, grandest, and most numerous monumental buildings in Mesopotamia. The Uruk period saw many innovations including the potter's wheel and the development of writing. (RIGHT) An artist's reconstruction of Anu Ziggurat and the White Temple at Uruk, around 3100 BCE. No written documents exist to indicate the amount of labor involved in constructing such monuments, but it was obviously substantial.

height during the first few centuries of the Common Era. At this time, other civilizations were flourishing throughout the Andes, supported by a successful form of agriculture that was well adapted to high altitudes. It relied on a system of raised fields interspersed by canals. This form of agriculture, over time, fell out of practice, but archaeologists discovered evidence of it. Through their efforts, raised field farming is now reviving in the Andes and helping to provide increased food yields (see the Lessons Applied box).

At the time of the Spanish Conquest in 1532, the Inca had formed the largest empire in the world (MacCormack 2001). The empire was vast, stretching from Colombia in the north to Chile in the south. The city of Cuzco was the empire's capital, and it was linked to distant provinces by a network of roads and bridges. Llamas and alpacas were important domesticated animals, used for their wool and meat and also as pack animals. Hundreds of varieties of potatoes, the most important food crop, were grown on terraced hillsides. The Inca, although a large and powerful empire, had no writing system. Instead, administrators used a system of knotted cords called *khipu* for recordkeeping.

In North America, many complex societies emerged, from the pueblo sites of the southwestern United States to the Iroquois nation of the northeast into Canada. They developed extensive trade networks, engaged in long-distance warfare, and built massive and enduring earthwork monuments. Politically, these societies did not develop state-level institutions but, rather, remained as complex chiefdoms that functioned without urban centers (Earle 1993).

The *Mississippian cultures,* dated to the first century of the Common Era, were located on or near the floodplains of rivers and were based on maize cultivation. Mississippian centers had earthen platform mounds that supported elite residences, ceremonial areas, and burial mounds. Local leaders gained status through the exchange of prestige goods, in which exotic materials and finished goods were traded over large distances (Peregrine 1992). One of the largest Mississippian centers was Cahokia, in present-day Illinois, which gained regional prominence around the year 1000 (Pauketat 2004). Cahokia is located on a vast floodplain where the Mississippi, Ohio, and Missouri Rivers meet. Fish and waterfowl were plentiful, and maize grew in abundance in the fertile and well-watered soil of the floodplain. Terrestrial game was available in the forested uplands. Control over the intersection of several major exchange routes was a key factor in Cahokia's rise to prominence. Enormous for its time and place, Cahokia covered an area of 13 square kilometers, with a peak population of several thousand people. The site contains a large rectangular plaza surrounded by more than 100 earthwork mounds. The largest, Monk's Mound, was 30 meters (over 98 feet) high and is the largest earthwork in North America. Monk's Mound was built in stages between 900 and 1200 CE. The extent of mound construction at Cahokia is a testament to the organizational capacity of the Cahokian political system to harness labor for construction on a grand scale.

Like other powerful chiefdoms, Cahokia had marked social inequality. This inequality is evident in burials, with abundant prestige goods marking high-status burials. Status and gender differences in diet confirm dietary inequalities (Ambrose et al. 2003). High-status people ate more animal protein and less maize, whereas the diet of low-status people was more dependent on maize. Men ate more protein and less maize than women. The diet of low-status women had the highest proportion of maize, about 60 percent.

Moche portrait vessels, considered a brilliant art style, flourished on the northern coast of Peru around the year 500. Many of the pieces depict high-status males with elaborate headdresses and face painting. This piece depicts a woman carrying a load.

▶ *Do research to learn whether the vessels are portraits of actual people or represent generic social categories.*

Dave Rudkin © Dorling Kindersley, Courtesy of the Birmingham Museum and Art Galleries

THINKING
OUTSIDE
THE BOX

Consider the importance of domesticated guinea pigs as food sources in Central and South America and as family pets in North America. What is the likelihood that guinea pigs will become a popular food source in North America and a popular household pet in Central and South America?

LESSONS applied

Archaeology Findings Increase Food Production in Bolivia

An archaeological research project near the shores of Lake Titicaca in highland Bolivia uncovered prehistoric remains of raised fields separated by an intricate system of canals (Straughan and Schuler 1991). When the Spanish colonialists arrived, they abandoned the raised-field system and replaced it with their own type of cultivation. In the later twentieth century, Bolivian farmers were struggling to produce adequate crops of potatoes from the boggy soil. Frosts also took their toll on the plants before they matured.

Two archaeologists who had been working in the region for several years convinced a local farmer to experiment with the indigenous raised-field system, suggesting that what worked a thousand years ago might succeed again. The other villagers were skeptical but watched with interest as the potato plants on the raised field grew taller than they had ever seen. Then, right before the harvest, 90 percent of the village crop was lost due to a heavy frost. Most of the potatoes in the experimental raised field, however, were fine. They had been protected by a thick mist that had formed over the field. The sun's warmth during the day heats up the canal water, which, in turn, warms the fields at night when the temperature drops.

The community eventually adopted the new–old system, and crop yields rose significantly. Moreover, algae and aquatic plants began to grow in the canals along with nitrogen-fixing bacteria. When the canals are cleaned annually, they yield a rich residue of organic material that can be used

Raised beds in Bolivia. This strategy helps prevent erosion, improves the organic content of the soil, captures moisture, and provides protection for crops from frosts. The main feature of the system, termed *waru waru* in the Quechua language, is a network of embankments and canals.

▷ *To find out more about this system, go to* http://www.loas.usde/publications/Unit/oca59ec/ch27.html.

to fertilize the fields. The Bolivian government has started a training program to promote the raised-field technique as a way to increase the nation's food supply. Local people now welcome the archaeologists with enthusiasm when they visit. The Lake Titicaca region, once the center of a rich civilization, was reduced to poverty by the effects of European colonialism. Now, through archaeological findings about the past, the agricultural economy is reviving and thriving.

The site of Cahokia suffered substantial damage in the late 1800s and early 1900s as a result of urban development, construction of roads and railways, expansion of farmland, and amateur collecting (Young and Fowler 2000). Many mounds were bulldozed, and their contents, including human bones and artifacts such as copper goods and shell beads, were used as land fill. Concern expressed by a few archaeologists raised public awareness and put a halt to the destruction and neglect. Cahokia is now a World Heritage Site, and Native American groups from across the United States hold regular ceremonies there.

---

anthropogenic   caused by humans.

An artist's reconstruction of Cahokia showing thatch-roofed houses and massive earthworks. The site reached prominence around the year 1000 CE (Common Era) and was largely abandoned by 1400 CE.

▶ *Visit the website* www.cahokiamounds.com/cahokia.html.

CIVILIZATIONS ARE NOT FOREVER Comparative analysis of many early states shows that all past states have gone through cycles of expansion and decline followed by the rise of new states. (Marcus 1998). In fact, periods of decline, rather than the more archaeologically visible episodes of powerful territorial states, are the norm. Why do even the most powerful states always collapse? The answer may lie in the difficulty states have of maintaining territorial integration and extreme social inequality over long periods. Another factor may be the environmental decline that accompanies state building and accumulation. Some archaeologists think that **anthropogenic** (caused by humans) effects on the environment, such as clearing forests and exhausting the soil, contributed to the collapse of many great and powerful civilizations. Changes during the Neolithic and urban revolutions shed light on humanity's prospects in the future and could provide important cautionary notes about the costs and sustainability of "civilization."

the BIG questions REVISITED

◆ What do living nonhuman primates tell us about human culture?

Humans belong to the category of primates. Primates vary in size from several ounces to over 400 pounds. All nonhuman primates in the wild provide for their food needs by foraging. Most primates live in a social group.

According to genetic data, modern humans are closely related to the living great apes with which we share a common ancestor between 4 and 8 million years ago. The category of great apes includes the four largest ape species: orangutans, gorillas, chimpanzees, and bonobos. Of these, chimpanzees and bonobos are genetically the most closely related to humans. Although chimpanzees and bonobos are alike in many ways, they also have several differences. Neither the chimpanzee or bonobo model applies neatly to all modern human cultures.

Many nonhuman primate species have behaviors that are learned and shared and are thus cultural. Examples include tool use for procuring food and symbolic forms of greeting and interaction.

◆ What role did culture play during hominin evolution?

Hominins is a category of primates that includes modern humans and extinct species of early human ancestors that are more closely related to humans than to living chimpanzees and bonobos. Hominin evolution can be divided into three stages: the early hominins, archaic *Homo,* and modern humans.

The early hominins span from 8 million years ago to 2 million years ago. The two oldest species, *Sahelanthropus tchadensis* and *Orrorin tugenensis* are important, respectively, for showing that early hominins extended from East Africa into West-Central Africa, and they were bipedal. Australopithecines refers to a category of several extinct species of early hominins found in East and southern Africa. The australopithecine era provides the first stone tools.

Archaic *Homo* includes extinct hominin species that lived from 2.4 million years to 19,000 years ago and had a more modern human-like body shape, larger brains, and smaller jaws and teeth. Stone tools are prominent in the culture of all archaic *Homo* species. One species, *Homo erectus,* is the first hominin species to live widely throughout the Old World. The last archaic *Homo* species, the Neanderthals, are known from many sites in Eurasia. They had some aspects of culture including the beginning of art and music and possibly verbal language.

According to archaeological evidence, modern humans evolved in Africa starting 300,000 years ago, though the earliest fossil evidence is from 160,000 years ago. From Africa, they migrated to the Middle East and Asia, later to Central Asia and Europe, and finally to the New World. The Upper Paleolithic is the period of modern human occupation in Eurasia. The first modern humans in Europe are the Cro-Magnons, who are associated with microlithic tools and cave art.

◆ How has modern human culture changed in the past 12,000 years?

Around 12,000 years ago, some people started changing their lives in ways that differed fundamentally from previous times. The first major change was a trend toward sedentism. With increased sedentism, people turned to plant and animal domestication instead of relying on only wild foods. Plant and animal domestication is a major defining feature of humanity's last several thousand years. It provided new types of foods, such as grains, and an increased level of food production that supported the growth of cities and states.

The Neolithic Revolution was a time of rapid transformation in technology, including tools such as sickle blades and grinding stones. The Neolithic began in Mesopotamia, where plants such as wheat, and barley were first domesticated along with animals such as sheep, goats, cattle, and pigs. Domestication of a different array of plants and animals occurred in the Middle East, Africa, China, and the New World.

Following sedentism and domestication, cities developed and then the state as a new form of political organization. Cities and states first emerged in Mesopotamia. In the New World, cities and states formed later than in the Old World. Some New World states operated without writing. In North America, complex societies emerged with extensive trade networks, long-distance warfare, and massive earthwork monuments, but without a state organization.

KEY CONCEPTS

Acheulian tradition

Anatomically Modern
   Humans (AMH) or *Homo*
   sapiens

anthropogenic

archaic *Homo*

artifact

australopithecines

bipedalism

brachiation

Clovis culture

Cro-Magnons

domestication

evolution

foraging

fossil

great apes

hominins

knuckle-walking

Mousterian tradition

natural selection

Neolithic Revolution

Oldowan tradition

primates

savanna

sedentism

sociality

tell

Upper Paleolithic

SUGGESTED READINGS

David W. Anthony. *The Horse, the Wheel, and Language.* Princeton, NJ: Princeton University Press, 2007. The author links the domestication of horses around 4800 years ago and then the invention of the wheel to the spread of the Proto-Indo-European language, which at the time existed only in spoken form.

Julian Caldecott and Lera Miles. *World Atlas of Great Apes and Their Conservation.* Berkeley: University of California Press, 2005. This overview describes the current distribution and status of the great apes and information on their ecology and behavior, habitat requirements, conservation efforts, and additional protection needed.

Thomas Dillehay. *The Settlement of the Americas: A New Prehistory.* New York: Basic Books, 2000. This book details efforts to determine who the first modern humans in the Americas were. It reviews dating, paleoenvironments, stone tools, and cultural and linguistic traditions from Paleoindian sites.

Frans de Waal and Frans Lanting. *Bonobo: The Forgotten Ape.* Berkeley: University of California Press, 1998. The book describes the behavior and ecology of bonobos. It covers social relationships, leadership, parent–offspring ties, sexuality, and the relevance of bonobos as the best model for humans.

William C. McGrew. *Chimpanzee Material Culture.* Cambridge: Cambridge University Press, 1992. McGrew discusses chimpanzee behavior as observed at several long-term field sites. Topics include chimpanzee culture and similarities and differences between humans and chimpanzees.

Jeffrey K. McKee. *The Riddled Chain: Chance, Coincidence, and Chaos in Human Evolution.* New Brunswick, NJ: Rutgers University Press, 2000. The author argues that the evidence for linking hominin evolution with changes in the paleoclimates is weak and suggests that paleoanthropologists should pay more attention to the role of chance.

Sarah Milledge Nelson, ed. *Worlds of Gender: The Archaeology of Women's Lives around the Globe.* New York: AltaMira Press, 2007. Chapters in this book provide case studies of gender in archaeology.

They show how much a "gendered past" reveals about the variety of ancient social structures.

Sue Savage-Rumbaugh, Stuart G. Shanker, and Talbot J. Taylor. *Apes, Language, and the Human Mind.* Oxford: Oxford University Press, 2001. This book discusses the upbringing of Kanzi, a bonobo who learned to understand spoken English and to communicate using pictorial symbols called lexigrams.

G. J. Sawyer and Viktor Deak, eds. *The Last Human: A Guide to Twenty-Two Species of Extinct Humans.* New York: Yale University Press, 2007. This book provides information on each species in terms of its emergence, chronology, habitat, lifestyle, and cultural capabilities.

Kathy D. Schick and Nicholas Toth. *Making Silent Stones Speak: Human Evolution and the Dawn of Technology.* New York: Simon and Schuster, 1993. The authors trace the prehistory of stone tools from their earliest appearance in the archaeological record up to modern humans.

Eugenie C. Scott. *Evolution vs. Creationism: An Introduction.* Berkeley: University of California Press, 2004. Scott surveys the debate in the United States about teaching evolution in schools. She discusses diverse religious points of view and the scientific evidence for human evolution.

Bruce D. Smith. *The Emergence of Agriculture.* New York: Scientific American Library, 1998. This volume offers an account of the rise of food production in eight world regions, seeking the common processes at work in this transition.

David Whitley, ed. *Handbook of Rock Art Research.* Walnut Creek, CA: AltaMira Press, 2001. An overview of prehistoric rock art worldwide, this volume addresses a wide range of topics from analysis of the meaning of rock art depictions to questions of conservation.

Gregory D. Wilson. *The Archaeology of Everyday Life at Early Moundville.* Tuscaloosa, AL: University of Alabama Press, 2008. This study describes life in a Mississippian polity in west-central Alabama between the twelfth and fifteenth centuries CE.

CHAPTER 3

RESEARCHING CULTURE

62

Cultural anthropologist Robert Bailey and biological anthropologist Nadine Peacock, members of a Harvard University fieldwork team, conversing with some Ituri people who live in the rainforests of the eastern part of the Democratic Republic of Congo.

RESEARCHING CULTURE

the BIG questions

- ◆ How do cultural anthropologists conduct research about culture?

- ◆ What does fieldwork involve?

- ◆ What are some urgent issues in cultural anthropology research today?

This chapter is about how cultural anthropologists do research to learn about people's shared and learned behavior and beliefs, and how they change over time. The first section discusses how methods in cultural anthropology have evolved since the late nineteenth century. The second section covers the steps involved in a research project. The chapter concludes by addressing two urgent topics in cultural anthropology research.

◆ ◆ ◆

Changing Research Methods in Cultural Anthropology

Methods in cultural anthropology today are different in several ways from those used during the nineteenth century. Most cultural anthropologists now gather data by doing **fieldwork**, going to the field, which is wherever people and cultures are, to learn about culture through direct observation. They also use a variety of specialized research techniques.

FROM THE ARMCHAIR TO THE FIELD

The term *armchair anthropology* refers to how early cultural anthropologists conducted research by sitting and reading about other cultures. They read reports written by travelers, missionaries, and explorers but never visited those places or had any kind of direct experience with the people. Sir Edward Tylor, who proposed the first definition of culture in 1871, was an armchair anthropologist. Sir James Frazer, another famous founding figure of anthropology, was also an armchair anthropologist. He wrote *The Golden Bough* (1978 [1890]), a multivolume collection of myths, rituals, and symbols that he compiled from his wide reading.

In the late nineteenth and early twentieth centuries, anthropologists hired by European colonial governments moved a step closer to learning directly about the people of other cultures. They traveled to colonized countries in Africa and Asia, where they lived near, but not with, the people they were studying. This approach is called *verandah anthropology* because, typically, the anthropologist would send out for

---

fieldwork research in the field, which is any place where people and culture are found.

participant observation basic fieldwork method in cultural anthropology that involves living in a culture for a long period of time while gathering data.

multisited research fieldwork conducted in more than one location in order to understand the behaviors and ideas of dispersed members of a culture or the relationships among different levels such as state policy and local culture.

A. R. Radcliffe-Brown, The Andaman Islanders. Cambridge: Cambridge University Press, 1964 [1922]

Ethnographic research in the early twentieth century often involved photography. The girl shown here wears the skull of her deceased sister. Indigenous people of the Andaman Islands revere the bones of their dead relatives and would not want them to be taken away, studied, or displayed in a museum.

"natives" to come to his verandah for interviewing (verandah anthropologists, like armchair anthropologists, were men). A classic example of verandah anthropology is A. R. Radcliffe-Brown's research on the Andaman Islanders (see Culturama). When he went to South Andaman Island at the turn of the twentieth century, the indigenous population had been greatly reduced by diseases brought in by the British colonizers and by the effects of direct colonial violence. Radcliffe-Brown's assignment was to do *salvage anthropology*, to collect what data he could from the remaining people in order to document their language, social life, and religious beliefs.

A bit earlier, in the United States during the mid-nineteenth century, Lewis Henry Morgan had taken steps toward learning about people through direct observation. A lawyer, Morgan lived in Rochester, New York, near the Iroquois territory. He became well acquainted with many of the Iroquois (Tooker 1992). These experiences provided Morgan with important insights into their everyday lives. His writings changed the prevailing Euro-American perception of the Iroquois, and other Native American tribes, as "dangerous savages." Morgan showed that Iroquois behavior and beliefs make sense if an outsider spends time learning about them through direct experience.

PARTICIPANT OBSERVATION

A major turning point in how cultural anthropologists do research occurred in the early twentieth century, during World War I, laying the foundation for the current cornerstone method in cultural anthropology: fieldwork combined with participant observation. **Participant observation** is a research method for learning about culture that involves living in a culture for an extended period while gathering data.

The "father" of participant observation is Bronislaw Malinowski. He adopted what was, at the time, an innovative approach to learning about culture while he was in the Trobriand Islands in the South Pacific during World War I (see Culturama). For two years, he lived in a tent alongside the local people, participating in their activities and living, as much as possible, as one of them. Through this process adopted by Malinowski, the key elements of participant observation were established:

- Living with the people
- Participating in their everyday life
- Learning the language

By living with the people and participating in their daily round of life, Malinowski learned about their culture in context rather than through secondhand reports. By learning the local language, he could talk with the people without the use of interpreters and thus gain a much more accurate understanding of their culture.

In this early phase of fieldwork and participant observation, a primary goal was to record as much as possible of a people's language, songs, rituals, and social life because many cultures were disappearing. Most early cultural anthropologists did fieldwork in small, relatively isolated cultures. They thought they could study everything about such cultures; those were the days of holism. Typically, the anthropologist (a White man) would go off with his notebooks to collect data on a standardized list of topics including economics, family life, politics, religion, language, art and crafts, and more.

Today, few if any such seemingly isolated cultures remain. Cultural anthropologists have devised new research methods so that they can study larger-scale cultures, global–local connections, and cultural change. One methodological innovation of the late twentieth century is especially important in addressing these new issues: **multisited research**, which is fieldwork conducted on a topic in more than one location (Marcus 1995). Although especially helpful in studying migrant populations in their place of origin and their new location, multisited research is useful for studying many topics.

Lanita Jacobs-Huey conducted multisited fieldwork in order to learn about the language and culture of hairstyles among African American women (2002). She chose a range of sites throughout the United States and in London, England, in order to explore the many facets of the far-from-simple topic of hair: beauty salons, regional and international hair expos and training seminars, Bible study meetings of a nonprofit group of Christian cosmetologists, standup comedy clubs, a computer-mediated discussion about the

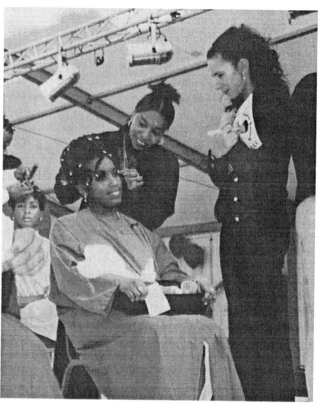

Lanita Jacobs-Huey's fieldsites include hairstyling competitions throughout the United States and in London, England. Here, a judge evaluates the work of a student stylist at the Afro Hair & Beauty Show in London.

politics of Black hair, and a cosmetology school in Charleston, South Carolina.

◆◆◆

Doing Fieldwork in Cultural Anthropology

Fieldwork in cultural anthropology can be exciting, frustrating, scary, boring, and sometimes dangerous. One thing is true: It transforms the lives of everyone involved. This section explores the stages of a fieldwork research project, starting with the initial planning and ending with the analysis and presentation of the findings.

THINKING
OUTSIDE
THE BOX

As you read this chapter, consider the similarities and differences between research in cultural anthropology and research in other disciplines such as biology, psychology, political science, economics, and history.

Before going to the field, the prospective researcher must select a research topic and prepare for the fieldwork itself. These steps are critical to the success of the project.

PROJECT SELECTION Finding a topic for a research project is a basic first step. The topic should be important and feasible. Cultural anthropologists often find a topic to research by carrying out a *literature review*, or reading what others have already written assessing its adequacy. Conducting a literature review often exposes a gap in previous research. For example, cultural anthropologists realized during the 1970s that anthropological research had bypassed women and girls, and this is how feminist anthropology began (B. Miller 1993).

Notable events sometimes inspire a research topic. The HIV/AIDS epidemic and its rapid spread continue to prompt research. The recent rise in the numbers of international migrants and refugees is another pressing area for study. The fall of state socialism in Russia and Eastern Europe shifted attention to that region. Conflict situations in Afghanistan, Iraq, Sudan, and other places spur cultural anthropologists to ask what causes such conflicts and how post-conflict reconstruction can be most effectively accomplished (Lubkemann 2005).

Some cultural anthropologists choose to study the cultural context of a particular material item, such as sugar (Mintz 1985), cars (D. Miller 2001), beef (Caplan 2000), money (R. Foster 2002), shea butter (Chalfin 2004), wedding dresses (Foster and Johnson 2003), coca (Allen 2002), or cocaine (Taussig 2004). The material item provides a focus for understanding the social relations surrounding its production, use, and trade, and what it means in terms of people's changing identities.

Another idea for a research project is a *restudy*, fieldwork conducted in a previously researched community. Many decades of previous research provide baseline information on which later studies can build. It makes sense to examine changes that have occurred or to look at the culture from a new angle. For her doctoral dissertation research, Annette Weiner (1976) decided to go to the Trobriand Islands, following in the footsteps of Malinowski, to learn what people's lives were like over 50 years after his fieldwork. What she found there prompted her to change her original research plans (see Critical Thinking and Culturama, this chapter).

Even luck can lead to a research topic. Spanish anthropologist María Cátedra (1992) stumbled on an important issue during exploratory fieldwork in rural northern Spain (see Map 5). A suicide occurred in a village in the mountains near where she was staying. The local people did not consider the suicide remarkable or strange. In fact, the area had a high rate of suicide. Later she went back and did long-term research on the social dynamics of suicide in this area.

In focusing on a single commodity, cultural anthropologists reveal much about local and global cultures. (TOP) Children working on a sugarcane plantation in the Philippines. (CENTER) A model dressed as "Miss Chiquita" stands in front of the Brandenburg Gate in Berlin during Germany's International Green Week and agricultural fair. (BOTTOM) Villagers chewing coca leaves in highland Peru.

---

informed consent an aspect of fieldwork ethics requiring that the researcher inform the research participants of the intent, scope, and possible effects of the study and seek their consent to be in the study.

PREPARING FOR THE FIELD   After defining the research topic, it is important to secure funding to carry out the research. Academic anthropologists can apply for grants from a variety of sources, governmental and nongovernmental. Several sources of funding are also available for advanced graduate students. Undergraduate students have a more difficult time finding grants to support fieldwork, but many succeed.

Related to the funding question is whether it is appropriate for an anthropologist to conduct research while employed in the research setting. Employment provides financial support for the research, but it raises some problems. A basic dilemma, discussed later in the chapter, is the ethical principle that anthropologists cannot do "undercover" research. If you are working in a factory, for example, while studying what goes on in the factory, you must get people's permission for your study, something that is not always easy. More positively, a work role can help gain people's trust and respect. A British graduate student worked as a bartender in a tourist town in Ireland (Kaul 2004). This position placed him at the center of the village, and people respected him as a hardworking person, thus greatly adding to his ability to learn about the local culture, at least as revealed from a bartender's perspective.

If the project involves international travel, the host government may require a visa and an application for permission to conduct research. These formalities may take a long time and may even be impossible to obtain. The government of India, for example, restricts research by foreigners, especially research related to "sensitive" topics such as tribal people, border areas, and family planning. China's restrictions against foreign anthropologists doing fieldwork have been eased since the 1980s, but it is still not easy to get permission to do fieldwork and participant observation.

Many countries require that researchers follow official guidelines for *protection of human subjects*. In the United States, universities and other institutions that support or conduct research with living people must establish *institutional review boards* (IRBs) to monitor research to make sure it conforms to ethical principles. IRB guidelines follow a medical model related to the need to protect people who participate as "subjects" in medical research. Normally, IRBs require informed consent, in writing, of the research participants. **Informed consent** is an aspect of research ethics requiring that the researcher inform the research participants of the intent, scope, and possible effects of the study and seek their agreement to be in the study. Obtaining written consent of research participants is reasonable and feasible in many anthropological research projects. Written consent, however, is often not reasonable or feasible, especially in oral-based cultures where most people are not literate. Fortunately, IRBs are gaining more experience with the contexts in which most cultural anthropologists do research. Some universities' IRBs

will waive the requirement for written informed consent, allowing oral informed consent instead. IRB guidelines do change, so check your institution's website for the latest policy.

Depending on the project location, preparation for the field may involve buying specialized equipment, such as a tent, warm clothing, waterproof clothing, and sturdy boots. Health preparations may require immunization against contagious diseases such as yellow fever. For research in a remote area, a well-stocked medical kit and basic first-aid training are essential. Research equipment and supplies are another important aspect of preparation. Cameras, video recorders, tape recorders, and laptop computers are now basic field equipment. Unlike the traditional paper notebook and pen, though, these machines require batteries and other inputs.

If a researcher is unfamiliar with the local language, intensive language training before going to the field is critical. Even with language training in advance, cultural anthropologists often find that they cannot communicate in the local version of the standardized language they studied in a classroom. Therefore, many fieldworkers rely on help from a local interpreter throughout their study or at least in its early stages.

WORKING IN THE FIELD

A basic first step in establishing a fieldwork project is to decide on the particular location or locations for the research. The second is to find a place to live.

SITE SELECTION   A research *site* is the place where the research takes place, and sometimes a project involves more than one site. The researcher often has a basic idea of the area where the fieldwork will occur—for example, a shantytown in Rio de Janeiro, a village in Scotland, or a factory in Malaysia. It is often impossible to know in advance exactly where the project will be located. Selecting a research site depends on many factors. It may be necessary to find a large village if the project involves class differences in work patterns, or a clinic if the study concerns health-care behavior. It may be difficult to

THINKING OUTSIDE THE BOX

At the author's university, the Department of Anthropology has a research fund that supports about a dozen student research projects annually. Visit the website http://www.gwu.edu/~anth/atgw/cotlow_awards.cfm and review the list of student projects. What might you propose to research?

CRITICAL thinking

Shells and Skirts in the Trobriand Islands

A lasting contribution of Bronislaw Malinowski's ethnography *Argonauts of the Western Pacific* (1961 [1922]) is its detailed examination of the **kula**, a trading network linking many islands in the region, in which men have long-standing partnerships for the exchange of everyday goods such as food as well as highly valued necklaces and armlets.

More than half a century later, Annette Weiner (1976) traveled to the Trobriand Islands to study woodcarving. She settled in a village less than a mile from where Malinowski had done his research. She immediately began making startling observations: "On my first day in the village, I saw women performing a mortuary [death] ceremony in which they distributed thousands of bundles of strips of dried banana leaves and hundreds of beautifully decorated fibrous skirts" (1976:xvii).

Nowhere in Malinowski's voluminous writings did he mention the women's activities. Weiner was intrigued and decided to change her research project to investigate women's goods, exchange patterns, and prestige. Men, as Malinowski showed, exchange shells, yams, and pigs. Women, as Weiner learned, exchange bundles of banana leaves and intricately made skirts. Power and prestige derive from both exchange networks.

Pearson Education

Bronislaw Malinowski during his fieldwork in the Trobriand Islands, 1915–1918.

▶ *What are some of the differences between what his field research revealed about men's lives in the Trobriand Islands compared to what a "verandah anthropologist" would have learned?*

Reading Malinowski alone informs us about the world of men's status systems and describes them in isolation from half of the islands' population: women. Weiner's book *Women of Value, Men of Renown* (1976) provides an account of women's trading and prestige activities as well as how they are linked to those of men. Building on the work of her predecessor, Weiner shows how a full understanding of one domain requires knowledge of the other.

◆ CRITICAL THINKING QUESTIONS

* Is it possible that Malinowski overlooked women's exchange patterns?
* Do the findings of Annette Weiner simply provide another one-sided view?
* What might a cultural anthropologist discover in the Trobriand Islands now?

---

find a village, neighborhood, or institution in which the people welcome the researcher and the project. Often, housing shortages mean that even the most welcoming community cannot provide space for an anthropologist.

Here is an example in which a combination of factors came together in a positive way. Jennifer Robertson was seeking a research site in Japan for a study of urban popula-

tion change. She selected Kodaira, a suburb of Tokyo (see Map 2), because of advice from a Japanese colleague. It had available housing and offered a good fit with her research interests. By happy coincidence, she was also familiar with the area:

> I spent my childhood and early teens in Kodaira [but] my personal past did not directly influence my selection of Kodaira as a fieldsite and home. . . . That I wound up living in my old neighborhood in Kodaira was determined more by the availability of a suitable apartment than by a nostalgic curiosity about my childhood haunts. As it turned out, I could not have landed at a better place at a better time. (1991:6)

---

kula a trading network, linking many of the Trobriand Islands, in which men have long-standing partnerships for the exchange of everyday goods such as food as well as highly valued necklaces and armlets.

CULTURAMA

The Trobriand Islanders of Papua New Guinea

The Trobriand Islands are named after eighteenth-century French explorer Denis de Trobriand. They include 22 flat coral atolls east of the island of New Guinea. The indigenous Trobriand population lives on four main islands. Kiriwina is by far the most populated, with about 28,000 people (digim'Rina, personal communication 2006). The Papua New Guinea (PNG) district office and an airstrip are located on Kiriwina at Losuia.

The islands were first colonized by Great Britain and then ceded to Australia in 1904 (Weiner 1988). The British attempted to stop local warfare and to change many other aspects of Trobriand culture. Christian missionaries introduced the game of cricket as a substitute for warfare. In 1943, Allied troops landed as part of their Pacific operations. In 1975, the islands became part of the state of Papua New Guinea.

Island-to-island cultural differences exist. Even within one island, people may speak different dialects, although everyone speaks a version of the language called Kilivila (Weiner 1988). The Trobrianders grow much of their own food, including root crops such as yams, sweet potatoes, and taro; beans and squash; and bananas, breadfruit, coconuts, and betel nut. Pigs are the main animal raised for food and as prestige items. In the latter part of the twentieth century, Trobrianders were increasingly dependent on money sent to them by relatives working elsewhere in PNG. Current development projects are encouraging people to plant more fruit trees, such as mango (digim'Rina 2005).

Kinship emphasizes the female line, meaning that mothers and daughters form the core of co-residential groups. Fathers, though not co-residential, are nonetheless important family members and spend as much time caring for children as women do (Weiner 1988). Fathers of political status give their babies and children, both boys and girls, highly valued shell earrings and necklaces to wear. Mothers give daughters prized red skirts. Trobriand children attend Western-style schools on the islands, and many go to mainland PNG and beyond for further studies.

Today, elders worry that young people do nothing but dream about "money" and fail to care for the heritage of their ancestors. Another concern is that commercial overfishing is endangering the coral reefs.

Thanks to Linus S. digim'Rina, University of Papua New Guinea, and Robert Foster, University of Rochester, for reviewing this material.

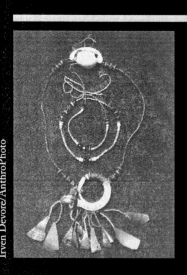

Irven Devore/AnthroPhoto

© Albrecht G. Schaefer/CORBIS

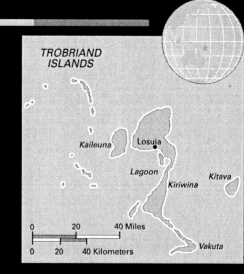

MAP 1 Trobriand Islands of Papua New Guinea. Also known as the Kiriwina Islands, these islands are an archipelago of coral atolls lying off the eastern coast of the island of New Guinea.

(LEFT) Trobriand men's coveted trade goods include this shell necklace and armlet. (CENTER) A Trobriand girl wears a valued skirt at a dance in honor of the ancestors on Kiriwina Island. She and other female participants coat their skin with coconut oil and herbs and wear decorative flowers.

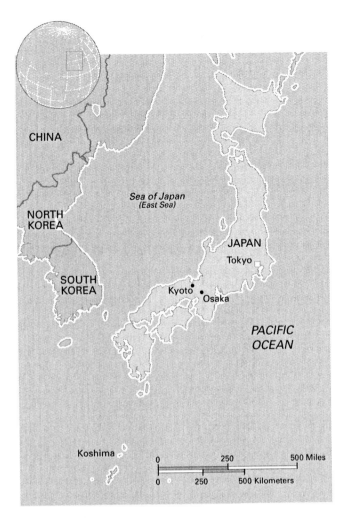

MAP 2 Japan.
The State of Japan, or Nihon-koku or Nippon-koku, encompasses over 3000 islands, most of which are mountainous. Its population is nearly 129 million. Greater Tokyo, with over 30 million residents, is the largest metropolitan area in the world. Japan has the world's second largest economy.

Jennifer Robertson (FAR LEFT) celebrates the publication of her book, *Native and Newcomer* (1991), with several administrators from Kodaira City Hall. This informal gathering at a local restaurant followed a formal ceremony at the City Hall, where Robertson presented her book to the mayor of Kodaira, an event covered by city and regional newspapers.

▶ *What cultural features are noteworthy about this gathering?*

GAINING RAPPORT **Rapport** is a trusting relationship between the researcher and the study population. In the early stages of research, the primary goal is to establish rapport with key leaders or decision makers in the community who may serve as *gatekeepers* (people who formally or informally control access to the group or community).

Gaining rapport involves trust on the part of the study population, and their trust depends on how the researcher presents herself or himself. In many cultures, people have difficulty understanding why a person would come to study them because they do not know about universities and research and cultural anthropology. They may provide their own explanations based on previous experience with outsiders

---

rapport a trusting relationship between the researcher and the study population.

whose goals differed from those of cultural anthropologists, such as tax collectors, family planning promoters, and law-enforcement officials.

Stories about *false role assignments* can be humorous. During his 1970s fieldwork in northwest Pakistan, Richard Kurin reports that in the first stage of his research, the villagers thought he was an international spy from America, Russia, India, or China (1980). Over time, he convinced them that he was not a spy. So what was he? The villagers came up with several roles for Kurin. First, they speculated that he was a teacher of English because he was tutoring one of the village boys. Second, they guessed that he must be a doctor because he gave people aspirin. Third, they thought he might be a lawyer who could help them in local disputes because he could read court orders. Last, they decided he was a descendant of a local clan because of the similarity of his last name and that of an ancestral king. For Richard Kurin, the last of these—being a true "Karan"—was best of all.

Being labeled a spy continues to be a problem for anthropologists. Christa Salamandra, a Western-trained doctoral student in anthropology, went to Damascus, Syria (see Map 3) to do research for her dissertation in anthropology (2004). Although Damascus has an ancient history, it is increasingly cosmopolitan. Damascenes, however, have little

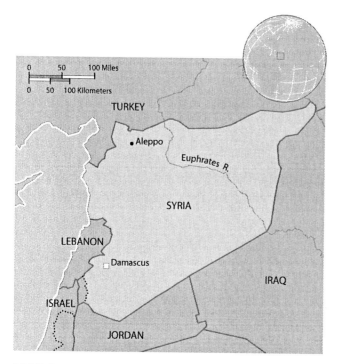

MAP 3 Syria.
The Syrian Arabic Republic historically included the present-day territories of Lebanon, Israel, the Palestinian Territories, and parts of Jordan, but not the Jazira region in Syria's northeast. Its population is 19 million people. Syria's capital city, Damascus, with a population of 3 million people, is one of the oldest continually occupied cities in the world.

exposure to anthropology. Syria has no university with a department of anthropology, and there are no Syrian anthropologists. Salamandra's research interests in popular culture (movies, cafés, and fashion) perplexed the local people, who decided she must be a foreign spy. One person said to her, "Your question is CIA, not academic" (2004:5). Nevertheless, she managed to carry out her study and write a book about popular culture in Damascus.

Another situation of an assumed spying role arose in North Carolina, even though the anthropologist, Mary Anglin, shared citizenship with the people (2002). During her fieldwork in a mica-processing factory in the western part of the state, some people thought she was an industrial spy. Anglin came from the northeastern United States, so she was not a "southerner." Moreover, she had no kin connections in the region and no "family" (she was single). The Irish-Scottish residents of the area did not quickly welcome her, but she managed to get the factory owner to let her spend time in the factory as a participant-observer. Several of the women factory workers befriended her, but many of the local people continued to be suspicious. At one point, a rumor circulated that Anglin was an industrial spy, intent on learning about mica processing in order to sell the information to competitors. The rumor died down, but the factory owner later banned her from entering the factory.

GIFT GIVING AND EXCHANGE   Giving gifts to people involved in the research can help the project proceed, but gifts should be culturally and ethically appropriate. Learning the local rules of exchange is important (see Figure 1).

Matthews Hamabata, a Japanese American who did fieldwork in Japan, learned about the complexities of gift giving among Japanese business families (1990). He developed a close relationship with one family, the Itoos, and helped their daughter apply for admission to universities in the United States. When the applications were completed, Mrs. Itoo invited him to an expensive restaurant to celebrate. After the dinner, she handed him a small, carefully wrapped package, expressing her embarrassment at the inadequacy of her gift in relation to all that he had done for her daughter. When he returned home, he opened the gift. It was a box of chocolates. Upon opening the box, he discovered 50,000 yen (about US$250). Hamabata felt insulted: "Who do the Itoos think they are? They can't buy me or my services!" (1990:21–22). He asked some Japanese friends what he should do. They told him that the gift signaled the Itoos' wish to have a long-standing relationship and that returning the money to the Itoos would be an insult. They advised him to give a return gift later on, in order to maintain the relationship. His gift should leave him ahead by about 25,000 yen, given his status as an anthropologist in relation to the Itoos' status as a rich business family. This strategy worked and the relationship between Hamabata and the Itoos remained intact.

MICROCULTURES AND FIELDWORK   Class, race, gender, and age all affect how the local people will perceive and welcome an anthropologist. Some examples illustrate how microcultures influence rapport and affect the research in other ways.

- What an appropriate or an inappropriate gift is
- How to deliver a gift
- How to behave as a gift giver
- How to behave when receiving a gift
- If and how to give a follow-up gift

FIGURE 1   Culture and Gift Giving in the Field

THINKING
OUTSIDE
THE BOX

Recall a situation in which either you did not know what would be an appropriate gift to give someone (in terms of quality, cost, or some other factor) or you were faced with some other puzzling situation related to gift exchange. What were the cultural meanings underlying the situation?

CLASS In most fieldwork situations, the anthropologist is more wealthy and powerful than the people studied. This difference is obvious to the people. They know that the anthropologist must have spent hundreds or thousands of dollars to travel to the research site. They see the anthropologist's expensive equipment (camera, tape recorder, video recorder, even a vehicle) and valuable material goods (stainless steel knives, cigarettes, flashlights, canned food, and medicines).

Many years ago, Laura Nader urged that anthropologists should also *study up* by doing research among powerful people such as members of the business elite, political leaders, and government officials (1972). As one example of this approach, research on the high-fashion industry of Japan placed the anthropologist Dorinne Kondo in touch with members of the Japanese elite—influential people capable of taking her to court if they felt she wrote something defamatory about them (1997). Studying up has contributed to awareness of the need, in all fieldwork situations, for recognition of the anthropologist's accountability to the people being studied, whether or not they are able to read what the anthropologist has written about them or wealthy enough to hire a lawyer if they do not like how they and their culture have been presented.

"RACE"/ETHNICITY For most of its history, cultural anthropology has been dominated by Euro-American White researchers who study "other" cultures that are mainly non-White and non-Euro-American. The effects of "Whiteness" on role assignments range from the anthropologist being considered a god or ancestor spirit to being reviled as a representative of a colonialist past or neocolonialist present. While doing research in a village in Jamaica called Haversham, Tony Whitehead learned how "race" and status interact (1986). Whitehead is an African American and from a low-income family. Being of a similar "race" and class as the rural Jamaicans with whom he was doing research, he assumed he would quickly build rapport because of a shared heritage. The people of Haversham, however, have a complex status system that relegated Whitehead to a position that he did not predict, as he explains:

> I was shocked when the people of Haversham began talking to me and referring to me as a "big," "brown," "pretty-talking" man. "Big" was not a reference to my weight but to my higher social status as they perceived it, and "brown" referred not only to my skin color but also to my higher social status. . . . More embarrassing than bothersome were the references to how "pretty" I talked, a comment on my Standard English speech pattern. . . . Frequently mothers told me that their children were going to school so that they could learn to talk as pretty as I did. (1986:214–215)

This experience prompted Whitehead to ponder the complexities of "race" and status cross-culturally.

Similarly, for Lanita Jacobs-Huey, in her research on African American women's hair culture, being an African American did not automatically gain her acceptance (2002). Hairstyle is a sensitive subject related to African American identity. For example, in one part of her research, she attempted to establish rapport with Internet-based participants. Before the women would take her into their confidence, they wanted to know how she styled her hair.

GENDER If a female researcher is young and unmarried, she is likely to face more difficulties than a young unmarried man or an older woman, married or single, because people in most cultures consider a young unmarried female on her own as extremely unusual. Rules of gender segregation may dictate that a young unmarried woman should not move about freely without a male escort, attend certain events, or be

Liza Dalby

American anthropologist Liza Dalby in formal geisha dress during her fieldwork on geisha culture in Kyoto, Japan.

▶ *Besides learning to dress correctly, what other cultural skills did Liza Dalby probably have to learn?*

culture shock persistent feelings of uneasiness, loneliness, and anxiety that often occur when a person has shifted from one culture to a different one.

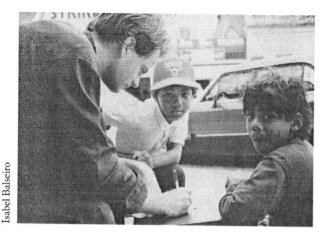

Tobias Hecht plays a game with some of the street children in his study in Rio de Janeiro, Brazil.

in certain places. A woman researcher who studied a community of gay men in the United States says:

> I was able to do fieldwork in those parts of the setting dedicated to sociability and leisure—bars, parties, family gatherings. I was not, however, able to observe in those parts of the setting dedicated to sexuality—even quasi-public settings such as homosexual bath houses. . . . Thus my portrait of the gay community is only a partial one, bounded by the social roles assigned to females within the male homosexual world. (Warren 1988:18)

Gender segregation may also prevent male researchers from gaining access to a full range of activities. Liza Dalby, a White American, lived with the geishas of Kyoto, Japan, and trained to be a geisha (1998). This research would have been impossible for a man to do.

AGE Typically, anthropologists are adults, and this fact may make it easier for them to gain rapport with people their age than with children or the aged. Although some children and adolescents welcome the participation of a friendly adult in their daily lives and respond to questions openly, others are more reserved.

OTHER FACTORS A researcher's role is affected by even more factors than those just discussed, including religion, dress, and personality. Being the same religion as the residents of a Jewish home for the aged in California helped a Jewish anthropologist establish rapport (Myerhoff 1978). This positive engagement is evident in a conversation between the anthropologist (A) and a woman named Basha (B):

B: "So, what brings you here?"

A: "I'm from the University of Southern California. I'm looking for a place to study how older Jews live in the city." At the word university, Basha moved closer and nodded approvingly. "Are you Jewish?" she asked.

A: "Yes, I am."

B: "Are you married?" she persisted.

A: "Yes."

B: "You got children?"

A: "Yes, two boys, 4 and 8," I answered.

B: "Are you teaching them to be Jews?" (1978:14)

The anthropologist was warmly accepted, and her plan for one year of research grew into a long-standing relationship. In contrast, being Jewish posed a potential problem in another context (Freedman 1986). Diane Freedman conducted research in rural Romania in the 1980s. Given the pervasiveness of anti-Semitism there, she was reluctant to tell the villagers that she was Jewish and also reluctant to lie. Early in her stay, she attended the village church. The priest asked what her religion was. She opted for honesty and found, to her relief, that being Jewish had no negative effects on her research.

CULTURE SHOCK **Culture shock** is the feeling of uneasiness, loneliness, and anxiety that occurs when a person shifts from one culture to a different one. The more different the two cultures are, the more severe the shock is likely to be. Culture shock happens to many cultural anthropologists, no matter how much they have tried to prepare themselves for fieldwork. It also happens to students who study abroad, Peace Corps volunteers, and anyone who spends time living and participating in another culture.

Culture shock can range from problems with food to language barriers and loneliness. Food differences were a major problem in adjustment for a Chinese anthropologist who came to the United States (Shu-Min 1993). American food never gave him a "full" feeling. An American anthropologist who went to Pohnpei, an island in the Federated States of Micronesia, found that her lack of skills in the local language caused her the most serious adjustment problems (Ward 1989). She says, "Even dogs understood more than I did. . . . [I will never] forget the agony of stepping on a woman's toes. Instead of asking for forgiveness, I blurted out, 'His canoe is blue'" (1989:14).

A frequent psychological aspect of culture shock is the feeling of reduced competence as a cultural actor. At home, the anthropologist is highly competent, carrying out everyday tasks such as shopping, talking with people, and mailing a package without thinking. In a new culture, the simplest tasks are difficult, and one's sense of self-efficacy is undermined. In extreme cases, an anthropologist may have to abandon a project because of an inability to adapt to the fieldwork situation. For most, however, culture shock is a temporary

THINKING OUTSIDE THE BOX

Think of an occasion in which you experienced culture shock, even if as the result of just a brief cross-cultural encounter. How did you feel? How did you cope? What did you learn from the experience?

affliction that subsides as the person becomes more familiar with the new culture.

Reverse culture shock may occur after coming home. An American anthropologist describes his feelings on returning to San Francisco after a year of fieldwork in a village in India:

> We could not understand why people were so distant and hard to reach, or why they talked and moved so quickly. We were a little frightened at the sight of so many white faces and we could not understand why no one stared at us, brushed against us, or admired our baby. (Beals 1980:119)

FIELDWORK TECHNIQUES

The goal of fieldwork is to collect information, or *data*, about the research topic. In cultural anthropology, variations exist about what kinds of data to emphasize and the best ways to collect data.

DEDUCTIVE AND INDUCTIVE RESEARCH AND DATA

A **deductive approach** is a form of research that starts from a research question or hypothesis and then involves collecting data related to the question through observation, interviews, and other methods. An **inductive approach** is a form of research that proceeds without a hypothesis and involves gathering data through unstructured, informal observation, conversation, and other methods. Deductive methods are

---

deductive approach (to research) a research method that involves posing a research question or hypothesis, gathering data related to the question, and then assessing the findings in relation to the original hypothesis.

inductive approach (to research) a research approach that avoids hypothesis formation in advance of the research and instead takes its lead from the culture being studied.

quantitative data numeric information.

qualitative data non-numeric information.

etic an analytical framework used by outside analysts in studying culture.

emic insiders' perceptions and categories, and their explanations for why they do what they do.

Hawthorne effect research bias due to participants changing their behavior to conform to expectations of the researcher.

interview a research technique that involves gathering of verbal data through questions or guided conversation between at least two people.

questionnaire a formal research instrument containing a pre-set series of questions that the anthropologist asks in a face-to-face setting, by mail, or by email.

---

more likely to collect **quantitative data**, or numeric information, such as the amount of land in relation to the population or numbers of people with particular health problems. The inductive approach in cultural anthropology emphasizes **qualitative data**, or nonnumeric information, such as recordings of myths, conversations, and filming of events. Most anthropologists, however, combine deductive and inductive approaches and quantitative and qualitative data.

Cultural anthropologists have labels for data collected in each approach. **Etic** (pronounced like the last two syllables of "phonetic") refers to data collected according to the researcher's questions and categories, with the goal of being able to test a hypothesis (see Figure 2). In contrast, **emic** (pronounced like the last two syllables of "phonemic") refers to data collected that reflect what insiders say and understand about their culture, and insiders' categories of thinking. Cultural materialists are more likely to collect etic data, whereas interpretivists are more likely to collect emic data. Again, however, most cultural anthropologists collect both types of data.

PARTICIPANT OBSERVATION The phrase *participant observation* includes two processes: participating, or being part of the people's lives, while carefully observing. These two activities may sound simple, but they are actually quite complex.

Being a participant means that the researcher adopts the lifestyle of the people being studied, living in the same kind of housing, eating similar food, wearing similar clothing, learning the language, and participating in the daily round of activities and in special events. The rationale is that participation over a long period improves the quality of the data. The more time the researcher spends living among the people, the more likely it is that the people will live their "normal" lives. In this way, the researcher is able to overcome the **Hawthorne effect**, a research bias that occurs when participants change their behavior to conform to the perceived expectations of the researcher. The Hawthorne effect was discovered in the 1930s during a study of an industrial plant in the United States. During the study, research participants altered their behavior in ways they thought would please the researcher.

An anthropologist cannot be everywhere, participate in everything, or observe everyone, so choices are involved in where to be and what to observe. As mentioned earlier, gender, age, and other microcultural factors may limit the anthropologist's participation in certain domains or activities. The sheer need for sleep may mean that the anthropologist misses something important that happens at night, such as a ritual or a moonlight hunting expedition.

Although participant observation is often equated with the casual term "hanging out," in fact, it means constant choices about where to be on a particular day at a particular time, what one observes, with whom, and what, by default, one misses. Depending on the research topic, participant observation may focus on who lives with whom, who interacts with whom

Research Approach	Process	Data
Deductive (Etic)	Hypothesis followed by data collection	Quantitative data for hypothesis testing
Inductive (Emic)	No hypothesis, data collection follows from participants' lead	Qualitative data for descriptive insights

FIGURE 2 Two Research Approaches in Cultural Anthropology

in public, who are leaders and who are followers, what work people do, how people organize themselves for different activities, rituals, arguments, festivals, funerals, and far more.

TALKING WITH PEOPLE Common sense tells you that participating and observing are important, but what about talking to people and asking questions such as "What is going on here?" "What does that mean?" "Why are you doing that?" The process of talking to people and asking them questions is such an important component of participant observation that the method should actually be called *participant observation and talking*. Cultural anthropologists use a variety of data-collection techniques that rely on talking with people, from informal, casual, and unplanned conversations, to more formal methods.

An **interview** is a technique for gathering verbal data through questions or guided conversation. It is more purposeful than a casual conversation. An interview may involve only two people, the interviewer and the interviewee, or several people in what are called group interviews or focus groups. Cultural anthropologists use different interview styles and formats, depending on the kinds of information they seek, the amount of time they have, and their language skills. The least structured type of interview is an *open-ended interview*, in which the respondent (interviewee) takes the lead in setting the direction of the conversation, topics to be covered, and the amount of time devoted to a particular topic. The interviewer does not interrupt or provide prompting questions. In this way, the researcher discovers what themes are important to the person.

A **questionnaire** is a formal research instrument containing a preset series of questions that the anthropologist asks in a face-to-face setting, or by mail or e-mail. Cultural anthropologists who use questionnaires favor a face-to-face setting. Like interviews, questionnaires vary in the degree to which the questions are *structured* (close-ended) or *unstructured* (open-ended). Structured questions limit the range of possible responses—for example, by asking research participants to rate their positions on a particular issue as "very positive," "positive," "negative," "very negative," or "no opinion." Unstructured interviews generate more emic responses.

When designing a questionnaire, the researcher should have enough familiarity with the study population to be able to design questions that make cultural sense (Fitchen 1990).

Researchers who take a ready-made questionnaire to the field with them should ask another researcher who knows the field area to review it in advance to see whether it makes cultural sense. Further revisions may be required in the field to make the questionnaire fit local conditions. A *pilot study* using the questionnaire among a small number of people in the research area can expose areas the need for revision.

COMBINING OBSERVATION AND TALKING A combination of observation of what people actually do with verbal data about what people say they do and think is essential for a well-rounded view of a culture (Sanjek 2000). People may say that they do something or believe something, but their behavior may differ from what they say. For example, people may say that sons and daughters inherit equal shares of family property when the parents die. Research into what really happens may reveal that daughters do not inherit equal shares. Similarly, an anthropologist might learn from people and their laws that discrimination on the basis of skin color is illegal. Research on people's behavior might reveal clear examples of discrimination. It is important for an anthropologist to learn about both what people say and what happens. Both are "true" aspects of culture.

SPECIALIZED METHODS Cultural anthropologists also use many more specific research methods. The choice depends on the anthropologist's research goals.

LIFE HISTORY A life history is a qualitative, in-depth description of an individual's life as narrated to the researcher. Anthropologists differ in their views about the value of the life history as a method in cultural anthropology. Early in the twentieth century, Franz Boas rejected this method as unscientific because research participants might lie or exaggerate (Peacock and Holland 1993). Others disagree, saying that a life history reveals rich information on individuals and how they think, no matter how "distorted" their reports are. For example, some

THINKING OUTSIDE THE BOX

Given the emphasis on observation in fieldwork, is it possible for a blind person to become a cultural anthropologist?

Marjorie Shostak (RIGHT) interviewing Nisa during fieldwork among the Ju/'hoansi in 1975.

▶ *What would you tell an anthropologist about your life?*

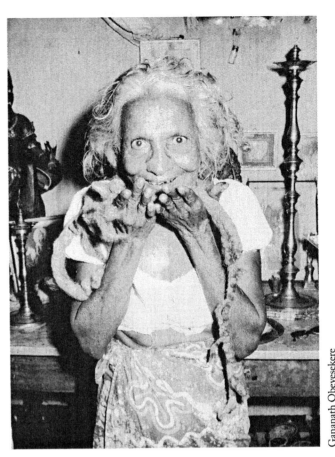

This Sri Lankan woman, whose life story Gananath Obeyesekere analyzed, is a priestess to a deity. She stands in the shrine room of her house, holding her matted, snaky hair.

▶ *How do hairstyles in your culture express a person's religion, marital status, or sexuality?*

anthropologists have questioned the accuracy of parts of *Nisa: The Life and Times of a !Kung Woman* (Shostak 1981), probably the most widely read life history in anthropology. It is a book-length story of a Ju/'hoansi woman of the Kalahari desert of southern Africa. Presented in Nisa's voice, the book offers rich details about her childhood and several marriages. The value of the narrative is not so much whether it is "true" or not; rather, the value is that we learn from Nisa what she wants to tell us, her view of her experiences. That counts as "data" in cultural anthropology, for it is "truly" what she reported to Marjorie Shostak.

In the early days of life history research, anthropologists tried to choose an individual who was somehow typical, average, or representative. It is not possible, however, to find one person who is representative of an entire culture in the scientific sense. Instead, anthropologists now seek individuals who occupy particularly interesting social niches. For example, Gananath Obeyesekere (oh-bay-yuh-SEK-eruh) analyzed the life histories of four Sri Lankan people, three women and one man (1981). Each became a Hindu religious devotee and ascetic, distinguished by their thickly matted hair, twisted into coils like a snake. Their snaky hair is permanently matted and impossible to comb. According to the devotees, a deity is present in their matted hair. Obeyesekere suggests that all four people had suffered deep psychological afflictions during their lives, including sexual anxieties. Their matted hair symbolizes their suffering and provides them with a special status as holy, thus beyond the rules of married life and conjugal sexual relations.

TIME ALLOCATION STUDY A *time allocation study* is a quantitative method that collects data on how people spend their time each day on particular activities. This method relies on standard time units as the basic matrix and then labeling or coding the activities that occur within certain time segments (Gross 1984). Activity codes must be adapted to fit local contexts. For example, activity codes for various kinds of work would not be useful in a time allocation study in a retirement home. Data can be collected through observation that may be continuous, at fixed intervals (for instance, every 48 hours), or on a random basis. Continuous observation is extremely time consuming and means that the number of people observed is limited. Spot observations help increase the number of observations but may inadvertently miss important activities. Another option for data collection is to ask people to keep daily time logs or diaries.

TEXTS Many cultural anthropologists collect *textual material*, a category that includes written or oral stories, myths, plays, sayings, speeches, jokes, and transcriptions of people's everyday conversations. In the early twentieth century, Franz Boas collected thousands of pages of texts from Native American groups of the Northwest Coast of Canada,

Michael Horowitz

A multidisciplinary team comprising anthropologists, engineers, and agricultural experts from the United States and Sudan meet to discuss a resettlement project.

including myths, songs, speeches, and accounts of how to perform rituals. These collections provide valuable records of cultures that have changed since the time of his fieldwork. Surviving tribal members have consulted them in order to recover forgotten aspects of their culture.

ARCHIVAL AND HISTORICAL SOURCES Many cultural anthropologists who work in cultures with a written history gain important insights about the present from records of the past preserved in archives maintained in institutions such as libraries, churches, and museums. Ann Stoler pioneered the use of archival resources in understanding the present in her study of Dutch colonialism in Java (1985, 1989). Her archival research exposed details about colonial policies, the culture of the colonizers, and relationships with indigenous Javanese people.

National archives in London, Paris, and Amsterdam, to name just a few places, contain records of colonial contact and relations. Regional and local archives contain information about land ownership, agricultural production, religious practices, and political activities. Parish churches throughout Europe keep detailed family histories extending back hundreds of years.

Important information about the past can also come from fieldwork among living people through an approach called the *anthropology of memory*. Anthropologists collect information about what people remember as well as gaps in their memory, revealing how culture shapes memories and how memories shape their culture. Jennifer Robertson's (1991) research about neighborhood people's memories of life in Kodaira, Japan, before the influx of immigrants is an example of this kind of research. She used both interview data and archival data.

MULTIPLE RESEARCH METHODS AND TEAM PROJECTS Most cultural anthropologists use a mix of several different methods. For example, consider what interviews with people in 100 households would provide in breadth of coverage, and then add what you could learn from life histories collected from a subset of five men and five women to provide depth, as well as what long-term participant observation with these people would contribute.

Anthropologists, with their in-depth insights about real people and real people's lives, are increasingly taking part in multidisciplinary research projects, especially projects with an applied focus. Such teamwork strengthens the research by adding more perspectives and methods. Combining data from group interviews, one-on-one interviews, participant observation, and mapping provides rich information on Inuit place names and environmental knowledge (see Eye on the Environment box).

RECORDING CULTURE

How does an anthropologist keep track of all the information collected in the field and record it for future analysis? As with everything else about fieldwork, things have changed since the early times when a notebook and typewriter were the major recording tools. Taking detailed notes, nonetheless, is still a cultural anthropologist's trademark method of recording data.

FIELD NOTES *Field notes* include daily logs, personal journals, descriptions of events, and notes about those notes. Ideally, researchers should write up their field notes each day. Otherwise, a backlog accumulates of daily "scratch notes," or rough jottings made on a small pad or note cards (Sanjek 1990). Trying to capture, in the fullest way possible, the events of even a single day is a monumental task and can result in dozens of pages of handwritten or typed field notes. Laptop computers now enable anthropologists to enter many of their daily observations directly into the computer.

TAPE RECORDING, PHOTOGRAPHY, AND VIDEOS Tape recorders are a major aid to fieldwork. Their use may raise problems, however, such as research participants' suspicions about a machine that can capture their voices, and the ethical issue of protecting the identity of people whose voices are preserved on tape. María Cátedra reports on her use of tape recording during her research in the Asturias region of rural Spain (see Map 5):

> At first the existence of the "apparatus," as they called it, was part wonder and part suspect. Many had never seen one before and were fascinated to hear their own voice, but all were worried about what I would do with the tapes. . . . I tried to solve the problem by explaining what I would do with the tapes: I would use them to record correctly what people told me, since my memory was not good enough and I could not take notes quickly enough. . . . One event helped people to accept my integrity in regard to the "apparatus."

Researching Inuit Place Names and Landscape Knowledge

The South Baffin Island Place Name Project is dedicated to collecting and recording Inuit place names and landscape knowledge as a means to preserving climatically important information (Henshaw 2003, 2006). Inuit is a cluster name for many indigenous peoples who live in the eastern Canadian Arctic. Before contact with Europeans, Inuit life was one of constant mobility. Now, most Inuit are settled in villages and towns. As a result, their detailed knowledge of migration routes, locations along these routes, and how to adapt to changing conditions when on the move are being lost.

Anthropologists and other researchers seek to work with Inuit people to document their traditional knowledge of places and routes. One project looks at **toponymy**, or the naming of places. Inuit toponymy is one aspect of a rich set of **indigenous knowledge**, or local understanding of the environment, climate, plants, and animals.

The South Baffin Place Names Project used several methods for collecting data. The first step was community-wide workshops, with 10 to 15 people gathered together in a community hall. The researchers laid out large maps, and the Inuit added place names to the map and explained their importance.

The second step was conducting one-on-one interviews with Inuit elders. These elders have lived in particular areas and can provide specialized knowledge about them in terms of use (for shelter, for fishing and hunting, and for storage), routes to and from the site, and likely weather conditions.

The third step was participant observation. The anthropologists, with Inuit collaborators, went to many of the sites. They gained first-hand experience about travel conditions to and from the sites and

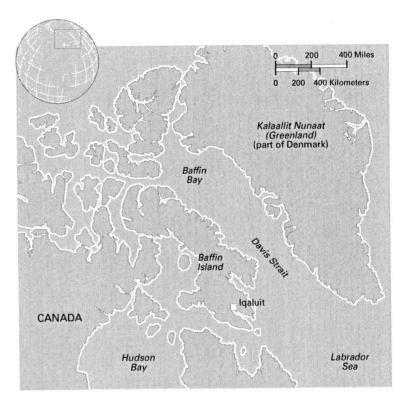

MAP 4 Baffin Island in Northeast Canada.
Baffin Island is the largest island in the Canadian Arctic. Iqaluit, a town of about 3,000 people, is the capital of the Nunavut territory. Kalaallit Nunaat, meaning The Human's Land, is the world's largest island and a self-governed Danish territory. Its population of 56,000 people is mainly of mixed descent between the indigenous Kalaallit (Inuit) and Danish people.

conditions at the sites themselves. They made video recordings and took photographs.

The fourth step was analytical and archival. The researchers created a computer database, linking the ethnographic data to maps.

This research project has many uses. It will provide a data baseline, starting with the memory of the elders, of important living sites and migration routes. It will show, over time, environmental changes that have occurred and how people are adapting to them. It will create an archive of indigenous knowledge that can be used by future

generations of Inuit in protecting their cultural heritage and ways of making a living.

◆ FOOD FOR THOUGHT

⊙ Choose an ordinary day in your week and create a map of where you go and how key locations are named (such as dorm room, dining hall, classroom, and other). What names do you use for key sites and what do the place names mean to you? How would you change your daily route depending on differences in the weather or season?

The "autonomous community" of Asturias is located in the far north of Spain. It has extensive coastal beaches but the inland is mainly mountainous. The traditional economy was based in fishing and agriculture. Coal mining and steel production were important in the mid-twentieth century but have declined.

> In the second braña [small settlement] I visited, people asked me to play back what the people of the first braña had told me, especially some songs sung by a group of men. At first I was going to do it, but then I instinctively refused because I did not have the first people's permission. . . . My stand was quickly known in the first braña and commented on with approval. (1992:21–22)

To be useful for analysis, tape recordings have to be transcribed (typed up), either partially or completely. Each hour of recorded talk takes between 5 and 8 hours to transcribe.

Like tape recordings, photographs or videos capture more detail than scratch notes. Any researcher who has watched people performing a ritual, taken scratch notes, and then tried to reconstruct the details of the ritual later on will know how much of the sequencing and related activity is lost to memory within just a few hours. Reviewing photographs or a video recording of the ritual provides a surprising amount of forgotten or missed material. The tradeoff, however, is that if you are using a camera or video recorder, you cannot take notes at the same time.

Kirsten Hastrup describes her use of photography in recording the annual ram exhibition in Iceland (see Map 6)

MAP 5   Spain.
The Kingdom of Spain is the largest of the three countries occupying the Iberian Peninsula. The geography is dominated by high plateaus and mountain ranges. Spain's population exceeds 40 million. Spain's administrative structure is complex, including autonomous communities, such as Andalucia and Catalonia, and provinces. The central government is granting more autonomy to some of the localities, including the Basque area.

that celebrates the successful herding in of the sheep from mountain pastures. This event is exclusively for men, but they allowed her to attend:

> The smell was intense, the light somewhat dim and the room full of indiscernible sounds from some 120 rams and about 40 men. A committee went from one ram to the next noting their impressions of the animal, in terms of its general beauty, the size of the horns and so forth. Measurements were made all over but the decisive measure (made by hand) was the size and weight of the ram's testicles. The air was loaded with sex and I realized that the exhibition was literally and metaphorically a competition of sexual potence. . . . I heard endless sexual jokes and very private remarks. The bursts of laughter followed by side-glances at me conveyed an implicit question of whether I understood what was going on. I did. (1992:9)

Hastrup took many photographs. After they were developed, she was disappointed by how little of the totality of the event they conveyed.

---

toponymy   the naming of places.

indigenous knowledge (IK)   local understanding of the environment, climate, plants, and animals.

© Catherine Karnow/CORBIS All Rights Reserved.

At the National Icelandic Ram Festival in Iceland.

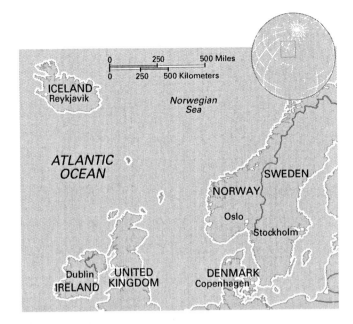

MAP 6 Iceland.
The Republic of Iceland has a population of 300,000. A volcanic island, Iceland is the fifth richest country in the world, according to GDP (gross domestic product) per capita. It has a high quality of life and ranked second in the 2005 United Nations Human Development Index. Iceland's economy is based in exporting fish and fish products, technology, and tourism.

DATA ANALYSIS

During the research process, an anthropologist collects a vast amount of data in many forms. How does he or she put the data into a meaningful form? In data analysis, as with data collection, two basic varieties exist: *qualitative* (prose-based description) and *quantitative* (numeric presentation).

ANALYZING QUALITATIVE DATA   Qualitative data include descriptive field notes, narratives, myths and stories, songs and sagas, and more. Few guidelines exist for undertaking a qualitative analysis of qualitative data. One procedure is to search for themes, or patterns. This approach involves exploring the data, or "playing" with the data, either "by hand" or with the use of a computer. Jennifer Robertson's analysis of her Kodaira data was inspired by writer Gertrude Stein's (1948) approach to writing "portraits" of individuals, such as Picasso. Robertson says that Stein was a superb ethnographer who was able to illuminate the "bottom nature" of her subjects and their worlds through a process that Stein referred to as "condensation." To do this, "she scrutinized her subjects until, over time, there emerged for her a repeating pattern of their words and actions. Her literary portraits . . . were condensations of her subjects' repeatings" (Robertson 1991:1). Like Stein, Robertson reflected on all that she had experienced and learned in Kodaira, beginning with the years when she lived there as a child. Emerging from all this was the dominant theme, *furusato*, which literally means "old village." References to *furusato* appear frequently in people's accounts of the past, conveying a sense of nostalgia for a more "real" past.

Many qualitative anthropologists use computers to help sort for such *tropes* (key themes). Computer scanning of data offers the ability to search vast quantities of data more quickly and perhaps accurately than with the human eye. The range of software available for such data management is expanding. The quality of the results, though, still depends on careful and complete inputting of the data and an intelligent coding scheme that will tell the computer what it should be scanning for in the data.

The presentation of qualitative data relies on people's own words—their stories, explanations, and conversations. Lila Abu-Lughod followed this approach in conveying Egyptian Bedu women's narratives in her book *Writing Women's Worlds* (1993). Abu-Lughod offers a light authorial framework that organizes the women's stories into thematic clusters such as marriage, production, and honor. Although Abu-Lughod provides an introduction to the narratives, she offers no conclusion, thereby prompting readers to think for themselves about the meanings of the stories and what they say about Egyptian Bedu women's life.

Some anthropologists question the value of such artistic, interpretive approaches because they lack scientific verifiability. Too much depends, they say, on the individual selection process of the anthropologist, and interpretation often depends on a small number of cases. Interpretive anthropologists respond that verifiability, in the scientific sense, is not their goal and is not a worthwhile goal for cultural anthropology. Instead, they seek to provide a plausible interpretation, or a fresh understanding into people's lives that offers detail and richness.

ANALYZING QUANTITATIVE DATA   Analysis of quantitative, or numeric, data can proceed in several directions. Some

---

ethnography   a firsthand, detailed description of a living culture, based on personal observation.

Item	Urban				Rural			
	Group 1	Group 2	Group 3	Total	Group 1	Group 2	Group 3	Total
Number of Households	26	25	16	67	32	30	16	78
Food	60.5	51.6	50.1	54.7	74.1	62.3	55.7	65.8
Alcohol	0.2	0.4	1.5	0.6	0.5	1.1	1.0	0.8
Tobacco	0.8	0.9	0.9	0.9	1.1	1.7	1.2	1.4
Dry Goods	9.7	8.1	8.3	8.7	8.8	10.2	14.3	10.5
Housing	7.3	11.7	10.3	9.7	3.4	5.7	3.9	4.4
Fuel	5.4	6.0	5.0	5.6	3.7	3.9	4.1	3.9
Transportation	7.4	8.2	12.4	8.9	3.0	5.3	7.6	4.9
Health	0.3	0.6	0.7	0.5	1.5	1.4	1.7	1.5
Education	3.5	2.8	3.1	3.2	1.2	2.1	3.0	1.9
Entertainment	0.1	0.9	1.1	0.6	0.0	0.1	0.3	0.2
Other	5.2	8.3	6.9	6.8	2.1	6.0	6.9	4.6
Total*	100.4	99.5	100.3	100.2	99.4	99.8	99.7	99.9

*Totals may not add up to 100 due to rounding.

Source: From "Social Patterns of Food Expenditure Among Low-Income Jamaicans" by Barbara D. Miller in *Papers and Recommendations of the Workshop on Food and Nutrition Security in Jamaica in the 1980s and Beyond*, ed. by Kenneth A. Leslie and Lloyd B. Rankine, 1987.

FIGURE 3   Mean Weekly Expenditure Shares (Percentage) in 11 Categories by Urban and Rural Expenditure Groups, Jamaica, 1983–1984

of the more sophisticated methods require knowledge of statistics, and many require the use of a computer and a software package that can perform statistical computations. The author's research on low-income household budgets in Jamaica involved the use of computer analysis: first, to divide the sample households into three income groups (lower, medium, and higher); second, to calculate percentages of expenditures in the three categories of goods and groups of goods, such as food, housing, and transportation (see Figure 3). Because the number of households was quite small (120), the analysis could have been done "by hand." But using the computer made the analysis proceed more quickly and more accurately.

REPRESENTING CULTURE   **Ethnography**, or a detailed description of a living culture based on personal observation and study, is the main way that cultural anthropologists present their findings about culture. In the early phase of cultural anthropology, in the first half of the twentieth century, ethnographers wrote about "exotic" cultures located far from their homes in Europe and North America. The early ethnographers tended to treat a particular local group or village as a unit unto itself with clear boundaries. Since the 1980s, ethnographies have changed in several ways:

- Ethnographers now treat local cultures as connected with larger regional and global structures and forces. Edward Fischer's book *Cultural Logics and Global Economics: Maya Identity in Thought and Practice* (2001) takes the topic of Maya political activism in Guatemala

as its focus and sets it within the context of changing economic systems more widely.

- Ethnographers focus on one topic of interest and avoid a more holistic approach. Laura Miller studied ideas and practices about the body and beauty in Japan. In her book *Body Up: Exploring Contemporary Japanese Body Aesthetics* (2006), she explores beauty salons, beauty products, changing ideas of female and male beauty, and ideas about diet.

- Ethnographers study Western, industrialized cultures as well as other cultures. Philippe Bourgois's research in East Harlem in New York City for his book *In Search of Respect: Selling Crack in El Barrio* (1995) explores how people in one neighborhood cope with poverty and dangerous living conditions. Although this topic sounds like it fits more in sociology than anthropology, a cultural anthropologist will provide rich contextual details about the everyday experiences and perspectives of the people based on participant observation.

THINKING OUTSIDE THE BOX

Have you ever had the experience of taking photographs of a place, event, or people and then being terribly disappointed because the results did not capture the essence of your experience? What was missing from the photographs?

Urgent Issues in Cultural Anthropology Research

This section considers two urgent issues in cultural anthropology research: fieldwork ethics and safety during fieldwork.

ETHICS AND COLLABORATIVE RESEARCH

Anthropology was one of the first disciplines to devise and adopt a code of ethics. Two events in the 1950s and 1960s prompted cultural anthropologists to reconsider their role in research in relation to the sponsors of their research and to the people with whom they were studying. The first was Project Camelot of the 1950s; it was a plan of the U.S. government to influence political leadership in South America in order to strengthen U.S. interests (Horowitz 1967). The U.S. government employed several anthropologists to collect information on political leaders and events, without revealing their purpose.

The second major event was the Vietnam War (or the American War, as people in Vietnam refer to it). It brought to the forefront of anthropology questions about government interests in ethnographic information, the role of anthropologists during wartime, and the protection of the people with whom anthropologists conduct research. Two bitterly opposed positions emerged within anthropology. On one side was the view that all Americans as citizens should support the U.S. military effort in Vietnam. People on this side said that any anthropologist who had information that could help subvert communism should provide it to the U.S. government. The other position stated that an anthropologist's responsibility is first and always to protect the people being studied, a responsibility that takes priority over politics. These anthropologists opposed the war and saw the people of South Vietnam as victims of Western imperialism. They uncovered cases in which anthropologists submitted information about people's political affiliations to the U.S. government, with the result being military actions and death of the people exposed by the research.

This period was the most divisive in the history of U.S. anthropology. It led, in 1971, to the adoption by the American Anthropological Association (AAA) of a code of ethics. The AAA code of ethics states that an anthropologist's primary responsibility is to ensure the safety of the people participating in the research. A related principle is that cultural anthropology does not condone covert or "undercover" research. Further, anthropologists should inform potential research participants about the purposes and scope of the study.

COLLABORATIVE RESEARCH   A new direction in methods explicitly seeks to involve members of the study population in collaborative research—from data collection to analysis and presentation. **Collaborative research** is an approach to learning about culture that involves the anthropologist working with members of the study population as partners and teammates rather than as "subjects." This strategy, from the start, forces reconsideration of how anthropologists refer to the people being studied, especially the long-standing term "informant." The term sounds hauntingly and negatively related to espionage or war and implies a passive role on handing over information to someone else. As noted earlier in this chapter, IRBs use the term "human subject," which cultural anthropologists reject for similar reasons. Cultural anthropologists favor the term *research participant*.

Luke Eric Lassiter is a pioneer in collaborative methods. In a recent project, Lassiter involved his undergraduate anthropology students in a collaboration with members of the African American community of Muncie, Indiana. This project resulted in a book with shared authorship between Lassiter, the students, and the community members (2004). The project collected information about African American life that is now housed in a library archive.

Cultural anthropologists are working to find better ways to share the benefits of research with the people and places we study. Research methods in cultural anthropology have come a long way from the armchair to new strategies for nonhierarchical research. More progress lies ahead, however, in democratizing anthropology and making everyone a "barefoot anthropologist."

SAFETY IN THE FIELD

Fieldwork can involve serious physical and psychological risks to the researcher and to members of his or her family. The image of "the anthropologist as hero" has muffled, to a large degree, both the physical dangers and the psychological risks of fieldwork.

The collaborative research team led by Luke Eric Lassiter includes Muncie community members (far left and far right) and students and faculty from Ball State University.

---

collaborative research   an approach to learning about culture that involves anthropologists working with members of the study population as partners and participants rather than as "subjects."

The food ration queue at an emergency clinic near Buedu, Sierra Leone in 2001. While conducting his dissertation research in war-torn Sierra Leone, Danny Hoffman combined traditional fieldwork techniques such as participant observation and interviews. He also had to be alert to sudden danger and other risks specific to research during war. Hoffman believes that anthropologists must be willing to take such risks in order to provide essential knowledge about the complex causes and consequences of war that are overlooked by war correspondents writing for the media.

Dangers from the physical environment are often serious and can be fatal. In the 1980s, the slippery paths of the highland Philippines claimed the life of Michelle Zimbalist Rosaldo, a major figure in late twentieth-century cultural anthropology. Disease is a frequent problem. Many anthropologists have contracted infectious diseases that have chronic effects or that may be fatal.

Violence figures prominently in some, but not most, fieldwork experiences. During the five years that Philippe Bourgois lived in East Harlem, New York, he witnessed the following: a shooting outside his window, a bombing and machine-gunning of a numbers joint, a shoot-out and police car chase in front of the pizza parlor where he was eating, the aftermath of a fire-bombing of a heroin house, a dozen serious fights, and "almost daily exposure to broken-down human beings, some of them in fits of crack-induced paranoia, some suffering from delirium tremens, and others in unidentifiable pathological fits of screaming and shouting insults to all around them" (1995:32). He was rough-handled by the police several times because they did not believe that he was a professor doing research. He was once mugged for the sum of $8. Although his research placed him in danger, it also enabled him to gain an understanding, from the inside, of everyday violence in the lives of desperately poor and addicted people.

Likewise, some anthropological research involves danger from political violence or even war. A new specialty, *war zone anthropology*, or research conducted within zones of violent conflict, can provide important insights into topics such as the militarization of civilian lives, civilian protection, the cultural dynamics of military personnel, and postconflict reconstruction (Hoffman and Lubkemann 2005). This kind of research requires skills and judgment that anthropology classes or research methods books do not typically address (Nordstrom 1997, Kovats-Bernat 2002). Previous experience in conflict zones as workers in international aid organizations or the military is helpful.

What about fieldwork danger in supposedly normal situations? After more than 20 years of fieldwork in the Kalahari desert, southern Africa, Nancy Howell (1990) suddenly had to confront the issue of danger in the field when one of her teenage sons was killed and another injured in a truck accident in Botswana, southern Africa, while with their father, Richard Lee, who was doing fieldwork there at the time. In the months following the accident, she heard from many anthropologist friends who shared stories about other fieldwork accidents.

Howell contacted the American Anthropological Association (AAA) to see what advice it provides about fieldwork safety. The answer, she learned, was not much. The AAA responded with financial support for her to undertake a detailed inquiry into fieldwork hazards in anthropology. Howell drew a sample of 311 anthropologists listed as employed in the AAA's *Guide to Departments*. She sent them a questionnaire asking for information on gender, age, work status, health status, and work habits in the field; and she asked for information on health problems and other hazards they had experienced. She received 236 completed questionnaires, a high response rate indicating strong interest in the study.

In her analysis, she found regional variation in risk and danger. The highest rates were in Africa, followed by India, the Asia/Pacific region, and Latin America. Howell offers recommendations about how anthropologists can prepare themselves more effectively for preventing and dealing with fieldwork risks. They include these:

- Increasing risk awareness among fieldworkers
- Training fieldworkers in basic medical care
- Learning about fieldwork safety in anthropology classes

Research methods in cultural anthropology have come a long way from the time of the armchair anthropologists. Topics have changed, as have techniques of data gathering and data analysis. New concerns about ethical research and responsibility and fieldworkers' safety continue to reshape research practices.

THINKING
OUTSIDE
THE BOX

To see the entire AAA Code of Ethics, go to http://www.aaanet.org.

the BIG questions REVISITED

◆ How do cultural anthropologists conduct research on culture?

Cultural anthropologists conduct research by doing fieldwork and using participant observation. In the nineteenth century, early cultural anthropologists did armchair anthropology, meaning that they learned about other cultures by reading reports written by explorers and other untrained observers. The next stage was verandah anthropology, in which an anthropologist went to the field but did not live with the people. Instead, the anthropologist would interview a few members of the study population where he (there were no women cultural anthropologists at this time) lived, typically on his verandah.

Fieldwork and participant observation became the cornerstones of cultural anthropology research only after Malinowski's innovations in the Trobriand Islands during World War I. His approach emphasized the value of living for an extended period in the field, participating in the daily activities of the people, and learning the local language. These features are the hallmarks of research in cultural anthropology today.

New techniques continue to develop in response to changing times. One of the most important is multisited research, in which the anthropologist studies a topic at more than one location.

◆ What does fieldwork involve?

Research in cultural anthropology involves several stages. The first is to choose a research topic. A good topic is timely, important, and feasible. Ideas for topics can come from literature review, restudies, current events and pressing issues, and even sheer luck. Once in the field, the first steps include site selection, gaining rapport, and dealing with culture shock. Microcultures affect how the anthropologist will gain rapport and will shape access of the anthropologist to particular cultural domains. Participating appropriately in the culture involves learning local forms of gift giving and other exchanges to express gratitude for people's hospitality, time, and trust.

Specific research techniques may emphasize gathering quantitative or qualitative data. Cultural materialists tend to focus on quantitative data, whereas interpretivists gather qualitative data. When in the field, anthropologists take daily notes, often by hand but now also using a computer. Several other methods of documenting culture include photography, audio recording, and video recording. The anthropologist's theoretical orientation and research goals affect the approach to data analysis and presentation.

Quantitative data may involve statistical analysis and presentation in graphs or tables. The presentation of qualitative data is more likely to be descriptive.

◆ What are some urgent issues in cultural anthropology research today?

Questions of ethics have been paramount to anthropologists since the 1950s. In 1971, U.S. anthropologists adopted a set of ethical guidelines for research to address their concern about what role, if any, anthropologists should play in research that might harm the people being studied. The AAA code of ethics states that an anthropologist's primary responsibility is to maintain the safety of the people involved. Further, cultural anthropologists should never engage in covert research and should always explain their purpose to the people in the study and preserve the anonymity of the location and of individuals. Collaborative research is a recent development that responds to ethical concerns by pursuing research that involves the participants as partners rather than as subjects.

Safety during fieldwork is another important issue. Danger to anthropologists can come from physical sources such as infectious diseases and from social sources such as political violence. A survey of anthropologists in the 1980s produced recommendations about increasing safety during fieldwork.

KEY CONCEPTS

collaborative research
culture shock
deductive approach
  (to research)
emic
ethnography
etic
fieldwork

Hawthorne effect
indigenous knowledge
inductive approach
  (to research)
informed consent
interview
kula
multisited research

participant observation
qualitative data
quantitative data
questionnaire
rapport
toponymy

SUGGESTED READINGS

Michael V. Angrosino. *Projects in Ethnographic Research.* Long Grove, IL: Waveland Press, 2005. This brief manual provides students with ideas about what conducting research in anthropology is like. It discusses the fundamental stages of three projects, with insights about how students can conduct their own research.

H. Russell Bernard. *Research Methods in Cultural Anthropology: Qualitative and Quantitative Approaches,* 3rd ed. Newbury Park, CA: Sage Publications, 2002. This is a sourcebook of anthropological research methods providing information about how to design a research project, methods of data collection, and data analysis and presentation.

Kathleen M. DeWalt and Billie R. DeWalt. *Participant Observation: A Guide for Fieldworkers.* New York: AltaMira Press, 2002. This book is a comprehensive guide to doing participant observation.

Alexander Ervin. *Applied Anthropology: Tools and Perspectives for Contemporary Practice.* Boston: Allyn and Bacon, 2005. Chapters discuss links between anthropology and policy, the history of applied anthropology, ethics, and specialized methods.

Carolyn Fluehr-Lobban. *Ethics and the Profession of Anthropology: A Dialogue for Ethically Conscious Practice,* 2nd ed. Philadelphia: University of Pennsylvania Press, 2003. The chapters address topics such as covert research, indigenous people's cultural rights, informed consent, and ethics in researching culture in cyberspace.

Peggy Golde, ed. *Women in the Field: Anthropological Experiences,* 2nd ed. Berkeley: University of California Press, 1986. Chapters in this classic collection discuss Margaret Mead's fieldwork in the Pacific, Laura Nader's fieldwork in Mexico and Lebanon,

Ernestine Friedl's fieldwork in Greece, and Jean Briggs's fieldwork among the Inuit of the Canadian Arctic.

Joy Hendry. *An Anthropologist in Japan: Glimpses of Life in the Field.* London: Routledge, 1999. This book describes the author's original research design, how her focus changed, and how she reached unanticipated conclusions.

Choong Soon Kim. *One Anthropologist, Two Worlds: Three Decades of Reflexive Fieldwork in North America and Asia.* Knoxville: University of Tennessee Press, 2002. The author reflects on his fieldwork, conducted over 30 years, on Japanese industry in the American South and on Korean families displaced by the Korean war and partition.

Luke Eric Lassiter. *The Chicago Guide to Collaborative Ethnography.* Chicago: University of Chicago Press, 2005. This handbook for doing collaborative anthropology includes historical and theoretical perspectives on collaborative anthropology, exposing its roots in feminist, humanist, and critical anthropology.

Carolyn Nordstrom and Antonius C. G. M. Robben, eds. *Fieldwork under Fire: Contemporary Studies of Violence and Survival.* Berkeley: University of California Press, 1995. The chapters discuss fieldwork experiences in Palestine, China, Sri Lanka, the United States, Croatia, Guatemala, and Ireland.

Tom Ric with Mette Louise Berg, eds. *Future Fields,* special issue of the online journal *Anthropology Matters,* Vol. 6, No. 2, 2004. This issue includes 11 articles that address a range of methodological issues cultural anthropologists face today, including emotional, financial, and ethical challenges as well as how to cope in situations of physical danger. The journal is accessible at no charge at http://www.anthropologymatters.com.

CHAPTER 4

MAKING A LIVING

A family living in a village in the interior Amazon region of Brazil preparing farinha (fuh-reen-yuh), a food staple made from manioc, a root crop. The villagers also eat fruit and vegetables harvested from the rainforest, but these foods are no longer easily available due to extensive clearing of the rainforest by illegal loggers, for cattle ranching, and for industrial farms that grow export crops such as soybeans.

MAKING A LIVING

the BIG questions

◆ How do cultural anthropologists study economic systems?

◆ What are the five modes of livelihood?

◆ How are the five modes of livelihood changing?

89

During the many thousands of years of human prehistory, people made their living by collecting food and other necessities from nature. All group members had equal access to life-sustaining resources. Most people throughout the world now live in economies much different from this description.

◆◆◆
Culture and Economic Systems

In anthropology, the term **economic system** includes three components:

- *Livelihood* or production—making goods or money
- *Consumption*—using up goods or money
- *Exchange*—the transfer of goods or money between people or institutions

Economic anthropology is the subfield of cultural anthropology that focuses on economic systems cross-culturally. It differs from the discipline of economics in several ways. First, the subject matter of economic anthropology is much wider. It covers all economics systems, not just modern capitalism. Second, economic anthropologists' methods are different. They tend to collect qualitative data and quantitative data, and they rely on fieldwork and participant observation rather than analyzing "canned" statistical datasets or census information. Third, economic anthropologists believe that it is important to gather emic data in order to understand people's own concepts and categories related to making a living, rather than applying Western concepts and categories.

In spite of these differences between economics and economic anthropology, some shared territory exists. Some economists do learn a foreign language and some try to learn about people's actual economic behavior and thought by conducting fieldwork. In turn, some economic anthropologists analyze large, quantitative datasets. Most fruitfully, some economists and some economic anthropologists work together on research and policy issues.

CATEGORIZING LIVELIHOODS

Many years of ethnographic research on economic systems has produced a rich body of knowledge about livelihoods in diverse settings, the topic of this chapter. Anthropologists organize this information by sorting it into categories, called *modes*. The next section describes five major modes of livelihood. A **mode of livelihood** is the dominant way of making a living in a culture.

---

economic system   the linked processes of livelihood, consumption, and exchange.

mode of livelihood   the dominant way of making a living in a culture.

During his fieldwork among the Hare Indians in Northwest Canada, anthropologist Joel Savishinsky holds a 25-pound trout. His dog team is resting behind him.

Categorizing a certain society as having a particular mode of livelihood implies an emphasis on a particular type of livelihood, but it does not mean that only one kind of economic activity exists. In a given society, some people will be involved in the prevailing productive activity, and others will not. A particular individual may be involved in more than one way of making a living. For example, a person could be a farmer and a herder. Another point to keep in mind is that the five modes of livelihood, in reality, blend with and overlap each other. Therefore, some cultures do not fit well within any one mode. Real life is always more complicated than the categories researchers create.

Figure 1 presents the five modes of livelihood in order of their historical appearance in the human record. This diagram does not mean that a particular mode evolves into the one following it—for example, foragers do not necessarily transform into horticulturalists, and so on. Nor does this ordering imply a judgment about the sophistication or superiority of more recent modes of livelihood. Figure 1 is not a model of "progress" from left to right. The oldest system involves complex and detailed knowledge about the environment that a contemporary city dweller would find difficult to learn quickly enough to ensure survival.

Foraging	Horticulture	Pastoralism	Agriculture	Industrialism/Informatics
Reason for Production Production for use				**Reason for Production** Production for profit
Division of Labor Family-based Overlapping gender roles				**Division of Labor** Class-based High degree of occupational specialization
Property Relations Egalitarian and collective				**Property Relations** Stratified and private
Resource Use Extensive and temporary				**Resource Use** Intensive and expanding
Sustainability High degree				**Sustainability** Low degree

FIGURE 1   Modes of Livelihood

MODES OF LIVELIHOOD AND GLOBALIZATION

Although economic anthropologists focus on local economic systems, they are increasingly involved in researching how global and local systems are linked. The spread of Western capitalism in recent centuries has had, and continues to have, marked effects on all other livelihood patterns that it meets.

The intensification of global trade in the past few decades has created a global division of labor, or *world economy,* in which countries compete unequally for a share of the wealth (Wallerstein 1979). In this view, the modern world economy is stratified into three major areas:

- Core
- Periphery
- Semiperiphery

Core areas monopolize the most profitable activities, such as the high-tech service, manufacturing, and financial activities. They have the strongest governments, which play a dominating role in the affairs of other countries. *Peripheral areas* are relegated to the least profitable activities, including livelihood of raw materials, foodstuffs, and labor-intensive goods, and they must import high-tech goods and services from the core. They tend to have weak governments and are dominated, either directly or indirectly, by core states. *Semiperipheral areas* stand in the middle.

In this model, economic benefits are highly unequal across regions, with core areas profiting most. Core states have about 20 percent of the world's population and control 80 percent of the world's wealth (and they create 80 percent of world's pollution). Politically, the core continues to increase its economic power and political influence through international

Monterrey, Mexico, is the second most important city in Mexico after the capital. Because of its strong steel industry, it is called "the Pittsburgh of Mexico." It has several major beer breweries and is home to the Mexican Baseball Hall of Fame. The city center has monuments of both Spanish colonialism and cosmopolitan modernity.

organizations such as the World Trade Organization (WTO) and regional arrangements such as the North American Free Trade Agreement (NAFTA). The last section of this chapter returns to the topic of globalization and livelihood change.

◆ ◆ ◆

Making a Living: The Five Modes of Livelihood

While reading this section, please bear in mind that most anthropologists are uneasy about typologies because they often do not reflect the complexity of life in any particular context. The purpose of the categories is to help you organize the ethnographic information presented in this book.

FORAGING

Foraging is a mode of livelihood based on resources that are available in nature through gathering, fishing, or hunting. The oldest way of making a living, foraging, is a strategy that humans share with our nonhuman primate relatives.

Although foraging supported humanity since our beginnings, it is in danger of extinction. Only around 250,000 people worldwide provide for their livelihood predominantly from foraging now. Most contemporary foragers live in what are considered marginal areas, such as deserts, tropical rainforests, and the circumpolar region. These areas, however, often contain material resources that are in high demand in core areas, such as oil, diamonds, gold, and expensive tourist destinations. Thus, the basis of their survival is threatened by what is called "the resource curse": People in rich countries desire the natural resources in their areas, which leads to conversion of foraging land to mines, plantations, or tourist destinations, in turn leading to the displacement of foragers from their homeland.

Depending on the environmental context, foragers' food sources include nuts, berries and other fruits, and surface-growing vegetables such as melons, roots, honey, insects, and eggs. They trap and hunt a wide variety of birds, fish, and animals. Successful foraging requires sophisticated knowledge of the natural environment and seasonal changes in it. Most critical is knowledge about the location of water sources and of various foods, how to follow animal tracks, how to judge the weather, and how to avoid predators. This unwritten knowledge is passed down over the generations.

Foragers rely on a diverse set of tools used for gathering, transporting, and processing wild foods. Tools include digging sticks for removing roots from the ground and for penetrating the holes dug by animals in order to get the animals out, bows and arrows, spears, nets, and knives. Baskets are important for carrying food. For processing raw materials into edible food, foragers use stones to mash, grind, and pound. Meat can be dried in the sun or over fire, and fire is used for cooking either by boiling or by roasting. These activities involve few nonrenewable fuel sources beyond wood or other combustible substances for cooking. Foraging is an **extensive strategy**, a mode of livelihood requiring access to large areas of land and unrestricted population movement. Cultural anthropologists distinguish two major varieties of foraging that are related to different environmental contexts: temperate-climate foraging and circumpolar foraging.

The Ju/'hoansi people of southern Africa, as studied in the early 1960s, moved several times during a year, depending on the seasonal availability of water sources. Each cluster of families regularly returned to "their" territory, reconstructing or completely rebuilding their shelters with sticks for frames, and leaf or thatch coverings. Shelters are sometimes attached to two or three small trees or bushes for support. The amount of time involved in gathering and processing food and constructing shelters is modest.

In contrast to foragers of temperate climates, those living in the circumpolar regions of North America, Europe, and Asia devote more time and energy to obtaining food and providing shelter. The specialized technology of circumpolar peoples includes spears, nets, and knives, as well as sleds and the use of domesticated animals to pull them. Dogs or other

	Temperate-Region Foragers	Circumpolar-Region Foragers
Diet	Wide variety of nuts, tubers, fruits, small animals, and occasional large game	Large marine and terrestrial animals
Gender division of labor in food procurement	Men and women forage; men hunt large game	Men hunt and fish
Shelter	Casual construction, nonpermanent, little maintenance	Time-intensive construction and maintenance, some permanent

FIGURE 2 Temperate and Circumpolar Foraging Systems Compared

A Ju/'hoansi traditional shelter.

animals used to pull sleds are an important aspect of circumpolar peoples' technology and social identity (see Everyday Anthropology box). Considerable amounts of labor are needed to construct and maintain igloos or log houses. Protective clothing, including coats, gloves, and boots, is another feature of circumpolar foraging that is time intensive in terms of making and maintaining.

DIVISION OF LABOR Among foraging peoples, the *division of labor,* or occupational specialization (assigning particular tasks to particular individuals), is based on gender and age. Among temperate foraging cultures, a minimal gender-based division of labor exists. Temperate foragers get most of their everyday food by gathering roots, berries, grubs, small birds and animals, and fish, and both men and women collect these basic foods. Hunting large animals, however, tends to involve only men, who go off together in small groups on long-range expeditions. Large game provides a small and irregular part of the diets of temperate-climate foragers. In circumpolar groups, a significant part of people's diet comes from large animals (such as seals, whales, and bears) and fish. Hunting and fishing tend to involve only men. Among circumpolar foragers, therefore, the division of labor is strongly gender-divided.

Age is a basis for task allocation in all modes of livelihood, including foraging. Young boys and girls help collect food. Elderly people tend to stay at the camp area where they are responsible for caring for young children.

PROPERTY RELATIONS The concept of *private property,* in the sense of owning something that can be sold to someone else, does not exist in foraging societies. Instead, the term **use rights** is more appropriate. It means that a person or group has socially recognized priority in access to particular resources such as gathering areas, hunting and fishing areas, and water holes. This access is willingly shared with others by permission. Among the Ju/'hoansi, family groups control access to particular water holes and the territory surrounding them (Lee 1979:58–60). Visiting groups are welcome and will be given food and water. In turn, the host group, at another time, will visit other camps and be offered hospitality there. In India's Andaman Islands (see Culturama), each family group controls a known offshore area for fishing. Sharing access to these resources is expected but only if permission has been requested and granted. Encroaching on someone else's area without permission is a serious misdemeanor and is likely to result in violence.

FORAGING AS A SUSTAINABLE SYSTEM When untouched by outside influences and with abundant land available, foraging systems are *sustainable,* which means that crucial resources are regenerated over time in balance with the demand that the population makes on them. North Sentinel Island, one island in the Andaman Islands, provides a clear case because its inhabitants have long lived in a "closed" system. So far, the few hundred indigenous people live in almost complete isolation from the rest of the world, other than the occasional helicopter flying overhead and the occasional attempt by outsiders to land on their territory.

---

extensive strategy a form of livelihood involving temporary use of large areas of land and a high degree of spatial mobility.

use rights a system of property relations in which a person or group has socially recognized priority in access to particular resources such as gathering, hunting, and fishing areas and water holes.

everyday ANTHROPOLOGY

The Importance of Dogs

Dogs were the first domesticated animal, with evidence of their domestication from sites in eastern Europe and Russia dating to around 18,000 years ago. In spite of dogs' long-standing importance to humans around the world, few cultural anthropologists have focused attention on humans and their dogs. One of the rare ethnographies to do so provides insights about the economic, social, and psychological importance of dogs among a group of circumpolar foragers.

Fewer than 100 Hare Indians constitute the community of Colville Lake in Canada's Northwest Territories (Savishinsky 1974). They live by hunting, trapping, and fishing in one of the harshest environments in the world. Joel Savishinsky went to Colville Lake to study stress, tension, and anxiety among the Hare and how people cope with environmental stress. Environmental stress factors include extremely cold temperatures, long and severe winters, extended periods of isolation, hazardous travel conditions along with the constant need for mobility during the harshest periods of the year, and sometimes food scarcity. Social and psychological stress factors also exist, including contact with White fur traders and missionaries.

Savishinsky discovered the importance of dogs to the Hare people early in his research:

> Later in the year when I obtained my own dogteam, I enjoyed much greater freedom of movement, and was able to camp with many people whom I had previously not been able to keep up with. Altogether I travelled close to 600 miles by dogsled between mid-October and early June. This constant contact with dogs, and the necessity of learning how to drive, train and handle them, led to my recognition of the social and psychological, as well as the ecological, significance of these animals in the lives of the people. (1974:xx)

Among the fourteen households, there are a total of 224 dogs. Some households have as many as four teams, with an average of six dogs per team, corresponding to people's estimation that six dogs are required for travel.

More than being economically useful, dogs play a significant role in people's emotional lives. They are a frequent topic of conversation:

> Members of the community constantly compare and comment on the care, condition, and growth of one another's animals, noting special qualities of size, strength, color, speed, and alertness (1974:169).

Emotional displays, uncommon among the Hare, are significant between people and their dogs:

> The affectionate and concerned treatment of young animals is participated in by people of all ages, and the nature of the relationship bears a striking resemblance to the way in which people treat young children. Pups and infants are, in essence, the only recipients of unreserved positive affect in the band's social life. . . (1974:169–170)

One reason for the sustainability of foraging is that foragers' needs are modest. Anthropologists have typified the foraging lifestyle as the *original affluent society* because needs are satisfied with minimal labor efforts. This term is used metaphorically to remind people living in contemporary consumer cultures that foraging is not a miserable, inadequate way to make a living, contrary to most ethnocentric thinking. In the 1960s, when the Ju/'hoansi people were still foragers, their major food source was mongongo nuts. At that time, these nuts were so abundant that there was never a shortage (Howell 1986). In addition, hundreds of species of edible plants and animals were available, with seasonal variations. The Ju/'hoansi were slender and often complained of hunger throughout the year. Their thinness may be an adaptation to seasonal fluctuations in food supply. Rather than maximizing food intake during times of plenty, they minimize it. Mealtime is not an occasion for stuffing oneself. Ju/'hoansi culture taught that it is good to have a hungry stomach, even when food is plentiful.

Because foragers' needs for goods are limited, minimal labor efforts are required to satisfy them. Foragers typically work fewer hours a week than the average employed North American. In traditional (undisturbed) foraging societies, the people spend as few as five hours a week collecting food and making and repairing tools. They have much time for storytelling, playing games, and resting. Foragers also traditionally enjoyed good health. During the early 1960s, the age structure and health status of the Ju/'hoansi compared well with people in the United States of around 1900 (Lee 1979:47–48). They had few infectious diseases or degenerative diseases (health problems related to aging, such as arthritis).

HORTICULTURE

Both horticulture and pastoralism are recent modes of livelihood, having emerged only as recently as 12,000 years ago in

---

horticulture   a mode of livelihood based on growing domesticated crops in gardens, using simple hand tools.

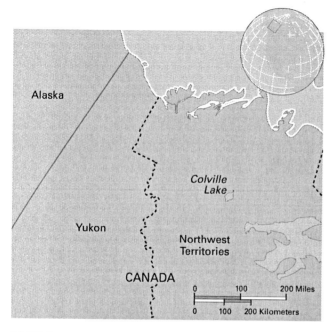

MAP 1 Hare Region near Colville Lake in Northwest Canada.
Early European colonialists named the local people Hare because of their reliance on snowshoe hares for food and clothing. The Hare people became involved in the wage-labor economy and were afflicted by alcoholism, tuberculosis, and other diseases. Efforts to reestablish claims to ancestral lands began in the 1960s.

Joel Savishinsky

Hare Indian children use their family's sled to haul drinking water to their village.

▶ *What tasks are children responsible for in a microculture that you know?*

◆ **FOOD FOR THOUGHT**

• Think of a culture (perhaps yours) in which dogs or some other domesticated animals are a focus of intense human interest. How do people and the animals in question interact? Are there age and gender differences in human relationships with domesticated animals? Hare children use their family's sled to haul drinking water to their village. What tasks are children responsible for in a microculture that you know? (Source: Joel Savishinsky)

the Middle East and then later in Africa, Asia, Europe, and the Western Hemisphere. Both depend on the domestication of plants and animals—that is, the process by which human selection causes genetic changes in plants and animals and leads to their greater control by humans in terms of their location and their reproduction.

Horticulture is a mode of livelihood based on cultivating domesticated plants in gardens using hand tools. Garden crops are often supplemented by foraging and by trading with pastoralists for animal products. Horticulture is still practiced by many thousands of people throughout the world. Prominent horticultural regions are found in sub-Saharan Africa, South Asia, Southeast Asia and the Pacific, Central America, South America, and the Caribbean islands. Major horticultural crops include yams, corn, beans, grains such as millet and sorghum, and several types of roots, all of which are rich in protein, minerals, and vitamins.

Horticulture involves the use of handheld tools, such as digging sticks, hoes, and carrying baskets. Rain is the sole

Cassava, also called manioc, is a root crop grown extensively in western Africa. This man displays a cassava plant grown in Niger. Cassava and millet, a grain, are the staple foods for many West Africans.

▶ *Do research to find some West African recipes that include cassava or millet.*

MAKING A LIVING

The Andaman Islanders of India

The Andaman Islands are a string of islands in the Bay of Bengal that belong to India. For unknown numbers of centuries, many of the islands were inhabited by people who fished, gathered, and hunted for their livelihood. During the eighteenth century, when European countries were expanding trade routes to the Far East, the Andaman Islands were of major strategic importance as a stopping place.

At the time of the first, small settlements of the British in the late eighteenth century, the total indigenous population was estimated at between 6000 and 8000 (B. Miller 1997). Today, over 400,000 people live on the islands, mostly migrants from the Indian mainland. The total number of indigenous people is about 400. British colonialism brought contagious diseases and increased death from violence among disrupted Andaman groups and between the Andaman people and the British.

Only four surviving clusters of indigenous Andamanese now exist. The smallest group, just a few dozen people, consists of the remnants of the so-called Great Andamanese people. They live on a small island near Port Blair, the capital, in what is essentially a reservation area. Several groups of Great Andamanese people formerly lived throughout North and Middle Andaman Islands, but no indigenous people inhabit these islands now. The so-called Jarawa, numbering perhaps 200, live in a reserved area on the southwest portion of South Andaman. Currently, no outsider knows their language or what name they use for themselves. Jarawa is a term that the Great Andamanese people use for them. The Onge, around 100 in number, live in one corner of Little Andaman Island. Another 100 people or so live on North Sentinel Island. Outsiders call them the "Sentinelese." No one has established communication with them, and almost no one from the outside has gotten closer than arrow-range of their shore.

The 2005 tsunami disrupted much of the Andaman Island landscape, particularly areas that had been cleared of mangroves and other trees. As far as anyone knows, none of the indigenous people died as a direct result of the tsunami, though many of the immigrant settlers did (Mukerjee 2005). The future of the indigenous people is more endangered by external culture, in the form of immigration and development, than from nature.

Thanks to Madhusree Mukerjee, independent scholar and activist, and Sita Venkateswar, Massey University, for reviewing this material.

Pankaj Sekhsaria

Pankaj Sekhsaria

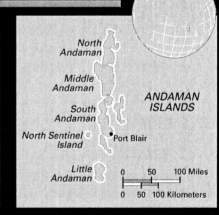

North Andaman
Middle Andaman
South Andaman
North Sentinel Island
ANDAMAN ISLANDS
Port Blair
Little Andaman

0   50   100 Miles
0   50   100 Kilometers

(LEFT) A Jarawa woman receives a handout from a passenger bus driver on the Andaman Trunk Road (ATR). Part of the ATR passes through the Jarawa reservation on South Andaman Island.

(CENTER) Government officials from Pt. Blair make periodic visits by boat to the Jarawa area to attempt to build Jarawa trust. This landmark incident, of getting some Jarawa to board a government boat, occurred in 1998. The Jarawa occupy land that is rich in resources such as ancient hardwood trees. Rumors are that the administration wants to remove the Jarawa from their territory and exploit it for logging, tourism, and other commercial interests.

MAP 2 Andaman Islands of India. The 576 islands are geologically part of Myanmar and Southeast Asia. The British Empire controlled them until India's independence in 1947.

Clearing: A section of the forest is cleared, partially or completely, by cutting down trees and brush and then setting the area on fire to burn off other growth. The fire creates a layer of ash that is rich fertilizer. The term *slash and burn cultivation* refers to this stage of clearing.

Planting: People use digging sticks to loosen the soil. They place seeds though the broadcasting method (scattering the seeds by hand) or place slips of plants by hand into the loose soil.

Weeding: Horticulture involves little weeding because the ash cover and shady growing conditions keep weed growth down.

Harvesting: This phase requires substantial labor to cut or dig crops and carry them to the residential area.

Fallowing: Depending on the soil and the crop grown, the land must be left unused for a specified number of years so that it regains its fertility.

FIGURE 3 Five Stages in Horticulture

source of moisture. Horticulture requires rotation of garden plots in order for them to regenerate. Thus, another term for horticulture is *shifting cultivation.* Average plot sizes are less than 1 acre, and 2.5 acres can support a family of five to eight members for a year. Yields can support semipermanent villages of 200 to 250 people. Overall population density per square mile is low because horticulture, like foraging, is an extensive strategy. Horticulture is more labor intensive than foraging because of the energy required for plot preparation and food processing. Anthropologists distinguish five phases in the horticultural cycle (see Figure 3).

Surpluses in food supply are possible in horticulture. These surpluses enable trade relationships and can lead to greater wealth for some people. Horticulture was the foundation for complex and rich civilizations, such as the Maya civilization of Mexico and Central America, which flourished between 200 and 900 CE.

DIVISION OF LABOR Gender and age are the key factors structuring the division of labor, with men's and women's work roles often being clearly differentiated. Typically, men clear the garden area while both men and women plant and tend the staple food crops. This pattern exists in Papua New Guinea, much of Southeast Asia, and parts of West and East Africa. Food processing involves women often working in small groups, whereas men more typically form small groups for hunting and fishing for supplementary food. Among many horticultural groups, women grow the staple food crops while men grow the "prestige foods" used in ritual feasts. In such contexts, men have higher public status than women.

Two unusual horticultural cases involve extremes in terms of gender roles and status. The first is the precontact Iroquois of central New York State (Brown 1975) (see Map 3). Iroquois women cultivated maize, the most important food crop, and they controlled its distribution. This control meant that they were able to decide whether the men would go to war, because a war effort depended on the supply of maize to support it. A contrasting example is that of the Yanomami of the Venezuelan Amazon (see Map 4) (Chagnon 1992). Yanomami men clear the fields and tend and harvest the crops. They also do much of the cooking for ritual feasts. Yanomami women, though, are not idle. They play an important role in

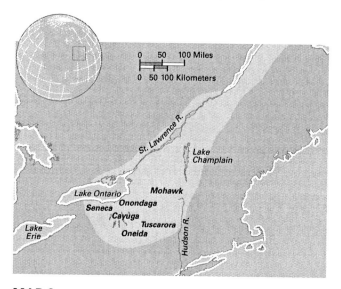

MAP 3 Precolonial Iroquois Region.
At the time of the arrival of the European colonialists, the six nations of the Iroquois extended over a wide area. The Mohawk stood guard over the eastern door of the confederacy's symbolic long house, and the Seneca guarded the western door. The six nations worked out a peace treaty among them and established a democracy. A great orator named Hiawatha promoted the plan throughout the tribes, and a Mohawk woman was the first to approve it.

This reconstruction of a pre-colonial Iroquois scene depicts longhouses in which many families lived and shows women in important productive roles.

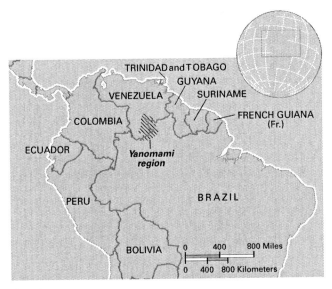

MAP 4 Yanomami Region in Brazil and Venezuela.
The Yanomami region is supposedly protected from outsiders. But miners, ranchers, loggers, and other commercial developers have encroached on the reserve, extracting natural resources and sexually exploiting women and children.

providing the staple food that comes from manioc, a starchy root crop that requires substantial processing work—it has to be soaked for a long time to remove toxins and then scraped into a mealy consistency. Among the Yanomami, however, men are the dominant decision makers and have more social power than Yanomami women do.

Although anthropologists cannot explain the origins of the different divisions of labor in horticulture, they do know that the differences are related to men's and women's status (Sanday 1973). Analysis of many horticultural societies shows that women's contribution to food production is a necessary but not sufficient basis for women's high status. In other words, if women do not contribute to producing food, their status will be low. If they do contribute, their status may, or may not, be high. The critical factor appears to be control over the distribution of what is produced, especially public distribution beyond the family. Slavery is a clear example of how a major role in production does not bring high status because slaves have no control over the product and its distribution.

Children do more productive work in horticultural societies than in any other mode of livelihood (Whiting and Whiting 1975). The *Six Cultures Study* is a research project that examined children's behavior in horticultural, farming, and industrial settings. Children among a horticultural group, the Gusii (goo-see-eye) of western Kenya, performed the most tasks at the youngest ages. Gusii boys and girls care for siblings, collect fuel, and carry water. Among the Gusii and in other

horticultural societies, children do so many tasks because adults, especially women, are busy working in the fields and markets. Children's work in the domestic domain fulfills what are adult roles in other economic systems.

PROPERTY RELATIONS Private property, as something that an individual can own and sell, is not characteristic of horticultural societies. Use rights are typically important, although they are more clearly defined and formalized than among foragers. By clearing and planting an area of land, a family puts a claim on it and its crops. The production of surplus goods allows the possibility of social inequality in access to goods and resources. Rules about sharing within the larger group decline in importance as some people gain higher status.

HORTICULTURE AS A SUSTAINABLE SYSTEM Fallowing is crucial in maintaining the viability of horticulture. Fallowing allows the plot to recover lost nutrients and improves soil quality by allowing the growth of weeds whose root systems keep the soil loose. The benefits of a well-managed system of shifting cultivation are clear, as are the two major constraints involved: the time required for fallowing and the need for access to large amounts of land so that some land is in use while other land is fallowed. Using a given plot for too many seasons or reducing fallowing time quickly results in depletion of soil nutrients, decreased crop production, and soil erosion.

PASTORALISM

Pastoralism is a mode of livelihood based on domesticated animal herds and the use of their products, such as meat and milk, for 50 percent or more of the diet. Pastoralism has long existed in the Middle East, Africa, Europe, and Central Asia, especially where rainfall is limited and unpredictable. In the Western Hemisphere, the only indigenous pastoralist system in existence before the arrival of the Spanish in the fifteenth century was in the Andean region of the New World; it was based on domesticated llamas (Barfield 2001). Sheep, goats, horses, and cattle became prominent after the Spanish conquest. Some Native American groups in the southwestern United States still rely on herding animals.

Worldwide, the six major species are sheep, goats, cattle, horses, donkeys, and camels. Three others have more restricted distribution: yaks at high altitudes in Asia, reindeer in northern sub-Arctic regions, and llamas in highland South America. Many pastoralists keep dogs for protection and for help with herding. Pastoralism can succeed in a variety of environments, depending on the animal involved. For example, reindeer herding is done in the circumpolar regions of Europe and Asia, and cattle and goat herding is common in India and Africa.

In terms of food, pastoralism provides primarily milk and milk products, with occasional slaughtering of animals for meat. Thus, pastoralists typically form trade links with

pastoralism a mode of livelihood based on keeping domesticated animals and using their products, such as meat and milk, for most of the diet.

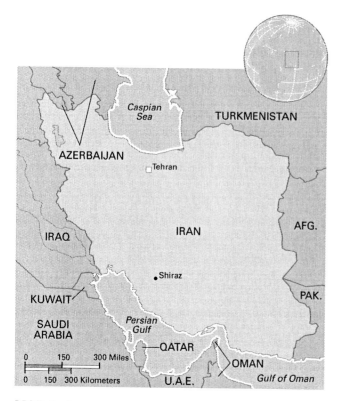

MAP 5 Iran.

The Islamic Republic of Iran is one of the world's most mountainous countries. Its economy is based on oil, family farming, and small-scale trading. Iran is OPEC's second-largest oil producer and has the second-largest natural gas reserves in the world after Russia. The population of Iran is over 68 million. The official language is Persian (Farsi) and Shi'a Islam is the official state religion.

foragers, horticulturalists, or farmers in order to obtain food and other goods that they cannot produce themselves. Prominent trade items are food grains and manufactured items, such as cooking pots, for which they offer milk, animals, hides, and other animal products.

Like foraging and horticulture, pastoralism is an extensive strategy. A common problem for all pastoralists is the continued need for fresh pasture and water for their animals. Herds must move or else the grazing area will become depleted. A distinction within the pastoralist category is based on whether the herds move over short or long distances (Fratkin, Galvin, and Roth 1994). The Qashqa'i of Iran are long-distance herders of sheep and camels (Beck 1986). Iran offers a varied and rich natural resource base that supports pastoralism, agriculture, and large urban centers, including the capital city of Shiraz (see Map 5). The pastoralism of the Qashqa'i involves seasonal migration to remote pastures separated by about 300 miles. The vast distances make the Qashqa'i vulnerable to raids and create the need for negotiation with village leaders along the route for permission to cross their land. To deal with this vulnerability, the Qashqa'i developed linkages across several tribes that can be mobilized, temporarily, to create a large political unit under one leader. The Qashqa'i are an example of a pastoralist system in which political organization is highly developed.

DIVISION OF LABOR Families and clusters of related families are the basic production unit. Gender and age are, again, key factors in the allocation of work. In many pastoralist cultures, gender roles are clearly divided. Men are in charge of herding—moving the animals from place to place. Women are responsible for processing the herd's products, especially the milk. A cultural emphasis on masculinity characterizes many herding populations. Reindeer herding among the Saami of Finland is closely connected to male identity to the extent that the definition of being a man is to be a reindeer herder. In contrast, women are the herders among the Navajo of the American Southwest. Navajo men's major work role is crafting silver jewelry.

The size of the animal involved is sometimes, but not always, related to the gender division of herding. Girls and women are often herders of smaller animals, perhaps because smaller animals need to graze less widely and can be kept penned near the house. Boys and men tend the animals that

(LEFT) Girls are in charge of herding water buffaloes to the Ganges River, at Varanasi, India, for watering. (RIGHT) Among the Ariaal, herders of northern Kenya, men are in charge of herding camels.

are pastured farther away. Children play important roles in tending herds. Among the cattle-herding groups of Eastern Africa, for example, parents want to have many children to help out with the herds.

PROPERTY RELATIONS The most important forms of property among pastoralists are, by far, animals, followed by housing (such as tents or yurts) and domestic goods (rugs and cooking ware). Depending on the group, ownership of animals is inherited through males, most commonly, or, less frequently, through females, as among the Navajo. A concept of private property exists for animals, which the family head may trade for other goods. A family's housing materials are also their own. Use rights, however, regulate pasture land and migratory routes, and these rights tend to be informally regulated through an oral tradition.

PASTORALISM AS A SUSTAINABLE SYSTEM Pastoralists have developed sustainable cultures in extremely varied environments, from the relative lushness of Iran to the more depleted situation of Mongolia. Pastoralism is a highly successful and sustainable economic system that functions in coexistence with other economic systems. As with foraging and horticulture, however, when outside forces squeeze the space available for migration, overexploitation of the environment soon results. A major external constraint on pastoralism is the goal of many governments to *sedentarize* (settle down) pastoralists. States do not like pastoralists to move across state lines, as they have done long before state boundaries were created. States want pastoralists to stay in one place so that they will be easier to keep track of, tax, and provide with services.

AGRICULTURE

Agriculture is a mode of livelihood that involves growing crops on permanent plots with the use of plowing, irrigation, and fertilizer; it is also called farming. In contrast to foraging, horticulture, and pastoralism, agriculture is an **intensive strategy**. Intensification involves the use of techniques that allow the same plot of land to be used repeatedly without losing its fertility. Crucial inputs include substantial amounts of labor for weeding, use of natural and chemical fertilizers, and control of water supply. The earliest agricultural systems are documented from the Neolithic period, beginning around 12,000 years ago in the Middle East.

---

agriculture   a mode of livelihood that involves growing crops with the use of plowing, irrigation, and fertilizer.

intensive strategy   a form of livelihood that involves continuous use of the same land and resources.

family farming (formerly termed peasant agriculture) a form of agriculture in which farmers produce mainly to support themselves and also produce goods for sale in the market system; formerly called *peasant farming*.

Agricultural systems now exist worldwide, on all continents except Antarctica.

Agriculture relies on the use of domesticated animals for plowing, transportation, and organic fertilizer either in the form of manure or composted materials. It is highly dependent on artificial water sources such as irrigation channels or terracing the land. Like the modes of livelihood already discussed, agriculture involves complex knowledge about the environment, plants, and animals, including soil types, precipitation patterns, plant varieties, and pest management. Long-standing agricultural traditions are now being increasingly displaced by methods introduced from the outside, and so the world's stock of indigenous knowledge about agriculture is declining rapidly. In many cases, it has become completely lost, along with the cultures and languages associated with it.

Occupational specialization increases in agricultural societies. Instead of people repairing their own tools and weapons, some people take on this work as a full-time job and no longer grow their own food, trading their skills for food with farmers. Other specializations that emerge as full-time occupations are political leaders, religious leaders or priests, healers, artisans, potters, musicians, and traders. Two types of agriculture are discussed next.

FAMILY FARMING **Family farming** (formerly termed peasant farming) is a form of agriculture in which production is geared to support the family and to produce goods for sale. Today, more than 1 billion people, or about one-sixth of the world's population, make their living from family farming. Found throughout the world, family farming is more common in countries such as Mexico, India, Poland, and Italy than in more industrialized countries. Family farmers exhibit much cross-cultural variety. They may be full-time or part-time farmers; they may be more or less closely linked to urban markets; and they may be poor and indebted or wealthy and powerful. Major activities in family farming include plowing, planting seeds and cuttings, weeding, caring for irrigation systems and terracing, harvesting crops, and processing and storing crops.

DIVISION OF LABOR   The family is the basic labor unit, and gender and age are important in organizing work. Most family farming societies have a marked gender-based division of labor. Cross-cultural analysis of gender roles in 46 cultures reveals that men perform most of the labor in over three-fourths of the societies (Michaelson and Goldschmidt 1971). Anthropologists have proposed various theories to explain why productive work on so many family farms is male dominated (see Figure 4). The remaining one-fourth of the sample includes cultures in which men's and women's roles are balanced and cultures in which women play the dominant role.

In farming systems where men play the major role in agriculture, women are likely to work in or near the home, processing food, maintaining the household, and caring for

Men and Plowing Hypothesis

This hypothesis is based on the importance of plowing fields in preparation for planting and on the fact that plowing is almost exclusively a male task (Goody 1976). Some anthropologists say that men plow because they are stronger than women and have the advantage of greater aerobic capacity. In southern India, for example, weather patterns require that plowing be accomplished in a very narrow time period (Maclachlan 1983). Assigning the task to the physically stronger gender ensures that the work is done more quickly and is thus an adaptive cultural strategy because it increases the chances for a good crop.

Women and Child Care Hypothesis

This hypothesis says that women are not involved in plowing and other agricultural field labor as much as men because such tasks are incompatible with child care (J. K. Brown 1970).

Women and Food Processing Hypothesis

This hypothesis notes that agriculture increases the demand for labor within and near the house (Ember 1983). Winnowing, husking, grinding, and cooking agricultural products are extremely labor-intensive processes. Linked to women's primary roles in child care and increased fertility in farm families, these labor demands restrict women to the household domain.

FIGURE 4   **Three Hypotheses to Explain Male Dominance in the Gender Division of Labor in Family Farming**

children (Ember 1983). This division of labor results in the *public/private dichotomy* in family farm societies, in which men are more involved with the outside, public world and women are more involved in the domestic domain. In this variety of family farming, men work more hours per week than in foraging, horticultural, and pastoralist systems. Women's work hours, in contrast, are as high as they are in horticultural and pastoralist systems.

In family farms in the United States and Canada, men typically have the main responsibility for daily farm operations; women's participation ranges from equal to minimal (Barlett 1989). Women do run farms in the United States and Canada, but generally only when they are divorced or widowed. Women are usually responsible for managing the domestic domain. On average, women's daily work hours are 25 percent more than those of men. A trend is for family farm women to take salaried jobs off the farm to help support the farm.

Balanced work roles between men and women in family farming frequently involve a pattern in which men do the agricultural work and women do marketing. This gender division of labor is common among highland indigenous groups of Central and South America. For example, among the Zapotec Indians of Mexico's southern state of Oaxaca (wuh-HAK-uh), men grow maize, the staple crop, and cash crops such as bananas, mangoes, coconuts, and sesame (Chiñas 1992). Women sell produce in the town markets, and they make tortillas, which they sell from their houses. The family thus derives its income from the labor of both men and women working interdependently. Male status and female status are quite equal in such contexts.

Female farming systems, in which women and girls play the major role in livelihood, are found mainly in southern India and Southeast Asia where wet rice agriculture is practiced. This is a highly labor-intensive way of growing rice that involves starting the seedlings in nurseries and transplanting them to flooded fields. Men are responsible for

plowing the fields using teams of water buffaloes. Women own land and make decisions about planting and harvesting. Women's labor is the backbone of this type of farming. Standing calf-deep in muddy water, they transplant rice seedlings, weed, and harvest the rice. Why women predominate in wet rice agriculture is an intriguing question but impossible to answer. Its consequences for women's status, however, are clear. In female farming systems, women have relatively high status. They own land, play a central role in household decision making, and have substantial personal autonomy (Stivens et al. 1994).

Children's roles in agricultural societies range from prominent to minor, depending on the context (Whiting and Whiting 1975). *The Six Cultures Study,* mentioned earlier, found low rates of child labor in agricultural villages in North India and Mexico compared to high rates among the horticultural Gusii in Kenya. In many agricultural contexts, however, children's labor participation is high. In villages in Java, Indonesia, and in Nepal, children spend more time caring for

Family farming in highland Ecuador. A man plows while women in the family follow, planting seed potatoes.

farm animals than adults do (Nag, White, and Peet 1978). Girls between 6 and 8 years old spend more time than adults in child care, and girls work more hours each day than boys. Children in the United States are not formally employed in farm work, but many family farms rely on children's contributions on weekends and during summer vacations. Amish farm families rely to a significant extent on contributions from all family members.

PROPERTY RELATIONS   Family farmers make substantial investments in land, such as clearing, terracing, and fencing, and these investments are linked to the development of firmly defined and protected property rights. Rights to land can be acquired and sold. Formalized, often written, guidelines exist about inheritance of land and transfer of rights to land through marriage. Social institutions such as law and police exist to protect private property rights.

In family farming systems where male labor and decision making predominate, women and girls are excluded from land rights. Conversely, in female farming systems, inheritance rules regulate the transmission of property rights more often through females.

INDUSTRIAL AGRICULTURE   **Industrial capital agriculture** produces crops through capital-intensive means, using machinery and inputs such as processed fertilizers instead of human and animal labor (Barlett 1989). It is commonly practiced in the United States, Canada, Germany, Russia, and Japan and is increasingly being adopted in developing countries such as India, Brazil, Mexico, and China.

Industrial agriculture has brought with it the *corporate farm,* a huge agricultural enterprise that produces goods solely for sale and are owned and operated by companies entirely reliant on hired labor. Industrial agriculture has major social effects (see Figure 5).

Much of the labor demand in industrial agriculture is seasonal, creating an ebb and flow of workers, depending on the task and time of year. Large ranches hire seasonal cowboys for roundups and fence mending. Crop harvesting is another high-demand point. Leo Chavez studied the lives of undocumented (illegal) migrant laborers from Central America who work in the huge tomato, strawberry, and avocado fields owned by corporate farms in southern California (1992). Many of the migrants are Maya people from Oaxaca, Mexico. They cross the border illegally in order to find work to support their families. In the San Diego area of southern California, they live temporarily in shantytowns, or camps. Here is what a men's camp is like on Sunday when they do not go to work in the fields:

> On Sundays, the campsites take on a community-like appearance. Men bathe, and wash their clothes, hanging them on trees and bushes, or on lines strung between the trees. Some men play soccer and basketball, using a hoop someone has rigged up. Others sit on old crates or tree-stumps as they relax, talk, and drink beer. Sometimes the men talk about fights from the night before. With little else to do, nowhere to go, and few outsiders to talk to, the men often drink beer to pass the time on Saturday nights and Sundays. Loneliness and boredom plague them during nonworking hours. (1992:65)

- Increased use of complex technology including machinery, chemicals, and genetic research on new plant and animal varieties.
  Social effects: This feature results in displacement of small landholders and field laborers. For example, replacing mules and horses with tractors for plowing in the U.S. South during the 1930s led to the eviction of small-scale share-croppers from the land because the landowners could cultivate larger units.

- Increased use of capital (wealth used in the production of more wealth) in the form of money or property.
  Social effects: The high ratio of capital to labor enables farmers to increase production but reduces flexibility. If a farmer invests in an expensive machine to harvest soybeans and then the price of soybeans drops, the farmer cannot simply switch from soybeans to a more profitable crop. Capitalization is most risky for smaller farms, which cannot absorb losses easily.

- Increased use of energy (primarily gasoline to run the machinery and nitrates for fertilizer) to grow crops. This input of energy often exceeds the calories of food energy yielded in the harvest. Calculations of how many calories of energy are used to produce a calorie of food in industrial agricultural systems reveal that some 2.5 calories of fossil fuel are invested to harvest 1 calorie of food—and more than 6 calories are invested when processing, packaging, and transport are taken into account.
  Social effects: This energy-heavy mode of production creates farmers' dependence on the global market of energy supplies.

Source: Adapted from "Industrial Agriculture" by Peggy F. Barlett in *Economic Anthropology,* ed. by Stuart Plattner. Copyright © 1989. Published by Stanford University Press.

FIGURE 5   **Three Features of Industrial Agriculture and Their Social Effects**

Migrant workers picking broccoli in Salinas, California.

© Morton Beebe/CORBIS

THE SUSTAINABILITY OF AGRICULTURE Agriculture requires more in the way of labor inputs, technology, and the use of nonrenewable natural resources than the economic systems discussed earlier. The ever-increasing spread of corporate agriculture worldwide is now displacing other long-standing practices and resulting in the destruction of important habitats and cultural heritage sites in its search for land, water, and energy sources. Intensive agriculture is not a sustainable system. Furthermore, it is undermining the sustainability of foraging, horticulture, and pastoralism. For many years, anthropologists have pointed to the high costs of agriculture to the environment and to humanity (see Critical Thinking).

INDUSTRIALISM AND THE INFORMATION AGE

Industrialism/informatics is the mode of livelihood in which goods and services are produced through mass employment in business and commercial operations and through the creation, manipulation, management, and transfer of information through electronic media. In industrial capitalism, the form of capitalism found in most industrialized nations, most goods are produced not to meet basic needs but to satisfy consumer demands for nonessential goods. Employment in agriculture decreases while jobs in manufacturing and the service sector increase. In some industrialized countries, the number of manufacturing jobs is declining, with more people being employed in service occupations and in the growing area of information processing such as computer programming, data processing, and communications.

An important distinction exists between the **formal sector**, which is salaried or wage-based work registered in official statistics, and the **informal sector**, which includes work that is outside the formal sector, not officially registered, and sometimes illegal. If you have done babysitting and were paid cash that was not formally recorded by your employer (for tax-deduction purposes) or by you (for income tax purposes), then you have participated in the informal sector. Informal sector activities that are illegal are referred to as being part of the underground economy, a huge and uncounted part of global and local economies worldwide.

THE FORMAL SECTOR: FACTORY STUDIES The formal sector includes a wide variety of occupations, ranging from stable and lucrative jobs to unstable or part-time and less lucrative jobs. Cultural anthropologists have done studies of small-scale workplaces, especially factories.

In one factory study, a team of cultural anthropologists and university graduate students studied the role of ethnicity in social relationships in a Miami clothing factory (Grenier et al. 1992). The clothing plant, a subsidiary of the largest U.S. clothing manufacturer, employs about 250 operators,

industrial capital agriculture   a form of agriculture that is capital-intensive, substituting machinery and purchased inputs for human and animal labor.

industrialism/informatics   a mode of livelihood in which goods are produced through mass employment in business and commercial operations and through the creation and movement of information through electronic media.

formal sector   salaried or wage-based work registered in official statistics.

informal sector   work that is not officially registered and sometimes illegal.

CRITICAL thinking

Was the Invention of Agriculture a Terrible Mistake?

Most Euro-Americans have a "progressivist" view that agriculture is a major advance in cultural evolution because it brought with it so many things that Westerners admire: cities, centers of learning and art, powerful state governments, and monumental architecture:

> Just count our advantages. We enjoy the most abundant and varied foods, the best tools, and material goods, some of the longest and healthiest lives, in history. . . . From the progressivist perspective on which I was brought up, to ask "Why did almost all our hunter–gatherer ancestors adopt agriculture?" is silly. Of course they adopted it because agriculture is an efficient way to get more food for less work. (Diamond 1994 [1987]:106)

Another claim about the advantage of agriculture is that it allows more leisure time, so art could flourish.

On the other hand, many scholars raise serious questions about the advantages of agriculture. These "revisionists" argue that agriculture may be "the worst mistake in the history of the human race," "a catastrophe from which we have never recovered" (Diamond 1994 [1987]: 105–106). Some of the "costs" of agriculture include social inequality; disease; despotism; and destruction of the environment from soil exhaustion and chemical poisoning, water pollution, dams and river diversions, and air pollution from tractors, transportation, and processing plants.

With agriculture, life did improve for many people, but not for all. Elites emerged with distinct advantages, but the gap between the haves and the have-nots increased. Health improved for the elites, but not for the landless poor and laboring classes. With the vast surpluses of food created by agricultural production, elaborate state systems developed with new forms of power exercised over the common people.

◆ **CRITICAL THINKING QUESTIONS**

* What is your definition of "the good life"?
* What are the benefits and costs of achieving the good life among, say, the Ju/'hoansi compared to your vision of the good life in your microculture?
* Who gets to live the good life in each type of economy?

---

mainly women. The majority of employees are Cuban women who, fleeing from the Castro regime, immigrated to Miami many years ago. As these employees have begun to retire, they are being replaced by new immigrants from Central America as well as Haitians and African Americans.

The workers are organized into a union, but members of the different ethnic groups have more solidarity with each other than with people in the union. Interethnic rivalry exists around the issue of management's treatment of members of different groups. Many non-Cuban workers claim that management favors Cuban employees. Some supervisors and managers expressed ethnic stereotypes, but not always consistent ones: "Depending on whom one listens to, Haitians are either too slow or too fast; Cubans may talk too much or be extraordinarily dedicated workers" (Grenier 1992:75). Managers see ethnic-based competition and lack of cooperation as a key problem that they attempt to deal with in various ways. For example, management banned workers from playing personal radios and installed a system of piped-in music by a radio station that supposedly alternates between "American" and "Latino" songs.

THE INFORMAL SECTOR: STREET VENDORS, DRUGS, AND SEX WORK Uncounted millions of people work in the informal sector. Many are involved in small-scale vending on the street, selling fruits and vegetables, beverages, cigarettes, snacks, books and magazines, ice cream, and souvenirs. Depending on the context, they may or may not have to pay for the location of their stand. Their rights to sell from a particular location are less secure than for someone who owns a shop. Some countries are seeking to remove street vendors in order to create a more modern city look.

Barbara Miller

A street vendor in Kingston, Jamaica. In many modernizing countries, city planners are taking steps to make street vending illegal on the grounds that such informal stands are unsightly.

▶ *If you were the mayor of Kingston, what position would you take on the street vending issue?*

Informal economies also operate at the global level, including the illegal trafficking of people and goods. The illegal drug industry links informal economies at the global level to the local level. Neither international drug dealers nor street sellers pay income tax on their profits, and their earnings are not part of the official gross national product (GNP) of any country. Currently, the drug traffic from Central and South America into North America is a multibillion-dollar business. Most of the supply moves through Mexico. Fieldwork in a small, rural town in Mexico's central highlands shows how the legal and illegal economies related to drug trafficking are intertwined (McDonald 2005). This ethnography of the local *narcoeconomy*, or an economy based on the production and sale of addictive drugs, reports, "None of this could happen without deep interconnections between drug traffickers, and networks of well-placed politicians, civil servants, and security forces of various kinds" (McDonald 2005:115).

How does the narcoeconomy affect local life in central Mexico? This ordinary town became a site of extraordinary inequalities: new, opulent houses for some, high-end clothing stores, a cybercafé, and a day spa. New farmers, willing to participate in the narcoeconomy, are moving in and gaining legitimacy in the community. These farmers are typically young men who come from local farm families and have worked in U.S. drug trafficking networks. They are hard working and interested in promoting local economic development. Through their experiences in the United States, they gained business skills and they understand the importance of networking. The positive features of this situation, however, are part of an economic system that is illegal.

In many parts of the world, sex work is illegal. In the United States, it is legal only in the state of Nevada, where income from sex work is taxable. In neighboring Mexico, options for legalized, state-controlled female sex work exist (Kelly 2008). Patty Kelly did fieldwork in a legal brothel in Chiapas, Mexico called the Zona Galactica. She uses the term *prostitution* as the exchange of sex for money, and it is therefore one form of *sex work*, which is a broader category that includes services such as erotic dancing, phone sex, and participation in erotic films and other media formats (2008:26). Although the women prostitutes' situation in the legal brothel in Chiapas is not ideal by any means, it has advantages compared to contexts in which prostitution is illegal and prostitutes have absolutely no security or protection.

In Thailand, laws about sex work are complicated (Jeffrey 2002). It is illegal to sell sex, but not to buy it. Recent legal reforms, however, pertain to the age of the sex seller and involve a prison sentence for anyone having sex with someone 15 years of age or younger. Nevertheless, child sex work in Thailand is an increasingly important part of the economy. The increased fear of HIV/AIDS among men who seek commercial sex leads to the demand for ever-younger sex workers, who are assumed to be less likely to be

Young sex workers in Thailand. With the advent of HIV/AIDS, men seeking sexual services increasingly want young sex workers, including children, because they are less likely to be contaminated with the disease. International human rights organizations consider sexual transactions with minors to constitute child abuse, and they seek to prevent sex work by minors.

▶ *What is the international definition of a "minor"? Is it universally applicable? If yes, why? If not, why not? Be prepared to support your view.*

carriers of the virus. Recruitment of children as young as 6 years old began in the 1990s.

How do children become involved in commercial sex work? Family poverty is a major part of the answer in Thailand. Low and declining incomes in rural northern Thailand continue to prompt parents to send children into sex work. Within the context of severe and increasing poverty in northern Thailand, however, a village-based study provides further details about how culture shapes family decisions about sending daughters into sex work (Rende Taylor 2005). In northern Thailand generally, and in the study village, daughters are valued members of the family. Along with their value come obligations to the family. From an early age, the eldest daughter is expected to assume major household responsibilities, including care of her younger siblings. The youngest daughter will inherit the house and, with it, the obligation to care for her aging parents. Middle daughters are the ones most likely to be sent outside to earn an income, often in commercial sex work. Parents are more concerned about the welfare of the family than about a daughter's involvement in commercial sex work. They

THINKING OUTSIDE THE BOX

Some people think that in order to protect child sex workers, they should be unionized. Others argue that unionization conveys a message of acceptance of this role for children. Where do you stand on this issue and why?

say, "The problem here isn't that our daughter sells her body . . . it's that we have no food to eat" (Rende Taylor 2005:416).

Research in a small slum community on the edge of a tourist town, frequented mainly by Europeans, reveals that the children reject the view of child prostitutes as mere victims (Montgomery 2001). They believe the work they do is moral because it is done in support of their family. The child sex workers and their pimps, also children, exercise some choice in deciding which clients to accept and which to reject. These insights do not deny the fact that the child sex workers are exploited and sometimes seriously harmed. They do, however, provide a fuller picture by showing how the children define their work as related to family obligations and how they seek to protect themselves within a context of limited options.

Certainly, the voices of the children should be heard. But scholars and activists must look beyond the children's emic worlds to the global, macroeconomic structures that generate and support the people who pay for sex with children and the poverty in the communities that send children into sex work. So far, the author of this textbook has not seen a study of the people who seek commercial sex.

◆◆◆
Changing Livelihoods

This section looks at recent changes in the five modes of livelihood. Contemporary economic globalization is the latest of many outside forces exerted on local economies. Most notably, European colonialism, starting in the fifteenth century, had dramatic effects on indigenous people's livelihood, mainly through the introduction of cash crops such as tea, coffee, and cotton; co-optation and control of local labor through slavery, indentureship, and hire; and taking over land for colonial plantations and other enterprises.

As noted at the beginning of this chapter, the spread of Western capitalism continues to have far-reaching effects on the local economies with which it comes in contact. In the later part of the twentieth century, surging economic growth in Asia, the demise of socialism in the former Soviet Union, and the increasing economic power of the United States throughout the world combined to spur the growth of a global economy. Social scientists vigorously debate the effects of economic globalization on poverty and inequality. Economists, relying on country-level figures about changing income levels and distribution, often take the view that economic globalization is beneficial, overall, because it increases economic growth. Cultural anthropologists, who work with local-level data and a more "on the ground" view tend to emphasize the negative effects of capitalist expansion into noncapitalist settings (Blim 2000). They point to three major transformations:

- Dispossession of local people of their land and other resource bases and substantial growth in the numbers of unemployed, displaced people. Global capitalism has displaced millions of people from their land and contributed to the growth of the unemployed urban poor.

- Recruitment of former foragers, horticulturalists, pastoralists, and family farmers to work in low levels of the industrialism/informatics sector and their exploitation in that setting. Such people become dependent wage workers as opposed to independent providers.

- Increases in export commodity production in periphery regions in response to the demands of a global market and decreases in food production for family use. This trend may provide higher incomes for people but it also reduces their independent ability to feed themselves. It also contributes to mono-cropping and the decline of biodiversity in food crops.

Examples exist of some foraging-horticultural groups choosing to become involved in the global economy on their own terms (Godoy et al. 2005). Far more often, however, these cultures have been destroyed by the intrusion of Western economic interests, their local knowledge has been lost, and the people have become demoralized, distressed, ill, and suicidal. The following cases illustrate how small-scale cultures react to and deal with Western capitalism and globalization.

FORAGERS: THE TIWI OF NORTHERN AUSTRALIA

The Tiwi (tee-wee) live on two islands off the north coast of Australia (see Map 6) (Hart, Pilling, and Goodale 1988). As foragers, the Tiwi gathered food, especially vegetables (such as yams), nuts, grubs, small lizards, and fish. Women provided the bulk of the daily diet with their gathered vegetables and nuts that they ground and cooked into porridge. Men sometimes hunted kangaroos, wild fowl, and other game such as goanna (large lizards). Vegetables, nuts, and fish were abundant year round. The Tiwi lived a more comfortable life than Aboriginal groups of the mainland, where the environment was less hospitable.

The Tiwi have long been in contact with foreign influences, beginning in the 1600s with the arrival of the Portuguese, who were attracted to the islands as a source of iron. Later, in 1897, an Australian buffalo hunter named Joe Cooper came to the islands and kidnapped two native women to train as mainland guides. Cooper and his group greatly changed the Tiwi by introducing a desire for Western goods, especially tobacco. Later, Japanese traders arrived and offered Tiwi men manufactured goods in return for Tiwi women. In the early 1900s, the French established a Catholic mission on one island. The missionaries promoted reading of the Bible and criticized local marriage customs, which allowed a man to have multiple wives. The year 1942 brought World War II to the Tiwi as the Japanese bombed and strafed a U.S. airstrip. Military bases were prominent on the islands, and Tiwi

Aboriginal artist Eymard Tungatalum retouches a traditional Tiwi carving in an art gallery in Australia's Northern Territory. Tungatalum's carvings, along with songs and poems, are an important part of the Aboriginal people's efforts to revive their culture.

dependency on Western manufactured goods increased. In just a few decades, the Tiwi had experienced major culture shocks from contact with outsiders.

In the second half of the twentieth century, Tiwi lifestyle changed substantially. Instead of being regularly on the move in the bush, the Tiwi became settled villagers living in houses built of corrugated iron sheets. Tiwi men now play football (soccer) and water polo and engage in competitive javelin throwing. Tiwi produce art, especially carving and painting, for sale in Australia and internationally. Tiwi are active in public affairs and politics, including the aboriginal rights movement.

Another major factor of change is international tourism, a force that the Tiwi are managing with dignity and awareness. One Tiwi commented that tourism may mean that "white people too will learn to live with and survive in the country" (Hart, Pilling, and Goodale 1988:144–145).

HORTICULTURALISTS: THE MUNDURUCU OF THE BRAZILIAN AMAZON

Outside economic and political factors have had major effects on horticultural societies throughout the world. In the Amazon, one force of change is the rubber industry. Its impact on indigenous peoples ranges from their being able to maintain many aspects of traditional life, to the complete loss of traditional lifeways. Like the Tiwi, the Mundurucu have experienced neither cultural preservation nor complete loss (Murphy and Murphy 1985).

After the arrival of Brazilians who were commercial rubber producers in the Amazon in the late nineteenth century, many Indians began to work for the Brazilians as latex tappers. For over a century, Mundurucu men combined their horticultural tasks with seasonal work collecting latex in the rubber area. Marked cultural change occurred when many Mundurucu people opted to leave their traditional villages, migrating to live in the rubber area year-round.

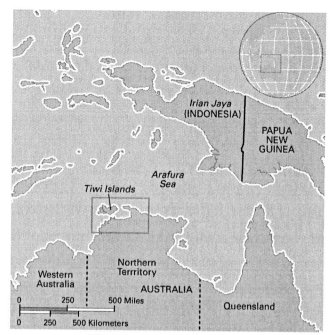

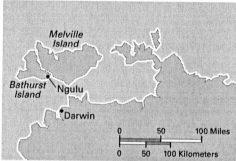

MAP 6 **Tiwi Region in Northern Australia.**
The Tiwi Islands consist of Bathurst and Melville Islands. The total number of Tiwi is about 2500 people. Most Tiwi live on Bathurst Island. In 2001, the Tiwi Islands Local Government Area was established, launching a new era of local government with statutory authority.

In the traditional villages, men live in a separate structure at one side of the village. Husbands visit wives and children in their houses. In the rubber settlement, husbands and wives live together in their own houses, and there is no separate men's house. In the traditional villages, women's communal work groups share water-carrying tasks. Such groups do not exist in the rubber settlement villages. Husbands in the new villages have taken on the task of carrying the water, so men work harder than they did in the traditional village. Although women in the settlement area work more hours per day than men, they believe that life is better because they like living in the same house with their husbands.

PASTORALISTS: THE HERDERS OF MONGOLIA

In the early 1990s, cultural anthropologist Melvyn Goldstein and biological anthropologist Cynthia Beall (1994) gained permission to do fieldwork among herders in Mongolia, a landlocked and mountainous country located between Russia and China (see Map 7). The Mongolian rural economy has long been, and still is, heavily dependent on animal herds. The "big five" animals are sheep, goats, yaks, horses, and camels. Sheep and goats provide meat and clothing and some milk; yaks are most important for dairy products because they give milk all year; and horses and camels provide transportation.

Goldstein and Beall wanted to study the effects of the transformation from a socialist, collectivized economy to a capitalist, market system. Starting in the 1950s, the (then) USSR ruled Mongolia and sought to transform it into an agricultural and industrial state. The government established urban centers, and the urban population began to grow while the rural population declined. The state provided all social services such as health and education. There was no homelessness or unemployment.

Official policy regarding pastoralism banned private ownership and collectivized all herds. The transition was difficult. Collectivization resulted in a 30 percent reduction of livestock, as owners chose to slaughter animals rather than collectivize them (Barfield 1993). Subsequently, state policy was altered to allow herders to control some animals as their own. By the early 1990s, the government's main policy was privatization, a process of transferring collective ownership and provision of goods and services to a system of private ownership. Collective ownership of herds was abandoned, and family-organized livelihood was reinstated.

Goldstein and Beall selected a remote region for their research: the Moost district in the Altai Mountain area in the southeastern part of the country, which is 99.9 percent pasture. At the time, the area contained about 4000 people and 115,000 head of livestock. Goldstein and Beall set up their tent and were immediately welcomed by an invitation to have milk-tea, a hot drink made of tea, water, milk, butter, and salt. During their stay, they spoke with many of the herders, participated in their festivals, and learned about people's

perceptions of economic change. First, the people had to adjust to the dramatic restructuring of their economy from private family herding to collectivized herding. Then, in just a few decades, they had to adjust back to private herding.

The transition to privatization created serious problems for the herders. Their standard of living declined markedly in the 1990s. Goods such as flour, sugar, candy, and cooking oil were no longer available. Prices for meat fluctuated widely, making it difficult for them to know how to manage their herd size efficiently. Social services such as health care and schools were less available and of lower quality.

FAMILY FARMERS: THE MAYA OF CHIAPAS, MEXICO

Frank Cancian, in 1960, did fieldwork among the Maya of Zinacantán, located in the Chiapas region of Mexico. He returned in 1983 to conduct a restudy and thus learned of changes that had taken place in the intervening twenty years (1989). At the time of his first research, most Zinacantecos were family farmers, making a living by growing corn and selling some of their crops in a nearby city. They were largely independent of outside forces in terms of their own food supply. The community was closely knit, its social boundaries defined by people's commitment to community roles and ceremonies. Twenty years later, both the local economy and the social system had changed dramatically.

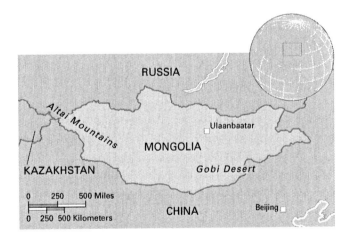

MAP 7 Mongolia.
Mongolia, with its population of 2.9 million and its vast territory, is the most sparsely populated country of the world. After Kazakhstan, it is the world's second largest landlocked country. Mountains lie to the north and west and the vast Gobi Desert to the south. The environment is well suited to pastoralism but not to farming. One-third of the population makes a living primarily from pastoralism. Ulan Bator is the capital and largest city, with nearly 40 percent of the population living in and around the city. Many residents are squatters who have migrated to the city in hope of employment and live in a circle of encampments surrounding the capital. Tibetan Buddhism is Mongolia's primary religion.

Even the most remote areas of Mongolia are now connected to the wider world through satellite dishes.

The main cause of change was a large increase in public spending by the government in the 1970s. This spending supported the construction of roads, dams, schools, and housing throughout the Chiapas region. The government also sponsored outreach programs to promote agricultural change, mainly crop diversification and ways to increase production. Another important factor was the oil boom in northern Chiapas and Tabasco province, which brought unprecedented amounts of cash into the local economy.

By the early 1980s, 40 percent of the households had no land at all and planted no corn. Most people had become involved in wage work, and unemployment, rather than a bad farming season, was the major threat to food security. Wage work included the new opportunities in road construction, government jobs, transportation (of people, food goods, and flowers), and full-time trading in urban markets reachable by the new roads.

This story, in its general outlines, is similar to that of many family farmers throughout the world, especially in developing countries. It involves transformation from production mainly for own use to production mainly for sale within a cash economy geared toward making a profit. Overall, the area became more prosperous, more monetized, and more dependent on the outside economy. A second characteristic is the dislocation of farm owners from their land and their recruitment in the wage labor force. Many self-employed farmers sold their land and entered the wage economy. A third trend is increasing social inequality. Although many Zinacantecos raised their incomes substantially during this period, many others did not. Those who had the ability to buy a truck and take advantage of the new opportunities for urban trade created by the roads were the ones who became rich. Households with the least access to cash were left behind, and these households were characteristically headed by single women.

INDUSTRIALISTS: FACTORY WORKERS IN OHIO

Increased mechanization is a major aspect of change in industry worldwide, and it has marked effects on labor demand and household income of workers. Unemployment and manufacturing declines in America's Rust Belt are well-known trends in industrial lifeways. Gregory Pappas studied unemployment in Barberton, a working-class Ohio town (1989). A tire company that had been the town's major employer closed in 1980, eliminating 1200 jobs. Pappas lived in Barberton for a year, interviewing many people. He also sent a questionnaire to over 600 displaced workers for further information. Pappas learned how unemployed workers cope either by migrating or by finding new ways to spend their time in Barberton. The unemployed factory workers of Barberton are faced with having to construct a new identity for themselves: "For factory workers the place of employment is crucial; their identities are bound up in a particular place, and plant shutdowns compromise their ability to understand themselves" (Pappas 1989:83). As one unemployed man commented, "I don't know who I am anymore." In this context of decline, levels of stress and mental disorder have increased for many people.

GLOBAL CAPITALISM: TAIWANESE INDUSTRIALISTS IN SOUTH AFRICA

In South Africa during the 1990s, after the dismantling of apartheid, political leaders adopted a Western-style, capitalist economic policy (Hart 2002). One step toward expanding production and trade was to forge links with Taiwanese businesses in hopes of transferring to South Africa the Asian economic "miracle." Several Taiwanese industries were established outside major urban areas. Although there is no simple explanation for the so-called Asian economic miracle, one component was family-based production in which power hierarchies based on age and gender ensure compliance among workers.

Taiwanese managers tried to use such a hierarchical family system in South Africa in order to ensure a smoothly functioning labor force. Research in Taiwanese knitwear factories in KwaZulu-Natal province, western South Africa, reveals substantial worker resentment against the Taiwanese managers. Women workers were especially vocal. Taiwanese patterns of communicating with women workers by using an idiom of family did not work with the South Africans. The women said they felt as though they were being treated like animals. The Taiwanese industrialists were separated from the workers by a wide racial, economic, and social divide. Imposing hierarchical family metaphors failed to create a cooperative workforce in South Africa. Many of the Taiwanese industrialists found themselves a focal point of local political conflict. In one town, a Chinese welcome monument was removed.

Karl Marx predicted that capitalism would wither away, but it has not yet done so. Through contemporary globalization, its effects are ever more powerfully felt in localities worldwide. Marx would be interested to observe how the Tiwi are developing international tourism, how the Maya people in Chiapas took up road construction for cash, and how Taiwanese knitwear manufacturers in KwaZulu-Natal encounter problems in cross-cultural labor management. He would perhaps also be amused to see how, at the same time, cultural anthropologists are trying to document and understand these changes.

the BIG questions REVISITED

◆ How do cultural anthropologists study economic systems?

Cultural anthropologists define economic systems as including three interrelated processes: production (making a living), consumption, and exchange. They study economic systems cross-culturally including systems other than modern capitalism. They divide cross-cultural patterns of making a living into five modes: foraging, horticulture, pastoralism, agriculture, and industrialism/informatics.

The current world system economy is increasingly competitive and unequal, placing some countries in the core, where their strong governments protect and expand their economic interests. Some countries are in the semiperiphery, and many are in the periphery. Anthropologists study local economic systems as well as regional and global economic factors that affect local economies.

◆ What are the five modes of livelihood?

Foraging relies on collecting food that is available in nature. In foraging societies, the division of labor is based on gender and age, with temperate foragers having more gender overlap in tasks than circumpolar foragers. All group members have equal rights to resources. Foraging has long-term sustainability when not affected by outside pressure.

Horticulture and pastoralism are extensive strategies that depend on domesticated plants (horticulture) and animals (pastoralism). Horticulture requires fallowing, and pastoralism requires the constant movement of animals to fresh pastures. The division of labor varies, including situations in which men do more productive work, those where women do more work, and those in which workloads are shared between men and women. Use rights are the prominent form of property relations. Both have long-term sustainability when not affected by encroachments.

Family farming systems produce crops for their own use and for sale in the market. Most family farming systems involve more male labor in the fields and more female labor in the domestic domain. Agriculture's sustainability is limited by the need to replenish the land.

In industrialism/informatics, the division of labor is highly differentiated by class, gender, and age. Widespread unemployment is found in many industrial economies. In capitalist societies, private property is the dominant pattern. Industrialism/informatics lacks sustainability, given its high demand for non-renewable energy.

◆ How are the five modes of livelihood changing?

Foragers are being incorporated into settled economies as their access to land is constricted by outside forces and as governments force them to sedentarize. Many former foraging people now work as farm laborers and in other jobs of low status in the mainstream cash economy. Others are advocating for the revitalization of their culture in the new global economy, producing art for sale on the world market, developing cultural tourism opportunities for outsiders, or gaining a share in profits related to commercialization of their indigenous knowledge.

Horticulture and pastoralism are under great pressure from the competing economic forms of agriculture and industrialism. Many former horticulturalists have migrated to plantations or urban areas and become part of the cash economy. States have pressured pastoralists to settle down. Family farms are declining worldwide in number as corporate farms increase. The labor supply has changed from being family based to including a high proportion of migrant laborers. The Information Age has only recently emerged, with its emphasis on economic processes that involve virtual workplaces and the movement of information, creating the new, combined mode of livelihood called industrialism/informatics.

Capitalism increasingly involves international investments and location of production sites in countries where wages are low. Such situations implicate culture in complex ways, including managerial issues and cross-cultural communication.

KEY CONCEPTS

agriculture	horticulture	intensive strategy
economic system	industrial capital agriculture	mode of livelihood
extensive strategy	industrialism/informatics	pastoralism
family farming	informal sector	use rights
formal sector		

SUGGESTED READINGS

Anne Allison. *Nightwork: Sexuality, Pleasure and Corporate Masculinity in a Tokyo Hostess Club.* Chicago: University of Chicago Press, 1994. Based on the author's participant observation, this book explores what it is like to work as a hostess in a club that caters to corporate male employees and discusses men's corporate work culture.

Mary K. Anglin. *Women, Power and Dissent in the Hills of Carolina.* Urbana: University of Illinois Press, 2002. This book addresses class, gender, and race issues in a mica processing factory in the Blue Ridge Mountains of North Carolina.

Michael Blim. *Equality and Economy: The Global Challenge.* New York: AltaMira Press, 2005. The author examines the relationships between global capitalism and social inequality at three levels: households, states, and international.

Jans Dahl Saqqaq: *An Inuit Hunting Community in the Modern World.* Toronto: University of Toronto Press, 2000. This ethnography of the Saqqaq, people of eastern Greenland, is based on fieldwork carried out at several times since 1980 in order to provide a diachronic perspective.

Daniel Dohan. *The Price of Poverty: Money, Work, and Culture in the Mexican American Barrio.* Berkeley: University of California Press, 2003. This ethnography explores poverty among Mexican Americans in two neighborhoods in California: undocumented immigrants in San Jose who work mainly in the Silicon Valley and urban Chicanos of Los Angeles.

Hallie Eakin. *Weathering Risk in Rural Mexico: Climatic, Institutional, and Economic Change.* Tucson: University of Arizona Press. 2007. Eakin documents the local effects of globalization and climate change through ethnographic studies of three agricultural communities in central Mexico.

J. A. English-Lueck. *Cultures@SiliconValley.* Stanford: Stanford University Press, 2002. A team of professors and anthropology students at San Jose State University conducted research for over a decade in Silicon Valley, and this book is the result of that work. The book describes what life is like for people in a "technology-saturated" environment, from working to shopping to family life.

Nandini Gunewardena and Ann Kingsolver, eds. *The Gender of Globalization: Women Navigating Culture and Economic Marginalization.* Albuquerque, NM: School of American Research Press, 2007. Contributing authors use feminist ethnographic methods to examine how neoliberal capitalist policies affect women in Argentina, Sri Lanka, Mexico, Ghana, the United States, India, Jamaica, and elsewhere.

Patty Kelly. *Lydia's Open Door: Inside Mexico's Most Modern Brothel.* Berkeley: University of California Press, 2008. This ethnography focuses on the personal histories and experiences of the women who work in a state-run brothel in the capital city of Chiapas, Mexico. Kelly shows how the brothel is a social experiment by the state to bring modernity to its poorest region through the business of sex.

Stephen A. Marglin. *The Dismal Science: How Thinking Like an Economist Undermines Community.* Cambridge, MA: Harvard University Press, 2008. Marglin provides an anthropological critique of economics, with attention to how economists' views of autonomous, self-interested individuals and market relationships erode a sense of community.

Heather Montgomery. *Modern Babylon? Prostituting Children in Thailand.* New York: Bergahn Books, 2001. The author conducted fieldwork in a tourist community in Thailand where many parents commit their children to prostitution. She gained a view of this system from the perspective of the children and the parents.

Katherine S. Newman. *Falling from Grace: The Experience of Downward Mobility in the American Middle Class.* New York: The Free Press, 1988. This book provides ethnographic research on downwardly mobile people of New Jersey as a "special tribe," with attention to loss of employment by corporate managers and blue-collar workers and the effects of downward mobility on middle-class family life.

Deborah Sick. *Farmers of the Golden Bean: Costa Rican Households and the Global Coffee Economy.* Dekalb, IL: Northern Illinois University Press, 1999. This book is about coffee-producing households in Costa Rica and the difficulties that coffee farmers face as a consequence of unpredictable global forces.

Michael K. Steinberg, Joseph J. Hobbs, and Kent Mathewson, eds. *Dangerous Harvest: Drug Plants and the Transformation of Indigenous Landscapes.* New York: Oxford University Press, 2004. The chapters in this book address opium and the people of Laos, opium production in Afghanistan and Pakistan, struggles over coca in Bolivia, marijuana growing by the Maya, use of kava in the Pacific, and policy questions.

CHAPTER 5

CONSUMPTION AND EXCHANGE

Nanjing Road in Shanghai, China. Nanjing Road is the main shopping street in Shanghai and the world's longest shopping street. Attracting over one million visitors a day, it is also one of the world's busiest shopping streets. In terms of status, it ranks with Fifth Avenue in New York City, Oxford Street in London, and the Champs-Elysées in Paris.

CONSUMPTION AND EXCHANGE

the BIG questions

◆ What is consumption in cross-cultural perspective?

◆ What is exchange in cross-cultural perspective?

◆ How are consumption and exchange changing?

115

Imagine that it is the late eighteenth century and you are a member of the Kwakwaka'wakw (KWA-kwuh-kayuh-wah-kwah) of British Columbia in Canada's Pacific Northwest region (see Culturama at the end of this chapter). You and your tribal group are invited to a **potlatch**, a feast in which the host lavishes the guests with abundant quantities of the best food and many gifts (Suttles 1991). The most honorable foods are fish oil, high-bush cranberries, and seal meat, and they will be served in ceremonial wooden bowls. Gifts include embroidered blankets, household articles such as carved wooden boxes and woven mats, canoes, and items of food. The more the chief gives, the higher his status rises and the more his guests are indebted to him. Later, when it is the guests' turn to hold a potlatch, they will give away as much as, or more than, their host did.

The Pacific Northwest region is rich in fish, game, berries, and nuts, among other foods. Nonetheless, given regional climatic variation, food supplies were often uneven, with some groups each year having surpluses while others faced scarcity. The potlatch system helped to smooth out these variations: Groups with a surplus would sponsor a potlatch and those experiencing a leaner year were guests. In this way, potlatching established a social safety net across a wide area of the Northwest. This brief sketch of potlatching shows the linkages among the three economic processes of making a livelihood, consumption, and exchange. Potlatches are related to food supply, they are opportunities for consumption, and they involve exchange.

This chapter provides cross-cultural examples of the modes of the other two components of economic systems:

---

potlatch   a grand feast in which guests are invited to eat and to receive gifts from the hosts.

mode of consumption   the dominant pattern, in a culture, of using things up or spending resources in order to satisfy demands.

mode of exchange   the dominant pattern, in a culture, of transferring goods, services, and other items between and among people and groups.

minimalism   a mode of consumption that emphasizes simplicity, is characterized by few and finite consumer demands, and involves an adequate and sustainable means to achieve them.

consumerism   a mode of consumption in which people's demands are many and infinite and the means of satisfying them are insufficient and become depleted in the effort to satisfy these demands.

leveling mechanism   an unwritten, culturally embedded rule that prevents an individual from becoming wealthier or more powerful than anyone else.

- **Mode of consumption**: the dominant way, in a culture, of using up goods and services.
- **Mode of exchange**: the dominant way, in a culture, of transferring goods, services, and other items between and among people and groups.

The chapter's last section provides examples of contemporary change in consumption and exchange.

◆◆◆
Culture and Consumption

This section examines the concept of consumption, cross-cultural patterns of consumption budgets, and consumption inequalities. It also presents two theoretical positions on food *taboos*, or rules about forbidden food.

WHAT IS CONSUMPTION?

Consumption has two meanings: First, it is a person's "intake" in terms of eating or other ways of using things; second, it is "output" in terms of spending or using resources to obtain those things. Thus, for example, "intake" is eating a sandwich; "output" is spending money at the store to buy a sandwich. Both activities fit within the term "consumption."

People consume many things. Food, beverages, clothing, and shelter are the most basic consumption needs in most cultures. People also may acquire tools, weapons, means of transportation, computers, books and other items of communication, art and other luxury goods, and energy for heating and cooling their residence. In noncash economies, such as that of foragers, people "spend" time or labor in order to provide for their needs. In money-based economies, such as industrialized contexts today, most consumption depends on having cash or some virtual form of money.

MODES OF CONSUMPTION

In categorizing varieties of consumption, it makes sense to consider two contrasting modes, with mixed modes in the middle (see Figure 1). They are based on the relationship between demand (what people want) and supply (the resources available to satisfy demand):

- **Minimalism**: a mode of consumption characterized by few and finite consumer demands and an adequate and sustainable means to achieve them. It is most characteristic of free-ranging foragers but is also found to some degree among horticulturalists and pastoralists.
- **Consumerism**: a mode of consumption in which people's demands are many and infinite, and the means of satisfying them are never sufficient, thus driving

Foraging	Horticulture	Pastoralism	Agriculture	Industrialism/Informatics
Mode of Consumption Minimalism Finite needs				**Mode of Consumption** Consumerism Infinite needs
Social Organization of Consumption Equality/sharing Personalized products are consumed				**Social Organization of Consumption** Class-based inequality Depersonalized products are consumed
Primary Budgetary Fund Basic needs				**Primary Budgetary Fund** Rent/taxes, luxuries
Mode of Exchange Balanced exchange				**Mode of Exchange** Market exchange
Social Organization of Exchange Small groups, face-to-face				**Social Organization of Exchange** Anonymous market transactions
Primary Category of Exchange The gift				**Primary Category of Exchange** The sale

FIGURE 1 Modes of Livelihood, Consumption, and Exchange

colonialism, globalization, and other forms of expansionism. Consumerism is the distinguishing feature of industrial/informatic cultures. Globalization is spreading consumerism throughout the world.

The social organization and meaning of consumption varies cross-culturally. Foragers are generally egalitarian, whereas social inequality characterizes most agricultural and industrialism/informatics societies. In foraging peoples, sharing within the group is the norm, and everyone has equal access to all resources. Among the Ju/'hoansi: "Even though only a fraction of the able-bodied foragers go out each day, the day's return of meat and gathered foods are divided in such a way that every member of the camp receives an equitable share" (Lee 1979:118).

The distribution of personal goods such as clothing, beads, musical instruments, or smoking pipes is also equal. An important process that operates among small-scale societies and works to keep people equal with each other is called a leveling mechanism. **Leveling mechanisms** are unwritten, culturally embedded rules that prevent an individual from becoming wealthier or more powerful than anyone else. They are maintained through social pressure and gossip. An important leveling mechanism among the Ju/'hoansi requires that any large game animal killed be shared with the group and its killer must be modest, insisting that the meat is meager (Lee 1969). Ju/'hoansi hunters gain no social status or power through their provision of meat. The same applies to other

foragers. Leveling mechanisms are important in horticultural and pastoralist societies, too. For example, when someone's herd grows "too large," that person will be subject to social pressure to sponsor a large feast in which many of the herd animals are eaten.

Sharing is also a key value among many contemporary Indian tribes such as the Cheyenne of the Great Plains region of the United States (Moore 1999). Within the family, exchange goes on continuously and includes not just food but also tools, jewelry, and even vehicles. Sharing extends to people beyond the family who are considered part of the group. A Cheyenne woman told anthropologist John Moore about her observations at a child-care center where Anglo people also took their children: "'White people are funny,' she said. 'They spend half their time telling kids which toys are theirs, and the other half trying to get them to share'" (1999:179).

At the other end of the consumption continuum is consumerism, with the United States as the primary example, being the major consumerist country of the world. Since the 1970s, consumption levels in the United States have been the highest of any society in human history, and they show no sign of decline. The mass media send out seductive messages promoting consumerism as the way to happiness. Since China began to adopt aspects of capitalism, it has quickly become a consumerist giant. In the world's poorest countries, too, rising numbers of middle- and upper-class people pursue consumerism.

Well-stocked and brightly lit candy shops are a prominent part of urban nightlife in Valencia, Spain. Sugarcane was introduced into Spain by the Arabs. Later, the Spanish established the first sugarcane plantations on Madeira and the Canary Islands using enslaved laborers from Africa.

▶ *Log your food and drink consumption every day for a week and assess the role that sugar plays in the results.*

Minimalism was sustainable over hundreds of thousands of years, for most of humanity's time on earth. The amount of goods that the world's population consumed in the past 50 years equals what was consumed by all previous generations in human history. The growth of consumerism worldwide has some major costs:

- To the *environment and biological species diversity:* natural features such as rivers and lakes, forests, mountains, and beaches; nonhuman primates and hundreds of other species; and substances such as oil, gold, and diamonds

- To the world's *cultural diversity:* people who live in environments being destroyed by consumerism (these people currently occupy the tropical rainforests, circumpolar regions, deserts, and mountain areas)

- To the *poor* everywhere: people whose real and relative incomes place them in poverty and who experience an ever-widening gap between themselves and the well-off and the super-rich

In the United States, concern about the negative effects of consumerism tends to focus on the natural environment (especially "unspoiled" places for vacations such as national parks and beaches) and endangered nonhuman species rather than on the endangerment and possible extinction of indigenous

peoples and other nonindustrialized people—minimalists who "tread lightly on the land." The tragic irony is that more people in North America probably know about an endangered bird species, the spotted owl, than about any single endangered human group.

Some countries have policies that seek to control consumerism and its negative effects. The government of Sweden has invested in public transportation and bicycle paths in cities in order to reduce the use of cars. London recently placed a tax on cars entering the city. San Francisco is working on a plan to recycle dog waste and use it to create energy.

As consumerism spreads throughout the world, changes in the social relations involved in consumption also occur. In small-scale societies—such as those of foragers, horticulturalists, and pastoralists—consumption items are typically produced by the consumers themselves for their own use. If not, they are likely to be produced by people with whom the consumer has a personal, face-to-face relationship—in other words, *personalized consumption*. Everyone knows where products came from and who produced them. This pattern contrasts markedly with consumption in our contemporary globalized world, which is termed *depersonalized consumption*. Multinational corporations manage the production of most of the goods that people in industrialized countries consume. These products often are multi-sourced, with parts assembled in diverse parts of the world by hundreds of unknown workers. Depersonalized consumption, by distancing consumers from workers who actually produce goods, makes it more possible for workers to be exploited.

---

consumption fund   a category of a personal or household budget used to provide for consumption needs and desires.

(LEFT) Seoul, capital of the Republic of Korea. The demand for electricity in urban centers worldwide has prompted construction of many large dams to generate power. Food must be shipped to urban markets. In general, cities have high energy costs compared to rural areas. (RIGHT) In Rome, as elsewhere in Europe, mini-cars are popular due to their fuel efficiency and ease of parking.

➤ *Do research to discover the gas mileage of an average new car in the United States or Canada and compare it to that of a mini-car.*

Even in the most industrialized/informatics contexts, though, depersonalized consumption has not completely replaced personalized consumption. The popularity of farmers' markets in urban centers is an example of personalized consumption in which the consumer buys produce from the person who grew it and with whom the consumer may have a friendly conversation, perhaps while sampling one of the farmer's apples.

CONSUMPTION FUNDS

Anthropologists define a **consumption fund** as a category within a person's or household's budget used to provide for his

or her needs and desires. Cross-cultural analysis reveals five categories that appear to be relevant universally:

- *Basic needs fund:* for food, beverages, shelter, clothing, fuel, and the tools involved in producing or providing for them
- *Recurrent costs fund:* for maintenance and repair of tools, animals, machinery, and shelter
- *Entertainment fund:* for leisure activities
- *Ceremonial fund:* for social events such as rituals
- *Rent and tax fund:* for payments to landowners or governments for use of land, housing, or services

The categories apply universally, but the proportion of the budget allocated to each category varies widely and in relation to the mode of consumption. Remember: The "spending" involved may be in time, labor, or money, depending on the cultural context.

In the budget of free-ranging foragers, the largest share of expenditures goes into the basic needs fund. Foragers in temperate climates, however, spend far fewer hours per week collecting food than those in circumpolar climates. The next most important consumption fund among foragers is the recurrent costs fund, which supports repair and maintenance

Child labor is prominent in many modes of production. In this photograph, a girl picks coffee beans in Guatemala.

➤ *Should a child have the right to work, or should more international pressure be brought to bear against child labor?*

THINKING OUTSIDE THE BOX

Estimate your monthly expenditures in terms of the five funds. What proportion of your total expenditures goes to each fund? Do your expenditures fit well within the five categories or are different categories needed?

of tools and baskets, weapons, and shelter. Smaller shares are devoted to the entertainment fund and the ceremonial fund. Nothing goes into the rent and tax fund, because access to all land and other resources is free.

Consumption budgets in consumerist cultures differ in several ways from those in foraging, minimalist cultures. First, the absolute size of the budget is larger. People in agricultural and industrial/informatics societies work longer hours (unless they are unemployed), so they "spend" more of their time and labor providing for their consumption than foragers. Depending on their class position, they may have weekly cash budgets that are worth far more than their earnings due to stored wealth. Second, the relative size of the consumption funds varies in household budgets cross-culturally. Take as an example an imagined middle-class person in the United States. His or her consumption funds, compared to those of a forager, might look like this: The basic needs fund is a small portion of the total budget, given the increased overall size of the budget. This finding is in line with the economic principle that budgetary shares for food and housing (basic needs) decline as income rises. For example, someone who earns a total of $1000 a month and spends $800 on food and housing spends 80 percent of his budget in that category. Someone who makes $10,000 a month and spends $2000 a month on food and housing spends only 20 percent of her budget in this category, even though she spends more than twice as much as the first person, in an absolute sense. The largest share of the budget is the rent and tax fund. In some agricultural contexts, tenant farmers have to pay one-third to one-half of their crops to the landlord as rent. Income taxes claim well over 50 percent of personal income in countries such as Japan, Sweden, the Netherlands, and Italy. The entertainment fund receives a larger share than the ceremonial fund.

THEORIZING CONSUMPTION INEQUALITIES

Amartya Sen, an economist and a philosopher, proposed the theory of entitlements in order to explain why some groups suffer more than others during a famine (1981). An **entitlement** is a culturally defined right to provide for one's life needs. According to Sen, everyone has a set, or "bundle," of entitlements. For example, a person might own land, earn cash from a job, be on welfare, or live off an inheritance. Some entitlements are more secure and lucrative than others. *Direct entitlements* are the most secure form. In an agricultural society, for example, owning land that produces food is a direct

entitlement. *Indirect entitlements* depend on exchanging something in order to obtain consumer needs: labor, animal hides, money, or food stamps. Because indirect entitlements involve dependency on other people or institutions, they are riskier bases of support than direct entitlements are. When a factory shuts down, animal hides drop in value, or a food stamp program ends, a person depending on those entitlements is in trouble. During times of economic decline, scarcity, or disaster, people with indirect entitlements are the most vulnerable to impoverishment, hunger, and forced displacement.

ENTITLEMENTS CROSS-CULTURALLY   Entitlements vary depending on the type of economic system. In foraging societies, everyone has the same entitlement bundle. Entitlements are mainly direct, with the exception of infants and very old people who depend on sharing from group members for food and shelter. In industrial capitalist societies, entitlements are mainly indirect. People who grow all their own food are a small proportion of the total population. Even they depend on indirect entitlements for electricity and inputs required for maintaining their lifestyles. In highly monetized economies, the most powerful entitlements are those that provide a large and steady cash income, such as a good job. Other strong entitlements include home ownership, savings, stocks and bonds, and a retirement fund.

Internationally, entitlement theory exposes contrasts between countries that have secure and direct access to life-supporting resources and those that do not. Countries that produce food surpluses have a more secure entitlement to food than nations that are dependent on imports, for example. Replacing food crops with **cash crops**—plants grown primarily for sale, such as coffee or tobacco, rather than for own use—shifts a country from having mainly direct food entitlements to having mainly indirect entitlements. The same applies to access to energy sources that may be important for transportation to work or for heating homes. Direct access to energy resources is preferable to indirect access. This formula, however, leaves out the important factor of political power as exercised by the core countries of today's global economy. Many core countries lack direct access to critical resources, notably oil, yet they use political force to maintain access to such resources.

At the state (country) level, governments affect people's entitlements through policies related to employment, welfare programs, health care, and tax structures, among others. Political leaders and powerful policy makers decide how many people will live in poverty and how many will be allowed to become rich, or even super-rich. They decide on whether to fund programs that transfer wealth from the rich to the poor or to enact regressive tax structures that tax lower-income people at higher rates than the rich.

The entitlement concept can also be applied to *intra-household* entitlements, or shares of important resources that

---

entitlement   a culturally defined right to life-sustaining resources.

cash crop   a plant grown primarily for sale rather than for one's own use.

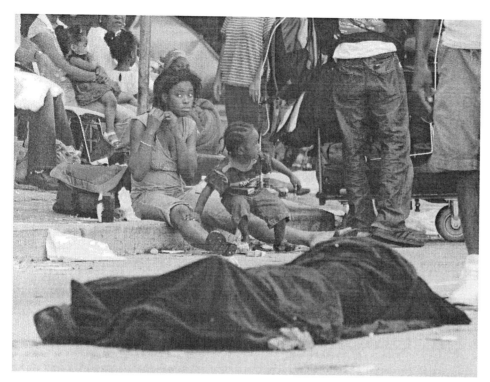

In the aftermath of Hurricane Katrina in 2005, a corpse lies covered as evacuees line the streets outside the convention center in New Orleans, Louisiana. After acknowledging that the initial federal effort to aid victims had failed, President George W. Bush deployed additional U.S. troops to the area.

▶ *Using the Internet, learn what roles cultural anthropologists played in the post-hurricane situation in the Gulf Coast area.*

© Shannon Stapleton/CORBIS

are allocated to particular household members. Households do not always provide equal entitlements for all members. A household member who is employed and earns wages, for example, may have a more secure position in terms of resources such as preferred food than someone who does not. Commonly, men have more secure intra-household entitlements than women. For example, inheritance practices may ensure that sons receive assets such as land or the family business, whereas daughters are excluded. Intra-household entitlements may also affect expenditures on health care depending on the status and value of particular members.

During crises, entitlement structures often become glaringly clear. Famines are a good example. Famine is defined as massive levels of death resulting from food deprivation in a geographically widespread area. Most people think that famines are caused by overpopulation or by natural disasters such as droughts and floods. Comparative analyses of many famine situations prove, however, that neither overpopulation nor natural disasters are sufficient explanations for famine (Sen 1981). Calculations of world food supply in relation to population prove that there is enough food produced every year to feed the world's population. Furthermore, although natural factors are often catalysts of famine, they do not always cause famine.

Hurricane Andrew of 1992 devastated much of Florida, but state and federal agencies rushed aid to the stricken area. In Louisiana and Mississippi, the hurricanes of 2005 caused many deaths, massive loss of private and commercial property, and displacement of thousands of people. But they did not cause a famine. Anthony Oliver-Smith, an anthropologist

who specializes in disasters, has said that there is no such thing as a purely *natural* disaster (2002). His point is that culture always shapes the patterns of human suffering and loss following a "natural" disaster. The social pattern of population displacement as a result of the 2005 hurricanes is testimony to the cultural shaping of disasters.

Entitlement analysis can help improve the effectiveness of humanitarian aid during famines and other crises (Harragin 2004). During the famine in southern Sudan in 1988, relief workers failed to understand the local cultural pattern of sharing, which extends to the last cup of rice. As food supplies decreased, local people continued to share whatever food was available. As a result, many people were surviving, but barely. When the food supply declined even more, the social safety net was unable to stretch further. Suddenly hundreds of people were dying. If relief workers had known about the culture of sharing unto death, they might have been able to forecast the breaking point before it happened and to bring in food aid sooner.

THINKING OUTSIDE THE BOX

What is in your personal entitlement bundle? Conduct a self-analysis of your daily consumption needs (food, shelter, entertainment, and other things) and how you provide for them. Then, imagine how you would provide for these needs if, starting today, your usual entitlements no longer had any value.

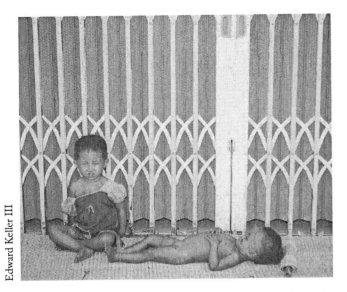

Homeless children rest by a storefront grate in Ho Chi Minh City, Vietnam.

▶ Consider how the entitlement system affected children under pure socialism compared to the current transition to a more capitalist system.

THREE CONSUMPTION MICROCULTURES This section provides examples of three consumption microcultures: class, gender, and "race." Microcultures have distinct entitlement patterns, related levels of health and welfare, and identity associated with consumption. Depending on the cultural context, social inequality may play an important role and have major effects on human welfare.

CLASS AND THE GAME OF DISTINCTION IN ISRAELI BIRTHDAY PARTIES Class differences, defined in terms of levels of income, are reflected in distinctive consumption patterns. Although class differences in consumption may seem too obvious to be worth studying, they constitute an important and growing area in anthropology.

A landmark study about consumer preferences, or "tastes," was conducted by a team of French researchers led by French anthropologist/sociologist Pierre Bourdieu (1984). They sent questionnaires to several thousand people, based on a national sample, and received 1000 responses. Statistical analysis of the responses revealed clear class patterns in, for example, choice of favorite painters or pieces of music. Preferences corresponded with educational level and father's occupation. An overall pattern of *distance from necessity* in tastes and preferences characterized members of the educated upper classes, who were more likely to prefer abstract art. Their goal was to keep "necessity" at a distance. In comparison, the working classes were closer to "necessity," and they preferred realist art. Bourdieu provides the concept of the *game of distinction* in which people of the upper classes continually adjust their preferences to distance themselves from the lower classes, whereas members of the lower classes tend to adopt aspects of upper-class preferences in order to gain status.

Cross-culturally, events such as weddings, funerals, and children's birthday parties are often occasions requiring large expenditures that send messages about the status (real or aspired) of the hosts. Children's birthday parties are a less studied topic but one with much potential, especially because such parties are becoming increasingly popular in cultures around the world. In Israel, children's birthday parties have recently become expensive events among middle-class and upper-class urbanites (Goldstein-Gidoni 2003). Parents hire birthday party professionals to create special themes. "Around the World" themes are popular, especially those drawing on Japanese, Spanish, South American, and Middle Eastern motifs. A current craze for Japanese culture, such as gardens and food, means that the Japanese theme is one of the most

Skiers and snowboarders line up to ride the lift to the top of the Middle East's first indoor ski resort, Ski Dubai, at the Mall of the Emirates in Dubai. Ski Dubai is housed in one of the world's largest malls and features a snow park with a twin track bobsled ride and a ski slope with five runs.

▶ Plan a fantasy two-week trip to Dubai: How will you get there, where will you stay, where will you eat, what will you do, and how much will the trip cost?

popular. "Around the World" birthday party themes are ostensibly to help the children learn about other places and people. At the same time, they make a statement about how cosmopolitan, well-off, and stylish the hosts are.

Not everyone, everywhere, buys into the game of distinction. Many individuals and wider social movements actively resist the spread of upper-class consumption patterns and promote alternative cultural practices.

WOMEN'S DEADLY DIET IN PAPUA NEW GUINEA
Consumption patterns are often marked by gender and related to discrimination and inequality. Specific foods may be considered "men's food" or "women's food." An example of lethal gender inequalities in food consumption comes from highland Papua New Guinea (see Map 1).

The story begins with the eruption of a mysterious disease, with the local name of *kuru*, among the Fore (for-ay), a horticultural people of the highlands (Lindenbaum 1979). Between 1957 and 1977, about 2500 people died of kuru. Most victims, however, were women. The first signs of kuru are shivering tremors, followed by a progressive loss of motor ability along with pain in the head and limbs. Kuru victims could walk unsteadily at first but would later be unable to get up. Death occurred about a year after the first symptoms appeared.

American medical researchers revealed that kuru was a neurological disease. Australian cultural anthropologist Shirley Lindenbaum pinpointed the cultural cause of kuru: cannibalism. Kuru victims had eaten the flesh of deceased people who had died of kuru.

Why were most of the kuru victims women? Lindenbaum learned that among the Fore, it was considered acceptable to cook and eat the meat of a deceased person, although it was not a preferred food. The preferred source of animal protein is meat from pigs, and men receive preferential

access to the best food. Fore women had begun to eat human flesh more often because of increased scarcity of pigs. Population density in the region had risen, more land was being cultivated, and forest areas had decreased. Pigs live in forest areas, so as their habitat became more restricted, their numbers declined. The Fore could not move to more pig-abundant areas because they were bounded on the east, west, and north sides by other groups. The south was a harsh and forbidding region. These factors, combined with the Fore's male-biased system of protein consumption, forced women to turn to the less preferred protein source of human flesh. By eating the flesh, including brains, of kuru victims, they contracted the disease.

"RACE" AND CHILDREN'S SHOPPING IN NEW HAVEN
Throughout the world, in countries with "race"-based social categories, inequalities in consumption and quality of life exist, often in spite of anti-discrimination legislation. In the United States, racism and racial discrimination affect many areas of life from access to housing, neighborhood security and services, schooling, health, and whether a person is likely to be ignored by a taxi or stopped by a police officer for speeding. Racial inequality between Black and White Americans has risen steadily since the 1970s in terms of income, wealth, and property ownership, especially house-ownership (Shapiro 2004). Those at the top of the income distribution have increased their share of the wealth most. The share of total income that goes to the top 1 percent of families is nearly the same size as the total income share of the bottom 40 percent.

How is this happening in a country dedicated to equality of opportunity? A large part of the answer lies in the simple fact that, in a capitalist system, inequality leads to more inequality through the transfer of wealth and property across generations. Those who have wealth and property are able to establish their children's wealth through college tuition payments, house down payments, and other financial gifts. The children of poor parents have to provide for their education and housing costs from their wages alone, a fact that makes it far less likely that they will be able to pursue higher education or buy a home.

As a graduate student in anthropology at Yale University, Elizabeth Chin decided to do her dissertation research on consumption patterns among schoolchildren in a poor, African American neighborhood in New Haven, Connecticut (2001) (see Map 2). In terms of per capita income, Connecticut is the wealthiest state in the United States. It also harbors some of the most severe poverty and racial inequality in its major cities. Chin describes New Haven as a "patchwork of clearly delineated neighborhoods that can veer quite suddenly from the abjectly poor to the fabulously wealthy" (2001:vii). These zones are largely divided into White and Black groups who are fearful and suspicious of

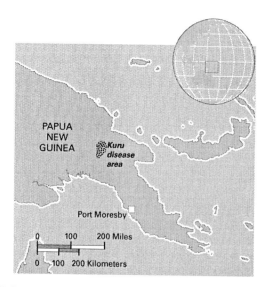

MAP 1 Location of the Kuru Epidemic in Papua New Guinea.

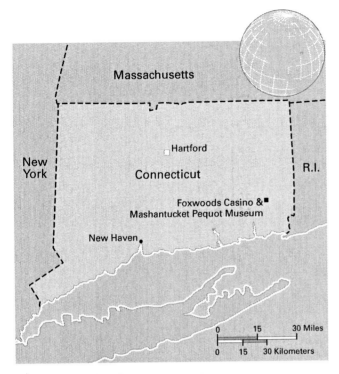

MAP 2 Connecticut, United States.
In terms of per capita income, Connecticut is the wealthiest state in the United States. Its population of about 3.5 million includes a majority of Whites (76 percent), predominantly of Italian, Irish, and English descent. Blacks and Latinos constitute about 10 percent of the population each. Indian tribal peoples are 0.3 percent.

each other. During her research in "Newhallville," Chin found that the Black and White cultural worlds are clearly separate and deeply unequal. In the Black neighborhood, 50 percent of children age 5 and under were living in poverty.

Chin formed a relationship with one fifth-grade class of 22 students. She spent time in the classroom. She explored the neighborhood with some of the children, visited with them and their families in their homes, and accompanied them on shopping trips to the mall. The children are bombarded with media messages about consumption but they have little money to spend. Some receive an allowance for doing household chores; some receive small amounts of pocket money on an ad hoc basis; and some earn money from small-scale ventures such as a cucumber stand. They learn about the basics of household finances and the costs of daily life early on. Seeing their families strain every day to put meals on the table teaches them about the negative effects of overindulgence: "From divvying up the milk to figuring out where to sleep there is an emphasis on sharing and mutual obligation" (2001:5).

These practical lessons shape how the children spend their money when they go to the mall. Practicality and generosity guide their shopping choices. In order to learn about the children's decisions, Chin would give a child $20 and go

with him or her to the mall. Most of the girls spent over half their money on gifts for family members, especially their mothers and grandmothers (2001:139). The girls knew their mothers' shoe sizes and clothing sizes. One boy, just before school was to start in the fall, spent $10 on a T-shirt to wear on the first day of school, $6 on a pair of shorts, and the rest on school supplies: pencils, pens, notebook paper, and a binder (2001:135). In her two years of research, Chin never heard a Newhallville child nag a caretaker about buying him or her something or whine about personal consumption desires.

Birthday parties are rare events in Newhallville. The one birthday party Chin observed involved an $18 ice-cream cake. Birthday gifts are few. One girl received three gifts on her tenth birthday: a jump rope and a bingo game from her mother, wrapped in brown paper made from a grocery bag, and an inexpensive plastic toy from her grandmother (2001:72). There was no party, but her mother baked a chocolate cake for her.

FORBIDDEN CONSUMPTION: FOOD TABOOS

Cultural anthropologists have a long-standing interest in trying to explain culturally specific food taboos, or rules about prohibited foods. Cultural materialists and symbolic anthropologists disagree about why food taboos exist.

WHAT CULTURAL MATERIALISM SAYS Cultural materialist Marvin Harris asks why there are Jewish and Muslim taboos on eating pig when pig meat is so enthusiastically consumed in many other parts of the world (1974). He says, "Why should gods so exalted as Jahweh and Allah have bothered to condemn a harmless and even laughable beast whose flesh is relished by the greater part of mankind?" (1974:36). Harris proposes that we consider the role of environmental factors during early Hebrew times and the function of this prohibition in terms of its fit to the local ecology.

Within the overall pattern of this mixed farming and pastoralist complex, the divine prohibition of pork constituted a sound ecological strategy. The pig is thermodynamically ill-adapted to the hot, dry climate of the Negev, the Jordan Valley, and the other lands of the Bible and the Koran. Compared to cattle, goats, and sheep, the pig has an inefficient system for regulating its body temperature. Despite the expression "to sweat like a pig," it has been proved that pigs can't sweat at all (1974:41–42).

Raising pigs in this context would be a luxury. On the other hand, in "pig-loving" cultures of Southeast Asia and the Pacific, climatic factors, including temperature, humidity, and the presence of forest cover (good for pigs) promote raising pigs. There, pigs offer an important protein source that complements the major root crops: yams, sweet potatoes, and taro. Harris acknowledges that not all religiously sanctioned food

Preparation for a feast in the highlands of Papua New Guinea, where people place much value on consuming roasted pig meat.

▶ *What are the high-status foods in your cultural world(s)?*

© David Austen/Stock Boston LLC

practices can be explained ecologically and that food practices often serve to communicate and promote social identity. But analysis of food consumption should always consider ecological and material factors of production as basic.

WHAT SYMBOLIC ANTHROPOLOGISTS SAY   Symbolic anthropologist Mary Douglas argues, in contrast to Harris, that what people eat has less to do with the material conditions of life (the environment or hunger) than with what food means and how food communicates meaning and identity (1966). For Douglas, people's emic categories about food provide a mental map of the world and people's place in it. *Anomalies*, or things that do not fit into culturally defined categories, become reminders to people of moral problems or things to avoid.

Douglas uses a symbolic approach in examining food categories and anomalies as laid out in the Old Testament book of Leviticus. One rule says that people may eat animals with cloven hoofs and that chew a cud. On the basis of this rule, animals that do not satisfy both criteria are anomalies, and such animals are considered unclean and are taboo as food. These anomalies include camels, pigs, and hares. A pig, for example, has cloven hoofs, but it does not chew a cud. In the interpretation of Douglas, the food rules in Leviticus are a symbolic system defining completeness and purity (the animals one can eat) in contrast to incompleteness and impurity (the animals one cannot eat). By extension, she argues, people who know these rules and follow them are constantly reminded of God's perfection, completeness, and purity. When people follow these rules, they communicate their identity as pure and godly to other people. Thus, according to Douglas, food choices are not about the nutritional content of the food; rather, they have to do with symbols and meaning. She down-

plays studying the "practical" aspects of food because, she says, that distracts analysts from studying the meaning of food.

Anthropologists, no matter which theoretical perspective they favor about food taboos, recognize that there is more to food than just eating. Douglas emphasizes the importance of food rules as codes, ways of communicating meaning, and this interpretation is clearly valid. Harris says that economic and political aspects of food choices must be considered for a full understanding, and this point is valid, too.

◆ ◆ ◆

Culture and Exchange

Exchange is the transfer of something that may be material or immaterial between at least two persons, groups, or institutions. Cultural anthropologists have done much research on gifts and other forms of exchange, starting with Malinowski's work on the kula in the South Pacific and Boas's research on potlatching among Northwest Coast Indians. In all economic systems, individuals and groups exchange goods and services with others, so. But variation exists in what is exchanged, how goods are exchanged, when exchange takes place, and the meaning of exchange.

THINKING OUTSIDE THE BOX

You have invited Jesus, the Buddha, Muhammad, and Moses to dinner. What are you serving?

everyday ANTHROPOLOGY

The Rules of Hospitality

In much of the Middle East, where women spend most of their time in the domestic domain, social visits among women are eagerly anticipated and carefully planned events with complex rules about what foods and drinks should be served (Wikan 1982). In Oman, when women go outside the home, they wear head veils, face masks, and full-length gowns. Their main social activity consists of visits to other women in their homes. A typical visit involves sitting, chatting, and eating snacks.

Social etiquette dictates what should be served and how. Coffee and dates are the traditional entertainment foods offered to close neighbors. Biscuits (cookies), caramel candies, and popcorn are favored snacks. Beyond the particular snack item, the number of dishes offered is important. For neighbors who interact on a daily basis, a single dish is typical. All other visitors should be offered at least two plates with different contents, or else the hostess will be considered stingy. In the case of many guests, the number of plates must be increased, with a minimum of four plates, and the variety of snacks must be greater. Another rule of visitor etiquette requires that guests should leave approximately half of the food served to them; it will be consumed by members of the hostess' household (1982:130–132).

Cooked food, such as meat and sweets, is served when entertaining guests at weddings, seasonal feasts, and burials. In such situations, when cooked food is served, the hosts may never eat with their guests: "Even if the consequence is that the guest must eat all alone, in a separate room, it would be disrespectful to arrange it otherwise" (1982:133).

◆ FOOD FOR THOUGHT

- How do these Omani rules of hospitality resemble or contrast with your rules of hospitality? Think about your choices of items served, numbers of items, and other choices you make about what to serve and how to serve it when entertaining guests.

A Bedu (Bedouin) woman of Muscat, Oman.

▶ Assume you are going to Oman for a semester abroad. What should you know about the culture before you go?

WHAT IS EXCHANGED?

The items that people exchange range from seashells to stocks and bonds and may be purely utilitarian (see Figure 2). Items of exchange may carry meanings and have a history, or "social life," of their own, as prized kula items do (Appadurai 1986).

Category	Selected Examples
Material Goods	Food to family and group members
	Gifts for special occasions such as weddings
	Money
Nonmaterial Goods	Myths, stories, rituals
	Time, labor
People	Offspring in marriage
	Slavery

FIGURE 2 Items of Exchange

In contemporary industrialized societies, money is the major item of exchange, and such economies are referred to as *monetized*. In nonmarket economies, money plays a less important role, and time, labor, and goods are prominent exchange items. As nonmarket economies are connected, through globalization, they are confronted with the (to them) peculiar and mysterious meaning of Western money. Often, they localize the meanings of money, by treating particular bills as more special than others. In many cultures, money has completely replaced other valued items of exchange, such as shell wealth in Papua New Guinea.

Nonmonetary exchange exists in contemporary industrial societies, too. Hosting dinner parties, exchanging gifts at holiday times, and sharing a bag of potato chips with a friend are examples of common forms of nonmonetary exchange. Some scholars also include kisses, glances, and loyalty (Blau 1964).

MATERIAL GOODS Cross-culturally, food is one of the most common exchange goods both in everyday life and on ritual occasions. Daily meals involve some form of exchange,

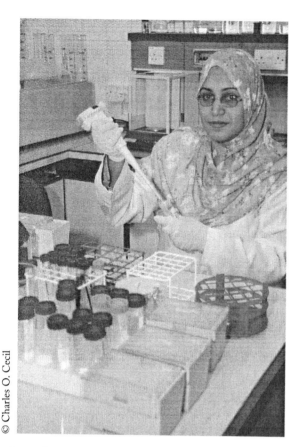
Omani biotech scientist, Ms. Wahida al-Amri, at work in her lab in the Omani Marine Science and Fisheries Center.

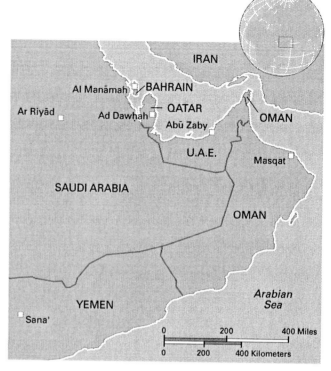

MAP 3 Oman.
The Sultanate of Oman is mainly a vast desert plain with a hot, dry climate. The population of nearly 3 million includes over 500,000 immigrant laborers. The economy is based mainly on crude oil. The major religion is Ibādī Islam, a more liberal version of Islam than Sunni or Shi'a Islam. Arabic is the official language, with English a widely spoken second language. Several local dialects are spoken including the Omani dialect of Arabic.

as do most ceremonies and rituals. In many cultures, arranging a marriage involves many stages of food gifts and countergifts exchanged between the families of the couple.

Wedding exchanges among the Nias of northern Sumatra, Indonesia provide an illustration of a complex set of exchanges. From the betrothal to the actual marriage, a scheduled sequence of events occurs at which culturally stipulated food and other gifts are exchanged between the families of the bride and groom (Beatty 1992). At the first meeting between the families, when the prospective groom expresses his interest in a betrothal, he and his party visit the bride's house and are fed. The guests receive the lower jaw of a pig (the portion of honor), and they take away with them raw and cooked portions of the pig for the father of the groom-to-be (1992:121). Within the next week or two, the prospective groom brings a gift of 3 to 12 pigs to confirm the engagement. He returns the container used for the pig meat given to him on the previous visit, filled with a certain kind of nut. The groom gives more pigs and gold as the major gift to seal the marriage. For many years following the wedding, the two families continue to exchange gifts.

On an everyday level, exchanges of food and beverages are important in friendships. Among friends, food exchanges involve their own, largely unconscious rules of etiquette (see Everyday Anthropology).

Exchanging alcoholic beverages is an important feature of many community ritual events in Latin America. In a highland village in Ecuador, the San Juan fiesta is the high point of the year (Barlett 1980). The fiesta consists of four or five days during which small groups of celebrants move from house to house, dancing and drinking. The anthropologist reports on the event:

I joined the groups consisting of the president of the community and the elected *alcaldes* (councilmen and police), who were accompanied by their wives, a few friends, and some children. We met each morning for a hearty breakfast at one house, began drinking there, and then continued eating and drinking in other homes throughout the day and into the evening. . . . Some people drink for only one or two days, others prefer to make visits mainly at night, some people drink day and night for four days. (1980:118–119)

Guests who drink at someone's house will later serve their former hosts alcohol in return.

SYMBOLIC GOODS Intangible valuables such as myths (sacred stories) and rituals (sacred practices) may be exchanged in ways similar to material goods. In the Balgo Hills region of Australia (see Map 4), long-standing exchange networks transfer myths and rituals among regionally dispersed groups of women (Poirier 1992). The women may keep important narratives and rituals for a limited time and then must pass them on to other groups. One is the *Tjarada*, a love-magic ritual with an accompanying narrative. The Tjarada came to the women of Balgo Hills from the north. They kept it for about 15 years and then passed it on to another group in a ceremony that lasted for three days. During the time that the Balgo Hills women were custodians of the Tjarada, they incorporated some new elements into it. These elements are retained even after its transfer to the next group. Thus, the Tjarada contains bits of local identity of each group that has had it. A sense of community and responsibility thereby develops and is sustained among the groups that have held the Tjarada.

LABOR In labor-sharing groups, people contribute labor to other people on a regular basis (for seasonal agricultural work such as harvesting) or on an irregular basis (in the event of a crisis such as the need to rebuild a barn damaged by fire). Labor-sharing groups are part of what has been called a "moral economy" because no one keeps formal records on how much any family puts in or takes out. Instead, accounting is socially regulated. The group has a sense of being a moral community based on years of trust and sharing. In Amish communities of North America, sharing labor is a central part of life. When a family needs a new barn that requires group labor, a barn-raising party is called. Many families show up to help. Adult men provide manual labor, and adult women provide food for the event.

MONEY For most of humanity's existence, people did not purchase things. They collected or made things they needed themselves, shared, or exchanged items for other things. The invention of money is recent, only a few thousand years ago. **Money** is a medium of exchange that can be used for a variety of goods (Godelier 1971). Money exists cross-culturally in such diverse forms as shells, salt, cattle, furs, cocoa beans, and iron hoes.

Modern money, in the form of coins and paper bills, has the advantages of being portable, divisible, uniform, and recognizable (Shipton 2001). On the other hand, modern money

MAP 4 The Balgo Hills (Wirrimanu) Region in Western Australia.
The Balgo Hills community is located on the northern edge of the Tanami and Great Sandy Deserts. One of Australia's most isolated indigenous desert settlements, it nevertheless has a flourishing art center. Balgo paintings and glass are highly sought after by collectors. To learn about Balgo art and artists, visit http://www.aboriginalartonline .com/regions/balgo.php.

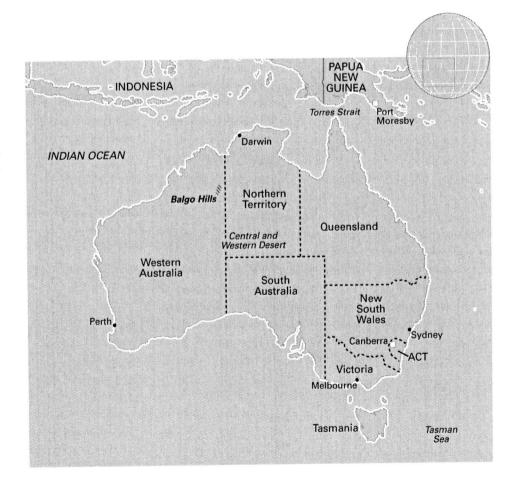

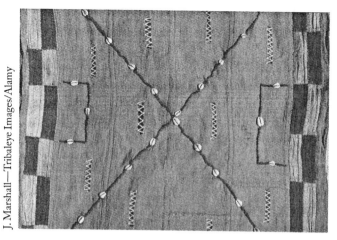

J. Marshall—Tribaleye Images/Alamy

This raffia cloth, from the Democratic Republic of Congo, is woven from palm fibers. Throughout central Africa, raffia cloth functions as limited-purpose money, or money that can be used only for specific purposes, such as marriage or compensation for wrongdoing. It cannot be used for commercial transactions such as buying food, a house, or a car.

is vulnerable to economic changes such as inflation, which reduce its value. The use of modern money is spreading throughout the world. Nonmonetary cultures, however, often adopt modern money in limited ways. They may prohibit its use in religious exchanges or in life-cycle rituals such as marriages. All forms of money, even modern money, are symbolic. They have meaning to the user, and they are associated with the user's identity and sense of self. The color and design of a credit card, for example, may signify status, such as "platinum" for the biggest spenders. As the European Union was forming, lengthy discussion was devoted to what the new currency would look like. As e-money becomes increasingly used, it will be interesting to see what kinds of meaning are attached to it.

PEOPLE Exchange in human beings relegates humans to objects. Throughout history, some people have been able to gain control of other people and treat them as items of exchange, as in slavery and human trafficking. The enslavement of people from many regions of Africa during European colonialism from the fifteenth to nineteenth centuries stands as one of the most heinous processes of treating humans as commodities in the full light of day, with no legal sanctions involved for slave traders or owners. This process cruelly transformed thousands of people into property that could be bought and sold, used and abused, and even murdered.

A long-standing debate in anthropology concerns women as objects of exchange in marriage. Lévi-Strauss proposed many years ago that the exchange of women between men is one of the most basic forms of exchange among humans (1969 [1949]). He based his assertion on the universality of some sort of *incest taboo,* which he defined as a rule

preventing a man from marrying or cohabiting with his mother or sister. Such a rule, he says, is the logic driving the exchange of women among men: "The fact that I can obtain a wife is, in the final analysis, the consequence of the fact that a brother or father has given her up" (1969:62). Thus, the avoidance of incest forces men to develop exchange networks with other men and, by extension, leads to the emergence of social solidarity more widely. For Lévi-Strauss, the incest taboo provides the foundation for human social organization.

Feminist anthropologists say that this theory overlooks much ethnographic evidence to the contrary. Men do not have rights over women in many foraging societies; instead, women make their own choices about partners (Rubin 1975). In many horticultural and agricultural societies of Southeast Asia, men do not exchange women (Peletz 1987). Instead, women select grooms for their daughters. This pattern turns Lévi-Strauss's theory on its head because it involves women organizing the exchange of men.

MODES OF EXCHANGE

Parallel to the two contrasting modes of consumption described earlier (minimalism and consumerism), two distinct modes of exchange can be delineated (see Figure 3):

- **Balanced exchange:** a system of transfers in which the goal is either immediate or eventual balance in value.
- **Unbalanced exchange:** a system of transfers in which one party attempts to make a profit.

BALANCED EXCHANGE The category of balanced exchange contains two subcategories based on the social relationship of the two parties involved in the exchange and the degree to which a "return" is expected. **Generalized reciprocity** is a transaction that involves the least conscious sense of interest in material gain or thought of what might be received in return, and when. Such exchanges often involve goods and services of an everyday nature, such as a cup of coffee. Generalized reciprocity is the main form of exchange between people who know each other well and trust each other. Therefore, it is the main form of exchange in foraging societies. It is also found among close kin and friends cross-culturally.

---

money   a medium of exchange that can be used for a variety of goods.

balanced exchange   a system of transfers in which the goal is either immediate or eventual equality in value.

unbalanced exchange   a system of transfers in which one party seeks to make a profit.

generalized reciprocity   exchange involving the least conscious sense of interest in material gain or thought of what might be received in return.

	Balanced Exchange			Unbalanced Exchange	
	Generalized Reciprocity	Expected Reciprocity	Redistribution	Market Exchange	Theft, Exploitation
Actors	Kin, friends	Trading partners	Leader and pooling group	Buyers/sellers	Nonkin, nonfriends, unknown
Return	Not calculated or expected	Expected at some time	Feast and give-away	Immediate payment	No return
Example	Buying coffee for a friend	Kula	Moka	Internet shopping	Shoplifting

FIGURE 3   Keeping Track of Exchange

A **pure gift** is something given with no expectation or thought of a return. The pure gift is an extreme form of generalized reciprocity. Examples of a pure gift include donating money for a food drive, or making donations to famine relief, blood banks, and religious organizations. Some people say that a truly pure gift does not exist because one always gains something, no matter how difficult to measure, in giving—even if it is just the good feeling of generosity. Parental care of children is said to be a pure gift by some, but others do not agree. Those who say that parental care is a pure gift argue that most parents do not consciously calculate how much they have spent on their children with the intention of "getting it back" later on. Those who do not consider parental care a pure gift say that even if the "costs" are not consciously calculated, parents have unconscious expectations about what their children will "return" to them, whether the return is material (care in old age) or immaterial (making the parent feel proud).

Expected reciprocity is the exchange of approximately equally valued goods or services, usually between people of

---

pure gift   something given with no expectation or thought of a return.

expected reciprocity   an exchange of approximately equally valued goods or services, usually between people roughly equal in social status.

redistribution   a form of exchange that involves one person collecting goods or money from many members of a group, who then, at a later time and at a public event, "returns" the pooled goods to everyone who contributed.

market exchange   the buying and selling of commodities under competitive conditions in which the forces of supply and demand determine value.

trade   the formalized exchange of one thing for another according to set standards of value.

roughly equal social status. The exchange may occur simultaneously between both parties, or it may involve an understanding about the time period within which the exchange will be completed. This aspect of timing contrasts with generalized reciprocity, in which there is no fixed time limit for the return. In expected reciprocity, if the second party fails to complete the exchange, the relationship will break down. Balanced reciprocity is less personal than generalized reciprocity and, according to Western definitions, more "economic."

The kula is an example of a system of expected reciprocity. Men exchange necklaces and armlets, giving them to their exchange partners after keeping them for a while. Partners include neighbors as well as people on faraway islands who are visited via long canoe voyages on high seas. Trobriand men are distinguished by the particular armlets and necklaces that they exchange, and certain armlets and necklaces are more prestigious than others. One cannot keep one's trade items for long because the kula code dictates that "to possess is great, but to possess is to give." Generosity is the essence of goodness, and stinginess is the most despised vice. Kula exchanges should involve items of equivalent value. If a man trades a very valuable necklace with his partner, he expects to receive in return a very valuable armlet as an equivalent gift). At the time, if one's partner does not possess an equivalent item, he may have to give an intermediary gift, which stands as a token of good faith until a proper return gift can be given. The clinching gift comes later and balances the original gift. The equality of exchange ensures a strong bond between the trading partners and is a statement of trust. When a man arrives in an area where it may be dangerous because of previous raids or warfare, he can count on having a friend to give him hospitality.

Redistribution is a form of exchange in which one person collects goods or money from many members of a group and provides a social return at a later time. At a public event, even several years later, the organizer "returns" the pooled goods to everyone who contributed by sponsoring a generous

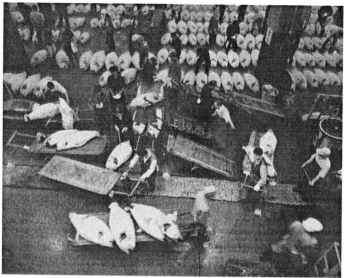

(LEFT) In China, many marketers are women. These two women display their wares in a permanent food market in a city about an hour's drive from Shanghai. (RIGHT) Workers at Tsukiji, the world's largest fish market in Tokyo, transport frozen tuna on hand carts for the upcoming auction.

▶ *For a research project, learn more about Ted Bestor's research on Tsukiji.*

feast. Compared to the two-way pattern of exchange involved in reciprocity, redistribution involves some "centricity." It contains the possibility of inequality because what is returned may not always equal, in a material sense, what each individual contributed. The pooling group may continue to exist, however, because it benefits from the leadership skills of the person who mobilizes contributions. If a neighboring group threatens a raid, people turn to their redistributive leader for political leadership.

UNBALANCED EXCHANGE **Market exchange**, a prominent form of unbalanced exchange, is the buying and selling of commodities under competitive conditions in which the forces of supply and demand determine value and the seller seeks to make a profit (Dannhaeuser 1989:222). In market transactions, the seller and buyer may or may not have a personal relationship. They may or may not be social equals. Their exchange is not likely to generate social bonding. Many market transactions take place in a marketplace, a physical location in which buying and selling occur. The market system evolved from other, less formal contexts of **trade**, formalized exchange of one thing for another according to set standards of value.

The market system is associated with regional specialization in producing particular goods and trade between regions. Certain products are often identified with a town or region. In Oaxaca, Mexico, some villages are known for their blankets, pottery, stone grinders, rope, and chili peppers (Plattner 1989). In Morocco, the city of Fez (see Map 3) is famous for its blue-glazed pottery, whereas the Berber people of the Atlas Mountains are known for their fine wool blankets and rugs. Increasingly, producers of regionally distinct products, such as

champagne, are legally copyrighting the regional name to protect it from use by producers of similar products from outside the region. Specialization develops with illegal commodities too. For example, Jamaican marijuana is well known for its high quality, and many tourists travel to Jamaica, especially the Negril area in the west, in order to buy this product in its many forms.

Marketplaces range from informal, small stands that appear in the morning and disappear at night, to huge multistoried shopping centers. One variety found in many parts of the world is a *periodic market,* a site for buying and selling that takes place on a regular basis (for example, monthly) in a particular location but without a permanent physical structure. Sellers appear with their goods and set up a table with perhaps an awning. In contrast, permanent markets are built structures situated in fixed locations. Marketplaces, however, are more than just places for buying and selling. They involve social interactions and even performances. Sellers solicit customers, shoppers meet and chat, government officials drop by, religious organizations may hold services, and traditional healers may treat toothaches. The particularities of how markets are structured, spatially and socially, and how culture shapes market transactions are rich topics for ethnographic research.

THINKING
OUTSIDE
THE BOX

Propose some examples of what might qualify as a "pure gift."

Barbara Miller

Ted Bestor conducted research over many years in Tsukiji (tsee-kee-jee), the world's largest fish market, located in Tokyo (2004). Tsukiji connects large-scale corporations that supply most of the seafood with small-scale family-run firms that continue to dominate Tokyo's retail food trade. Bestor describes the layout of the huge market, with inner and outer sections as a basic division. The outer market attracts younger, more hip shoppers looking for unusual, trendy gourmet items and a more authentic-seeming shopping experience. It contains sushi bars, noodle stalls, knife shops, and chopstick dealers, as well as temples and graveyards. The inner market contains 11 fresh produce market subdivisions. The seafood section by far overshadows the "veggie" markets in size and transaction level. It is subdivided into several main buildings where auctions occur, activities such as deliveries and dispatches take place, and rows of retail stalls serve 14,000 customers each morning. Bestor gained insight into the verbally coded conversations between experienced buyers and sellers in the stalls that are more likely to yield a better price than what an inexperienced first-time buyer will get. Stalls do not typically post prices, so buyers and sellers have to negotiate them. The verbal codes involve phrases such as "morning mist on a white beach," which, depending on the number of syllables in the phrase, conveys a price offer.

OTHER FORMS OF UNBALANCED EXCHANGE

Several forms of unbalanced exchange other than market transactions exist. In extreme instances, no social relationship is involved; in others, sustained unequal relationships are maintained over time between people. These forms include taking something with no expectation of giving any return. They can occur in any mode of production but are most likely to be found in large-scale societies where more options (other than face-to-face) for balanced exchange exist.

GAMBLING *Gambling,* or gaming, is the attempt to make a profit by playing a game of chance in which a certain item of value is staked in hopes of acquiring the much larger return that one receives if one wins the game. If one loses, that which was staked is lost. Gambling is an ancient practice and is common cross-culturally. Ancient forms of gambling include dice throwing and card playing. Investing in the stock market can be considered a form of gambling, as can gambling of many sorts through the Internet. Although gambling may seem an odd category within unbalanced exchange, its goals of making a profit seem to justify its placement here. The fact that gambling within "high" capitalism is on the rise justifies anthropological attention to it. In fact, some scholars have referred to the present stage of Western capitalism as casino capitalism, given the propensity of investors to play risky games in the stock market (Klima 2002).

Indian tribal gambling establishments in the United States have mushroomed in recent years. Throughout the United States, Indian casinos are so financially successful that they are perceived as an economic threat to many state lotteries. The Pequot Indians of Connecticut (see Map 2), a small tribe of around 200 people, now operate the most lucrative gaming establishment in the world, Foxwoods Resort and Casino, established in 1992. Through gaming, many Indian tribal groups have become successful capitalists. An important question is what impact casinos will have on Indian tribal people, and anthropologists are involved in trying to answer this question (see Lessons Applied).

THEFT *Theft* is taking something with no expectation or thought of returning anything to the original owner for it. It is the logical opposite of a pure gift. Anthropologists have neglected the study of theft, no doubt a reasonable response because theft is an illegal activity that is difficult to study and might involve danger.

A rare study of theft focused on food stealing by children in West Africa (Bledsoe 1983). During fieldwork among the Mende people of Sierra Leone, Caroline Bledsoe learned that children in town stole fruits such as mangoes, guavas, and oranges from neighborhood trees. Bledsoe at first dismissed cases of food stealing as rare exceptions, but then she realized that she "rarely walked through town without hearing shouts of anger from an adult and cries of pain from a child being whipped for stealing food" (1983:2). Deciding to look into children's food stealing more closely, she asked several children to keep diaries. Their writings were dominated by themes of *tiefing,* the local term for stealing. Fostered children, who are temporarily placed in the care of friends or relatives, do more food tiefing than children living with their birth families do. Such food stealing can be seen as children's attempts to compensate for their less-than-adequate food shares in their foster homes.

Although much theft worldwide is motivated by skewed entitlements and need, much is also driven by greed. Cultural anthropologists, for obvious reasons, have not done research on high-level theft involving expensive commodities such as drugs, gems, and art, nor have they examined corporate financial malpractice as a form of theft. Given the ethical requirement of informed consent, it is unlikely that any anthropologist would be given permission to study such criminal activity.

EXPLOITATION *Exploitation,* or getting something of greater value for less in return, is a form of extreme and persistent unbalanced exchange. Slavery is a form of exploitation in which people's labor power is appropriated without their consent and with no recompense for its value. Slavery is rare among foraging, horticultural, and pastoralist societies. Social relationships that involve sustained unequal exchange do exist between members of different social groups that, unlike pure slavery, involve no overt coercion and entail a certain degree of return by the dominant member to the subdominant member.

LESSONS applied

Evaluating Indian Gaming in California

In 2006, the Center for California Native Nations (CCNN) at the University of California at Riverside released an evaluation of the effects of Indian gaming in California (Spilde Contreras 2006). *Note:* According to current preferences of the people involved, the terms Indian or Indian tribe are used instead of Native American.

Kate Spilde Contreras, applied cultural anthropologist, directed the multidisciplinary team of anthropologists, political scientists, economists, and historians. The research objective was to evaluate the social and economic effects of Indian gaming operations on tribal and local governments in California. The study relies mainly on public data, especially the 1990 and 2000 U.S. Censuses, to supply a "before" and "after" picture during the initial growth phase of Indian gaming in the state. To learn about more recent changes, the research team conducted surveys of tribal and local government officials and in-depth case studies of individual tribal governments.

Findings indicate two important factors that shape the effects of Indian gaming in California: gaming establishments are owned by tribal governments, and gaming establishments are located on existing tribal trust lands. Therefore, gaming revenues support community and government activities of the tribal communities, and employment generation is localized within the tribal communities.

Indian reservations in California are more economically heterogeneous than elsewhere in the United States.

Casino Sandia, located in the Sandia Pueblo in northern New Mexico, is one of many casinos in the state established in the hope of raising funds to improve the lives of Indian people.

Since the development of gaming, California also has greater economic inequality between gaming and nongaming reservations than is found in other states. By 2000, the fastest average income growth on California reservations occurred on gaming reservations. A policy response to this situation is a tribal-state gaming contract, the Revenue Sharing Trust Fund (RSTF) that provides for sharing of gaming revenue with nongaming communities.

Spilde Contreras's team considered the effects on gaming beyond the reservation. They found that areas within 10 miles of gaming reservations experienced significant employment increases, greater income growth, and more educational expansion than those farther away. Given the fact that reservations in California are located in the poorest regions, this location effect is progressive; that is, it helps poorer communities in favor of helping better-off communities.

Although the income and other effects of gaming in California are clearly substantial for Indians and their neighbors, Spilde Contreras points to the large gaps that still exist between conditions on Indian reservations and those for most Americans.

◆ FOOD FOR THOUGHT

- How does the recent development of Indian casinos connect with the theoretical perspective of structure versus agency?

Some degree of covert compulsion or dependence is likely to be present, however, in order for relationships of unequal exchange to endure.

Relationships between the Efe (eff-ay), who are "pygmy" foragers, and the Lese (less-ay), who are farmers, in the Democratic Republic of Congo exemplify sustained unequal exchange (Grinker 1994) (see Map 5). The Lese live in small villages. The Efe are seminomadic and live in temporary camps near Lese villages. Men of each group maintain long-term, hereditary exchange partnerships with each other. The Lese give cultivated foods and iron to the Efe, and the Efe give meat, honey, and other forest goods to the Lese.

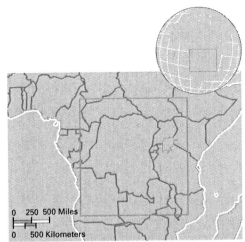

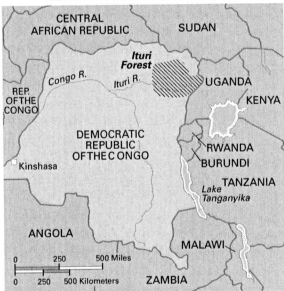

MAP 5   Lese and Efe Region in the Democratic Republic of Congo.
The Lese and Efe live in the Ituri Forest, a dense tropical rainforest in the northern part of the Congo River Basin. Cultural Survival supports the Ituri Forest Peoples Fund, which promotes the health and education of Efe foragers and Lese farmers. Go to the Internet to learn about the projects of the Ituri Forest Peoples Fund.

Each Efe partner is considered a member of the "house" of his Lese partner, although he lives separately. Their main link is the exchange of food items, a system conceptualized by the Lese not as trade but as sharing of co-produced goods by partners living in a single unit. Evidence of inequality exists, however, in these relationships, with the Lese having the advantage. The Efe provide much-wanted meat to the Lese, but this role gives them no status. Rather, it is the giving of cultivated foods by the Lese to the Efe that conveys status. Another area of inequality is marital and sexual relationships. Lese men may marry Efe women, and their children are considered Lese. Efe men, however, cannot marry Lese women.

Changing Patterns of Consumption and Exchange

Powerful market forces controlled by the core countries are the main factors affecting changing patterns of consumption and exchange. Local cultures, though, variously adopt and adapt globalizing products and their meanings. Sometimes they resist them outright.

SUGAR, SALT, AND STEEL TOOLS IN THE AMAZON

Katherine Milton, a biological anthropologist, has studied the nutritional effects of Western contact on the consumption patterns and health of indigenous foragers in the Brazilian Amazon. She comments:

> Despite the way their culture traditionally eschews possessions, forest-living people embrace manufactured goods with amazing enthusiasm. They seem to appreciate instantly the efficacy of a steel machete, ax, or cooking pot. It is love at first sight.... There are accounts of Indian groups or individuals who have turned their backs on manufactured goods, but such people are the exception. (1992:40)

The attraction to Western goods has its roots in the early decades of the twentieth century, when the Brazilian government sought to "pacify" Amazonian groups by placing cooking pots, machetes, axes, and steel knives along trails. This technique proved so successful that it is still used to "contact" remote groups. According to Milton:

> Once a group has been drawn into the pacification area, all its members are presented with various trade goods—standard gifts include metal cooking pots, salt, matches, machetes, knives, axes, cloth hammocks, T-shirts, and shorts.... Once the Indians have grown accustomed to these new items, the next step is to teach them that these gifts will not be repeated. The Indians are now told that they must work to earn money or must manufacture goods for trade so that they can purchase new items.
>
> Unable to contemplate returning to life without steel axes, the Indians begin to produce extra arrows or blowguns or hunt additional game or weave baskets beyond what they normally need so that this new surplus can be traded. Time that might, in the past, have been used for other tasks—subsistence activities, ceremonial events, or whatever—is now devoted to production of barter goods. (1992:40)

Adoption of Western foods has negatively affected the nutrition and health of indigenous Amazonian peoples. They have begun to use table salt and refined sugar. Previously, they consumed small quantities of salt made by burning certain leaves and collecting the ash, and sugar came from wild fruits,

A member of the Kayapo tribe of Brazil eats a popsicle during a break in a meeting of indigenous peoples to protest a dam-building project. Tooth decay, diabetes, and obesity are rising among indigenous peoples worldwide as a result of changing consumption patterns.

in the form of fructose. Sucrose, in contrast, tastes exceptionally sweet, and the Indians get hooked on it. Tooth decay, obesity, and diabetes are new and growing health risks. Milton comments, "The moment manufactured foods begin to intrude on the indigenous diet, health takes a downward turn" (1992:41).

SOCIAL INEQUALITY IN RUSSIA AND EASTERN EUROPE

As the countries of the former Soviet Union entered the global market economy, income inequality within those countries grew dramatically. The new rich own mansions and Mercedes-Benz cars. The influx of Western goods, including sugared soft drinks and junk food, was nicknamed *pepsistroika* by an anthropologist who did fieldwork in Moscow around the time of the transition to capitalism (Lempert 1996). Advertising messages encourage people to adopt new diets that include unhealthy amounts of rich food.

From 1961 to 1988, the consumption of calories, proteins, and fats in what are now Russia and Eastern Europe were above the level recommended by the World Health Organization and exceeded those of most middle-income countries worldwide (Cornia 1994). These countries had full

employment and little income inequality, so the high consumption levels were widely shared. This is not to say that diets were perfect. Especially in urban areas and among lower-income groups, people's diets contained less good-quality meat, fruits, vegetables, and vegetable oils. People tended to overconsume cholesterol-heavy products such as eggs and animal fats, sugar, salt, bread, and alcohol.

Income levels and consumption quality have fallen among the newly created poor. Now, there are two categories of poor people: the ultra-poor (those whose incomes are below the subsistence minimum, or between 25 and 35 percent of the average wage) and the poor (those whose incomes are above the subsistence minimum, but below the social minimum, or between 35 and 50 percent of the average wage). The largest increases in the number of ultra-poor occurred in Bulgaria, Poland, Romania, and Russia, where between 20 and 30 percent of the population are ultra-poor and another 20 to 40 percent are poor. Overall calorie and protein intake fell significantly. People in the ultra-poor category substitute less expensive sources of nutrients. They now consume more animal fats and starch, and less milk, animal proteins, vegetable oils, minerals, and vitamins. Rates of low-birthweight babies rose in Bulgaria and Romania, reflecting the deterioration in maternal diets, and the rate of childhood anemia rose dramatically in Russia.

GLOBAL NETWORKS AND ECSTASY IN THE UNITED STATES

In the late 1990s, a sharp increase in the use of ecstasy occurred in the United States (Agar and Reisinger 2003). Ecstasy, or MDMA (an abbreviation for its chemical name), is an illicit drug that produces a high without, apparently, leading to clinical dependence. Fieldwork and interviews in Baltimore, Maryland, revealed that ecstasy use "took off" in the late 1990s as the "up and coming" drug of choice among youth. As one research participant commented, "A lot of people I know like rolling, taking a pill of ecstasy and going to, like, a club or going to a school dance. I mean, alcohol is up and coming among like teenagers, like it's always been, but I think ecstasy's making a pretty powerful fight" (2003:2).

Official statistics confirmed this rise: In 1998, 10 percent of Baltimore County high school seniors reported that they had tried ecstasy; in 2001, the number had increased to nearly 20 percent. Nationwide statistics on reported use, arrests of distributors, and numbers of MDMA-related seizures reveal a similar pattern of increased use during this period. What accounts for this change? Two anthropologists conducted research to assess their hypothesis that there was a major change in the systems that produced and delivered the drug, leading to increased availability.

The standard story of the supply chain goes like this: Ecstasy is produced in the Netherlands and Belgium, distributed to the United States by Israelis, with a fuzzy role for

Russian organized crime along the way. Two anthropologists studied websites and media reports in 2000 and discovered a much more complicated story. They found a network of multiple and shifting production sites all over the world, including the largest illicit drug lab ever reported in Canadian history. Distribution channels are also highly diffuse. Although the simpler story may have been true in 1998, it was no longer true two years later. Perhaps as demand rose in the United States and elsewhere, this rise prompted the development of a wider network of production and distribution.

ALTERNATIVE FOOD MOVEMENTS IN EUROPE AND NORTH AMERICA

Starting in Europe in the 1980s, several alternative food movements have grown in Europe and North America (Pratt 2007). *Alternative food movements* seek to reestablish direct links between food producers, consumers, and marketers by promoting consumption of locally grown food and food that is not mass produced. Such movements exist in direct opposition to the agro-industrial food system, which:

- leads to economic ruin of small-scale producers who promote biodiversity
- shifts diet to fast foods, convenience food, take-away food, and microwave preparation
- transforms meals into eating on the run
- promotes a depersonalized, global market and supply chain, with Wal-Mart as the prime example
- has little regard for the environmental consequences of mass production and global marketing

Many alternative food movements exist. One of the first, Italy's Slow Food Movement, started in the late 1980s and has spread around the world. Naming itself in opposition to Western "fast food," the Slow Food Movement celebrates local agricultural traditions, seeks to protect consumers in terms of food quality, and advocates for social cooking, dining, and conviviality.

CONTINUITIES AND RESISTANCE: THE ENDURING POTLATCH

Potlatching among native peoples of the northwest coast of the United States and Canada was subjected to decades of opposition from Europeans and Euro-Americans (Cole 1991). The missionaries opposed potlatching as an unChristian practice. The government thought it was wasteful and excessive, out of line with their goals for the "economic progress" of the Indians. In 1885, the Canadian government outlawed the potlatch. Of all the Northwest Coast tribes, the Kwakwa̱ka̱'wakw (see Culturama) resisted this prohibition

Barbara Miller

The weekly market in Pistoia, a small town near Firenze (Florence), Italy, is set up each Saturday next to the main church. According to government regulations, all food items are supposed to have labels that identify where they were grown.

most strongly and for the longest time. In Canada, potlatches are no longer illegal. But it took a long battle to remove restrictions.

Reasons for giving a potlatch today are similar to those in the past: naming children, mourning the dead, transferring rights and privileges, celebrating marriages, and raising totem poles (Webster 1991). The length of time devoted to planning a potlatch, however, has changed. In the past, several years were involved compared to about a year now. Still, it takes much organization and work to accumulate enough goods to ensure that no guest goes away empty-handed, and the guest list may include between 500 and 1000 people. Another change is in the kinds of goods exchanged. Typical potlatch goods now include crocheted items (such as cushion covers, blankets, and potholders), glassware, plastic goods, manufactured blankets, pillows, towels, articles of clothing, and sacks of flour and sugar. The potlatch endures but changes.

CULTURAMA

The Kwakwaka'wakw of Canada

Several Northern First Nations recently adopted the name Kwakwaka'wakw to refer to a cluster of 20 linguistically related groups of Canada's Pacific Northwest region (Macnair 1995). Kwakwaka'wakw means "the people who speak Kwak'wala." It replaces the earlier term "Kwakiutl," which refers to only one of the several groups, and is therefore insulting to members of the other groups.

Their territory includes many islands as well as the waterways and deep inlets penetrating the Coast Mountains, a region of dense forests and sandy beaches. In earlier times, travel was mainly by canoe. Families moved seasonally with all their belongings packed in the canoe (Macnair 1995).

The Kwakwaka'wakw are famous for aspects of their material culture, including tall, carved wooden totem poles,

canoes, masks, and serving bowls, as well as richly decorated capes, skirts, and blankets.

Cedar is vital to the Kwakwaka'wakw. They use its wood for the objects just mentioned and the inner bark for garments. Women pounded the bark strips with a whale-bone beater until the fibers separated and became soft. They wove the strips on a loom or handwove them into mats used for sleeping on.

The first contact with Whites occurred in 1792, when explorer Captain George Vancouver arrived (Macnair 1995). At that time, the Kwakwaka'wakw numbered around 8000 people. Franz Boas arrived in 1886 and carried out research with the help of George Hunt, born of an English father and a high-ranking Tlingit (Northwest Coast) mother.

In the late nineteenth century, colonial authorities and missionaries disapproved of matters such as marriage arrangements and the potlatch, and enacted legislation to promote change, including a ban on potlatching from 1884 to 1951. The people continued, however, to potlatch in secret.

The Royal British Columbia Museum (RBCM) in Victoria, British Columbia, Canada, worked closely with Kwakwaka'wakw communities to document their potlatches and promote cultural revitalization (Kramer, personal communication 2006). The first legal potlatch of recent times, hosted by Mungo Martin in 1953, was held outside the RBCM.

Thanks to Jennifer Kramer, University of British Columbia, for reviewing this material.

© Vickie Jensen

(LEFT) Canoes and their crews from other Kwakwaka'wakw villages gather at Alert Bay in 1999 to help celebrate the opening of the newly built Big House.

(CENTER) Kwakwaka'wakw students practice the hamat'sa dance at a school in Alert Bay, under the tutelage of K'odi Nelson.

MAP 6 **The Kwakwaka' wakw Region in Canada.** The total number of Kwakwaka' wakw is over 5000 people.

the BIG questions REVISITED

◆ What is consumption in cross-cultural perspective?

Consumption includes a person's "intake" in terms of eating or other ways of using things and "output" in terms of spending or using resources to obtain those things. Anthropologists delineate two major modes of consumption. The first is minimalism, which is characterized by finite needs, the means of satisfying them, and sustainability. The second is consumerism, the mode of consumption with infinite needs, the inability to satisfy all needs, and lack of sustainability. Foraging societies typify the minimalist mode of consumption. Horticulture, pastoralism, and farming are associated with mixed patterns of consumption, with a rising trend toward consumerism. The consumerist mode of consumption is most clearly associated with industrialism/informatics.

In nonmarket economies, most consumers either produce the goods they use themselves or know who produced them. This is called personalized consumption. In market economies, consumption is largely depersonalized through globalized mass production.

Anthropologists define five consumption funds, the proportions of which vary in different economic systems. Microcultures such as "race"/ethnicity, class, and gender are linked to specific consumption patterns. Such patterns may involve inequalities that affect human welfare.

A long-standing area of interest in cultural anthropology is cross-cultural patterns of food taboos and why such taboos exist. Cultural materialists provide interpretations that consider the ecological and environmental contexts of such food taboos and how taboos make sense to people's material lives. Symbolic/interpretive anthropologists interpret food taboos as systems of meaning that give people a sense of identity and communicate that identity to others.

◆ What is exchange in cross-cultural perspective?

Exchange refers to the transfer of goods, both material and intangible, or services between people, groups, or institutions. Cross-culturally, people and groups exchange a wide variety of goods and services. Nonmarket exchange long existed without the use of money. Modern money is now found throughout most of the world, though some groups restrict its use.

Anthropologists define two modes of exchange. In balanced exchange, items of roughly equal value are exchanged over time between people who have a social relationship. In unbalanced exchange, the value of items transferred is unequal and there may or may not be a social relationship between the seller and buyer.

Market exchange, the main form of unbalanced exchange, is a transaction in which the seller's goal of making a profit overrides social relationships. Markets exist in many forms. Some are impermanent and irregular; some are impermanent and regular, as in a weekly farmer's market; and others are permanent. Recent technological developments have led to the creation of virtual marketplaces.

◆ How are consumption and exchange changing?

Globalizing capitalism is leading to many changes in consumption and exchange around the world. Globalization appears to provide benefits to securely entitled people in core countries. In other areas, it affects production, consumption and exchange in complex ways.

Many indigenous peoples are attracted by Western goods, such as steel axes and processed food. In order to obtain these goods, they must have cash, so they are lured into the cash economy and subject to the fluctuations of the world labor market. The nutritional and health status of many such groups has declined with the adoption of Western-style foods, especially large amounts of sugar and salt in food.

Other examples of change include the decline in consumption of nutritious food and increase in alcohol consumption in countries of the post-USSR, the rising popularity of the drug ecstasy among youth in the United States, and the rise of new food movements promoting small farm food production and local food consumption.

In spite of the powerful effects of globalization, some local cultures are standing up and claiming rights to their traditional forms of production, consumption, and exchange. The revitalization of the potlatch in Canada is an example.

KEY CONCEPTS

balanced exchange	generalized reciprocity	money
cash crop	leveling mechanism	potlatch
consumerism	market exchange	pure gift
consumption fund	minimalism	redistribution
entitlement	mode of consumption	trade
expected reciprocity	mode of exchange	unbalanced exchange

SUGGESTED READINGS

Theodore C. Bestor. *Tsukiji: The Fish Market at the Center of the World*. Berkeley: University of California Press, 2004. This ethnography of Tsukiji, the huge fish market in Tokyo, describes how it is a workplace for thousands of people, a central node in the Japanese fishing industry, and part of the global economy.

Denise Brennan. *What's Love Got to Do with It? Transnational Desires and Sex Tourism in the Dominican Republic*. Durham, NC: Duke University Press, 2004. This is an account of global sex tourism in the town of Sosúa, Dominican Republic, where Afro-Dominican and Afro-Haitian women sell sex to foreign, White tourists.

Michael F. Brown. *Who Owns Native Culture?* Cambridge, MA: Harvard University Press, 2003. This book documents the efforts of indigenous peoples to redefine heritage as a resource over which they claim proprietorship. It considers specific cases and proposes strategies for defending the rights of indigenous people within a market system.

Elizabeth Chin. *Purchasing Power: Black Kids and American Consumer Culture*. Minneapolis: University of Minnesota Press, 2001. The author did research with a fifth-grade class in a low-income, African American neighborhood in New Haven, Connecticut. These 10-year-olds, motivated by a strong sense of family responsibility, spend their money mainly on practical items and gifts for family members rather than status symbols.

Maris Boyd Gillette. *Between Mecca and Beijing: Modernization and Consumption among Urban Chinese Muslims*. Stanford, CA: Stanford University Press, 2000. For centuries, the Han majority have labeled Chinese Muslims, or Hui, of northwest China as a "backward" minority. Although the government seeks to "modernize" the Hui, the Hui challenge government policy by maintaining Islamic values.

Dwight B. Heath. *Drinking Occasions: Comparative Perspectives on Alcohol and Culture*. New York: Taylor & Francis, 2000. This book provides an ethnological review of alcohol consumption and looks at questions such as when people drink alcohol, where people drink, who drinks and who does not, what people drink, and why people drink.

Ann Kingsolver. *NAFTA Stories: Fears and Hopes in Mexico and the United States*. Boulder, CO: Lynne Reiner Publishers, 2001. The author collected and followed stories about NAFTA (North American Free Trade Agreement) during the early 1990s as told by everyday people in Mexico City and two cities in Morelos, Mexico. She worked collaboratively with a Mexican anthropologist for both ethical reasons and legal requirements and considers her research, and her book, an example of activist social documentation.

Bill Maurer. *Mutual Life, Limited: Islamic Banking, Alternative Currencies, Lateral Reason*. Princeton, NJ: Princeton University Press, 2005. This comparison of Islamic bankers who seek to avoid interest with local currency proponents who seek to provide an alternative to capitalist financial mechanisms shows how both resist and sometimes replicate Western capitalism.

Lisa Rofel. *Desiring China: Experiments in Neoliberalism, Sexuality, and Public Culture*. Durham, NC: Duke University Press, 2007. Fieldwork in Beijing and Hangzhou informs this study of new material and sexual desires in contemporary China.

Linda J. Seligmann, ed. *Women Traders in Cross-Cultural Perspective: Mediating Identities, Marketing Wares*. Stanford, CA: Stanford University Press, 2001. The chapters include attention to historic patterns of women's participation in Mexico's markets, and case studies of contemporary women marketeers in Java, South India, Ghana, the Philippines, Morocco, and Hungary.

Parker Shipton. *The Nature of Entrustment: Intimacy, Exchange, and the Sacred in Africa*. New Haven, CT: Yale University Press, 2007. This ethnographic study of the Luo people of western Kenya shows how the Luo assess obligations to others, including intimates and strangers.

CHAPTER 6

KINSHIP AND DOMESTIC LIFE

142

A Minangkabau bride in Sumatra, Indonesia, wears an elaborate gold headdress. Women play a central role among the Minangkabau, the world's largest matrilineal culture.

KINSHIP AND DOMESTIC LIFE

the BIG questions

- ◆ How do cultures create kinship ties through descent, sharing, and marriage?

- ◆ What are cross-cultural patterns of households and domestic life?

- ◆ How are kinship and households changing?

Learning how another kinship system works is as challenging as learning another language. Robin Fox became aware of this challenge during his research among the Tory Islanders of Ireland (see Map 1) (1995 [1978]). Some Tory Island kinship terms are similar to American English usage; for example, the word *muintir* means "people" in its widest sense, as in English. It can also refer to people of a particular social category, as in "my people," and to close relatives. Another similarity is in *gaolta*, the word for "relatives" or "those of my blood." Its adjectival form refers to kindness, like the English word kin, which is related to "kindness." Tory Islanders have a phrase meaning "children and grandchildren," also like the English term "descendants." One major difference is that the Tory Island word for "friend" is the same as the word for "kin." This usage reflects the cultural context of Tory Island with its small population, all related through kinship. So, logically, a friend is also kin.

All cultures have ways of defining *kinship*, or a sense of being related to another person or persons. Rules about kinship, the combination of rules about who are kin and the expected behavior of kin, are either informal or formalized in law or both. Starting in infancy, people learn about their particular culture's **kinship system**, the predominant form of kin relationships in a culture and the kinds of behavior involved. Like language, one's kinship system is so ingrained that it is taken for granted as something natural rather than cultural.

This chapter first considers cultural variations in three key features of kinship systems. It then focuses on a key unit of domestic life: the household. The last section provides examples of contemporary change in kinship patterns and household organization.

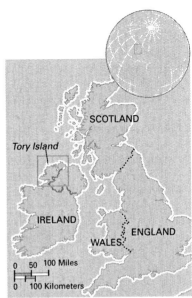

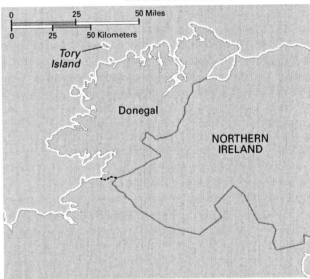

◆ ◆ ◆

How Cultures Create Kinship

In all cultures, kinship is linked with modes of livelihood and reproduction (see Figure 1). Nineteenth-century anthropologists found that kinship was the most important organizing principle in nonindustrial, nonstate cultures. The kinship group performs the functions of ensuring the continuity of the group by arranging marriages; maintaining social order by setting moral rules and punishing offenders; and providing for the basic needs of members by regulating production, consumption, and distribution. In large-scale industrial/informatics societies, kinship ties exist, but many other kinds of social ties draw people together.

Nineteenth-century anthropologists also discovered that definitions of who counts as kin differed widely from those of Europe and the United States. Western cultures emphasize "blood" relations as primary, or relations through birth from a

---

kinship system the predominant form of kin relationships in a culture and the kinds of behavior involved.

MAP 1 Ireland.
Ireland's population is about 4 million. The geography is low central plains surrounded by a ring of mountains. Membership in the European Union (EU) and the rising standard of living earned Ireland the nickname of the Celtic Tiger. Its economic opportunities are attracting immigrants from places as diverse as Romania, China, and Nigeria. Most people are Roman Catholics, followed by the Anglican Church of Ireland.

biological mother and biological father (Sault 1994). "Blood" is not a universal basis for kinship, however. Even in some cultures with a "blood"-based understanding of kinship, variations exist in defining who is a "blood" relative and who is not. For example, in some cultures, male offspring are considered of one "blood," whereas female offspring are not.

Among the Inuit of northern Alaska, behavior is a nonblood basis for determining kinship (Bodenhorn 2000). In this context, people who act like kin are kin. If a person stops acting like kin, then he or she is no longer a kinsperson. So, among the Inuit, someone might say that a certain person "used to be" his or her cousin.

Foraging	Horticulture	Pastoralism	Agriculture	Industrialism/Informatics
Descent and Inheritance				**Descent and Inheritance**
Bilineal	Unilineal (matrilineal or patrilineal)			Bilineal
Marital Residence				**Marital Residence**
Neolocal or bilocal	Matrilocal or patrilocal			Neolocal
Household Type				**Household Type**
Nuclear	Extended			Nuclear or single-parent or single-person

FIGURE 1 Modes of Livelihood, Kinship, and Household Structure

STUDYING KINSHIP: FROM FORMAL ANALYSIS TO KINSHIP IN ACTION

Anthropologists in the first half of the twentieth century focused on finding out who, in a particular culture, is related to whom and in what way. Typically, the anthropologist would conduct an interview with a few people, asking questions such as "What do you call your brother's daughter? Can you (as a man) marry your father's brother's daughter? What is the term you use to refer to your mother's sister?" The anthropologist would ask an individual to name all his or her relatives, explain how they are related to the interviewee, and provide the terms by which they refer to him or her.

From this information, the anthropologist would construct a *kinship diagram,* a schematic way of presenting the kinship relationships of an individual, called *ego,* using a set of symbols to depict all the kin relations of ego (see Figure 2). A kinship diagram depicts ego's relatives, as remembered by ego. In cultures where kinship plays a major role in social relations, ego may be able to provide information on dozens of relatives. When I (the author) took a research methods course as an undergraduate, I interviewed my Hindi language teaching assistant for a class assignment to construct a kinship diagram. He was from an urban, middle-class business family in India. He recalled over 60 relatives on both his father's and mother's sides, providing information for a much more extensive kinship diagram than I would have been able to provide for my middle-class, Euro-American relatives.

In contrast to a kinship diagram, a *genealogy* is a schematic way of presenting a family tree, constructed by beginning with the earliest ancestors that can be traced, then working down to the present. A genealogy, thus, does not begin with ego. When Robin Fox attempted to construct kinship diagrams beginning with ego, the Tory Islanders were uncomfortable with the approach. They preferred to proceed genealogically, so he followed their preference. Tracing a family's complete genealogy may involve archival research

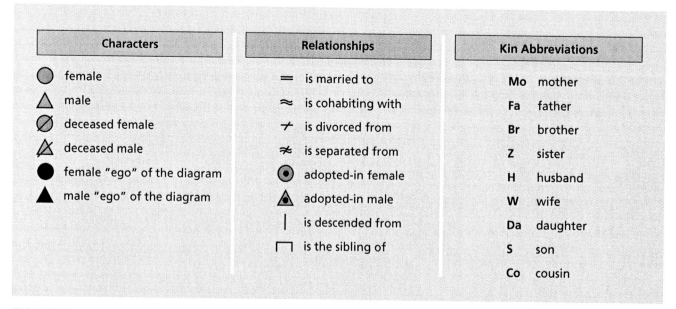

FIGURE 2 Symbols Used in Kinship Diagrams

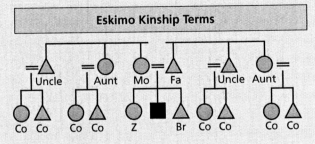

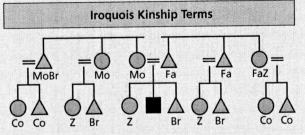

Eskimo kinship terminology, like that of most Euro-Americans, has unique terms for kin within the nuclear family that are not used for any other relatives: mother, father, sister, brother. This fact is related to the importance of the nuclear family. Another feature is that the same terms are used for relatives on both the mother's side and the father's side, a property that is related to bilineal descent.

Iroquois kinship terminology operates in unilineal systems. One result is that there are different terms for relatives on the mother's and father's sides and distinctions between cross and parallel cousins. Another feature is the "merging" of one's mother with one's mother's sister (both are referred to as "mother") and of one's father with one's father's brother (both are referred to as "father").

FIGURE 3 Two Kinship Naming Systems

in the attempt to construct as complete a history as possible. In Europe and the United States, Christians have long followed a practice of recording their genealogy in the front of the family Bible. Many African Americans and other people are consulting DNA analysts to learn about their ancestry and cultural heritage.

Decades of anthropological research have produced a mass of information on kinship terminology, or the words people use to refer to kin. For example, in Euro-American kinship, a child of one's father's sister or brother or one's mother's sister or brother is referred to by the kinship term "cousin." Likewise, one's father's sister and one's mother's sister are both referred to as "aunt," and one's father's brother and one's mother's brother are both referred to as "uncle." "Grandmother" and "grandfather" refer to the ascending generation on either one's father's or one's mother's side. This

---

descent the tracing of kinship relationships through parentage.

bilineal descent a kinship system in which a child is recognized as being related by descent to both parents.

unilineal descent a kinship system that traces descent through only one parent, either the mother or the father.

patrilineal descent a kinship system that highlights the importance of men in tracing descent, determining marital residence with or near the groom's family, and providing for inheritance of property through the male line.

matrilineal descent a kinship system that highlights the importance of women by tracing descent through the female line, favoring marital residence with or near the bride's family, and providing for property to be inherited through the female line.

---

merging pattern is not universal. In some cultures, different terms apply to kin on one's mother's and father's sides, so a mother's sister has a different kinship term than a father's sister. Another type of kinship system emphasizes solidarity along lines of siblings of the same gender. For example, among the Navajo of the American southwest. one's mother and one's mother's sisters have the same term, which translates as "mother."

Early anthropologists classified the cross-cultural variety in kinship terminology into six basic types, named after groups first discovered to have those systems. Two of the six types, for illustration, are the Iroquois type and the Eskimo type (see Figure 3). Anthropologists place various cultures with similar kinship terminology, no matter where they lived, into one of the six categories. Thus, the Yanomami people of the Amazon are classified as having an Iroquois naming system. Contemporary anthropologists who study kinship have moved beyond these categories because they feel that the six kinship types do not shed light on actual kinship dynamics. This book, therefore, presents only the two examples and avoids going into detail on the six classic types.

Current interest in the study of kinship shows how it is related to other topics, such as globalization, ethnic identity, and even terrorism. Anthropologists have come a long way from classifying kinship to showing how it matters. They focus on three key factors that, cross-culturally, construct kinship relations: descent, sharing, and marriage.

DESCENT

Descent is the tracing of kinship relationships through parentage. It is based on the fact that everybody is born from someone else. Descent creates a line of people from whom someone is descended, stretching through history. But not all cultures reckon descent in the same way. Some cultures have a **bilineal descent** system, in which a child is recognized as being related by descent to both parents. Others have a **unilineal descent** system, which recognizes descent through only one parent, either the father or the mother. The distribution of bilineal and unilineal systems is roughly correlated with different modes of livelihood (see Figure 1). This correspondence makes sense because economic systems—production, consumption, and exchange—are closely tied to the way people are socially organized.

UNILINEAL DESCENT Unilineal descent is the basis of kinship in about 60 percent of the world's cultures, making it the most common form of descent. This system tends to be found in societies with a fixed resource base. Thus, unilineal descent is most common among pastoralists, horticulturalists, and farmers. Inheritance rules that regulate the transmission of property through only one line help maintain cohesiveness of the resource base.

Unilineal descent has two major forms. One is **patrilineal descent**, in which kinship is traced through the male line. The other is **matrilineal descent**, in which kinship is traced through the female line. In a patrilineal system, only male children are considered members of the kinship lineage. Female children "marry out" and become members of the husband's lineage. In matrilineal descent systems, only daughters are considered to carry on the family line, and sons "marry out."

Patrilineal descent is found among about 45 percent of all cultures. It occurs throughout much of South Asia, East Asia, the Middle East, Papua New Guinea, northern Africa, and among some horticultural groups of sub-Saharan Africa. The world's most strongly patrilineal systems are found in East Asia, South Asia, and the Middle East (see Everyday Anthropology).

Matrilineal descent exists in about 15 percent of all cultures. It traces kinship through the female line exclusively, and the lineage consists of mothers and daughters and their daughters. It is found among many Native North American groups; across a large band of central Africa; among many groups of Southeast Asia and the Pacific, and Australia; in parts of eastern and southern India; in a small pocket of northern Bangladesh; and in parts of the Mediterranean coast of Spain and Portugal. Matrilineal societies are found among foragers and in agricultural societies. Most matrilineal cultures, however, are horticulturalist economies in which women dominate the production and distribution of food and other goods. Often, but not always, matrilineal kinship is associated with recognized public leadership positions for women, as among the Iroquois and Hopi. The Minangkabau (mee-NAN-ka-bow, with the last syllable rhyming with "now") of Indonesia are the largest matrilineal group in the world (see Culturama).

(TOP) Some members of a Bedu household in Yemen. Yemen is the most densely populated country of the Arabian peninsula. The Bedu are a small proportion of the Yemeni population. (BOTTOM) Boys playing in Hababa, Yemen. In this patrilineal culture, public space is segregated by gender.

▶ *If you were a cultural anthropologist working in Yemen, how would you proceed to learn about how Yemeni girls spend their time?*

BILINEAL DESCENT Bilineal descent traces kinship from both parents equally to the child. Bilineal descent is found in about one-third of the world's cultures (Murdock 1965 [1949]:57). The highest frequency of bilineal descent is found at the opposite ends of the modes of livelihood diagram (see Figure 1). For example, Ju/'hoansi foragers have bilineal descent as do most urban professionals in North America.

Both foraging and industrialism/informatics cultures rely on a flexible gender division of labor in which both males and females contribute, more or less equally, to making a living. Bilineal descent makes sense for foraging and industrial/informatics groups because it fits with small family units that are spatially mobile.

Marital residence rules tend to follow the prevailing direction of descent rules (see Figure 1). *Patrilocality*, or

everyday ANTHROPOLOGY

What's in a Name?

Naming children is always significant. Parents may follow cultural rules that a first-born son receives the name of his father's father or a first-born daughter receives the name of her mother's mother. Some parents believe that a newborn should not be formally named for a year or two, and the child is instead referred to by a nickname. Others think that a name must convey some special hoped-for attribute for the child, or that a name should be unique.

The village of Ha Tsuen is located in the northwest corner of a rural area of Hong Kong (Watson 1986). About 2500 people live in the village. All the males belong to the same patrilineage and all have the same surname of Teng. They are descended from a common male ancestor who settled in the region in the twelfth century. Daughters of Ha Tsuen marry into families outside the village, and marital residence is patrilocal.

Women do not own property, and they have no control of the household economy. Few married women are employed in wage labor. They depend on their husbands for financial support. Local politics is male-dominated, as is all public decision making. A woman's status as a new bride is low, and the transition from daughter to bride can be difficult psychologically. Women's primary role is in reproduction, especially of sons. As a woman bears children, especially sons, her status in the household rises.

The local naming system reflects the power, importance, and autonomy of males. All children are first given a name referred to as their *ming* when they are a few days old. If the baby is a boy, the 30-day ceremony is as elaborate as the family can afford. It may include a banquet for many neighbors and the village elders and the presentation of red eggs to everyone in the community. For a girl, the 30-day ceremony may involve only a special meal for close family members. Paralleling this expenditure bias toward sons is the thinking that goes into selecting the *ming*. A boy's ming is distinctive and flattering. It may have a classical literary connection. A girl's ming often has negative connotations, such as "Last Child," "Too Many," or "Little Mistake." One common ming for a daughter is "Joined to a Brother," which implies the hope that she will be a lucky charm, bringing the birth of a son next. Sometimes, though, people give an uncomplimentary name to a boy such as "Little Slave Girl." The reason behind this naming practice is protection—to trick the spirits into thinking the baby is only a worthless girl so that the spirits will do no harm.

Marriage is the next formal naming occasion. When a male marries, he is given or chooses for himself a *tzu*, or marriage name. Gaining a tzu is a key marker of male adulthood. The tzu is not used in everyday address, but appears mainly on formal documents. A man also has a *wai hao*, "outside name," which is his public nickname. As he enters middle age, he may take a *hao*, or courtesy name, which he chooses and which reflects his aspirations and self-perceptions.

---

marital residence with or near the husband's family, occurs in patrilineal societies, whereas *matrilocality* or marital residence with or near the wife's family, occurs in matrilineal societies. *Neolocality,* or marital residence in a place different from either the bride's or groom's family, is common in Western industrialized society. Residence patterns have political, economic, and social implications. Patrilineal descent and patrilocal residence, for example, promote the development of cohesive male-focused lineages associated with warfare.

SHARING

Many cultures emphasize kinship ties based on acts of sharing and support. These relationships may be either informal or formally certified. Godparenthood and blood brotherhood are examples of sharing-based kinship that are ritually formalized.

KINSHIP THROUGH FOOD SHARING Sharing-based kinship is common in Southeast Asia, Papua New Guinea, and Australia (Carsten 1995). Among inhabitants of one of Malaysia's many small islands, sharing-based kinship starts in the womb when the mother's blood feeds the fetus. After birth, the mother's breast milk nourishes the infant. This tie is crucial. A child who is not breastfed will not "recognize" its mother. Breastfeeding is also the basis of the incest rule. People who have been fed from the same breast are kin and may not marry. After the baby is weaned, its most important food is cooked rice. Sharing cooked rice, like breast milk, becomes another way that kinship ties are created and maintained, especially between women and children. Men are often away on fishing trips, in coffee shops, or at the mosque and so are not likely to have rice-sharing kinship bonds with children.

ADOPTION AND FOSTERING Another form of sharing-based kinship is the transfer of a child or children from the birth parent(s) to the care of someone else. Adoption is a formal and permanent form of child transfer. Common motivations for adoption include infertility and the desire to

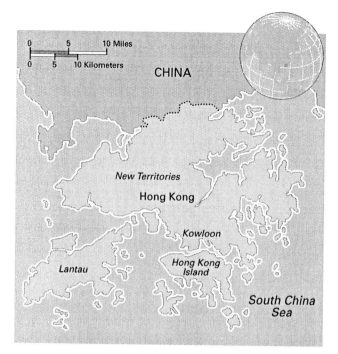

MAP 2 Hong Kong.
The formal name of Hong Kong is the Hong Kong Special Administrative Region of the People's Republic of China. A world center of finance and trade, it lacks natural resources and agricultural land, so it imports most of its food and raw materials. With 7 million residents, Hong Kong's population density is high. Most of the population is ethnic Chinese, and many practice ancestor worship. Ten percent of the population is Christian. Religious freedom is protected through its constitution.

In the case of a woman, her ming ceases to exist when she marries. She no longer has a name. Instead, her husband refers to her as *nei jen*, "inner person," because now her life is restricted to the domestic world of household, husband's family, and neighborhood. People may also refer to her by *teknonyms*, or names for someone based on their relationship to someone else, such as "Wife of So and So" or "Mother of So and So." In old age, she becomes *ah po*, "Old Woman".

Throughout their lives, men accumulate more and better names than women. They choose many of the names themselves. Over the course of their lives, women have fewer names than men. Women's names are standardized, not personalized, and women never get to choose any of their names.

◆ **FOOD FOR THOUGHT**

* Go to www.slate.com/id/2116505/ (Trading Up: Where Do Baby Names Come From? by Steven D. Levitt and Stephen J. Dubner) and read about the status game of child naming in the United States. How does your first name fit into this picture?

obtain a particular kind of child (often a son). Motivations for the birth parent to transfer a child to someone else include a premarital pregnancy in a disapproving context, having "too many" children, and having "too many" of a particular gender. Among the Maasai, a woman who has several children might give one to a friend, neighbor, or aged person who has no children to care for her or him.

Since the mid-1800s, adoption has been a legalized form of child transfer in the United States. Judith Modell, cultural anthropologist and adoptive parent, studied people's experiences of adoptees, birth parents, and adoptive parents in the United States (1994). She found that the legal process of adoption constructs the adoptive relationship to be as much like a biological one as possible. In *closed adoption*, the adopted child receives a new birth certificate, and the birth parent ceases to have any relationship to the child. A recent trend is toward *open adoption*, in which adoptees and birth parents have information about each other's identity and are free to interact with one another. Of the 28 adoptees Modell interviewed, most were interested in searching for their birth parents. The search for birth parents involves an attempt to discover "who I really am." For others, such a search is backward-looking instead of being a path toward identity formation. Thus, in the United States, adoption legalizes sharing-based kinship but does not always replace a sense of descent-based kinship for everyone involved.

Fostering a child is sometimes similar to a formal adoption in terms of permanence and a sense of kinship. Or it may be temporary placement of a child with someone else for a specific purpose, with little or no sense of kinship. Child fostering is common throughout sub-Saharan Africa. Parents foster out children to enhance the child's chances for formal education or so that the child will learn a skill such as marketing. Most foster children go from rural to urban areas and from poorer to better-off households. Fieldwork conducted in a neighborhood in Accra, Ghana (see Map 4), sheds light on the lives of foster children (Sanjek 1990). Child fostering in the neighborhood is common: About one-fourth of the children were foster children. Twice as many of the foster

KINSHIP AND DOMESTIC LIFE

scholars, merchants, and politicians. Inheritance of property, including

ditional house has upward curves that echo the shape of water buffalo horns.

Emory University, for reviewing this material.

© Wolfgang Kachler/CORBIS

© Lindsay Hebberd/CORBIS

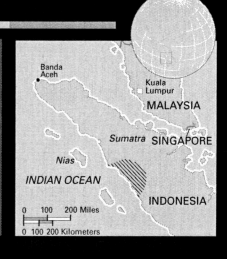

(LEFT) A traditional wooden Minangkabau longhouse with its distinctive upward-pointing roof. The house interiors are divided into separate "bays" for submatrilineal groups. Many are no longer places of residence but are used as meeting halls or are falling into ruin.

(CENTER) The symbolic importance of water buffaloes, apparent in the shape of traditional rooftops, is reiterated in the shape of girls' and women's ceremonial headdress. The headdress represents women's responsibilities for the growth and strength of Minangkabau culture.

MAP 3 **Minangkabau Region in Indonesia.** The shaded area shows the traditional heartland of Minangkabau culture in western Sumatra. Many Minangkabau people live elsewhere in Sumatra and in neighboring Malaysia.

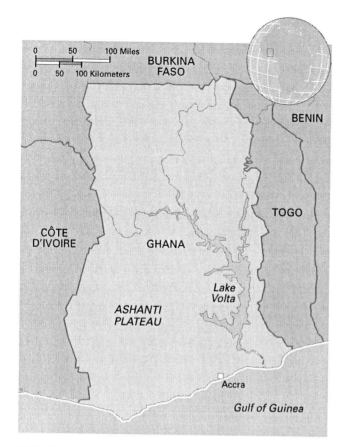

MAP 4 Ghana.
The Republic of Ghana has over 20 million people. Ghana has rich natural resources and exports gold, timber, and cocoa. Agriculture is the basis of the domestic economy. Several ethnic groups exist, with the Akan people constituting over 40 percent of the population. English is the official language, but another 80 or so languages are also spoken. Over 60 percent of the people are Christian, 20 percent follow traditional religions, and 16 percent are Muslim.

children were girls as boys. School attendance is biased toward boys. All of the boys were attending school, but only 4 of the 31 girls were. An important factor affecting the treatment of the child is whether the fostered child is related to his or her sponsor. Although 80 percent of the foster children as a whole were kin of their sponsors, only 50 percent of the girls were kin. People who sponsor nonkin girls make a cash payment to the girl's parents. These girls cook, do housecleaning, and assist in market work by carrying goods or watching the trading area. Fostered boys, most of whom are kin of their sponsors, do not perform such tasks because they attend school.

RITUALLY ESTABLISHED KINSHIP Ritually defined ties between adults and children born to other people are common among Christians, especially Catholics, worldwide. Relationships between godparents and godchildren often involve strong emotional ties and financial flows from the former to the latter. In Arembepe, a village in Bahia state in northeastern Brazil, children request a blessing from their godparents the first time they see them each day (Kottak

1992:61). Godparents give their godchildren cookies, candy, and money, and larger presents on special occasions.

Among the Maya of Oaxaca, Mexico, godparenthood is both a sign of the sponsor's status and the means to increased status for the sponsor (Sault 1985). A parent's request that someone sponsor his or her child is a public acknowledgment of the sponsor's standing. The godparent gains influence over the godchild and can call on the godchild for labor. Being a godparent of many children means that the godparent can amass a large labor force when needed and gain further status. Most godparents in Oaxaca are husband–wife couples, but many are women alone, a pattern that reflects the high status of Maya women.

MARRIAGE

The third major basis for forming close interpersonal relationships is through marriage or other forms of "marriage-like" relationships, such as long-term cohabitation. The following material focuses on marriage.

TOWARD A DEFINITION Anthropologists recognize that some concept of *marriage* exists in all cultures, though it may take different forms and serve different functions. What constitutes a cross-culturally valid definition of marriage is, however, open to debate. A standard definition from 1951 is now discredited: "Marriage is a union between a man and a woman such that children born to the woman are the recognized legitimate offspring of both parents" (Barnard and Good 1984:89). This definition says that the partners must be of different genders, and it implies that a child born outside a marriage is not socially recognized as legitimate. Exceptions exist to both these features cross-culturally. Same-gender marriages are legal in Denmark, Norway, and Holland. The legal status of same-gender marriage is a subject of ongoing debate in the United States and Canada. In the United States, as of 2008, the states of Massachusetts and California recognize same-sex marriage.

Deanne Fitzmaurice/San Francisco Chronicle/CORBIS

Jillian Armenante (LEFT), actress on *Judging Amy,* and her bride, Alice Dodd, call friends and family after their marriage ceremony in City Hall, San Francisco, in 2004.

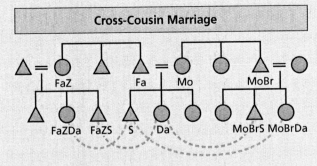
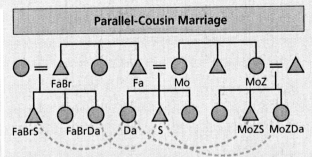

Cross-cousin marriage: A daughter marries either her father's sister's son or her mother's brother's son. A son marries either his father's sister's daughter or his mother's brother's daughter.

Parallel-cousin marriage: A daughter marries either her father's brother's son or her mother's sister's son. A son marries either his father's brother's daughter or his mother's sister's daughter.

FIGURE 4 Two Forms of Cousin Marriage

In many cultures no distinction is made between legitimate and illegitimate children on the basis of whether they were born within a marriage. Women in the Caribbean region, for example, typically do not marry until later in life. Before that, a woman has sequential male partners with whom she bears children. None of her children is considered more or less "legitimate" than any other.

Other definitions of marriage focus on rights over the spouse's sexuality. But not all forms of marriage involve sexual relations; for example, the practice of *woman–woman marriage* exists among the Nuer of southern Sudan and some other African groups (Evans-Pritchard 1951:108–109). In this type of marriage, a woman with economic means gives gifts to obtain a "wife," goes through the marriage rituals with her, and brings her into the residential compound just as a man would who married a woman. This wife contributes her productive labor to the household. The two women do not have a sexual relationship. Instead, the in-married woman will have sexual relations with a man. Her children, though, will belong to the compound into which she married.

---

marriage a union between two people (usually), who are likely to be, but are not necessarily, coresident, sexually involved with each other, and procreative.

incest taboo a strongly held prohibition against marrying or having sex with particular kin.

endogamy marriage within a particular group or locality.

parallel cousin offspring of either one's father's brother or one's mother's sister.

cross-cousin offspring of either one's father's sister or one's mother's brother.

The many practices that come under the heading of marriage make it impossible to find a definition that will fit all cases. One might accept the following as a working definition of **marriage**: a more or less stable union, usually between two people, who may be, but are not necessarily, coresidential, sexually involved with each other, and procreative with each other.

SELECTING A SPOUSE All cultures have preferences about whom one should and should not marry or with whom one should and should not have sexual intercourse. Sometimes these preferences are informal and implicit, and other times they are formal and explicit. They include both rules of exclusion (who one should not marry) and rules of inclusion (who is a preferred marriage partner).

An **incest taboo**, or rule prohibiting marriage or sexual intercourse between certain kinship relations, is one of the most basic and universal rules of exclusion. In his writings of the 1940s, Claude Lévi-Strauss proposes a reason for the universality of incest taboos by saying that, in premodern societies, incest avoidance motivated men to exchange women between families. In his view, this exchange is the foundation for all social networks and social solidarity beyond the immediate group. Such networks promote trade between areas with different resources and peace through ties established by bride exchange. So, for him, the incest taboo has important social and economic functions: It impels people to create social organization beyond the family.

Contemporary genetic research suggests an alternate theory for universal incest taboos. It says that larger breeding pools reduce the frequency of genetically transmitted conditions. Like the theory of Lévi-Strauss, the genetic theory is functional. Each theory attributes the universal existence of incest taboos to their adaptive contribution to human survival and success, though in two different ways. Anthropological data support both theories, but ethnographic data provide some puzzles to consider.

The most basic and universal form of incest taboo is against marriage or sexual intercourse between fathers and their children, and mothers and their children. Although most cultures forbid brother–sister marriage, exceptions exist. The most well-known example of brother–sister marriage comes from Egypt at the time of the Roman Empire (Barnard and Good 1984:92). Brother–sister marriage was the norm among royalty, but it was common among the general population, with between 15 and 20 percent of marriages between full brothers and sisters.

Further variations in close-relation marriage arise in terms of cousins. Incest taboos do not universally rule out marriage with cousins. In fact, some kinship systems promote cousin marriage, as discussed next.

Many preference rules exist cross-culturally concerning whom one should marry. Rules of **endogamy**, or marriage within a particular group, stipulate that the spouse must be from a defined social category. In kin endogamy, certain relatives are preferred, often cousins. Two major forms of cousin marriage exist. One is marriage between **parallel cousins**, children of either one's father's brother or one's mother's sister—the term *parallel* indicates that the linking siblings are of the same gender (see Figure 4). The second is marriage between **cross-cousins**, children of either one's father's sister or one's mother's brother—the term *cross* indicates the different genders of the linking siblings. Parallel-cousin marriage is favored by many Muslim groups in the Middle East and northern Africa, especially the subform called *patrilateral parallel-cousin marriage*, which is cousin marriage into the father's line.

In contrast, Hindus of southern India favor *matrilateral cross-cousin marriage*, which is cousin marriage into the mother's line. Although cousin marriage is preferred, it nonetheless is a minority of all marriages in the region. A survey of several thousand couples in the city of Chennai (formerly called Madras) (see Map 5) in southern India showed that three-fourths of all marriages involved unrelated people, whereas one-fourth were between first cross-cousins or between uncle and niece, which is considered to be the same relationship as that of cross-cousins (Ramesh, Srikumari, and Sukumar 1989).

Readers who are unfamiliar with cousin marriage may find it objectionable on the basis of the potential genetic disabilities from close inbreeding. A study of thousands of such marriages in southern India, however, revealed only a small difference in rates of congenital problems compared to cultures in which cousin marriage is not practiced (Sundar Rao 1983). Marriage networks in South India are diffuse, extending over a wide area and offering many options for "cousins." This situation contrasts to the much more closed situation of a single village or town. In cases where cousin marriage exists

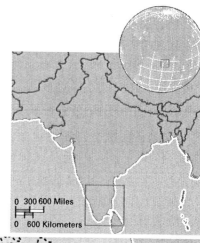

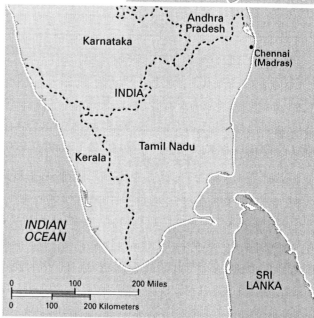

MAP 5 South India.
The states of southern India, compared to the northern states, have lower population density, lower fertility rates, higher literacy rates, and less severe gender inequality. Agriculture is the mainstay of the region's economy and the population is predominantly rural. Industry, information technology, and business process outsourcing (BPO) are of increasing importance in cities such as Chennai and Bangalore.

among a small and circumscribed population, then the possibility of negative genetic effects is high.

Endogamy may also be based on location. Village endogamy is preferred in the eastern Mediterranean among both Christians and Muslims. It is also the preferred pattern

THINKING
OUTSIDE
THE BOX

Do some research on www.match.com to learn what cultural preferences people mention in their profiles.

Hypergyny	The bride marries a groom of higher status.	The groom may be wealthier, more educated, older, taller.
Hypogyny	The bride marries a groom of lower status.	The bride may be wealthier, more educated, older, taller.
Isogamy	The bride and groom are status equals.	The bride and groom have similar wealth, education, age, height.

among Muslims throughout India and among Hindus of southern India. Hindus of northern India, in contrast, forbid village endogamy and consider it a form of incest. Instead, they practice village **exogamy**, or marriage outside a defined social group. For them, a spouse should live in a far-off village or town. In India, marriage distance is greater in the north than in the south, and northern brides are thus far less likely to be able to maintain regular contact with their birth family. Many songs and stories of northern Indian women convey sadness about being separated from their birth families.

Status considerations often shape spouse selection (see Figure 5). (The following discussion pertains to heterosexual marriage.) *Hypergyny,* or "marrying up," refers to a marriage in which the bride has lower status than the groom. Hypergyny is widely practiced in northern India, especially among upper-status groups. It is also prominent among many middle- and upper-class people in the United States. Women in top professions such as medicine and law have a difficult time finding an appropriate partner because there are few, if any, options for higher-status marriage partners. Women medical students in North America are experiencing an increased marriage squeeze because of status hypergyny. The opposite pattern is *hypogyny,* or "marrying down," a marriage in which the bride has higher status than the groom. Hypogyny is rare cross-culturally. *Isogamy,* marriage between partners who are status equals, occurs in cultures where male and female roles and status are equal.

Subtypes of status-based hypergyny and hypogyny occur on the basis of factors such as age and even height. Age hypergyny refers to a marriage in which the bride is younger than the groom, a common practice worldwide. In contrast, age hypogyny is a marriage in which the bride is older than the groom. Age hypogyny is rare cross-culturally but has been increasing in the United States due to the marriage squeeze on women who would otherwise prefer a husband of equal age or somewhat older.

Physical features, such as ability, looks, and appearance, are factors that may be explicitly or implicitly involved in spouse selection. Facial beauty, skin color, hair texture and length, height, and weight are variously defined as important. Height hypergyny (in which the groom is taller than the

bride) is more common in male-dominated contexts. Height-isogamous marriages are common in cultures where gender roles are relatively equal and where sexual dimorphism (differences in shape and size of the female body compared to the male body) is not marked, as in much of Southeast Asia.

People with physical disabilities, particularly women, face constraints in marrying nondisabled partners (Sentumbwe 1995). Nayinda Sentumbwe, a blind researcher, conducted fieldwork with participants in education and rehabilitation programs for blind people in Uganda, central Africa. He realized that all of the married blind women in his study had blind spouses. Many of the married blind men had wives who were not blind. In exploring the reason for this pattern, Sentumbwe considered Ugandan gender roles, especially that of the housewife. People said that blindness decreases women's competence as wives and mothers and therefore reduces their desirability as spouses. Ugandan housewives have many roles: mother, hostess, housekeeper, keeper of the homestead, provider of meals, and provider of home-grown food, among others. Because a man wants a "competent" wife, blind women as partners are avoided. Ugandan men, however, often choose blind women as lovers. The relationship between lovers is private and does not involve social competence in the woman.

© Rick Smolan/Stock Boston, LLC

Men and women in Southeast Asia are similar in height and weight, as is the case with this couple from Bali, Indonesia.

▶ *What are your cultural perceptions of the height of an ideal partner for you?*

---

exogamy marriage outside a particular group or locality.

Jack Heaton

The Taj Mahal, located in Agra, northern India, is a seventeenth-century monument to love. It was built by the Mughal emperor Shah Jahan as a tomb for his wife, Mumtaz Mahal, who died in childbirth in 1631.

The role of romantic love in spouse selection is debated by biological determinists and cultural constructionists. Biological determinists argue that feelings of romantic love are universal among all humans because they play an adaptive role in uniting males and females in care of offspring. Cultural constructionists, in contrast, argue that romantic love is an unusual factor influencing spouse selection (Barnard and Good 1984:94). The cultural constructionists point to variations in male and female economic roles to explain cross-cultural differences in the emphasis on romantic love. Romantic love is more likely to be an important factor in relationships in cultures where men contribute more to subsistence and where women are therefore economically dependent on men. Whatever the cause of romantic love, biological or cultural or both, it is an increasingly common basis for marriage in many cultures (Levine et al. 1995).

Within the United States, microcultural variations exist in the degree to which women value romantic love as a basis for marriage (Holland and Eisenhart 1990). One study interviewed young American women entering college from 1979 to 1981 and again in 1987 after they had graduated and begun their adult lives. The research sites were two southern colleges in the United States, one attended mainly by White Euro-Americans and the other by African Americans. A contrast between the groups of women emerged. The White women were much more influenced by notions of romantic love than the Black women. The White women were also less likely to have strong career goals and more likely to expect to be economically dependent on their spouse. The Black women expressed independence and strong career goals. The theme of romantic love supplies young White women with a model of the heroic male provider as the ideal, with her role being one of attracting him and providing the domestic context for their married life. The Black women were brought up to be more economically independent. This pattern is related to African traditions in which women earn and manage their own earnings and the racially discriminatory job market in the United States that places African American men at a severe disadvantage.

Arranged marriages are formed on the basis of parents' considerations of what constitutes a "good match" between the families of the bride and groom. Arranged marriages are common in many Middle Eastern, African, and Asian countries. Some theorists claim that arranged marriages are "traditional" and love marriages are "modern." They believe arranged marriages will disappear with modernity. Japan presents a case of an industrial/informatics economy with a highly educated population in which arranged unions still constitute a substantial proportion of all marriages, about 25 to 30 percent (Applbaum 1995). In earlier times, marriage partners would be found through personal networks, perhaps with the help of an intermediary who knew both families. Now, in large cities such as Tokyo and Osaka, professional matchmakers play an important role in finding marriage partners. The most important criteria for a spouse are the family's reputation and social standing, the absence of undesirable traits such as a case of divorce or mental illness in the family, education, occupation, and income.

The new billionaires of China (multimillionaires in terms of dollars) are men with wealth and interest in marrying a virgin woman (French 2006). They have turned to advertising to seek applications from prospective brides. In Shanghai, an enterprising lawyer began a business by managing the advertising and applicant screening for over 50 billionaires. On average, the process takes three months.

MARRIAGE GIFTS Most marriages are accompanied by exchanges of goods or services between the partners, members of their families, and friends (see Figure 6). The two major forms of marital exchanges cross-culturally are dowry and brideprice.

THINKING
OUTSIDE
THE BOX

What is your opinion about the relative merits of love marriages versus arranged marriages, and on what do you base your opinion?

FIGURE 6 Major Types of
Marriage Exchanges

Dowry	Goods and money given by the bride's family to the married couple	European and Asian cultures; agriculturalists and industrialists
Groomprice	Goods and money given by the bride's family to the married couple and to the parents of the groom	South Asia, especially northern India
Brideprice	Goods and money given by the groom's family to the parents of the bride	Asian, African, and Central and South American cultures; horticulturalists and pastoralists
Bride service	Labor given by the groom to the parents of the bride	Southeast Asian, Pacific, and Amazonian cultures; horticulturalists

Dowry is the transfer of goods, and sometimes money, from the bride's side to the new married couple for their use. The dowry includes household goods such as furniture, cooking utensils, and sometimes rights to a house. Dowry is the main form of marriage transfer in farming societies throughout Eurasia, from Western Europe through the northern Mediterranean and into China and India. In much of India, dowry is more accurately termed *groomprice* because the goods and money pass not to the new couple but rather to the groom's family (Billig 1992). In China during the Mao era, the government considered dowry a sign of women's oppression and made it illegal. The practice of giving dowry in China has returned with increased personal wealth and consumerism, especially among the newly rich urban populations (Whyte 1993).

Brideprice, or bridewealth, is the transfer of goods or money from the groom's side to the bride's parents. It is common in horticultural and pastoralist cultures. **Brideservice**, a subtype of brideprice, is a transfer of labor from the groom to his parents-in-law for a designated time period. It is practiced in some horticultural societies, especially in the Amazon.

The Hausa are an important ethnic group of Ghana. This photograph shows a display of Hausa dowry goods in Accra, the capital city. The most valuable part of a Hausa bride's dowry is the *kayan dak'i* ("things of the room"). It consists of bowls, pots, ornamental glass, and cookware, which are conspicuously displayed in the bride's marital house so that the local women can get a sense of her worth. The bride's parents pay for these status items and for utilitarian items such as everyday cooking utensils.

brideservice a form of marriage exchange in which the groom works for his father-in-law for a certain period of time before returning home with the bride.

monogamy marriage between two people.

polygamy marriage involving multiple spouses.

polygyny marriage of one husband with more than one wife.

polyandry marriage of one wife with more than one husband.

family a group of people who consider themselves related through a form of kinship, such as descent, marriage, or sharing.

household a group of people, who may or may not be related by kinship, who share living space.

nuclear household a domestic unit containing one adult couple (married or partners), with or without children.

extended household a coresidential group that comprises more than one parent–child unit.

KINSHIP AND DOMESTIC LIFE

Many marriages involve gifts from both the bride's and the groom's side. For example, a typical pattern in the United States is that the groom's side is responsible for paying for the rehearsal dinner the night before the wedding, whereas the bride's side bears the costs of everything else.

FORMS OF MARRIAGE Cultural anthropologists distinguish two forms of marriage on the basis of the number of partners involved. **Monogamy** is marriage between two people—a male or female if the pair is heterosexual, or two people of the same gender in the case of a homosexual pair. Heterosexual monogamy is the most common form of marriage cross-culturally, and in many countries it is the only legal form of marriage.

Polygamy is marriage involving multiple spouses, a pattern allowed in many cultures. Two forms of polygamous marriage exist. The more common of the two is **polygyny**, marriage of one man with more than one woman. **Polyandry**, or marriage between one woman and more than one man, is rare. The only place where polyandry is commonly found is in the Himalayan region that includes parts of Tibet, India, and Nepal. Nonpolyandrous people in the area look down on the people who practice polyandrous marriage as backward (Haddix McCay 2001).

◆◆◆
Households and Domestic Life

In casual conversation, North Americans might use the words *family* and *household* interchangeably to refer to people who live together. Social scientists, however, propose a distinction between the two terms. A **family** is a group of people who consider themselves related through kinship. In North American English, the term includes both close or immediate relatives and more distant relatives. All members of a family do not necessarily live together or have strong bonds with one another.

A related term is the **household**, a person or persons who occupy a shared living space and who may or may not be related by kinship. Most households consist of members who are related through kinship, but an increasing number do not. An example of a nonkin household is a group of friends who live in the same apartment. A single person living alone also constitutes a household. This section of the chapter looks at household forms and organization cross-culturally and relationships between and among household members.

THE HOUSEHOLD: VARIATIONS ON A THEME

This section considers three forms of households and the concept of household headship. The topic of female-headed households receives detailed attention because this pattern of headship is widely misunderstood.

The woman on the lower right is part of a polyandrous marriage, which is still practiced among some Tibetan peoples. She is married to several brothers, two of whom stand behind her. The older man with the sash in the front row is her father-in-law.

HOUSEHOLD FORMS Household organization is divided into types according to how many married adults are involved. The **nuclear household** (which many people call the nuclear family) is a domestic group that contains one adult couple (married or "partners"), with or without children. An **extended household** is a domestic group that contains more than one adult married couple. The couples may be related through the father–son line (making a *patrilineal extended household*), through the mother–daughter line (a *matrilineal extended household*), or through sisters or brothers (a *collateral extended household*). Polygynous (multiple wives) and polyandrous (multiple husbands) households are *complex households*, domestic units in which one spouse lives with or near multiple partners and their children.

The precise cross-cultural distribution of these various types is not known, but some broad generalizations can be offered. First, nuclear households are found in all cultures but are the exclusive household type in only about one-fourth of the world's cultures (Murdock 1965 [1949]:2). Extended households are the most important form in about half of all cultures. The distribution of these two household forms corresponds roughly with the modes of livelihood (see Figure 1). The nuclear form is most characteristic of economies at the two extremes of the continuum: foraging groups and industrialized/informatic societies. This pattern reflects the need for spatial mobility and flexibility in both

THINKING OUTSIDE THE BOX

In your microculture, what are the prevailing ideas about wedding expenses and who should pay for them?

In China, the stem household system is changing because many people have one daughter and no son as a result of lowered fertility and the One-Child-Per-Family Policy.

▶ *Speculate about what the next generation of this household might contain.*

modes of production. Extended households constitute a substantial proportion of households in horticultural, pastoralist, and farming economies.

In Japan and other parts of East Asia, a subtype of the extended household structure has endured within the context of an industrial/postindustrial and urban economy. The *ie*, or **stem household**, is a variation of an extended household containing two (and only two) married couples related through the male line. Only one son remains in the household, bringing in his wife, who is expected to perform the important role of caretaker for the husband's parents as they age. Although people throughout East Asia still prefer the *ie*, it is increasingly difficult to achieve due to changing economic aspirations of children, who do not want to dedicate their lives to caring for their aging parents. Aging parents who find that none of their children is willing to live with them and take responsibility for their care exert considerable pressure on an adult child to come and live with them (Traphagan 2000). A compromise is for an adult child and his or her spouse to live near the parents but not with them.

HOUSEHOLD HEADSHIP The question of who heads a household is often difficult to answer. This section reviews some approaches to this question and provides insights into how cross-cultural perceptions about household headship differ.

The *household head* is the primary person, or persons, responsible for supporting the household financially and making major decisions. This concept of household head is based on a Euro-American view that emphasizes the income contribution of the head, traditionally a man. European colonialism spread the concept of the male, income-earning head of household around the world, along with laws that placed household authority in male headship.

The model of a male household head influences the way official statistics are gathered worldwide. If a household has a coresident man and woman, there is a tendency to report the household as male headed. In Brazil, for example, the official definition of household head considers only a husband to be head of the household, regardless of whether he contributes to the household budget. Single, separated, or widowed women who are responsible for household support are deprived of the title of household head. If they happen to have a man visiting them on the day the census official arrives, he is considered to be the household head (de Athayde Figueiredo and Prado 1989:41). Similarly, according to official reports, 90 percent of households in the Philippines are headed by males (Illo 1985). Filipino women, however, play a prominent role in income generation and budgetary control, and both partners share major decision making. Thus co-headship would be a more appropriate label for many households in the Philippines and elsewhere.

Matrifocality refers to a household pattern in which a woman (or women) is the central, stable domestic figure around whom other members cluster (González 1970). In a matrifocal household, the mother is likely to be the primary or only income provider. The concept of matrifocality does not exclude the possibility that men may be part of the household, but they are not the central income providers or decision makers.

The number of woman-headed households is increasing worldwide, and these households tend to be poorer than other households. In general, a woman-headed household can come

---

stem household a coresidential group that comprises only two married couples related through males, commonly found in East Asian cultures.

matrifocality a household pattern in which a female (or females) is the central, stable figure around whom other members cluster.

This matrifocal household in rural Jamaica includes two sisters and their children.

about if a partner never existed, if a partner existed at one time, but for some reason—such as separation, divorce, or death—is no longer part of the household, or if a partner exists but is not a coresident because of migration, imprisonment, or some other form of separation.

In terms of the healthy functioning of households, it is not simply the gender of the household head that is critical. What matters are the resources to which the head has access, both material and social, such as property ownership, a decent job, kinship and other supportive social ties, and living in a safe neighborhood.

INTRAHOUSEHOLD DYNAMICS

How do household members interact with each other? What are their emotional attachments, rights, and responsibilities? What are the power relationships between and among members of various categories, such as spouses, siblings, and those of different generations? Kinship systems define what the content of these relationships should be. In everyday life, people may conform more or less to the ideal.

SPOUSE/PARTNER RELATIONSHIPS This section discusses three areas of spousal relationships: marital satisfaction, sexual activity over the life course, and satisfaction within marriage and the "too good" wife in Japan.

A landmark study of marriages in Tokyo in 1959 compared marital satisfaction of husbands and wives in love marriages and arranged marriages (Blood 1967). In all marriages, marital satisfaction declined over time, but differences between the two types emerged. The decline was greatest for wives in arranged marriages and least for husbands in arranged marriages. In love-match marriages, both partners' satisfaction dropped dramatically (a bit earlier for wives and a bit later for husbands), but both husbands and wives reported nearly equal levels of satisfaction after they had been married nine years or more.

Sexual activity of couples can be both an indication of marital satisfaction and a cause of marital satisfaction. Analysis of reports of marital sex from a 1988 survey in the United States shows that frequency per month steadily declines with the duration of marriage, from an average of twelve times per month for people ages 19 to 24 years, to less than once a month for people 75 years of age and older (Call, Sprecher, and Schwartz 1995). Older married people have sex less frequently. Less happy people have sex less frequently. Within each age category, sex is more frequent among three categories of people:

- Those who are cohabiting but not married
- Those who cohabited before marriage
- Those who are in their second or later marriage

In seeking to learn whether such decline is more widespread, an anthropologist and a statistician joined forces to analyze data from a survey conducted with over 90,000 women in 19 developing countries (Brewis and Meyer 2004). One of the survey questions was "When was the last time you had sexual intercourse [with a spouse]?" The *honeymoon effect* (having more frequent sex in the first year of marriage) is significant in only five countries: Brazil, Benin, Ethiopia, Mali, and Kazakhstan. Significant reductions in frequency after the first year of marriage occur in all countries but one: Burkina Faso in West Africa. What is going on here? One factor is that Burkina Faso couples have a significantly lower frequency of reported marital sex during the first year of marriage; in other words, couples do not go through a honeymoon phase of frequent sexual intercourse, and so activity in following years is not that much lower. These intriguing results at the country level need to be followed up by research on local cultural practices and patterns.

Cultures everywhere also define the proper role of a wife or husband. In Japan, a "good wife" should care for her husband's needs and make sure that any problems in the household do not erupt into the public domain (Borovoy 2005). Many Japanese salarymen (corporate workers) consume substantial amounts of alcohol after work. They return home late and drunk. It is the duty of the "good wife" to provide dinner for her husband and get him to go to bed, so he can make it to work the next day. The wives face a profound cultural dilemma: If they continue to perform well the role of the "good wife," they are "codependent" in the husband's alcohol abuse, and contribute to the continuance of the problem. Many middle-class Japanese wives are joining support groups to help them deal with their situation by building new roles for themselves beyond that of the "good wife."

SIBLING RELATIONSHIPS Sibling relationships are an understudied aspect of intrahousehold dynamics. One example comes from research in a working-class neighborhood of Beirut, Lebanon (Joseph 1994). The anthropologist became friendly with several families and was especially close to Hanna, the oldest son in one of them. Hanna was an attractive

Japanese salarymen singing karaoke.

young man, considered a good marriage choice, with friends across religious and ethnic groups. Therefore, the author reports her shock when she once heard Hanna shouting at his 12-year-old sister Flaur and slapping her across the face. Further observation of the relationship between Hanna and Flaur suggested that Hanna was playing a fatherly role to Flaur. He was especially irritated with her if she lingered on the street near their apartment building, gossiping with other girls: "He would forcibly escort her upstairs to their apartment, slap her, and demand that she behave with dignity" (1994:51). Adults in the household thought nothing was wrong. They said that Flaur enjoyed her brother's aggressive attention. Flaur herself commented, "It doesn't even hurt when Hanna hits me." She said that she hoped to have a husband like Hanna.

An interpretation of this kind of brother–sister relationship, common in Arab culture, is that it is part of a socialization process that maintains and perpetuates male domination in the household: "Hanna was teaching Flaur to accept male power in the name of love . . . loving his sister meant taking charge of her and that he could discipline her if his action was understood to be in her interest. Flaur was reinforced in learning that the love of a man could include that male's violent control and that to receive his love involved submission to control" (1994:52).

DOMESTIC VIOLENCE BETWEEN PARTNERS Violence between domestic partners, with males dominating as perpetrators and women as victims, is found in nearly all cultures, although in varying forms and frequencies (Brown 1999). Wife beating is more common and more severe in contexts where men control the wealth. It is less common and less severe where women's work groups and social networks exist

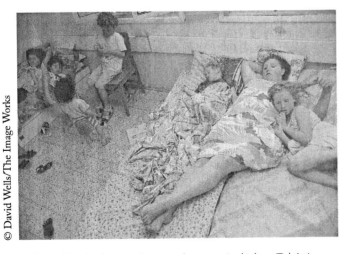

© David Wells/The Image Works

A shared bedroom in a battered woman's shelter, Tel Aviv, Israel. Many people wonder why abused women do not leave their abusers. Part of the answer lies in the unavailability and low quality of shelters throughout much of the world.

(Levinson 1989). The presence of women's work groups is related to a greater importance of women in production and matrifocal residence. These factors provide women with the means to leave an abusive relationship. For example, among the Garifuna, an African-Indian people of Belize, Central America, incidents of spouse abuse occur, but they are infrequent and not extended (Kerns 1999). Women's solidarity in this matrifocal society limits male violence against women.

Increased domestic violence worldwide throws into question the notion of the house as a refuge or place of security. In the United States, evidence exists of high and increasing rates of intrahousehold abuse of children (including sexual abuse), violence between spouses or partners, and abuse of aged family members. Anthropological research helps policy makers and social workers better understand the factors affecting the safety of individuals within households so they are able to design more effective programs to promote personal safety (see Lessons Applied).

HOUSEHOLD TRANSFORMATIONS The composition and sheer existence of a particular household can change as a consequence of several factors, including divorce, death, and possible remarriage.

Divorce and separation, like marriage and other forms of long-term union, are cultural universals, even though they may be frowned on or forbidden. Important research questions about marital dissolution include the causes for it, the reasons why divorce rates appear to be rising worldwide, and the implications for the welfare of children of divorced parents and other dependents.

Marriages may break up for several reasons: The most common are voluntary separation and death of one of the partners. Globally, variations exist in the legality and propriety of divorce. Some religions, such as Roman Catholicism, prohibit divorce. In Muslim societies, divorce by law is easier for a husband to obtain than for a wife.

One hypothesis for why divorce rates vary cross-culturally says that divorce rates will be lower in cultures with unilineal descent. In such cultures, a large descent group has control over and interests in offspring and control over in-marrying spouses due to their dependence (Barnard and Good 1984:119). Royal lineages, with their strong interests in maintaining the family line, are examples of groups especially unlikely to favor divorce, because divorce generally means losing control of offspring. In bilineal foraging societies, there is more flexibility in both marriage and divorce.

Another question is the effect of multiple spouses on divorce. A study in Nigeria, West Africa, found that two-wife arrangements are the most stable, whereas marriages involving three or more wives have the highest rates of disruption (Gage-Brandon 1992). Similar results come from an analysis of household break-up in a polyandrous group of

Ethnography for Preventing Wife Abuse in Rural Kentucky

Domestic violence in the United States is reportedly highest in the state of Kentucky. An ethnographic study of domestic violence in Kentucky reveals several cultural factors related to the high rate of wife abuse (Websdale 1995). The study included interviews with 50 abused wives in eastern Kentucky and with battered women in shelters, police officers, shelter employees, and social workers.

Three categories of isolation exist in rural Kentucky making domestic violence particularly difficult to prevent:

1. *Physical isolation:* The women reported a feeling of physical isolation in their lives. Abusers' tactics were more effective because of geographical isolation. They include disabling motor vehicles so the wife cannot leave the residence; destroying motor vehicles; monitoring the odometer reading on motor vehicles; locking the thermostat in winter; driving recklessly to intimidate the wife; and discharging firearms, for example, at a pet (1995:106–107).

It is difficult or impossible for an abused woman to leave a home located many miles from the nearest paved road, and especially so if the woman has children. No public transportation serves even the paved road. Nearly one-third of households had no phones. Getting to a phone to report abuse results in delay and gives police the impression that the call is less serious and increases a woman's sense of hopelessness. Sheriffs have acquired a very poor reputation among battered women in the region for not attending domestic calls at all.

2. *Social isolation:* Aspects of the rural culture, including gender roles, promote a system of "passive policing." Men are seen as providers and women are tied to domestic work and child rearing. When women do work outside the home, their wages are about 50 percent of men's wages. Marital residence is often in the vicinity of the husband's family. Thus a woman is separated from the potential support of her natal family and limited in seeking help in the immediate vicinity because the husband's family is likely to be nonsupportive of her. Local police officers view the family as a private unit, and so they are not inclined to intervene in family problems. Because the home is the man's world and men are supposed to be dominant in the family, police are unwilling to arrest husbands accused of abuse. In some instances, the police take the batterer's side because they share the belief in a husband's right to control his wife.

3. *Institutional isolation:* Social services for battered women in Kentucky are scarce and especially so in rural areas. The fact that abused women often know the people who run the services ironically inhibits the women from approaching them, given the value of family privacy. Other institutional constraints include low levels of schooling, lack of child-care centers to allow mothers the option to work outside the home, inadequate health services, and religious teaching of fundamentalist Christianity that supports values such as the idea that it is a woman's duty to stay in a marriage and "weather the storm."

These findings suggest some recommendations. First, rural women need more and better employment opportunities to reduce their economic dependency on abusive partners. To address this need, rural outreach programs should be strengthened. Expanded telephone subscriptions would decrease rural women's institutional isolation. Because of the complexity of the social situation in Kentucky, however, no single solution will be sufficient.

◆ **FOOD FOR THOUGHT**

• How do conditions in Kentucky differ from or resemble those in another cultural context where wife beating is frequent.

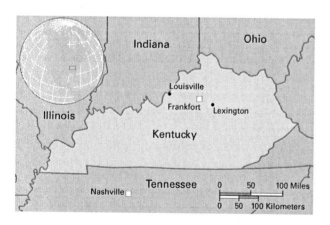

MAP 6 Kentucky, United States.
Located in the southeastern United States, in the wider Appalachian region, Kentucky's population is over 4 million. It has more farmers per square mile than any other state. Per capita income is 43rd in the 50 states. Before being occupied by British settlers in the late eighteenth century, Kentucky was the hunting grounds of the Shawnees and Cherokees. The current population is about 91 percent White, 7 percent Black, 0.6 percent American Indian, and 0.9 percent Asian. Kentucky is known for thoroughbred horse breeding and racing, bourbon and whiskey distilling, and bluegrass music.

Tibetan people living in northwestern Nepal (Haddix McCay 2001). Wealth of the household is an important factor affecting household stability, but the number of brothers is another strong factor. Polyandrous households comprising two brothers are far less likely to break up than those with four or more brothers. An additional factor, although more difficult to quantify, is the social support and networks that a brother has beyond the polyandrous household. Only with such social support will he be able to build a house and establish a separate household on his own.

The position of a widow or widower carries altered responsibilities and rights. Women's position as widows is often marked symbolically. In Mediterranean cultures, a widow must wear modest, simple, and black-colored clothing, sometimes for the rest of her life. Her sexuality is supposed to be virtually dead. At the same time, her new "asexual" status allows her greater spatial freedom than before. She can go to public coffeehouses and taverns, something not done by women whose husbands are living.

Extreme restrictions on widows are recorded for parts of South Asia where social pressures on a widow enforce self-denial and self-deprivation, especially among the propertied class. A widow should wear a plain white sari, shave her head, eat little food, and live an asexual life. Many widows in India are abandoned, especially if they have no son to support them. They are considered polluting and inauspicious. Widows elsewhere also experience symbolic and life-quality changes much more than do widowers. For example, in South Africa, a widower's body is not marked in any significant way except to have his head shaved. He is required to wear a black button or armband for about six months. A widow's body is marked by shaving her head, smearing a mixture of herbs and ground charcoal on her body, wearing black clothes made from an inexpensive material, and covering her face with a black veil and her shoulders with a black shawl. She may wear her clothes inside out, wear one shoe, eat with her left hand, or eat from a lid instead of a plate (Ramphele 1996).

◆◆◆

Changing Kinship and Household Dynamics

This section provides examples of how marriage and household patterns are changing. Many of these changes have roots in colonialism, whereas others are the result of recent changes effected by globalization.

CHANGE IN DESCENT

Matrilineal descent is declining worldwide as a result of both European colonialism and contemporary Western globalization. European colonial rule in Africa and Asia contributed to the decline in matrilineal kinship by registering land and other property in the names of assumed male heads of household, even where females were the heads (Boserup 1970). This process eroded women's previous rights and powers. Western missionaries further contributed to transforming matrilineal cultures into patrilineal systems (Etienne and Leacock 1980). For example, European colonial influences led to the decline of matrilineal kinship among Native North Americans. Before European colonialism, North America had one of the largest distributions of matrilineal descent worldwide. A comparative study of kinship among three reservation-based Navajo groups in Arizona shows that matrilineality is stronger where conditions most resemble the pre-reservation era (Levy, Henderson, and Andrews 1989).

Among the Minangkabau of Indonesia (review Culturama), three factors explain the decline of matrilineal kinship (Blackwood 1995):

- Dutch colonialism promoted the image of male-headed nuclear families as an ideal.
- Islamic teachings idealize women as wives and men as household heads.
- The modernizing Indonesian state has a policy of naming males as household heads.

CHANGE IN MARRIAGE

Although the institution of marriage in general remains prominent, many of its details are changing including courtship, the marriage ceremony, and marital relationships.

New forms of communication are profoundly affecting courtship. In a village in western Nepal, people's stories of their marriages reveal that arranged marriages have decreased and elopement has increased since the 1990s (Ahern 2001). In the 1990s, love letters became the most important basis of establishing marital relationships. In this context, dating is not allowed, so sending love letters is how young people court. Of the 200 love letters Ahern collected, 170 were written by men and 30 by women. Typically, the man starts the correspondence. For example, one man's love letter contains the following lines: "I'm helpless and I have to make friends of a notebook and pen in order to place this helplessness before you. . . . I'll let you know by a 'short cut' what I want to say: Love is the union of two souls . . . I'm offering you an invitation to love" (2001:3). Love letters became possible only in the 1990s because of increased literacy rates in the village. Literacy facilitated self-selected marriages and thus supported an increasing sense of personal agency among the younger people of the village. Now, throughout the world, young people are courting through text messaging, even in the most conservative parts of the world such as the Middle East.

Nearly everywhere, the age at first marriage is rising. The later age at marriage is related to increased emphasis on completing a certain number of years of education before marriage

A newly married husband and wife and their relatives in front of a church in Seoul, Republic of Korea.

▶ *How does this wedding group resemble or differ from a wedding you have attended?*

and to higher material aspirations, such as being able to own a house. Marriages between people of different nations and ethnicities are increasing, partly because of growing rates of international migration. Migrants take with them many of their marriage and family practices. They also adapt to rules and practices in their area of destination. Pluralistic practices evolve, such as conducting two marriage ceremonies—one conforming to the "original" culture and the other to the culture in the place of destination.

Marriage crises are situations in which people who want to marry cannot do so for one reason or another. They are more frequent now than in the past, at least as perceived and reported by young people in the so-called marriage market. Two examples illustrate variations in how a marriage crisis comes about and how it plays out for those caught up in it.

In a town of about 38,000 in rural Niger, West Africa, the marriage crisis involves young men's inability to raise the necessary funds for the brideprice and additional gifts to the bride's family (Masquelier 2005). Among these Muslim, Hausa-speaking people, called Mawri, marriage is the crucial ritual that changes a boy into a man. Typically, a prospective groom receives financial assistance from his kin and friends. In Niger, the economy has been declining for some time, and typical farm or other wages are worth less than they were in earlier times. Marriage costs for the groom have not declined, however—quite the opposite. Wealthy young men can afford to give a car to the bride's parents as a wedding gift. But most

young Mawri men cannot afford such gifts and are caught in the marriage crisis. They remain sitting at home in their parents' house, something that only females do. The many young, marriage-age women who remain single gain a reputation of being immoral, as they occupy a new and suspect social space between girl and wife.

The marriage crisis for African American women in Syracuse is related to policies promoted by the government of President George W. Bush (Lane et al. 2004). The Bush government earmarked millions of dollars to promote two-parent, heterosexual families. Furthermore, during the George W. Bush era an increasing number of African American men were imprisoned. Besides high rates of imprisonment, African American men die violent deaths at much higher rates than other ethnic populations. In the population of Syracuse, a city in postindustrial decline, there are four African American women for every one African American man, compared to an equal ratio among Whites. Given the strong preference for ethnic endogamous marriages, it is statistically impossible for many African American women to get married.

Weddings are important, culture-revealing events. Style changes in weddings worldwide abound. Factors of changes to consider are the ceremony, costs, appropriate clothing, and the possibility of a honeymoon. Due to globalization, features of the Western-style *white wedding* (a long white gown for the bride, a multitiered wedding cake, and certain kinds of floral arrangements) are spreading around the world, though with fascinating local adaptations. Just considering what the bride and groom wear takes one into the complex connections between weddings and identity of the bride and groom and their families. Clothing choice may reflect adherence to "traditional" values or may reject those in favor of more "modern" values. Throughout much of East and Southeast Asia, advertisements and upscale stores display the Western-style white wedding gown (but less so in India, where white clothing for women signifies widowhood and is inauspicious). Resurgence of local styles is occurring in some contexts, such as in Morocco, where there is a trend for "modern" brides to wear a Berber costume (long robes and silver jewelry characteristic of the rural, mountain pastoralists) at one stage of the wedding ceremony.

CHANGING HOUSEHOLDS

Globalization is creating rapid change in household structure and intrahousehold dynamics. One assumption is that the frequency of extended households will decline with

THINKING OUTSIDE THE BOX

What forms of communication do young people use to court someone in your cultural world? For a class project, interview your parents about courtship communication that they used.

Matthew Amster   Matthew Amster

(LEFT) A modern-style Kelabit longhouse built in the 1990s. It is the home of six families who formerly lived in a 20-family longhouse, seen in the background, which is being dismantled. (RIGHT) Since the 1990s, houses built for a nuclear unit have proliferated in the highlands. These houses stand on the site of a former multiunit longhouse.

MAP 7   Kelabit Region in Malaysia.
The Kelabit people's homeland is the Kelabit Highlands in Sarawak, a plateau ringed by mountain peaks that are forest covered. One of Malaysia's smallest indigenous tribes, they number around 6000 people, or 0.4 percent of Sarawak's population of 1.5 million, and 0.03 percent of Malaysia's total population of 22 million. Less than one-third of the Kelabit people live in the highlands.

industrialization and urbanization, and the frequency of nuclear households will rise. Given what this chapter mentioned earlier about the relationship between nuclear households and industrialism/informatics, it is highly possible that with the spread of this mode of production, nuclear households will increase too.

This projection finds strong confirmation in the changes that have occurred in household structure among the Kelabit people of highland Borneo since the early 1990s (Amster 2000) (see Map 7). One Kelabit settlement was founded in 1963 near the Indonesian border. At the time, everyone lived in one longhouse with over 20 family units. It was a "modern" longhouse, thanks to roofing provided by the British army and the innovation of private sleeping areas. Like more traditional longhouses, though, it was an essentially egalitarian living space within which individuals could freely move. Today, that longhouse is no more. Most of the young people have migrated to coastal towns and work in jobs related to the offshore oil industry. Most houses are now single-unit homes with an emphasis on privacy. The elders complain of a "bad silence" in the village. No one looks after visitors with the old style of hospitality. There is no longer one common longhouse for communal feasts and rituals.

International migration is another major cause of change in household formation and internal relationships. Dramatic decline in fertility can occur in one generation when members of a farming household in, for example, Taiwan or Egypt, migrate to England, France, Canada, or the United States. Having many children makes economic sense in their homeland, but not in the new destination. Many such migrants

decide to have only one or two children. They tend to live in small, isolated nuclear households. International migration creates new challenges for relationships between parents and children. The children often become strongly identified with the new culture and have little connection with their ancestral culture. This rupture creates anxiety for the parents and conflict between children and parents over issues such as dating, dress, and career goals.

In 1997, the people of Norway were confronted with a case of kidnapping of an 18-year-old Norwegian citizen named "Nadia". Her parents took her to Morocco and held her captive there. The full story is complicated, but the core issues revolve around conflict between Moroccan and Norwegian family values. Nadia's parents felt that she should be under their control and that they had the right to arrange her marriage in Morocco. Nadia had a Norwegian concept of personal autonomy. In the end, Nadia and her parents returned to Norway, where the courts ruled that, for the sake of the family, the parents would not be jailed for kidnapping their daughter. The case brought stigma to Nadia among the Muslim community of Norway, who viewed her as a traitor to her culture. She now lives at a secret address and avoids publicity. An anthropologist close to this case who served as an expert cultural witness during the trial of her parents reports that, in spite of her seclusion, Nadia has offered help to other young women.

At the beginning of the twenty-first century, three kinds of households are most common in the United States: households composed of couples living in their first marriage, single-parent households, and households formed through remarriage. A new fourth category is the multigenerational household, in which an *adult child*, or *boomerang kid*, lives with his or her parents. About one in three unmarried adults between the ages of 25 and 55 share a home with their mother or father or both (*Psychology Today* 1995 [28]:16). In the United States, adult offspring spend over 2 hours a day doing household chores, with adult daughters contributing about 17 hours a week and adult sons 14.4 hours. Daughters spend most of their time doing laundry, cooking, cleaning, and washing dishes. Sons are more involved in yard work and car care. Parents in multigenerational households still do three-quarters of the housework.

Kinship and household formation are certainly not dull or static topics. Just trying to keep up with changing patterns in North America is a daunting task, to say nothing of tracking changes worldwide.

the BIG questions REVISITED

◆ How do cultures create kinship?

Key differences exist between unilineal and bilineal descent systems. Within unilineal systems, further important variations exist between patrilineal and matrilineal systems in terms of property inheritance, residence rules for married couples, and the relative status of males and females. Worldwide, unilineal systems are more common than bilineal systems. Within unilineal kinship systems, patrilineal kinship is more common than matrilineal kinship.

A second important basis for kinship is sharing. Sharing one's child with someone else through either informal or formal processes is probably a cultural universal. Sharing-based kinship is created through food transfers, including breastfeeding (in some cultures, children breastfed by the same woman are considered kin and cannot marry). Ritualized sharing creates kinship, as in the case of godparenthood.

The third basis for kinship is marriage, another universal factor, even though definitions of marriage may differ substantially. All cultures have rules of exclusion and preference rules for spouses.

◆ What are cross-cultural patterns of households and domestic life?

A household may consist of a single person living alone or may be a group comprising more than one person who may or may not be related by kinship; these individuals share a living space and, often, financial responsibilities for the household.

Nuclear households consist of a mother and father and their children, but they also can be just a husband and wife without children. Nuclear households are found in all cultures but are most common in foraging and industrial societies. Extended households include more than one nuclear household. They are most commonly found in cultures with a unilineal kinship system. Stem households, which are most common in East Asia, are a variant of an extended household in which only one child, usually the first born, retains residence with the parents.

Household headship can be shared between two partners or can be borne by a single person, as in a woman-headed household. Study of intrahousehold dynamics between parents and children and among siblings reveals complex power relationships as well as security, sharing, and sometimes violence. Household break-up comes about through divorce, separation of cohabiting partners, or death of a spouse or partner.

◆ How are kinship and households changing?

The increasingly connected world in which we live is having marked effects on kinship formation and household patterns and dynamics. Matrilineal systems have been declining in distribution since European colonialist expansion beginning in the 1500s.

Many aspects of marriage are changing, including a trend toward later age at marriage in many developing countries. Although marriage continues to be an important basis for the formation of nuclear and extended households, other options (such as cohabitation) are increasing in importance in many contexts, including urban areas in developed countries.

Contemporary changes in kinship and in household formation raise several serious questions for the future, perhaps most importantly about the care of dependent members such as children, the aged, and disabled people. As fertility rates decline and average household size shrinks, kinship-based entitlements to basic needs and emotional support disappear.

KEY CONCEPTS

bilineal descent
brideservice
cross-cousin
descent
endogamy
exogamy

extended household
family
household
incest taboo
kinship system
marriage

matrilineal descent
matrifocality
monogamy
nuclear household
parallel cousin
patrilineal descent

polyandry
polygamy
polygyny
stem household
unilineal descent

SUGGESTED READINGS

Irwin Altman and Joseph Ginat, eds. *Polygynous Families in Contemporary Society*. Cambridge: Cambridge University Press, 1996. This book provides a detailed account of polygyny as practiced in two fundamentalist Mormon communities of Utah, one rural and the other urban.

Dorothy Ayers Counts, Judith K. Brown, and Jacquelyn C. Campbell, eds. *To Have and to Hit: Cultural Perspectives on Wife Beating*. Champaign/Urbana: University of Illinois Press, 1999. Chapters include an introductory overview and cases from Australia, southern Africa, Papua New Guinea, India, Central America, the Middle East, and the Pacific.

Amy Borovoy. *The Too-Good Wife: Alcohol, Codependency, and the Politics of Nurturance in Postwar Japan*. Berkeley: University of California Press, 2005. This book explores the experiences of middle-class women in Tokyo who participated in a weekly support meeting for families of substance abusers. The women attempt to cope with their husbands' alcoholism while facing the dilemma that being a good wife may be part of the problem.

Deborah R. Connolly. *Homeless Mothers: Face to Face with Women and Poverty*. Minneapolis: University of Minnesota Press, 2000. Poor, White women on the margin of mainstream society in Portland, Oregon, describe how they attempt to be good mothers with no money, no home, and no help.

Charles N. Durran, James M. Freeman, and J.A. English-Lueck. *Busier Than Ever! Why American Families Can't Slow Down*. Stanford, CA: Stanford University Press, 2007. The authors followed the daily activities of 14 American families in California. Their findings show how people try to balance the demands of work and family in a cultural context in which "busyness," or always being busy, is an indication of success and the good life.

Helen Bradley Foster and Donald Clay Johnson, eds. *Wedding Dress across Cultures*. New York: Berg, 2003. Chapters examine the evolution and ritual functions of wedding attire in cultures such as urban Japan, Alaskan Indians, Swaziland, Morocco, Greece, and the Andes.

Jennifer Hirsch. *A Courtship after Marriage: Sexuality and Love in Mexican Transnational Marriages*. Berkeley: University of California Press, 2003. This study uses an innovative method of pairing 13 migrant women living in Atlanta, Georgia, with 13 nonmigrant counterparts in two rural towns in Mexico to learn about marriage and married life.

Suad Joseph, ed. *Intimate Selving in Arab Families: Gender, Self, and Identity*. Syracuse, NY: Syracuse University Press, 1999. Chapters discuss family life and relationships in Arab culture with attention to connectivity, gender inequality, and the self. Case studies are from Lebanon and Egypt.

Laurel Kendall. *Getting Married in Korea: Of Gender, Morality, and Modernity*. Berkeley: University of California, 1996. This book examines preferences about desirable spouses, matchmaking, marriage ceremonies and their financing, and the effect of women's changing work roles on their marital aspirations.

Sulamith Heins Potter. *Family Life in a Northern Thai Village: A Structural Study in the Significance of Women*. Berkeley: University of California Press, 1977. This ethnography of matrifocal family life in rural Thailand focuses on work roles, rituals, and intrafamily relationships.

Kanchana Ruwanpura. *Matrilineal Communities, Patriarchal Realities: A Feminist Nirvana Uncovered*. Ann Arbor: University of Michigan Press, 2007. This book describes Muslim, Sinhala, and Tamil households headed by women in Sri Lanka.

Margaret Trawick. *Notes on Love in a Tamil Family*. Berkeley: University of California Press, 1992. This reflexive ethnography takes a close look at the daily dynamics of kinship in one Tamil (South Indian) family. Attention is given to sibling relationships, the role of older people, children's lives, and love and affection.

Toby Alice Volkman, ed. *Cultures of Transnational Adoption*. Durham, NC: Duke University Press, 2005. Chapters discuss Korean adoptees as a global family, transnational adoption in North America, shared parenthood among low-income people in Brazil, and representations of "waiting children."

CHAPTER 7

SOCIAL GROUPS AND SOCIAL STRATIFICATION

SOCIAL GROUPS AND SOCIAL STRATIFICATION

the BIG questions

◆ What are social groups and how do they vary cross-culturally?

◆ What is social stratification?

◆ What is civil society?

171

In the early 1800s, when French political philosopher Alexis de Tocqueville visited the United States and characterized it as a "nation of joiners," he implied that people in some cultures are more likely to join groups than others. The questions of what motivates people to join groups, what holds people together in groups, and how groups deal with leadership and participation have intrigued scholars in many fields for centuries.

This chapter focuses on nonkin groups and microculture formation. Several factors related to microcultures are class, "race," ethnicity, indigeneity, gender, age, and institutions such as prisons and retirement homes. Microcultures affect fieldwork and they vary in different economies and reproductive and kinship systems. This chapter looks at how microcultures shape group identity and organization and the relationships among different groups in terms of hierarchy and power. It first examines a variety of social groups ranging from small scale to large scale and then considers inequalities among social groups. The last section considers the concept of civil society and provides examples.

◆ ◆ ◆
Social Groups

A **social group** is a cluster of people beyond the domestic unit who are usually related on grounds other than kinship, although kinship relationships may exist between people in the group. Two basic categories exist: the **primary group**, consisting of people who interact with each other and know each other personally, and the **secondary group**, consisting of people who identify with each other on some common ground but who may never meet with one another or interact with each other personally.

Members of all social groups have a sense of rights and responsibilities in relation to the group. Membership in a primary group, because of face-to-face interaction, involves more direct accountability about rights and responsibilities than secondary group membership. When discussing different kinds of groups, cultural anthropologists also draw a distinction

---

social group a cluster of people beyond the domestic unit who are usually related on grounds other than kinship.

primary group a social group in which members meet on a face-to-face basis.

secondary group people who identify with each other on some basis but may never meet with one another personally.

age set a group of people close in age who go through certain rituals, such as circumcision, at the same time.

---

between *informal groups* and *formal groups* (March and Taqqu 1986:5):

- Informal groups are smaller and less visible.
- Members of informal groups have close, face-to-face relationships with one another; members of formal groups may or may not know each other.
- Organizational structure is less hierarchical in informal groups.
- Informal groups do not have legal recognition.

Modes of livelihood affect the formation of social groups, with the greatest variety of groups found in agricultural and industrial/informatics societies (see Figure 1). One theory for this pattern is that mobile populations, such as foragers and pastoralists, are less likely to develop enduring social groups beyond kin relationships simply because they have less social density and continuous interaction than more settled populations. Although foragers and pastoralists do have less variety of social groups, they do not completely lack social groupings. A prominent form of social group among foragers and pastoralists is an **age set**, a group of people close in age who go through certain rituals, such as circumcision, at the same time.

Although it is generally true that settled populations have more social groups as a way to organize society, some important exceptions exist. In accordance with this generalization, many informal and formal groups are active throughout Africa, Latin America, and Southeast Asia. In northern Thailand's Chiangmai region, for example, many social groups exist (Potter 1976). Villagers support the Buddhist temple, irrigation canals, the cremation grounds, and village roads through donations of food, cash, and labor. Several more formal and focused groups exist: the temple committee that arranges festivals, the school committee, the Young People's Club (youth from about the age of 15 until marriage who assist at village ceremonial functions), the village dancers (about a dozen young, unmarried women who host intervillage events), and the funeral society (which provides financial aid for funeral services).

Social groups, however, are typically less prominent in South Asia, a region that includes Pakistan, India, Nepal, Bhutan, Bangladesh, and Sri Lanka. In Bangladesh (see Map 1), for example, a densely populated and agrarian country of South Asia, indigenous social groups are rare. The most prominent ties beyond the immediate household are kinship based (Miller and Khan 1986). In spite of the lack of indigenous social groups, however, Bangladesh has gained world renown since the later twentieth century for its success in forming local microcredit (small loans) groups through an organization called the Grameen Bank, which gives loans to poor people to help them start small businesses. Likewise,

Foraging	Horticulture	Pastoralism	Agriculture	Industrialism/Informatics
Characteristics				**Characteristics**
Informal and primary			Formal and secondary	
Egalitarian structure			Recognized leadership	
Ties based on balanced exchange		Ritual ties	Dues and fees	
Functions				**Functions**
Companionship			Special purposes	
			Work, war, lobbying government	
Types				**Types**
Friendship	Friendship		Friendship	
	Age-based work groups		Urban youth gangs	
	Gender-based work groups		Clubs, associations	
			Status Groups:	
			Class, race, ethnicity, caste, age, gender	
			Institutional Groups:	
			Prisons, retirement homes	
			Quasi-Political Groups:	
			Human rights, environmental groups	

FIGURE 1   Modes of Livelihood and Social Groups

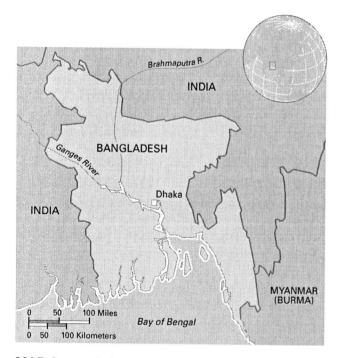

MAP 1   Bangladesh.
The People's Republic of Bangladesh is located on a deltaic floodplain with rich soil and risk of flooding. One of the world's most densely populated countries, its nearly 150 million people live in an area about the size of the state of Wisconsin. Bangladesh is the world's third-largest Muslim majority country.

throughout the rest of South Asia, the modern era has seen the rise of many active social groups including those dedicated to preserving traditional environmental knowledge, promoting women and children's health and survival, and advocating for lesbian/gay rights.

This section describes a variety of social groups, starting with the most face-to-face, primary groups of two or three people based on friendship. It then moves to larger and more formal groups such as countercultural groups and activist groups.

FRIENDSHIP

Friendship refers to close social ties between at least two people that are informal, voluntary, and involve personal, face-to-face interaction. Generally, friendship involves people who are nonkin, but in some cases kin are also friends. Friendship fits in the category of a primary social group. One question that cultural anthropologists ask is whether friendship is a cultural universal. Two factors make it difficult to answer this question. First, insufficient cross-cultural research exists to answer the question definitively. Second, defining friendship cross-culturally is problematic. It is likely, however, that something like "friendship" is a cultural universal but shaped in different degrees from culture to culture (see Everyday Anthropology).

everyday ANTHROPOLOGY

Making Friends

People's daily activities are often the basis of friendship ties. In Andalucia, southern Spain, men and women pursue separate kinds of work and, relatedly, have differing friendship patterns (Uhl 1991). Men's work takes place outside the house and neighborhood, either in the fields or in manufacturing jobs. Women devote most of their time to unpaid household work within the domestic domain. This dichotomy is somewhat fluid, however, as women's domestic roles sometimes take them to the market or the town hall.

For men, an important category of friend is an *amigo*, a friend with whom one casually interacts. This kind of friendship is acted out and maintained in the context in bars, as men drink together night after night. Bars are a man's world. Amigos share common experiences of school, sports and hobbies, and working together. In contrast, women refer to their friends either with kin terms or as *vecina*, "neighbor," reflecting women's primary orientation to family and neighborhood.

Differences also emerge in the category of *amigos(as) del verdad*, or "true friends." True friends are

A shepherd in Andalucia, southern Spain. In rural areas of Andalucia, as in much of the Mediterranean region, the gender of division of labor is distinct, with men working outside the home and women working inside or near the home. Friendship formation follows this pattern. Men form ties with men in cafes and bars after work, and women establish ties with other women in the neighborhood.

those with whom one shares secrets without fear of betrayal. Men have more true friends than women do, a pattern that reflects their wider social networks.

◆ FOOD FOR THOUGHT

* What categories of friends do you have? Are friends in some categories "closer" or "truer" than others? What is the basis of close friendship?

SOCIAL CHARACTERISTICS OF FRIENDSHIP People choose their friends, and friends remain so on a voluntary basis. Even so, the criteria for who qualifies as a friend may be culturally structured. For instance, gender segregation may prevent cross-gender friendships and promote same-gender friendships, and racial segregation limits cross-"race" friendships. Another characteristic of friendship is that friends are supportive of each other, psychologically and sometimes materially. Support is mutual, shared back and forth in an expectable way (as in balanced exchange). Friendship generally occurs between social equals, although there are exceptions, such as friendships between older and younger people, a supervisor and a staff worker, or a teacher and a student.

Sharing stories is often a basis of friendship groups. According to a study of men's friendship groups that focused on interactions in rumshops in Guyana (gai-ANN-uh)

In a low-income neighborhood in Rio de Janeiro, Brazil, men play dominoes and drink beer while others observe.

▶ *Discuss a comparable scene of female leisure activities in your microcultural experience.*

SOCIAL GROUPS AND SOCIAL STRATIFICATION

MAP 2 Caribbean Countries of South America.
The ethnically and linguistically diverse countries of the Caribbean region of South America include Guyana, Suriname, and French Guiana. Guyana, or the Co-operative Republic of Guyana, is the only South American country whose official language is English. Other languages are Hindi, Wai Wai, and Arawak. Its population is 800,000. The Republiek Suriname, or Surinam, was formerly a colony of the Netherlands and is the smallest independent state in South America. Its population is 440,000. Dutch is the official language but most Surinamese also speak Sranang Tongo, or Surinaams, a mixture of Dutch, English Portuguese, French, and local languages. French Guiana is an overseas department of France and is thus part of the European Union. The smallest political unit in South America, its population is 200,000. Its official language is French, but several other languages are spoken, including indigenous Arawak and Carib.

(see Map 2), Indo-Guyanese men who have known each other since childhood spend time every day at the rumshop, eating, drinking, and regaling each other with stories (Sidnell 2000). Through shared storytelling about village history and other aspects of local knowledge, men display their equality with each other. The pattern of storytelling, referred to as "turn-at-talk," in which efforts are made to include everyone as a storyteller in turn, also serves to maintain equality and solidarity. These friendship groups are tightly knit, and the members can call on one another for economic, social, political, and ritual help.

Participant observation and interviews with a sample of rural and urban, low-income Jamaicans reveals that cell phone use is frequent (Horst and Miller 2005). Jamaicans are keenly aware of their call lists and how often they have kept in touch with the many individuals on their lists. Cell phones allow for "linking up," or creating extensive networks that include close friends, possible future sexual partners, and members of one's church. Phone numbers of kin are also prominent on people's cell phone number lists. By linking up periodically with people on their lists, low-income Jamaicans

maintain friendship and other ties with people who they can call on when they need support. Cell phones allow a more extensive network of friends and other contacts than was previously possible.

FRIENDSHIP AMONG THE URBAN POOR Carol Stack's study of how friendship networks promote economic survival among low-income, urban African Americans is a landmark contribution (1974). She conducted fieldwork in the late 1960s in "The Flats," the poorest section of a Black community in a large, midwestern city. She found extensive networks of friends "supporting, reinforcing each other—devising schemes for self help, strategies for survival in a community of severe economic deprivation" (1974:28). Close friends, are referred to by kin terms.

People in the Flats, especially women, maintain a set of friends through exchange: "swapping" goods (food, clothing) needed by someone at a particular time, sharing "child keeping," and giving or lending food stamps and money. Such exchanges are part of a clearly understood pattern—gifts and favors go back and forth over time. Friends thus bound together are obligated to each another and can call on each other in time of need. In opposition to theories that suggest the breakdown of social relationships among the very poor, this research documents how poor people strategize and cope through social ties.

CLUBS AND FRATERNITIES

Clubs and fraternities are social groups that define membership in terms of a sense of shared identity and objectives. They may comprise people of the same ethnic heritage (such as the Daughters of the American Revolution in the United States), occupation or business, religion, or gender. Although many clubs appear to exist primarily to serve functions of sociability and psychological support, deeper analysis often shows that these groups have economic and political roles as well.

Women's clubs in a lower-class neighborhood in Paramaribo, Suriname (see Map 2), have multiple functions (Brana-Shute 1976). Here, as is common elsewhere in Latin America, clubs raise funds to sponsor special events and support individual celebrations, meet personal financial needs, and send cards and flowers for funerals. Members attend each other's birthday parties and death rites as a group. The clubs thus offer the women psychological support, entertainment, and financial help. A political aspect exists, too. Club members often belong to the same political party and attend political rallies and events together. The clubs therefore constitute political interest groups that can influence political outcomes. Politicians and party workers confirmed that real pressure is exerted on them by women individually and in groups.

College fraternities and sororities are highly selective groups that serve a variety of explicit functions, such as entertainment and social service. They also form bonds between

(LEFT) Students gather outside a fraternity house near the University of San Francisco campus for a weekend party.
(RIGHT) Members of a fraternity at the University of Texas at Austin engage in public service by planting trees at an elementary school.
▶ *What knowledge do you have of the positive and negative social aspects of college fraternities and sororities? How could anthropological research provide a clearer picture?*

members that may help in securing jobs after graduation. Few anthropologists have studied the "Greek system" on U.S. campuses. An exception is Peggy Sanday, who was inspired to study college fraternities after the gang rape of a woman student by several fraternity brothers at the campus where she teaches. In her book *Fraternity Gang Rape: Sex, Brotherhood, and Privilege on Campus* (1990), she explores initiation rituals and how they are related to male bonding solidified by victimization and ridicule of women. Gang rape, or a "train," is a prevalent practice in some, not all, fraternities. Fraternity party invitations may hint at the possibility of a "train." Typically, the brothers seek out a "party girl"—a somewhat vulnerable young woman who may be especially needy of acceptance or especially high on alcohol or other substances (her drinks may have been "spiked"). They take her to one of the brothers' rooms, where she may or may not agree to have sex with one of the brothers, and she often passes out. Then a "train" of men have sex with her. Rarely prosecuted, the male participants reinforce their sense of privilege, power, and unity with one another through a group ritual involving abuse of a female outsider.

In many indigenous Amazonian groups, the men's house is fiercely guarded from being entered by women. If a woman trespasses on male territory, men punish her by gang rape. One interpretation of this cultural practice is that men have a high degree of anxiety about their identity as fierce warriors and as sexually potent males (Gregor 1982). Maintaining their identity as fierce and forbidding toward outsiders in-

volves taking an aggressive position in relation to women of their own group.

Cross-culturally, women do not tend to form *androphobic* ("man-hating" or otherwise anti-male) clubs, the logical parallel of *gynophobic* ("woman-hating" or otherwise anti-female) men's clubs. College sororities, for example, are not mirror images of college fraternities. Although some sororities' initiation rituals are psychologically brutal to the pledges, bonding among the members does not involve abusive behavior toward men.

COUNTERCULTURAL GROUPS

Several kinds of groups comprise people who, for one reason or another, are outside the "mainstream" of society and resist conforming to the dominant cultural pattern, as in the so-called hippie movement of the 1960s. One similarity among these groups, as with clubs and fraternities, is the importance of bonding through shared initiation and other rituals.

YOUTH GANGS The term **youth gang** refers to a group of young people, found mainly in urban areas, who are often considered a social problem by adults and law enforcement officials (Sanders 1994).

Youth gangs vary in terms of how formally they are organized. Like clubs and fraternities, gangs often have a recognized leader, formalized rituals of initiation for new members, and symbolic markers of identity such as tattoos or special clothing. An example of an informal youth gang with no formal leadership hierarchy or initiation rituals is that of the "Masta Liu" in Honiara, the capital city of the Solomon Islands in the South Pacific (Jourdan 1995) (see Map 3). The primary unifying feature of the male youth who become Masta Liu is the fact that they are unemployed. Most have

youth gang a group of young people, found mainly in urban areas, who are often considered a social problem by adults and law enforcement officials.

migrated to the city from the countryside to escape what they consider an undesirable lifestyle there: working in the fields under control of their elders. Some Liu live with extended kin in the city; others organize Liu-only households. They spend their time wandering around town (*wakabaot*) in groups of up to ten: "They stop at every shop on their way, eager to look at the merchandise but afraid to be kicked out by the security guards; they check out all the cinemas only to dream in front of the preview posters . . . not even having the $2 bill that will allow them to get in; they gaze for hours on end, and without moving, at the electronic equipment displayed in the Chinese shops, without saying a word: One can read in their gaze the silent dreams they create" (1995:210).

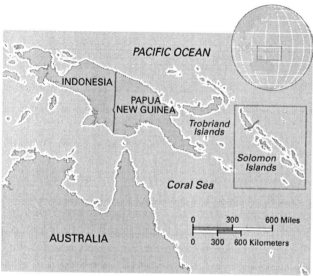

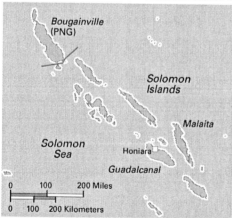

MAP 3 The Solomon Islands.
This country consists of nearly 1000 islands. Its capital, Honiara, is located on the island of Guadalcanal. The population is 540,000. Most of the people earn a living through small-scale farming and fishing. Commercial exploitation of local timber has led to severe deforestation. Over 70 languages are spoken, and 4 have recently gone extinct. The majority of the people are Christian, mainly Anglican. The Solomons were the site of some of the bitterest fighting during World War II.

Street gangs are a more formal variety of youth gang. They generally have leaders and a hierarchy of membership roles and responsibilities. They are named, and their members mark their identity with tattoos or "colors." Much popular thinking associates street gangs with violence, but not all are involved in violence. An anthropologist who did research among nearly 40 street gangs in New York, Los Angeles, and Boston learned much about why individuals join gangs, providing insights that also contradict popular thinking (Jankowski 1991). One common perception is that young boys join gangs because they are from homes with no male authority figure with whom they could identify. In the gangs studied, about half of the gang members were from intact nuclear households. Another common perception is that the gang replaces a missing feeling of family. This study showed that the same number of gang members reported having close family ties as those who did not.

Why, then, did young men join an urban gang? The research revealed that many gang members had a particular personality type called a *defiant individualist*. The defiant individualist type has five characteristics:

- Intense competitiveness
- Mistrust of others
- Self-reliance
- Social isolation
- Strong survival instinct

A structurist view suggests that poverty, especially urban poverty, leads to the development of this kind of personality, which is a reasonable response to the prevailing economic obstacles and uncertainty. In terms of explaining the global spread of urban youth gangs, structurists point to global economic changes in urban employment opportunities. In many countries, the declining urban industrial base has created persistent poverty in inner-city communities (Short 1996). At the same time, schooling and the popular media promote aspirations for a better life. Urban gang members, in this view, are the victims of large structural forces beyond their control that both inspire them to want aspects of a successful lifestyle while preventing them the legal means to obtain their aspirations. Many of these youth want to be economically successful, but social conditions channel their interests and skills into illegal pursuits rather than into legal pathways to achievement.

THINKING OUTSIDE THE BOX Think of some examples in which socially excluded groups have contributed to changing styles of music, dress, and other forms of expressive culture of so-called mainstream groups.

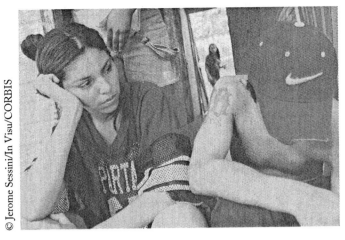

Members of the gang "18" in San Salvador, El Salvador, passing time on the street. The group's leader prohibits the use of alcohol and drugs except on Saturdays and Sundays.

▶ Consider how the social life of gangs worldwide is affected by contemporary globalization.

BODY MODIFICATION GROUPS One of the many countercultural movements in the United States includes people who have a sense of community strengthened through forms of body alteration. James Myers (1992) did research in California among people who feel they are a special group because of their interest in permanent body modification, especially genital piercing, branding, and cutting. Fieldwork involved participant observation and interviews: Myers was involved in workshops organized for the San Francisco SM (sadomasochist) community; he attended the Fifth Annual Living in Leather Convention held in Portland, Oregon, in 1990; he spent time in tattoo and piercing studios; and he talked with students and others in his hometown who were involved in these forms of body modification. The study population included males and females, heterosexuals, gays, lesbians, bisexuals, and SMers. The single largest group was SM homosexuals and bisexuals. The study population was mainly White, and most had either attended or graduated from college.

(LEFT) A Tahitian chief wears tattoos that indicate his high status. (RIGHT) A woman with tattooed arms and pierced nose in the United States.

▶ In your microcultural experience, what do tattoos mean to you when you see someone with them?

SOCIAL GROUPS AND SOCIAL STRATIFICATION

Myers witnessed many modification sessions at workshops: Those seeking modification go up on stage and have their chosen procedure done by a well-known expert. Whatever the procedure, the volunteers exhibit little pain—usually just a sharp intake of breath at the moment the needle passes through or the brand touches skin. After that critical moment, the audience breathes an audible sigh of relief. The volunteer stands up and adjusts clothing, and members of the audience applaud. This public event is a kind of initiation ritual that binds the expert, the volunteer, and the group together. Pain is an important part of many rites of passage. In this case, the audience witnesses and validates the experience and becomes joined to the initiate through witnessing.

The study revealed that a prominent motivation for seeking permanent body modification was a desire to identify with a specific group of people. As one participant said,

> It's not that we're sheep, getting pierced or cut just because everyone else is. I like to think it's because we're a very special group and we like doing something that sets us off from others. . . . Happiness is standing in line at a cafeteria and detecting that the straight-looking babe in front of you has her nipples pierced. I don't really care what her sexual orientation is, I can relate to her. (1992:292)

COOPERATIVES

Cooperatives are a form of economic group in which surpluses are shared among the members and decision making follows the democratic principle of one person/one vote (Estrin 1996). Agricultural and credit cooperatives are the most common forms of cooperatives worldwide, followed by consumer cooperatives. Two examples of cooperatives show how human agency, within different structures, can bring about positive results. In the first case, the cooperative gives its members economic strength and checks the power of the richest farmers in one region of India. In the second case, women craft producers in Panama achieve economic position within the world market and also build social ties and political leadership skills.

FARMERS' COOPERATIVES IN WESTERN INDIA
In India's western state of Maharashtra, the sugar industry is largely owned and operated through farmer cooperatives (Attwood 1992). Most shareholders are small farmers, producing just one or two acres of sugar cane. Yet the sugar industry, owned and managed cooperatively, is huge, almost as large as the state's iron and steel industry. In contrast, in the northern states where sugarcane is grown, cooperatives are not prominent.

How and why are sugar cooperatives so successful in this region? The answer lies in the different pattern of social stratification. The rural social stratification system in Maharashtra is simpler than in northern India. In most villages, the Marathas are the dominant caste, but here they constitute even more of a majority and control even more village land than is typical of dominant castes. They also have stronger local ties with each other because their marital arrangements are locally centralized. Thus, they have a better basis for cooperating with each other in spite of class differences among themselves. Large farmers dominate the elected board of directors of the cooperatives. These "sugar barons" use their position to gain power in state politics. However, within the cooperatives their power is held in check. They do not form cliques that exploit the cooperatives to the detriment of the less wealthy. In fact, large farmers cannot afford to alienate the small and midsize farmers, for that would mean economic ruin for the cooperative and the loss of their own profits.

The technology of sugarcane processing requires wide participation of the farmers. Mechanization involves investing in expensive heavy equipment. The machinery cannot be run at a profit unless it is used at full capacity during the crushing season. If small and midsize farmers were displaced with their treatment, they might decide to pull out of the cooperative and put their cane into other uses. Then capacity would be underused and profits would fall.

CRAFT COOPERATIVES IN PANAMA
In Panama's east coastal region, indigenous Kuna women have long sewn beautiful *molas*, or cloth with appliquéd designs (see Map 4). Kuna make this cloth for their own use as clothing, but since the 1960s, molas have been important items for sale both on the world market and to tourists who come to Panama (Tice 1995). Revenue from selling molas to tourists as well as internationally is now an important part of the household income of the Kuna. Some women continue to operate independently, buying their own cloth and thread and selling their molas either to an intermediary who exports them or in the local tourist market. But many women have joined cooperatives that offer them greater economic security. The cooperative buys cloth and thread in bulk and distributes it to the women. The women are paid almost the entire sale price for each mola, with only a small amount of the eventual sale prices being taken out for cooperative dues and administrative costs. Their earnings are steadier than what the fluctuating tourist season offers. Other benefits from being a member of the cooperative include the use of the cooperative as a consumer's cooperative (buying rice and sugar in bulk for members), a source of mutual strength and support, and a place for women

THINKING OUTSIDE THE BOX

Do research on the current global distribution of Alcoholics Anonymous.

Kuna Indian woman selling molas, San Blas Islands, Panama.

▷ *Learn more about molas from the Web.*

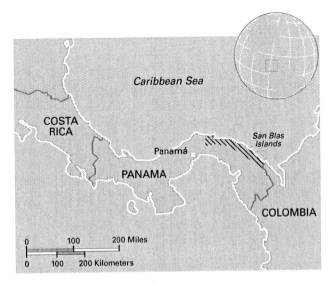

MAP 4 Kuna Region in Panama.
The Kuna are an indigenous people who live mainly in the eastern coastal region of Panama, including its offshore islands. Some live in cities and a few live in villages in neighboring Colombia. The Kuna population is around 150,000. Farming, fishing, and tourism are important parts of the economy. Each community has its own political organization, and the Kuna as a whole are organized into the Kuna General Congress. Most speak Kuna, or Dulegaya ("People's Language") and Spanish. They follow traditional religious practices, often with a mixture of Christian elements.

to develop greater leadership skills and to take advantage of opportunities for political participation in the wider society.

SELF-HELP GROUPS

Recent years have seen a worldwide proliferation of *self-help groups*, or groups formed to achieve specific personal goals, such as coping with illness or bereavement, or lifestyle change, such as trying to exercise more or lose weight. Self-help groups also increasingly use the Internet to form virtual support communities. Anthropologists who study these groups focus on why members join, on rituals of solidarity, and on leadership and organization patterns.

An ethnography of Alcoholics Anonymous groups in Mexico City reports that most members are low-income, working-class males (Brandes 2002). They migrated to Mexico City from rural areas several decades earlier to find work and improve their standard of living. Their drinking problems are related both to their poverty and to the close links between alcohol consumption and male gender identity in Mexico: A "real man" consumes a lot of alcohol. Through a dynamic of shared stories and regular meetings, AA members in Mexico City achieve a high rate of sobriety.

The success of AA in Mexico is leading to a rapid proliferation of groups. Membership is growing at about 10 percent a year, a remarkably high rate of growth for a self-help organization. At the end of the twentieth century, Latin America accounted for almost one-third of the world AA membership. Thus, a model of a middle-class self-help organization that originated in the United States has been adopted and culturally localized by low-income men throughout Latin America.

◆◆◆

Social Stratification

Social stratification consists of hierarchical relationships between different groups, as though they were arranged in layers or *strata*. Stratified groups may be unequal on a variety of measures, including material resources, power, human welfare, education, and symbolic attributes. People in groups in higher positions have privileges not experienced by those in lower-echelon groups, and they are likely to be interested in maintaining their privileged position. Social stratification appeared late in human history, most clearly with the emergence of agriculture. Now some form of social stratification is nearly universal.

Analysis of the categories—such as class, "race," gender, age, and indigeneity—that form stratification systems reveals a crucial difference among them in the degree to which membership in a given category is an **ascribed position**, based on qualities of a person gained through birth, or an **achieved position**, based on qualities of a person gained through action.

Ascribed positions may be based on one's "race," ethnicity, gender, age, and physical ability. These factors are generally out of the control of the individual, although some flexibility exists for gender (through surgery and hormonal treatments) and for certain kinds of physical conditions. Also, one can sometimes "pass" as a member of another "race" or ethnic group. Age is an interesting ascribed category because an individual goes through several different status levels associated with age. Achievement as a basis for group membership means that a person belongs on the premise of some valued attainment. Ascribed systems are thus more "closed" and achievement-based systems more "open" in terms of mobility within the system (either upward or downward). Some scholars of social status believe that increasing social complexity and modernization led to an increase in achievement-based positions and a decline in ascription-based positions. The following material explores how social categories define group membership and relations of inequality among groups.

Societies place people into categories—student, husband, child, retired person, political leader, or member of Phi Beta Kappa—referred to as a person's **status**, or position or standing in society (C. Wolf 1996). Each status has an accompanying role, which is expected behavior for someone of a particular status, and a "script" for how to behave, look, and talk. Some statuses have more prestige attached to them than others. Within societies that have marked status positions, different status groups are marked by a particular lifestyle, including goods owned, leisure activities, and linguistic styles. The maintenance of group position by higher-status categories is sometimes accomplished by exclusionary practices in relation to lower-status groups through a tendency toward group in-marriage and socializing only within the group. Groups, like individuals, have status, or standing in society.

ACHIEVED STATUS: CLASS

Social class refers to a person's or group's position in society defined primarily in economic terms. In many cultures, class is a key factor in determining a person's status, whereas in others, it is less important than, for example, birth into a certain family. Class and status, however, do not always match. A rich person may have become wealthy in disreputable ways and never gain high status. Both status and class groups are secondary groups, because a person is unlikely to know every other member of the group, especially in large-scale societies. In most instances, they are also informal groups; there are no recognized leaders or elected officials of the "urban elite" or the "working class." Subsegments of these large categories do organize themselves into formal groups, such as labor unions or exclusive clubs for the rich and famous. Class can be both ascribed and achieved because a person who is born rich has a greater than average chance of living an upper-class lifestyle.

In capitalist societies, the prevailing ideology is that the system allows for upward mobility and that every individual has the option of moving up. Some anthropologists refer to this ideology as *meritocratic individualism,* the belief that rewards go to those who deserve them (Durrenberger 2001). This ideology would seem to be most valid for people with decent jobs rather than menial workers or the unemployed, but in fact the ideology is widely held outside the middle class. In the United States, the pervasive popular belief in rewards for equal opportunity and merit is upheld and promoted in schools and universities, even in the face of substantial evidence to the contrary.

Conservative governments have long sought to weaken labor unions, and they continue to promote the fantasy of a classless society based on meritocratic individualism to support their antiunion policies. Anthropologists who take a structurist perspective point to the power of economic class position in shaping a person's lifestyle and his or her ability to choose a different one. Obviously, a person who was born rich can, through individual agency, become poor, and a poor person can become rich. In spite of exceptions to the rule, a person born rich is more likely to lead a lifestyle typical of that class, just as a person born poor is more likely lead a lifestyle typical of that class.

The concept of class is central to the theories of Karl Marx. Situated within the context of Europe's Industrial Revolution and the growth of capitalism, Marx wrote that class differences, exploitation of the working class by the owners of capital, class consciousness among workers, and class conflict are forces of change that would eventually spell the downfall of capitalism. In contrast to Marx's approach, French sociologist Emile Durkheim viewed social differences (including class) as the basis for social solidarity (1966 [1895]). He distinguished two major forms of societal cohesion: **mechanical solidarity**, social cohesion among similar groups, and **organic solidarity**, social cohesion among groups with different abilities and resources. Mechanical solidarity creates less enduring relationships because it involves little mutual need. Organic solidarity builds on need and provides

---

social stratification hierarchical relationships between different groups as though they were arranged in layers, or "strata."

ascribed position a person's standing in society based on qualities that the person has gained through birth.

achieved position a person's standing in society based on qualities that the person has gained through action.

status a person's position, or standing, in society.

mechanical solidarity social bonding among groups that are similar.

organic solidarity social bonding among groups with different abilities and resources.

(TOP) Salvatore Ferragamo headquarters in Firence (Florence), Italy. Top brand names such as Ferragamo are highly sought after by consumers internationally who can afford to buy these luxury goods. (BOTTOM) Warren Buffett, the world's richest man as of 2009. American businessman, investor, and philanthropist, Buffett is worth around US $62 billion. He is, however, known for his frugal life style.

▶ For a class project, do research for a report on Buffett's biography with attention to cultural context.

complementary resources to different groups, thus creating stronger bonds than mechanical solidarity does. Durkheim placed these two concepts in an evolutionary framework, saying that in nonindustrial times, the division of labor was only minimally specialized: Everyone did what everyone else did. With increasing social complexity and economic specialization, organic solidarity emerged as increasingly important.

ASCRIBED STATUS: "RACE," ETHNICITY, AND CASTE

Three major ascribed systems of social stratification are based on divisions of people into unequally ranked groups on the basis of "race," ethnicity, and caste, a ranked group, determined by birth, often linked to a particular occupation and to South Asian cultures. Like status and class groups, these three categories are secondary social groups, because no one can have a personal relationship with all other members of the entire group. Each system takes on local specificities depending on the context. For example, "race" and ethnicity are interrelated and overlap with conceptions of culture in much of Latin America, although differences in what they mean in terms of identity and status occur in different countries in the region (de la Cadena 2001). For some, the concept of **mestizaje** (mes-tee-ZAH-jay), mestizo, literally means "racial" mixture. In Central and South America, it refers to people who are cut off from their Indian roots, or literate and successful people who retain some indigenous cultural practices. One has to know the local system of categories and meanings attached to them to understand the dynamics of inequality that go with them.

Systems based in difference defined in terms of "race," ethnicity, and caste share with each other, and with class-based systems, some important features. First, they relegate large numbers of people to particular levels of entitlement to livelihood, power, security, esteem, and freedom (Berreman 1979 [1975]:213). This simple fact should not be overlooked. Second, those with greater entitlements dominate those with lesser entitlements. Third, members of the dominant groups tend to seek to maintain their position, consciously or unconsciously. They do this through institutions that control ideology among the dominated and through institutions that physically suppress potential rebellion or subversion by the dominated (Harris 1971, quoted in Mencher 1974:469). Fourth, in spite of efforts to maintain systems of dominance, instances of subversion and rebellion do occur, indicating the potential for agency among the oppressed.

"RACE" Racial stratification is a relatively recent form of social inequality. It results from the unequal meeting of two formerly separate groups through colonization, slavery, and other large-group movements (Sanjek 1994). Europe's "age of discovery," beginning in the 1500s, ushered in a new era of

Boys in a small town of Brazil exhibit some of the skin-color diversity in the Brazilian population.

global contact. In contrast, in relatively homogeneous cultures, ethnicity is a more important distinction than "race." In contemporary Nigeria, for example, the population is largely homogeneous, and ethnicity is the more salient term (Jinadu 1994). A similar situation prevails in other African states as well as in the Middle East, Central Europe and Eurasia, and China.

A key feature of racial thinking is its insistence that behavioral differences among peoples are "natural," inborn, or biologically caused (in this, it resembles sexism, ageism, and casteism). Throughout the history of racial categorizations in the West, such features as head size, head shape, and brain size have been accepted as the reasons for behavioral differences. Writing early in the twentieth century, Franz Boas contributed to de-linking supposed inborn, racial attributes from behavior. He showed that people with the same head size but from different cultures behaved differently and that people with various head sizes within the same cultures behaved similarly. For Boas and his followers, culture, not biology, is the key explanation for behavior. Thus "race" is not a biological reality; there is no way to divide the human population into "races" based on certain biological features. Yet social race and racism exist. In other words, the concept of "race" in many contexts has a social reality in terms of people's entitlements, status, and treatment. In spite of some progress in reducing racism in the United States in the twentieth century, racial discrimination persists. One way of understanding this persistence is to see racial discrimination as linked to class formation rather than separate from it (Brodkin 2000). In this view, racial stereotyping and discrimination function to keep people in less desirable jobs or unemployed, as necessary aspects of advanced industrial capitalism, which depends on

there being a certain number of low-paid workers and even a certain amount of unemployment.

Racial classifications in the Caribbean and in Latin America involve complicated systems of status classification. This complexity results from the variety of contact over the centuries between peoples from Europe, Africa, Asia, and indigenous populations. Skin tone is one basis of racial classification, but it is mixed with other physical features and economic status as well. In Haiti, for example, racial categories take into account physical factors such as skin texture, depth of skin tone, hair color and appearance, and facial features (Trouillot 1994). Racial categories also include a person's income, social origin, level of formal education, personality or behavior, and kinship ties. Depending on how these variables are combined, a person occupies one category or another—and may even move between categories. Thus, a person with certain physical features who is poor will be considered to be a different "color" than a person with the same physical features who is well-off.

An extreme example of racial stratification was the South African policy of apartheid, legally sanctioned segregation of dominant Whites from non-Whites. White dominance in South Africa (see Map 5) began in the early 1800s with White migration and settlement. In the 1830s, slavery was abolished. At the same time, increasingly racist thinking developed among Whites (Johnson 1994:25). Racist images, including visions of Africans as lazy, out of control, and sex driven, served as the rationale for colonialist domination in place of outright slavery. In spite of years of African resistance to White domination, the Whites succeeded in maintaining and increasing their control for nearly two centuries. In South Africa, Blacks constitute 90 percent of the population, a numerical majority dominated, through strict apartheid, by the White minority until only recently. Every aspect of life for the majority of Africans was far worse than for the Whites. Every measure of life quality—infant mortality, longevity, education—showed great disparity between the Whites and the Africans. In addition to physical deprivation, the Africans experienced psychological suffering through constant insecurity about raids from the police and other forms of violence. Now, they face the scourge of continuing poverty and disentitlement as well as excess death and suffering from HIV/AIDS.

In contrast to the explicitly racist discrimination of South African apartheid, racism exists even where it is against the law to discriminate against people on the basis of race. In such contexts, racism is often denied and therefore a challenge

---

mestizaje literally, racial mixture; in Central and South America, indigenous people who are cut off from their Indian roots, or literate and successful indigenous people who retain some traditional cultural practices.

In 2003, the Treatment Action Campaign (TAC) began a program of civil disobedience to prompt the government of South Africa to sign and implement a National Prevention and Treatment Plan for HIV/AIDS. The TAC uses images of Hector Peterson, the first youth killed in the Soweto uprising against apartheid, and slogans such as "The Struggle Continues: Support HIV/AIDS Treatment Now."

▶ *Take a position, and be prepared to defend it, on whether or not a country's government should take responsibility for preventing and treating HIV/AIDS.*

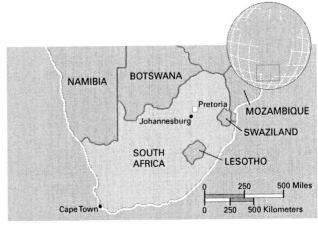

MAP 5 South Africa.
The Republic of South Africa experienced the highest level of colonial immigration of any African country. Its rich mineral wealth attracted interest from global powers through the Cold War era. Of its population of over 46 million, 80 percent are Black South Africans. The rest are of mixed ethnic backgrounds (referred to as "Coloureds"), Indian (from India), or White descendants of colonial immigrants. South Africa has 11 official languages, and it recognizes 8 nonofficial languages. Afrikaans and English are the major languages of the administration. Nonofficial languages include those of the San and other indigenous peoples.

to fight. In the United States, racism plays out in many areas of life including environmental pollution (see Eye on the Environment).

ETHNICITY Ethnicity is a sense of group membership based on a shared sense of identity (Comaroff 1987). Identity may be based on the perception of shared history, territory, language, religion, or a combination of these. Ethnicity can be a basis for claiming entitlements to resources (such as land, buildings, or artifacts) and for defending or regaining those resources.

States are interested in managing ethnicity to the extent that it does not threaten security. China has one of the most formalized systems for monitoring its many ethnic groups, and it has an official policy on ethnic minorities, meaning the non-Han groups (Wu 1990). The government lists a total of 54 groups other than the Han majority, which constitutes about 94 percent of the total. The other 6 percent of the population is made up of these 54 groups, about 67 million people. The non-Han minorities occupy about 60 percent of China's land mass and are located in border or "frontier" areas such as Tibet, Yunnan, Xinjiang, and Inner Mongolia. Basic criteria for defining an ethnic group include language, territory, economy, and "psychological disposition." The Chinese government establishes strict definitions of group membership and group characteristics; it even sets standards for ethnic costumes and dances.

---

diaspora population   a dispersed group of people living outside their original homeland.

The Chinese treatment of the Tibetan people is especially severe and can be considered *ethnocide,* or annihilation of the culture of an ethnic group by a dominant group.

The Chinese government's treatment of Tibetan traditional medicine over the past several decades illustrates how the Han majority exploits aspects of minority cultures. In 1951, China forcibly incorporated Tibet, and the Chinese government undertook measures to bring about the social and economic transformation of what was formerly a decentralized, Buddhist feudal regime. This transformation has caused increasing ethnic conflict between Tibetans and Han Chinese, including demonstrations by Tibetans and crackdowns from the Chinese. Traditional Tibetan medicine has become part of the Chinese–Tibetan conflicts because of its cultural significance and importance to religion in Tibetan society (Janes 1995:7). Previously based on a model of apprenticeship training, it is now westernized and involves several years of classroom-based, lecture-oriented learning followed by an internship. At Tibet University, only half of all formal lecture-based instruction is concerned with traditional Tibetan medicine. Curriculum changes have reduced the integrity of Tibetan medicine: It has been separated from its Buddhist content, and parts of it have been merged with a biomedical approach. Some might say that overall, traditional Tibetan medicine has been "revived" in China, but stronger evidence supports the argument that the state has co-opted it and transformed it for its own purposes.

Industrial Pollution and Activism in an African American Community in Georgia, the United States

"But I know it's true" is an often repeated phrase among African American residents of the Hyde Park area of Augusta, Georgia (Checker 2005, 2007). Following World War II, many rural African American families in Georgia bought land in Hyde Park, a swampy area, but nonetheless one that allowed them access to nearby jobs in factories or as domestic workers. The neighborhood was vibrant with shops and churches. It was, however, poorly serviced by the government and surrounded by several industrial enterprises including Southern Wood Piedmont (SWP), a wood-preserving factory.

In the 1980s, several residents fell ill with uncommon and mysterious forms of cancer and skin diseases. SWP was found to be polluting the ground water in the neighborhood with dioxins, chlorophenols, and other chemicals. The factory closed in 1988 and began efforts to remediate the contamination. A nearby low-income neighborhood that was predominantly White settled a class-action lawsuit against SWP and received compensation. The residents

of Hyde Park were not told of the lawsuit or asked to join it, and they therefore received no compensation.

Hyde Park residents began to learn of other sources of industrial pollution including PCBs. More cases emerged, especially among children, of rashes, lupus, respiratory and circulatory problems, and rare forms of cancer. People stopped letting their children play in the backyard, in order to avoid contact with contaminated ditch water and soil. They stopped growing vegetables in their home gardens. The value of their homes fell dramatically. In sum, they lost their health, their freedom to use their own property for play, and their economic security.

Over time, more studies showed high levels of chemicals and heavy metals in the groundwater and soil in Hyde Park. Georgia's Environmental Protection Division (EPD) continued to argue that levels were within normal ranges. Hyde Park residents, however, were convinced that the pollution was causing their health and other problems. They organized in order to make their claims heard.

Environmental justice activism refers to social movements dedicated to documenting the structural violence and inequality that place certain groups at risk of losing their entitlements to live in a safe and healthy environment and in helping such groups gain compensation or other forms of redress. Hyde Park residents, along with a nearby African American neighborhood, formed HAPIC, the Hyde and Aragon Park Improvement Committee. HAPIC activists use a unique blend of Black solidarity, church-based organizing principles, computers to bridge the digital divide, and connections with wider environmental groups such as the Sierra Club to make its voice heard in the state political arena.

◆ FOOD FOR THOUGHT

- Do Internet research to learn about the current status of the Hyde Park residents' efforts to make their neighborhood livable and gain compensation for damages to their health and household security.

People of one ethnic group who move from one niche to another are at risk of exclusionary treatment by the local residents. Roma (formerly called gypsies by outsiders but considered a derogatory term by the Roma), are a **diaspora population**, a dispersed group living outside their original homeland, and are scattered throughout Europe and the United States (see Culturama). A less difficult but still not easy adjustment is being experienced by Indo-Canadians (immigrants from India to Canada). In research among a sample of nearly 300 Indo-Canadians in Vancouver, British Columbia, about half of all the respondents reported experiencing some form of discrimination in the recent past (Nodwell and Guppy 1992). The percentage was higher among men (54 percent) than among women (45 percent). The higher level for men was consistent across the four categories: verbal abuse, property damage, workplace discrimination, and physical harm. Verbal abuse was the most frequent form of discrimination, reported by 40 percent of both men and women. Indo-Canadians of the Sikh faith who

were born in India say that they experience the highest levels of discrimination in Canada. Apparently, however, their actual experience of discrimination is not greater than for other Indo-Canadians. The difference is that Sikhs who were born in India are more sensitive to discrimination than others. Sikhism, as taught and practiced in India, supports a strong sense of honor, which should be protected and, if wronged, avenged. This study helps explain differences in perception of discrimination among ethnic migrants. It does not, however, explain why such high levels of discriminatory treatment exist in a nation committed to ethnic tolerance.

THINKING OUTSIDE THE BOX

With which ethnic or other kind of social group do you identify? What are the bases of this identification? Is your social group relatively high or low in terms of social status?

SOCIAL GROUPS AND SOCIAL STRATIFICATION

The Roma of Eastern Europe

The Roma, better known by the derogatory term "Gypsies," are Europe's largest minority population. They live in nearly all the countries of Europe and Central Asia. In Europe, their total is between 7 and 9 million people (World Bank 2003). They are most concentrated in the countries of Eastern Europe, where they constitute around 10 percent of the population.

Roma history is one of mobility and marginality ever since several waves of migrants left their original homeland in northern India between the ninth and fourteenth centuries CE (Crowe 1996). For many Roma in Europe, their lifestyle continues to involve movement. Temporary camps of their wagons often appear overnight on the outskirts of a town. Settled Roma typically live in marginalized areas that lack decent housing, clean water, and good schools. Most members of mainstream society look down on, and even despise, the Roma.

In Budapest, Hungary, the Roma minority is the most disadvantaged ethnic group (Ladányi 1993). Not all Roma in Budapest, however, are poor. About 1 percent have gained wealth. The other 99 percent live in substandard housing in the slums of inner Pest. Since the fall of state socialism in Hungary, discrimination against the Roma has increased. The government of Hungary has a policy that allows the Roma a degree of local minority self-government (Schaft and Brown 2000). Some Roma communities are mobilizing to improve their living conditions.

In Slovakia, one-third of the Roma live in ghetto-like enclaves called osada (Scheffel 2004). The heaviest concentration of osadas is in the eastern province. These settlements lack clean water, sewage treatment, reliable electricity, access to decent housing, good schools, and passable roads. They exist in close proximity to affluent neighborhoods of

ethnic Slovaks, or "Whites." In one village, Svinia (SVEEH-nee-yuh), roughly 700 Roma are crowded together on a hectare of swampy land while their 670 ethnic Slovak neighbors own over 1400 hectares of land (2004:8).

As more Eastern European countries seek to enter the European Union, they are initiating programs to improve Roma living conditions and enacting laws to prevent discrimination. Fieldwork in Slovakia indicates that the government there is doing little to improve the lives of the Roma. The situation in Hungary is better. After Hungary joined the European Union in 2004, it elected two Roma to the EU Parliament. In Bulgaria, the Roma won a court case in 2005 declaring that segregated schools were unconstitutional.

Thanks to David Z. Scheffel, Thompson Rivers University, for reviewing this material.

David Z. Scheffel

David Z. Scheffel

(LEFT) The Roma settlement of Svinia in 1993. The standard of living has not improved since the 1990s, but the population has increased by nearly 50 percent, resulting in overcrowding and high levels of stress.
(CENTER) Roma children's access to school facilities is severely restricted. A few Romani schoolchildren participate in the school lunch program but in a separate room next to the cafeteria.

MAP 6 Roma Population in Eastern Europe. Romania has the highest number of Roma of any country in the world, between 1 and 2 million. Macedonia has the highest percentage of Roma in its population.

CASTE The **caste system** is a social stratification system linked with Hinduism and based on a person's birth into a particular group. It exists in its clearest form in India, among its Hindu population, and in other areas of Hindu culture such as Nepal, Sri Lanka, and Fiji. The caste system is particularly associated with Hindu peoples because ancient Hindu scriptures are taken as the foundational sources for defining the major social categories called *varnas* (a Sanskrit word meaning "color") (see Figure 2). The four varnas are the *brahmans*, priests; the *kshatriya*, warriors; the *vaishya*, merchants; and the *shudras*, laborers. Men of the first three varnas go through a ritual ceremony of initiation and "rebirth," after which they may wear a sacred thread across their chest, indicating their purity and high status as "twice-born." Beneath the four varna groups are people considered so low that they are outside the caste system itself, hence the English term "outcast." Another English term for them is "untouchables," because people of the upper varnas avoided any kind of contact with them in order to maintain their purity. Mahatma Gandhi, himself a member of an upper caste, renamed them *harijans* ("children of god") in his attempt to raise their status into that of the shudras. Currently, members of this category have adopted the term **dalit** (dah-lit), which means "oppressed" or "ground down."

The four traditional varnas and the dalit category contain many hundreds of locally named groups called castes, or, more appropriately, *jatis* (birth group). The term "caste" is a Portuguese word meaning "breed" or "type." Portuguese colonialists first used it in the fifteenth century to refer to the closed social groups they encountered (Cohn 1971:125). Jati, a more emic term, conveys the meaning that a Hindu is born into his or her group. Jatis are ascribed status groups. Just as the four varnas are ranked relative to each other, so are all the jatis within them. For example, the jati of brahmans is divided into priestly and nonpriestly subgroups; the priestly brahmans are separated into household priests, temple priests, and

funeral priests; the household priests are broken down into two or more categories; and each of those are divided into subgroups based on lineage ties (Parry 1966:77). Within all these categories exist well-defined status hierarchies.

Status levels also exist among dalits. In western Nepal, which, like India, has a caste system, dalit artisans such as basket weavers and ironsmiths are the highest tier (Cameron 1995). They do not touch any of the people beneath them. The second tier includes leatherworkers and tailors. The bottom tier comprises people who are "untouchable" to all groups, including other dalits, because their work is extremely polluting according to Hindu rules. This category includes musicians (because some of their instruments are made of leather and they perform in public) and sex workers.

Indian anthropologist M. N. Srinivas (1959) contributed the concept of the *dominant caste* to refer to the tendency for one caste in any particular village to control most of the land and, often, to be numerically preponderant as well. Brahmans are at the top of the social hierarchy in terms of ritual purity, and they are often, but not always, the dominant caste. Throughout northern India, it is common for jatis of the kshatriya varna to be the dominant village group. This is the case in Pahansu village, where a group called the Gujars is dominant (Raheja 1988). The Gujars constitute the numerical majority, and they control most of the land. Moreover, they dominate in the *jajmani system*, a patron-provider system in which landholding patrons (*jajmans*) are linked, through exchanges of food for services, with brahman priests, artisans (blacksmiths, potters), agricultural laborers, and other workers such as sweepers. In Pahansu, Gujars have power and status as the major patrons, supporting many different service providers who are beholden to them.

Some anthropologists have described the jajmani service system as one of mutual interdependence (organic solidarity, to use Durkheim's term) that provides security for the less well-off. Others argue that the system benefits those at the top to the detriment of those at the bottom. This perspective, from "the bottom up," views the patron-service system and the entire caste system as one of exploitation by those at the top (Mencher 1974). The benign interpretation is based on research conducted among the upper castes who present this view. From low-caste people's perspective, it is the patrons who have the power. Dissatisfied patrons can dismiss service providers, refuse them loans, or not pay them. Service providers who are dissatisfied with the treatment they receive

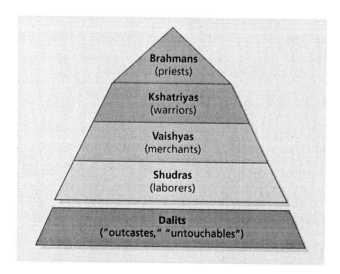

FIGURE 2 Model of India's Varna Categories

---

caste system a form of social stratification linked with Hinduism and based on a person's birth into a particular group.

dalit the preferred name for the socially defined lowest groups in the Indian caste system, meaning "oppressed" or "ground down."

(LEFT) Only a special category of brahman priests can officiate at the Chidambaram temple in Tamil Nadu, southern India. Here, members of a mixed-age group sit for a moment's relaxation. (RIGHT) A village carpenter in front of his house in a north Indian village. The status of carpenters is midlevel, between the landholding elites or brahman priests and those who deal with polluting materials such as animal hides or refuse.

▶ In your culture, what social status do carpenters, toolmakers, or other skilled manual laborers have?

from their patrons have little recourse. In addition, male patrons often demand sexual access to females of service-providing households.

Throughout South Asia, the growth of industrial manufacturing has reduced the need for some service providers, especially tailors, potters, and weavers. Many of these people have left their villages to work in urban areas. The tie that remains the strongest is between patrons and their brahman priests, whose ritual services cannot be replaced by machines.

The caste system involves several mechanisms that maintain it: marriage rules, spatial segregation, and ritual. Marriage rules strictly enforce jati endogamy (in-group marriage). Marriage outside one's jati, especially in rural areas and particularly between a higher-caste female and lower-caste male, is cause for serious, even lethal, punishment by caste elders and other local power-holders. Among urban educated elites, a trend toward inter-jati marriages is emerging.

Spatial segregation functions to maintain the privileged preserve of the upper castes and to remind the lower castes continually of their marginal status. In many rural contexts, the dalits live in a completely separate cluster; in other cases, they have their own neighborhood sections into which no upper-caste person will venture. Ritual rules and practices also serve to maintain dominance. The rich upper-caste leaders sponsor important annual festivals, thereby regularly restating their claim to public prominence (Mines 1994).

Social mobility within the caste system has traditionally been limited, but instances have been documented of group "up-casting." Several strategies exist, including gaining wealth, affiliation or merger with a somewhat higher jati, education, migration, and political activism (Kolenda 1978). A group that attempts to gain higher jati status takes on the behavior and dress of twice-born jatis. These include men wearing the sacred thread, vegetarianism, non-remarriage of widows, seclusion of women from the public domain, and the giving of larger dowries for the marriage of a daughter. Some dalits have opted out of the caste system by converting to Christianity or Buddhism. Others are becoming politically organized through the Dalit Panthers, a social movement seeking greater power and improved economic status for dalits.

The Indian constitution of 1949 declared that discrimination on the basis of caste is illegal. Constitutional decree, however, did not bring an end to these deeply structured inequalities. In the late twentieth century, the government of India instituted policies to promote the social and economic advancement of dalits, such as reserving for them places in medical schools, seats in the government, and public-sector jobs. This "affirmative action" plan has infuriated many of the upper castes, especially brahmans, who feel most threatened. Is the caste system on the decline? Surely aspects of it are changing. Especially in large cities, people of different jatis can "pass" and participate on a more nearly equal basis in public life—if they have the economic means to do so.

◆◆◆
Civil Society

Civil society consists of the social domain of diverse interest groups that function outside the government to organize economic, political, and other aspects of life. It has a long history in Western philosophy, and many different definitions have been proposed by thinkers such as John Locke, Thomas Paine, Adam Smith, and Karl Marx (Kumar 1996:89). According to the German philosopher Hegel, civil society encompasses the social groups and institutions between the individual and the state. Italian social theorist Gramsci wrote that there are two basic types of civic institutions: those that support the state, such as the church and schools, and those that oppose state power, such as trade unions, social protest groups, and citizens' rights groups.

CIVIL SOCIETY FOR THE STATE: THE CHINESE WOMEN'S MOVEMENT

In some instances, governments seek to build civil society to further their goals. The women's movement in China is an example of such a state-created organization. Canadian anthropologist Ellen Judd (2002) conducted a study of the women's movement in China, within the constraints that the government imposes on anthropological fieldwork by foreigners. Under the Mao leadership, foreign anthropologists were not allowed to do research of any sort in China. The situation began to change in the 1980s when some field research, within strict limitations, became possible.

Judd developed a long-term relationship with China over several decades, having lived there as a student from 1974 to 1977, undertaking long-term fieldwork there in 1986, and returning almost every year since for research or some other activity, such as being involved in a development project for women or attending the Beijing Fourth World Conference on Women. According to Judd, "These various ways of being in China all allowed me some interaction with Chinese women and some knowledge of their lives" (2002:14). In her latest project to study the Chinese women's movement, she wanted to conduct research as a cultural anthropologist would normally do, through intensive participant observation over a long period of time.

Even now, the Chinese government limits such research, keeping foreigners at a distance from everyday life. Judd was not allowed to join the local women's organization or to speak privately with any of the women. Officials accompanied her on all household visits and interviews. She was allowed to attend meetings, however, and she had access to all the public information about the goals of the women's movement, which is called the Women's Federations. A policy goal of the Chinese government is to improve the quality of women's lives, and the Women's Federations were formed to address that goal. The government oversees the operation at all levels, from the national level to the township and village. The primary objective is to mobilize women, especially rural women, to participate in literacy training and market activities.

Judd's fieldwork, constrained as it was by government regulations, nevertheless yielded insights. She learned, through interviews with women members, about some women who have benefited from the programs, and she discovered how important education for women is in terms of their ability to enter into market activities. The book she wrote is largely descriptive, focusing on the "public face" of the Women's Federations in one locale. Such a descriptive account is the most that can emerge from research in China at this time. Given that the women's organizations are formed by and for the government, this example stretches the concept of civil society.

ACTIVIST GROUPS

Activist groups are groups formed with the goal of changing certain conditions, such as political repression, violence, and human rights violations. In studying activist groups, cultural anthropologists are interested in learning what motivates the formation of such groups, what their goals and strategies are, and what leadership patterns they exhibit. Sometimes anthropologists join the efforts of activist groups and use their knowledge to support these groups' goals (see Lessons Applied).

Many activist groups are initiated and organized by women. CO-MADRES of El Salvador is an important, women-led social movement in Latin America (Stephen 1995). CO-MADRES is a Spanish abbreviation for an organization called, in English, the Committee of Mothers and Relatives of Political Prisoners, Disappeared and Assassinated of El Salvador. It was founded in 1977 by a group of mothers protesting the atrocities committed by the Salvadoran government and military. During the civil war that lasted from 1979 until 1992, a total of 80,000 people died and 7000 more disappeared, or one in every 100 El Salvadorans.

The initial group comprised nine mothers. A year later, it had grown to nearly 30 members, including some men. In 1979, the group made its first international trip to secure wider recognition. This developed into a full-fledged and successful campaign for international solidarity in the 1980s,

---

civil society the collection of interest groups that function outside the government to organize economic and other aspects of life.

LESSONS applied

Advocacy Anthropology and Environmental Activism in Papua New Guinea

A controversial issue in applied anthropology is whether an anthropologist should take on the role of community activist, acting as an advocate on behalf of the people among whom he or she has conducted research (Kirsch 2002). Some say that anthropologists should maintain a neutral position in a conflict situation and simply offer information on issues that may be used by either side. Others say that it is appropriate and right for anthropologists to take sides and help support less powerful groups against more powerful groups. Those who endorse anthropologists taking an activist or advocacy role argue that neutrality is never truly neutral: By seemingly taking no position, one indirectly supports the status quo, and information provided to both sides will generally serve the interests of the more powerful side in any case.

Stuart Kirsch took an activist role after conducting field research for over 15 years in a region of Papua New Guinea that has been negatively affected by a large copper and gold mine called the Ok Tedi mine. The mine releases 80,000 tons of mining wastes into the local river system daily, causing extensive environmental damage that in turn affects people's food and water sources. Kirsch has joined with the local community in its extended legal and political campaign to limit further pollution and to gain compensation for damages suffered. He explains his involvement with the community as a form of reciprocal exchange. The community members have provided him with information about their culture for over 15 years. He believes that his knowledge is part of the people's cultural property and that they have a rightful claim to its use.

Kirsch's support of the community's goals took several forms. First, his scholarly research provided documentation of the problems of the people living downstream from the mine.

Courtesy of Stuart Kirsch

Yonggom people gather at a meeting in Atkamba village on the Ok Tedi River, Papua New Guinea, to discuss legal proceedings in 1996. At the end of the meeting, leaders signed an agreement to an out-of-court settlement, which was presented to the Victorian Supreme Court in Melbourne, Australia. The current lawsuit concerns the Yonggom people's claim that the 1996 settlement agreement has been breached.

Community activists incorporated his findings in their speeches when traveling in Australia, Europe, and the Americas to spread awareness of their case and gather international support. During the 1992 Earth Summit, one leader presented the media with excerpts from an article by Kirsch during a press conference held aboard the Greenpeace ship, *Rainbow Warrior II*, in the Rio de Janeiro harbor. Second, he worked closely with local leaders, helping them decide how best to convey their views to the public and in the court. Third, Kirsch served as a cultural broker in discussions among community members, politicians, mining executives, lawyers, and representatives of nongovernmental organizations (NGOs) in order to promote solutions for the problems faced by people living downstream from the mine. Fourth, he convened an international meeting of environmental NGOs in Washington, DC, in 1999 and secured funding to bring a representative from the community to the meeting.

In spite of official reports recommending that the mine be closed in 2001, its future remains uncertain. No assessment of past damages to the community has been prepared. As the case goes on, Kirsch will continue to support the community's efforts by sharing with them the results of his research, just as they have for so long shared their culture with him. Indigenous people worldwide are increasingly invoking their rights to anthropological knowledge about themselves. According to Kirsch, these claims require anthropologists to rethink their roles and relationships with the people they study. It can no longer be a relationship in which the community provides knowledge and the anthropologist keeps and controls that knowledge for his or her intellectual development alone. Although the details are still being worked out, the overall goal must be one of collaboration and cooperation.

◆ FOOD FOR THOUGHT

- Consider the pros and cons of anthropological advocacy and decide what position you would take on the Ok Tedi case. Be prepared to defend your position.

with support in other Latin American countries, Europe, Australia, the United States, and Canada. The group's increased visibility earned it repression from the government. Its office was bombed in 1980 and then four more times after that. Forty-eight members of CO-MADRES have been detained since 1977; five have been assassinated. Harassment and disappearances continued even after the signing of the Peace Accords in January 1992: "In February 1993, the son and the nephew of one of the founders of CO-MADRES were assassinated in Usulutan. This woman had already lived through the experience of her own detention, the detention and gang rape of her daughter, and the disappearance and assassination of other family members" (1995:814).

In the 1990s, CO-MADRES focused on holding the state accountable for human rights violations during the civil war, providing protection for political prisoners, seeking assurances of human rights protection in the future, working against domestic violence, educating women about political participation, and initiating economic projects for women. The work of CO-MADRES, throughout its history, has incorporated elements of both the "personal" and the "political," concerns of mothers and other family members for lost kin and for exposing and halting abuses of the state and military. The lesson learned from the case of CO-MADRES is that activist groups formed by women can be based on issues related to the domestic domain (murdered sons and other kin), but their activities can extend to the top of the public political hierarchy.

Another example of activist group formation under difficult conditions comes from urban Egypt (Hopkins and Mehanna 2000). The Egyptian government frowns on overt political action outside the realm of the government. Although Egyptian citizens are deeply concerned about environmental issues such as waste disposal, clean air and water, and noise, group formation for environmental causes is not easily accomplished. People interviewed in Cairo reported that they rarely discuss environmental issues with one another. One case of environmental concern, however, did result in the closing of a highly polluting lead smelter. People in the affected neighborhood banded together around this particular issue and called attention to the situation in the public media, prompting high-level officials to take up their case. They were

A march of the "Mothers of the Disappeared" in Argentina. This organization of women combines activism motivated by personal causes (the loss of one's child or children to political torture and death) and the public issue of state repression.

▷ *How many activist groups in your culture can you name, and what are their goals?*

successful because their target was localized on one relatively small industry and because the industry was so clearly guilty of polluting the environment.

NEW SOCIAL MOVEMENTS AND CYBERPOWER

Social scientists have begun to use the term *new social movements* to refer to the many social activist groups that emerged in the late twentieth century around the world. These groups are often formed by oppressed minorities such as indigenous peoples, ethnic groups, women, and the poor.

New social movements are taking advantage of cybertechnology to broaden their membership, exchange ideas, and raise funds (Escobar 2002). Cyber-enhanced social movements are important new political institutions that offer new ways to question, resist, and transform current structures. The importance of cybernetworking has not gone unnoticed by formal political leaders, who are paying increased attention to enhancing their personal websites and those of their parties.

the BIG questions REVISITED

◆ What are social groups and how do they vary cross-culturally?

Social groups can be classified in terms of whether all members have face-to-face interaction with one another, whether membership is based on ascription or achievement, and how formal the group's organization and leadership structure are. They extend from the most informal, face-to-face groups, such as those based on friendship, to groups that have formal membership requirements and whose members are widely dispersed and never meet each other. All groups have criteria for membership, often based on a perceived notion of similarity in terms of gender or class identity, work roles, opposition to mainstream culture, economic goals, or self-improvement.

Many groups require a formal ritual of initiation of new members. In some cases, initiation into the group involves dangerous or frightening activities that serve to bond members to one another through a shared experience of helplessness.

◆ What is social stratification?

Social stratification consists of hierarchical relationships between and among different groups, usually based on some culturally defined concept of status. Depending on the context, categories such as class, "race," ethnicity, gender, sexual preference, age, and ability may determine group and individual status.

The degree of social inequality among different status groups is highly marked in agricultural and industrial/ informatics societies. Marked status inequalities are not characteristic of most foraging societies. Status inequalities are variable in pastoralist and horticultural societies, with leveling mechanisms typically at play to prevent the formation of severe inequalities.

India's caste-based system is an important example of a rigid structure of severe social inequality based on a person's birth group. According to ancient Hindu scriptures, the population is divided into mutually exclusive groups with different rights and privileges. Discrimination on the basis of caste is banned by the Indian constitution, yet it still exists, as does racism in other contexts even though formally illegal.

◆ What is civil society?

Civil society consists of groups and organizations that, although they are not part of the formal government, perform similar or complementary economic, political, or social functions. Civil society groups can be divided into those that support government policies and initiatives, and thus further the interests of government, and those that oppose government policies and actions.

Some anthropologists who study activist groups decide to take an advocacy role and apply their knowledge to further the goals of the community. This direction in applied anthropology is related to the view that anthropological knowledge is partly the cultural property of the people who have shared their lives and insights with the anthropologist.

New forms of information and communication technology help civil society groups gain visibility and stay in touch with their supporters.

KEY CONCEPTS

achieved position

age set

ascribed position

caste system

civil society

dalit

diaspora population

mechanical solidarity

mestizaje

organic solidarity

primary group

secondary group

social group

social stratification

status

youth gang

SUGGESTED READINGS

Sandra Bell and Simon Coleman, eds. *The Anthropology of Friendship*. New York: Berg, 1999. Following an introductory chapter by the editors on the anthropology of friendship, case studies discuss friendship in contemporary Melanesia, friendship as portrayed in Icelandic sagas, friendship in the context of a game of dominoes in a London pub, how friendship creates support networks in northern Europe, and the globalization of friendship ties in East Africa.

Gerald Berreman. *Caste and Other Inequities: Essays on Inequality*. Delhi, India: Folklore Institute, 1979. Berreman wrote these essays on caste and social inequality in India over a period of 20 years. Topics include caste and economy, caste ranking, caste and social interaction, and a comparison of caste with "race" in the United States.

Rosabelle Boswell. *Le Malaise Créole: Ethnic Identity in Mauritius*. New York: Bergahn Books, 2007. This book examines the marginalization of the Creole population in Mauritius. Most Creoles are descendants of slaves brought to the island from mainland Africa between the seventeenth and nineteenth centuries.

Stanley Brandes. *Staying Sober in Mexico City*. Austin: University of Texas Press, 2002. This ethnography of Alcoholics Anonymous groups in Mexico City focuses on how these groups help low-income men remain sober through social support. Although emphasizing the role of human agency in the men's attempts to remain sober, the author argues that the high rate of alcoholism among poor Mexican men must be viewed in the context of structural conditions.

Kia Lilly Caldwell. *Negras in Brazil: Re-Envisioning Black Women, Citizenship, and the Politics of Identity*. New Brunswick, NJ: Rutgers University Press, 2007. Fieldwork over more than a decade in several cities of Brazil informs this study of how Afro-Brazilian women see themselves as women, as Black, and as Brazilian. Narratives of 35 women show the connections between "race," gender, and social activism.

Liliana Goldin, ed. *Identities on the Move: Transnational Processes in North America and the Caribbean Basin*. Austin: University of Texas Press, 2000. This collection offers chapters on identity formation and change in the process of voluntary migration or

displacement and on how states label and exclude transnationals, often in racialized ways.

Thomas A. Gregor and Donald Tuzin, eds. *Gender in Amazonia and Melanesia: An Exploration of the Comparative Method*. Berkeley: University of California Press, 2001. Two anthropologists, one a specialist on indigenous peoples of Amazonia and the other on Papua New Guinea, edited this volume, which includes a theoretical overview chapter and several chapters addressing similarities and differences between the two regions in fertility cults, rituals of masculinity, gender politics, and age-based gender roles.

Steven Gregory and Roger Sanjek, eds. *Race*. New Brunswick: Rutgers University Press, 1994. Following an introductory chapter by each editor, chapters discuss topics including racism in the United States and the Caribbean, how "race" articulates with other inequalities, and racism in higher education and anthropology.

Jake Kosek. *Understories: The Political Life of Forests in Northern New Mexico*. Durham: Duke University Press, 2007. This book is based on fieldwork in New Mexico and archival research. It exposes the racial, class, and other factors that shape the political disputes over forest resources in the Española Valley.

Cris Shore and Stephen Nugent, eds. *Elite Cultures: Anthropological Perspectives*. New York: Routledge, 2002. This volume contains two introductory chapters and a concluding chapter framing 12 ethnographic cases from around the world. Issues addressed are how elites in different societies maintain their positions, how elites represent themselves to others, and how anthropologists study elites.

Karin Tice. *Kuna Crafts, Gender and the Global Economy*. Austin: University of Texas Press, 1995. This ethnography looks at how the tourist market has affected women's production of molas in Panama and how women have organized into cooperatives to improve their situation.

Kevin A. Yelvington. *Producing Power: Ethnicity, Gender, and Class in a Caribbean Workplace*. Philadelphia, PA: Temple University Press, 1995. This ethnography examines class, "race," and gender inequalities as linked processes of social stratification within the context of a factory in Trinidad and in the wider social sites of households, neighborhoods, and global interconnections.

CHAPTER 8

SEX, GENDER, AND CULTURE

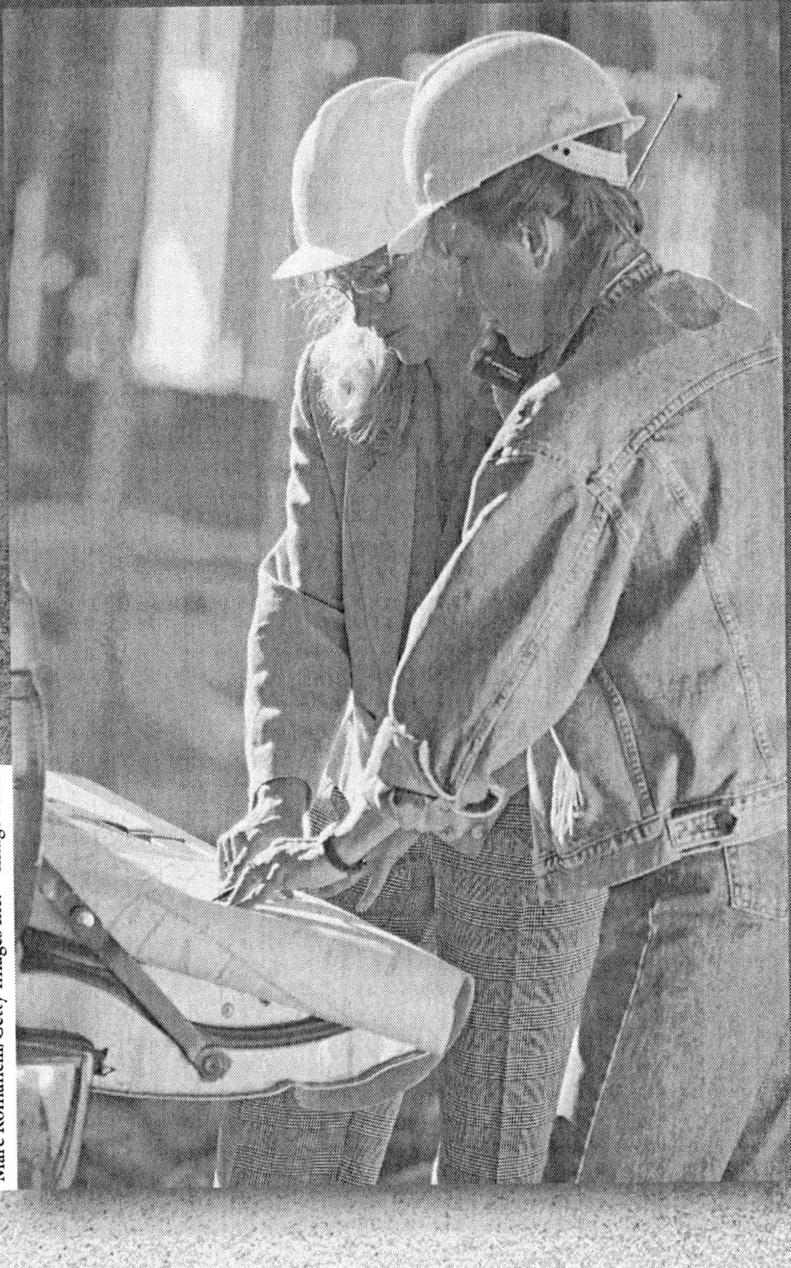

Marc Romanelli/Getty Images Inc.—Image Bank

Sex, Gender, and Culture

e all know that humans come in two major varieties—female and male. The contrast between them is one of the facts of life we share with most animal species. But the fact that males and females always have different organs of reproduction does not explain why males and females may also differ in other physical ways. After all, there are many animal species—such as pigeons, gulls, and laboratory rats—in which the two sexes differ little in appearance.[1] Thus, the fact that we are a species with two sexes does not really explain why human females and males typically look different. Also, the fact that humans reproduce sexually does not explain why human males and females should differ in behavior or be treated differently by society. Yet no society we know of treats females and males in exactly the same way; indeed, females usually have fewer advantages than males. That is why we are careful to say that egalitarian societies have no *social groups* with unequal access to resources, power, and prestige. But within social groups (e.g., families), even egalitarian societies usually allow males greater access to economic resources, power, and prestige.

Because many of the differences between females and males may reflect cultural expectations and experiences, many researchers now prefer to speak of **gender differences,** reserving the term **sex differences** for purely biological differences.[2] Unfortunately, biological and cultural influences are not always clearly separable, so it is sometimes hard to know which term to use. As long as societies treat males and females differently, we may not be able to separate the effects of biology from the effects of culture, and both may be present. As we focus our discussion on differences and similarities between females and males, keep in mind that not all cultures conceive of gender as including just two categories. Sometimes "maleness" and "femaleness" are thought of as opposite ends of a continuum, or there might be three or more categories of gender, such as "female," "male," and "other."[3]

In this chapter we discuss what we know cross-culturally about how and why females and males may differ physically, in gender roles, and in personality. We also discuss how and why sexual behavior and attitudes about sex vary from culture to culture. First we focus on culturally varying concepts about gender.

CHAPTER OUTLINE

- Gender Concepts
- Physique and Physiology
- Gender Roles
- Relative Contributions to Work
- Political Leadership and Warfare
- The Relative Status of Women
- Personality Differences
- Sexuality

Gender Concepts

In the United States and many Western societies your gender is thought of as female or male. There is no other category. In the instances where the baby's genitalia are ambiguous or when an adult desires a sex-change operation, there is a strong value on having the individual fit clearly into one or the other category. Many societies around the world share the male/female dichotomy when it comes to gender concepts. But a strict dichotomy is far from universal.

Some societies, like the Cheyenne Native Americans of the Great Plains, recognized male, female, and a third gender, referred to by the Cheyennes as "two-spirits." "Two-spirit" persons were usually young males. Their status as "two-spirit" persons was often recognized after their pre-adolescent vision quest. A two-spirit person would then wear women's dress and take on many of the activities of women. A two-spirit might even be taken as a second wife by a man, but whether the man and the two-spirit engaged in sex is not known. The role of a "two-spirit" person was not equivalent to becoming a woman; two-spirits played special roles at weddings and childbirth. Europeans referred to a two-spirit individual as a *berdache*.[4] Accounts of "two-spirit" biological females who take on the role of men are relatively rare, but they do occur in a number of native North American societies, such as the Kaska of Yukon Territory, the Klamath of southern Oregon, and the Mohave of the Colorado River area in the southwestern United States. These biological female "two-spirits" could marry women and such relationships were known to be lesbian relationships.[5]

In Oman there is a third gender role called *xanith*. Anatomically male, *xaniths* speak of themselves as "women." However, *xaniths* have their own distinctive dress—they wear clothes that are neither male nor female. In fact, their clothes and dress seem in-between. Men wear white clothes, women bright patterns, and *xaniths* wear unpatterned pastels. Men have short hair, women long, and *xaniths* are medium-length. Women are generally secluded in their houses and can only go out with permission from their husbands, but the *xanith* is free to come and go and works as a servant and/or a homosexual prostitute. But the *xanith* gender role is not necessarily forever. A *xanith* may decide to marry, and if he is able to have intercourse with his bride he becomes a "man." An older *xanith* who is no longer attractive may decide to become an "old-man."[6]

 Physique and Physiology

As we noted at the outset, biological males and females of many animal species cannot readily be distinguished. Although they differ in chromosome makeup and in their external and internal organs of reproduction, they do not differ otherwise. In contrast, humans are **sexually dimorphic**—that is, the females and males of our species are generally different in size and appearance. Females have proportionately wider pelvises. Males typically are taller and have heavier skeletons. Females have a larger proportion of their body weight in fat; males have a larger proportion of body weight in muscle. Males typically have greater grip strength, proportionately larger hearts and lungs, and greater aerobic capacity (greater intake of oxygen during strenuous activity).

There is a tendency in our society to view "taller" and "more muscled" as better, which may reflect the bias toward males in our culture. Natural selection may have favored these traits in males but different ones in females. For example, because females bear children, selection may have favored earlier cessation of growth, and therefore less ultimate height, in females so that the nutritional needs of a fetus would not compete with a growing mother's needs.[7] (Females achieve their ultimate height shortly after puberty, but boys continue to grow for years after puberty.) Similarly, there is some evidence that females are less affected than males by nutritional shortages, presumably because they tend to be shorter and have proportionately more fat.[8] Natural selection may have favored those traits in females because they resulted in greater reproductive success.

Both female and male athletes can build up their muscle strength and increase their aerobic work capacity through training. Given that fact, cultural factors, such as how much a society expects and allows males and females to engage in muscular activity, could influence the degree to which females and males differ muscularly and in aerobic capacity.

Training can greatly increase muscle strength and aerobic capacity.

Pete Saloutos/Corbis/Stock Market

Similar training may account for the recent trend toward decreasing differences between females and males in certain athletic events, such as marathons and swim meets. Even when it comes to female and male physique and physiology, then, what we see may be the result of both culture and genes.[9]

 Gender Roles

Productive and Domestic Activities

All societies assign or divide labor somewhat differently between females and males. Because role assignments have a clear cultural component, we speak of them as **gender roles.** What is of particular interest here about the gender division of labor is not so much that every society has different work for males and females but rather that so many societies divide up work in similar ways. The question, then, is why there are universal or near-universal patterns in such assignments.

Table 1 summarizes the worldwide patterns. We note which activities are performed by which gender in all or almost all societies, which activities are usually performed by one gender, and which activities are commonly assigned to either gender or both. Does the distribution of activities in the table suggest why females and males generally do different things?

One possible explanation may be labeled the **strength theory.** The greater strength of males and their superior capacity to mobilize their strength in quick bursts of energy (because of their greater aerobic work capacity) have commonly been cited as the reason for the universal or near-universal patterns in the division of labor by gender. Certainly, activities that require lifting heavy objects (hunting large animals, butchering, clearing land, working with stone, metal, or lumber), throwing weapons, and running with great speed (as in hunting) may generally be performed best by males. And none of the activities females usually perform, with the possible exception of collecting firewood, seems to require the same degree of physical strength or quick bursts of energy. But the strength theory is not completely convincing, if only because it cannot readily explain all the observed patterns. For example, it is not clear that the male activities of trapping small animals, collecting wild honey, or making musical instruments require much physical strength.

Table 1 — Worldwide Patterns in the Division of Labor by Gender

Type of Activity	Males Almost Always	Males Usually	Either Gender or Both	Females Usually	Females Almost Always
Primary subsistence activities	Hunt and trap animals, large and small	Fish Herd large animals Collect wild honey Clear land and prepare soil for planting	Collect shellfish Care for small animals Plant crops Tend crops Harvest crops Milk animals	Gather wild plants	
Secondary subsistence and household activities		Butcher animals	Preserve meat and fish	Care for children Cook Prepare vegetable foods drinks dairy products Launder Fetch water Collect fuel	Care for infants
Other	Lumber Mine and quarry Make boats musical instruments bone, horn, and shell objects Engage in combat	Build houses Make nets rope Exercise political leadership	Prepare skins Make leather products baskets mats clothing pottery	Spin yarn	

Source: Mostly adapted from George P. Murdock and Caterina Provost, "Factors in the Division of Labor by Sex: A Cross-Cultural Analysis," *Ethnology,* 12 (1973): 203–25. The information on political leadership and warfare comes from Martin K. Whyte, "Cross-Cultural Codes Dealing with the Relative Status of Women," *Ethnology,* 17 (1978): 217. The information on child care comes from Thomas S. Weisner and Ronald Gallimore, "My Brother's Keeper: Child and Sibling Caretaker," *Current Anthropology,* 18 (1977): 169–80.

Another possible explanation of the worldwide patterns in division of labor can be called the **compatibility-with-child-care theory.** The argument here is that women's tasks tend to be those that are compatible with child care. Although males can take care of infants, most traditional societies rely on breast-feeding of infants, which men cannot do. (In most societies, women breast-feed their children for two years on the average.) Women's tasks may be those that do not take them far from home for long periods, that do not place children in potential danger if they are taken along, and that can be stopped and resumed if an infant needs care.[10]

The compatibility theory may explain why *no* activities other than infant care are listed in the right-hand column of Table 1. That is, it may be that there are practically no universal or near-universal women-only activities because until recently most women have had to devote much of their time to nursing and caring for infants, as well as caring for other children. The compatibility theory may also explain why men usually perform tasks such as hunting, trapping, fishing, collecting honey, lumbering, and mining. Those tasks are dangerous for infants to be around, and in any case would be difficult to coordinate with infant care.[11]

Finally, the compatibility theory may also explain why men seem to take over certain crafts in societies with full-time specialization. Although the distinction is not shown in Table 1, crafts such as making baskets, mats, and pottery are women's activities in noncommercial societies but tend to be men's activities in societies with full-time craft specialists.[12] Similarly, weaving tends to be a female activity unless it is produced for trade.[13] Why should commercial activities change the gender division of labor? Full-time specialization and production for trade may increase incompatibility with child care. Cooking is a good example in our own society. Women may be fine cooks, but chefs and bakers tend to be men, even though women traditionally do most of the cooking at home. Women might be more likely to work as cooks and chefs if they could leave their babies and young children in safe places to be cared for by other people.

But the compatibility theory does not explain why men usually prepare soil for planting, make objects out of wood, or work bone, horn, and shell. All of those tasks could probably be stopped to tend to a child, and none of them is any more dangerous to children nearby than is cooking. Why, then, do males tend to do them? The **economy-of-effort theory** may help explain patterns that cannot readily be explained by the strength and compatibility theories. For example, it may be advantageous for men to make musical instruments because men generally collect the hard materials involved (e.g., by lumbering).[14] And because they collect those materials, men may be more knowledgeable about the physical properties of the materials and so more likely to know how to work with them. The economy-of-effort interpretation also suggests that it would be advantageous for one gender to perform tasks that are located near each other. Thus, if women have to be near home to take care of young children, it would be economical for them to perform other chores that are located in or near the home.

A fourth explanation of division of labor is the **expendability theory.** This theory suggests that men, rather than women, will tend to do the dangerous work in a society because men are more expendable, because the loss of men is less disadvantageous reproductively than the loss of women. If some men lose their lives in hunting, deep-water fishing, mining, quarrying, lumbering, and the like, reproduction need not suffer as long as most fertile women have sexual access to men—for example, if the society permits two or more women to be married to the same man.[15] When would anybody, male or female, be willing to do dangerous work? Perhaps only when society glorifies those roles and endows them with high prestige and other rewards.

Although the various theories, singly or in combination, seem to explain much of the division of labor by gender, there are some unresolved problems. Critics of the strength theory have pointed out that in some societies women do engage in very heavy labor.[16] If women in some societies can develop the strength to do such work, perhaps strength is more a function of training than traditionally has been believed.

The compatibility theory also has some problems. It suggests that labor is divided to conform to the requirements of child care. But sometimes it seems the other way around. For example, women who spend a good deal of time in agricultural work outside the home often ask others to watch and feed their infants while they are unavailable to nurse.[17]

Jorgen Shytte/Peter Arnold, Inc.

In many farming societies, women can do some agriculture and take care of their young children at the same time, as this mother in Zambia demonstrates.

Consider, too, the mountain areas of Nepal, where agricultural work is incompatible with child care; heavy loads must be carried up and down steep slopes, fields are far apart, and labor takes up most of the day. Yet women do this work anyway and leave their infants with others for long stretches of time.[18]

Furthermore, in some societies women hunt—one of the activities most incompatible with child care and generally not done by women. Many Agta women of the Philippines regularly hunt wild pig and deer; women alone or in groups kill almost 30 percent of the large game.[19] The women's hunting does not seem to be incompatible with child care. Women take nursing babies on hunting trips, and the women who hunt do not have lower reproductive rates than the women who choose not to hunt. Agta women may find it possible to hunt because the hunting grounds are only about a half-hour from camp, the dogs that accompany the women assist in the hunting and protect the women and babies, and the women generally hunt in groups, so others can help carry babies as well as carcasses. Hunting by women is also fairly common among the Aka, forest foragers in the Central African Republic. Aka women participate in and sometimes lead in organizing cooperative net-hunting, in which an area is circled and animals are flushed out and caught in nets. Women spend approximately 18 percent of their time net-hunting, which is more than men do.[20]

As the cases just described suggest, we need to know a lot more about labor requirements. More precisely, we need to know exactly how much strength is required in particular tasks, how dangerous those tasks are, and whether a person could stop working at a task to care for a child. So far, we have mostly guesses. When there is more systematically collected evidence on such aspects of particular tasks, we will be in a better position to evaluate the theories we have discussed. In any case, it should be noted that none of the available theories implies that the worldwide patterns of division of labor shown in Table 1 will persist. As we know from our own and other industrial societies, when machines replace human strength, when women have fewer children, and when women can assign child care to others, a strict gender division of labor begins to disappear.

Relative Contributions to Work

In the United States there has been a tendency to equate "work" with a job that brings in income. Until relatively recently, being a "homemaker" was not counted as an occupation. Anthropologists have not been immune from ignoring household work; indeed, most of the research on division of labor by gender has focused on **primary subsistence activities**—gathering, hunting, fishing, herding, and farming—and relatively less attention has been paid to gender contributions to **secondary subsistence activities** that involve the processing and preparation of food for eating or storing.

Overall Work

If we count all kinds of economic work, whether it be for primary subsistence, secondary subsistence, manufacturing, crafts, or for maintainance of the household, the studies that have been done largely suggest that women typically work more total hours per day than men in both intensive agricultural and horticultural societies.[21] We do not have that many studies yet—so we do not know if this is a cross-cultural universal. We do know though that in many societies, where women earn wages, they are still responsible for the bulk of household work as well as child care at home.

Subsistence Work

Researchers have focused mostly on primary subsistence activities, and they usually measure how much each gender's work in these primary activities contributes to the diet in terms of caloric intake. Alternatively, contribution to primary subsistence activities—generally outside activities, away from the home—can also be measured in terms of time spent doing them. Measures of caloric versus time contribution can yield different results. More time is spent by the Yanomamö in hunting than in horticulture, but horticulture yields more calories.

In some societies women traditionally have contributed more to the economy than men by any measure. For example, among the Tchambuli of New Guinea in the 1930s, the women did all the fishing—going out early in the morning by canoe to their fish traps and returning when the sun was hot. Some of the catch was traded for sago (a starch) and sugarcane, and it was the women who went on the long canoe trips to do the trading.[22]

In contrast, men did almost all of the primary subsistence work among the Toda of India. As they were described

Grinding corn is very time-consuming hard work. Women near Lake Titicaca in Peru grind corn between two large stones.

Laurence Fordyce/Corbis/Bettmann

early in the 20th century, they depended for subsistence almost entirely on the dairy products of their water buffalo, either by using the products directly or by selling them for grain. Women were not allowed to have anything to do with dairy work; only men tended the buffalo and prepared the dairy products. Women's work was largely household work. Women prepared the purchased grain for cooking, cleaned house, and decorated clothing.[23]

A survey of a wide variety of societies has revealed that both women and men typically contribute to primary food-getting activities, but men usually contribute more in terms of calories.[24] Women are almost always occupied with infant- and child-care responsibilities in most societies, so it is not surprising that men usually do most of the primary food-getting work, which generally has to be done away from the home.

Some of the variation in gender contribution to primary subsistence relates directly to the type of food-getting activities in the society. In societies that depend on hunting, fishing, and herding—generally male activities—for most of their calories, usually contribute more than women.[25] For example, among the Inuit, who traditionally depended mostly on hunting and fishing, and among the Toda, who depended mostly on herding, men did most of the primary subsistence work. In societies that depend on gathering, primarily women's work, women tend to do most of the food-getting in terms of calories. The !Kung are an example. But the predominant type of food-getting is not always predictive. Among the Tchambuli, who depended mostly on fishing, women did most of the work. Most societies known to anthropology depend primarily on plant cultivation for their calories, not on hunting, gathering, fishing, or herding. And, with the exception of clearing land, preparing the soil, and herding large animals, which are usually men's tasks, the work of planting, crop tending (weeding, irrigating), and harvesting is done by men, women, or both (see Table 1). So we need some explanation of why women do most of the farming work in some societies but men do it in others. Different patterns predominate in different areas of the world. In Africa south of the Sahara, women generally do most of the farming. But in much of Asia and Europe and the areas around the Mediterranean, men do more.[26]

One explanatory factor is the kind of plant cultivation. Many have pointed out that with intensive agriculture, particularly plow agriculture, men's caloric contribution to primary subsistence tends to be much higher than women's. In horticultural societies, in contrast, women's contribution is relatively high compared with men's. Women usually contribute the most when horticulture is practiced, either root and tree crop horticulture or shifting/slash-and-burn cultivation. According to Ester Boserup, when population increases and there is pressure to make more intensive use of the land, cultivators begin to use the plow and irrigation, and males start to do more.[27] But it is not clear why.

Why should women not continue to contribute a lot to farming just because plows are used? In trying to answer this question, most researchers shift to considering how much time males and females spend in various farming tasks, rather than estimating the total caloric contribution of females versus males. The reason for this shift is that gender contribution to farming varies substantially over the various phases of the production sequence, as well as from one crop to another. Thus, the total amount of time females versus males work at farming tasks is easier to estimate than how much each gender contributes to the diet in terms of calories. How would caloric contribution be judged, for example, if men do the clearing and plowing, women do the planting and weeding, and both do the harvesting?

One suggestion about why males contribute more to agriculture when the plow is used is that plow agriculture involves a great deal of labor input in the clearing and preparation phases of cultivation and at the same time minimizes subsequent weeding time. Men usually clear land anyway, but clearing is a more time-consuming process if intensive agriculture is practiced. It has been estimated that in one district in Nigeria, 100 days of work are required to clear one acre of virgin land for plowing by tractor; only 20 days are required to prepare the land for shifting cultivation. Weeding is a task that probably can be combined with child care, and perhaps for that reason it may have been performed mostly by women previously.[28] But the fact that men do the plowing, which may take a lot of time, does not explain why women do relatively fewer farming tasks, including weeding, in societies that have the plow.[29]

Another explanation for why women contribute less time than men to intensive agriculture is that household chores increase with intensive agriculture and thus limit the time women can spend in the fields. Intensive agriculturalists typically rely heavily on grain crops, which take much more work to make edible. Cereal grains (corn, wheat, oats) are usually dried before storing and thus take a long time to cook if they are left whole. More cooking requires more time to collect water and firewood (usually women's work) and more time to clean pots and utensils. A variety of techniques can reduce cooking time (such as soaking, grinding, or pounding), but the process that speeds up cooking the most—grinding—is itself time-consuming (unless done by machine).[30] Finally, household work may increase substantially with intensive agriculture because women in such societies have more children than women in horticultural societies.[31] If household work increases in these ways, it is easy to understand why women cannot contribute more time than men, or as much time as men, to intensive agriculture. But women's contribution, although less than men's, is nonetheless substantial; they seem to work outside the home four and a half hours a day, seven days a week, on the average.[32]

We still have not explained why women contribute so much to horticulture in the first place. They may not have as much household work as intensive agricultural women, but neither do the men. Why, then, don't men do relatively more in horticulture also? One possibility is that in horticultural societies men are often drawn away from cultivation into other types of activities. There is evidence that if males are engaged in warfare when primary subsistence work has to be done, the women must do that work.[33] Men may also be withdrawn from primary subsistence work if they have to work in distant towns and cities for wages or if they periodically go on long-distance trading trips.[34]

When women contribute a lot to primary food-getting activities, we might expect their behavior and attitudes concerning children to be affected. Several cross-cultural studies suggest that this expectation is correct. In societies with a high female contribution to primary subsistence (in terms of contributing calories), infants are fed solid foods earlier (so that other persons besides mothers can feed them) than in societies with a low female contribution.[35] Girls are likely to be trained to be industrious (probably to help their mothers), and girl babies are more valued.[36]

Political Leadership and Warfare

In almost every known society, men rather than women are the leaders in the political arena. One cross-cultural survey found that, in about 85 percent of the surveyed societies, only men were leaders. In the societies in which some women occupied leadership positions, the women were either outnumbered by or less powerful than the male leaders.[37] If we look at countries, not cultures, women on the average make up only around 10 percent of the representatives in national parliaments or legislative bodies.[38] Whether or not we consider warfare to be part of the political sphere of life, we find an almost universal dominance of males in that arena. In 87 percent of the world's societies, women

never participate actively in war.[39] (See the box "Why Do Some Societies Allow Women to Participate in Combat?" for a discussion of women in combat in the remaining 13 percent of societies.)

Even in *matrilineal* societies, which seem to be oriented around women (see the chapter on marital residence and kinship), men usually occupy political positions. For example, among the Iroquois of what is now New York State, women had control over resources and a great deal of influence, but men, not women, held political office. The highest political body among the League of the Iroquois, which comprised five tribal groups, was a council of 50 male chiefs. Although women could not serve on the council, they could nominate, elect, and impeach their male representatives. Women also could decide between life and death for prisoners of war, forbid the men of their households to go to war, and intervene to bring about peace.[40]

Why have men (at least so far) almost always dominated the political sphere of life? Some scholars have suggested that men's role in warfare gives them the edge in all kinds of political leadership, particularly because they control weapons, an important resource.[41] But evidence suggests that force is rarely used to obtain leadership positions[42]; superior strength is not the deciding factor. Still, warfare may be related to political leadership for another reason. Warfare clearly affects survival, and it occurs regularly in most societies. Therefore, decision making about war may be among

Women as well as men serve on political councils in many Coast Salish communities. Here we see a swearing-in ceremony for the Special Chief's Council in Sardis, British Columbia.

Ann Mohs/Bruce Miller

NEW PERSPECTIVES ON GENDER

Why Do Some Societies Allow Women to Participate in Combat?

U.S. women can serve in the military but are not in units directly engaged in combat. Some women feel that such exclusion is unfair and decreases their chances of promotion in the military. Other people, including some women, insist that female participation in combat would be detrimental to military performance or is inappropriate for women. Women in the U.S. military have been attacked in the course of their duties in Iraq and some have died. Some countries currently allow women to engage in combat. And in the 18th and 19th centuries women made up one wing of the standing army in the West African Kingdom of Dahomey and at one point constituted one-third of the armed forces. Most societies, however, have excluded women from combat and some have excluded women from any involvement in military activities or planning.

Why, then, do some societies allow women to be warriors? Psychologist David Adams compared about 70 societies studied by anthropologists to try to answer that question. Although most societies exclude women from war, Adams found that women are active warriors, at least occasionally, in 13 percent of the sample societies. In native North America, such societies included the Comanche, Crow, Delaware, Fox, Gros Ventre, and Navajo. In the Pacific, there were active warrior women among the Maori of New Zealand, on Majuro Atoll in the Marshall Islands, and among the Orokaiva of New Guinea. In none of these societies were the warriors usually women, but women were allowed to engage in combat if they wanted to.

How are the societies with women warriors different from those that exclude women from combat? They differ in one of two ways. Either they conduct war only against people in other societies (this is called "purely external" war) or they marry within their own community. Adams argues that these two conditions, which are not particularly common, preclude the possibility of conflicts of interest between wives and husbands, and therefore women can be permitted to engage in combat because their interests are the same as their husbands'. Because marriages in most cases involve individuals from the same society, husbands and wives will have the same loyalties if the society has purely external war. And even

if war occurs between communities and larger groups in the same society (what we call "internal" war), there will be no conflict of interest between husband and wife if they both grew up in the same community. In contrast, there is internal war at least occasionally in most societies, and wives usually marry in from other communities. In this situation, there may often be a conflict of interest between husband and wife; if women were to engage in combat, they might have to fight against their fathers, paternal uncles, and brothers. And wouldn't we expect the wives to try to warn kin in their home communities if the husbands planned to attack them? Indeed, the men's likely fear of their wives' disloyalty would explain why women in these societies are forbidden to make or handle weapons or go near meetings in which war plans are discussed.

Many countries today engage in purely external war; so other things being equal, we would not expect conflicts of interest to impede women's participation in combat. Therefore, extrapolating from Adams's findings, we might expect that the barriers against female participation in combat will disappear completely. But other conditions may have to be present before women and men participate equally in combat. In Adams's study, not all societies with purely external war or intracommunity marriage had women warriors. So we may also have to consider the degree to which the society seeks to maximize reproduction (and therefore protect women from danger) and the degree to which the society depends on women for subsistence during wartime.

There are other related questions to explore: Does military participation by women increase women's participation in politics? Does the presence of war in a society decrease or increase women's political participation? Does women's participation in politics or in the military change the nature of war?

Source: From David B. Adams, "Why There Are So Few Women Warriors," in *Behavior Science Research,* 18 (1983): 196–212; Joshua S. Goldstein, "War and Gender," in Carol R. Ember and Melvin Ember, eds. *Encyclopedia of Sex and Gender: Men and Women in the World's Cultures,* Vol. 1 (New York: Kluwer Academic/Plenum Publishers, 2004), pp. 107–116.

the most important kinds of politics in most societies. If so, then the persons who know the most about warfare should be making the decisions about it.

To explain why males and not females usually engage in fighting, let us refer to three of the possible explanations of the worldwide patterns in the gender division of labor. Warfare, like hunting, probably requires strength (for throwing weapons) and quick bursts of energy (for running). And certainly combat is one of the most dangerous and uninterruptible activities imaginable, hardly compatible with child care. Also, even if they do not at the time have children, women may generally be kept out of combat because their potential fertility is more important to a population's reproduction and survival than their potential usefulness as warriors.[43] So the strength theory, the compatibility theory, and the expendability theory might all explain the predominance of men in warfare.

Two other factors may be involved in male predominance in politics. One is the generally greater height of men. Why height should be a factor in leadership is unclear, but studies suggest that taller persons are more likely to be leaders.[44] Finally, there is the possibility that men dominate politics because they get around more in the outside world than do women. Men's activities typically take them farther from home; women tend to work more around the home. If societies choose leaders at least in part because of what they know about the larger world, then men will generally have some advantage. In support of this reasoning, Patricia Draper found that in !Kung bands that had settled down, women no longer engaged in long-distance gathering, and they lost much of their former influence in decision making.[45] Involvement in child care may also detract from such influence. In a study of village leadership among the Kayapo of Brazil, Dennis Werner found that women with heavy child-care burdens were less influential than women not as involved in child care; perhaps they had fewer friends and missed many details of what was going on in the village.[46]

These various explanations suggest why men generally dominate politics, but we still need to explain why women participate in politics more in some societies than in others. Marc Ross investigated this question in a cross-cultural survey of 90 societies.[47] In that sample, the degree of female participation in politics varied considerably. For example, among the Mende of Sierra Leone, women regularly held high office, but among the Azande of Zaire, women took no part in public life. One factor that appeared to predict the exclusion of women from politics was the organization of communities around male kin. As we will see later, when they marry, women usually have to leave their communities and move to their husband's place. If women are "strangers" in a community with many related males, then the males will have political advantages because of their knowledge of community members and past events.

The Relative Status of Women

There are probably as many definitions of status as there are researchers interested in the topic. To some, the relative status of the sexes means how much importance society confers on females versus males. To others, it means how much power and authority men and women have relative to each other. And to still others, it means what kinds of rights women and men possess to do what they want to do. In any case, many social scientists are asking why the status of women appears to vary from one society to another. Why do women have few rights and little influence in some societies and more of each in other societies? In other words, why is there variation in degree of **gender stratification?**

In the small Iraqi town of Daghara, women and men live very separate lives.[48] In many respects, women appear to have very little status. Like women in much of the Islamic world, women in Daghara live their lives mostly in seclusion, staying in their houses and interior courtyards. If women must go out, which they can do only with male approval, they must shroud their faces and bodies in long black

In some cultures, wives defer to their husbands in many contexts.

205

NEW PERSPECTIVES ON GENDER

Women's Electoral Success on the Northwest Coast

Political life has changed dramatically since first contact with Europeans for most Native American groups, including the Coast Salish of western Washington State and British Columbia. With impetus from the U.S. and Canadian governments, each of the recognized Coast Salish communities now has an elected council. But who is getting elected? Even though women did not have much of a role in traditional politics, now the Coast Salish groups are electing a lot of women. From the 1960s to the 1980s, women held over 40 percent of the council seats in the 12 Washington State groups, and in the 1990s women held 28 percent of the seats in the 50 British Columbian groups. The proportion of women on the councils varies from 6 percent among the Tulalip to 62 percent among the Stillaguamish. What accounts for the women's electoral success? And why does that success vary from one group to another, even though the groups are closely related culturally?

According to Bruce Miller, who did a comparative study of women's electoral success in Coast Salish communities, women generally have more of a political role now perhaps because new economic opportunities in the service and technical sectors allow women to contribute more to the household economy. But why do women win proportionately more council seats in some communities than in others? Miller found that women win proportionately more seats in communities with less income, the least income derived from fishing, and the smallest populations. Why should lower household income predict more electoral success for women? Miller

suggests that it is not so much the amount of income but rather the degree to which women (compared with men) contribute to household income. In groups with economic difficulties, the jobs women are able to get play a vital role in the household. Women were helped by federally funded programs such as the War on Poverty to acquire technical skills and jobs. Simultaneously, many men in some communities lost their jobs in logging and agriculture.

But a high dependence on fishing income seems to favor men politically. Families that operate vessels with a large drawstring net to catch fish at sea can make hundreds of thousands of dollars a year. Such fishing is predominantly done by men, and where there is such lucrative fishing, the successful men dominate the councils. Even though women may have jobs too, their income is not as great as the successful fisherman's.

Why should women be more successful politically in smaller communities? Miller suggests that women have a better chance to be known personally when the community is small, even though working outside the home in technical or service jobs cuts down on the time women can devote to tribal ceremonials and other public events.

Does female income relative to male and community size help explain the relative political success of women elsewhere? We do not know yet, but subsequent research may help us find out.

Source: Bruce G. Miller, "Women and Politics: Comparative Evidence from the Northwest Coast," *Ethnology,* 31 (1992): 367–82.

cloaks. These cloaks must be worn in mixed company, even at home. Women are essentially excluded from political activities. Legally, they are considered to be under the authority of their fathers and husbands. Even the sexuality of women is controlled. There is strict emphasis on virginity before marriage. Because women are not permitted even casual conversations with strange men, the possibilities for extramarital or even premarital relationships are very slight. In contrast, hardly any sexual restrictions are imposed on men.

But some societies such as the Mbuti seem to approach equal status for males and females. Like most food collectors, the Mbuti have no formal political organization to make decisions or to settle disputes. Public disputes occur, and both women and men take part in the uproar that is part of such disputes. Not only do women make their positions known, but their opinions are often heeded. Even in domestic quarrels involving physical violence between husband and wife,

others usually intervene to stop them, regardless of who hit whom first.[49] Women control the use of dwellings; they usually have equal say over the disposal of resources they or the men collect, over the upbringing of their children, and about whom their children should marry. One of the few signs of inequality is that women are somewhat more restricted than men with respect to extramarital sex.[50]

There are many theories about why women have relatively high or low status. One of the most common is that women's status will be high when they contribute substantially to primary subsistence activities. According to this theory, then, women should have very little status when food-getting depends largely on hunting, herding, or intensive agriculture. A second theory suggests that where warfare is especially important, men will be more valued and esteemed than women. A third theory suggests that where there are centralized political hierarchies, men will have higher status. The reasoning in this theory is essentially the same as the reasoning in the warfare theory: Men usually play the dominant role in political behavior, so men's status should be higher wherever political behavior is more important or frequent. Finally, there is the theory that women will have higher status where kin groups and couples' place of residence after marriage are organized around women.

One of the problems in evaluating these theories is that decisions have to be made about the meaning of *status*. Does it mean value? Rights? Influence? And do all these aspects of status vary together? Cross-cultural research by Martin Whyte suggests that they do not. For each sample society in his study, Whyte rated 52 items that might be used to define the relative status of the sexes. These items included such things as which sex can inherit property, who has final authority over disciplining unmarried children, and whether the gods in the society are male, female, or both. The results of the study indicate that very few of these items are related. Therefore, Whyte concluded, we cannot talk about status as a single concept. Rather, it seems more appropriate to talk about the relative status of women in different spheres of life.[51]

Even though Whyte found no necessary connection between one aspect of status and another, he decided to ask whether some of the theories correctly predict why some societies have many, as opposed to few, areas in which the status of women is high. Let us turn first to the ideas that are not supported by the available cross-cultural evidence. The idea that generally high status derives from a greater caloric contribution to primary subsistence activities is not supported at all.[52] Women in intensive agricultural societies (who contribute less than men to primary subsistence) do tend to have lower status in many areas of life, just as in the Iraqi case described earlier. But in societies that depend mostly on hunting (where women also do little of the primary subsistence work), women seem to have higher status, which contradicts the theoretical expectation. Similarly, there is no consistent evidence that a high frequency of warfare generally lowers women's status in different spheres of life.[53]

What does predict higher status for women in many areas of life? Although the results are not strong, there is some support in Whyte's study for the theory that where kin groups and marital residence are organized around women, women have somewhat higher status. The Iroquois are a good example. Even though Iroquois women could not hold political office, they had considerable authority within and beyond the household. Related women lived together in longhouses with husbands who belonged to other kin groups. In the longhouse, the women's authority was clear, and they could ask objectionable men to leave. The women controlled the allocation of the food they produced. Allocation could influence the timing of war parties, since men could not undertake a raid without provisions. Women were involved in the selection of religious leaders, half of whom were women. Even in politics, although women could not speak or serve on the council, they largely controlled the

selection of councilmen and could institute impeachment proceedings against those to whom they objected.[54]

If we look at nonindustrial or preindustrial societies, a generally lower status for women is more likely in societies with political hierarchies.[55] Lower status for women appears to be associated with other indicators of cultural complexity—social stratification, plow and irrigation agriculture, large settlements, private property, and craft specialization tend to have lower status for women. One type of influence for women increases with cultural complexity—informal influence. But, as Whyte pointed out, informal influence may simply reflect a lack of *real* influence.[56] Why cultural complexity is associated with women having less authority in the home, less control over property, and more restricted sexual lives is not yet understood. However, the relationship between cultural complexity and gender equality appears to change when we include industrial and postindustrial societies. Judging by a comparative study of gender attitudes in 61 countries, it seems that countries relying on agriculture such as Nigeria and Peru have the least favorable attitudes toward gender equality, industrial societies such as Russia and Taiwan have moderately favorable attitudes, and postindustrial societies such as Sweden and the United States have the most favorable attitudes toward gender equality.[57]

Western colonialism appears to have been generally detrimental to women's status, perhaps because Westerners were accustomed to dealing with men. There are plenty of examples of Europeans restructuring landownership around men and teaching men modern farming techniques, even in places where women were usually the farmers. In addition, men more often than women could earn cash through wage labor or through sales of goods (such as furs) to Europeans.[58] Although the relative status of men and women may not have been equal before the Europeans arrived, colonial influences seem generally to have undermined the position of women.

We are beginning to understand some of the conditions that may enhance or decrease certain aspects of women's status. If we can understand which of these conditions are most important, society may be able to reduce gender inequality if it wants to.[59]

Personality Differences

Much of the research on gender differences in personality has taken place in the United States and other Western countries where psychology is a major field of study. While such studies are informative, they do not tell us whether the observed differences hold true in cultures very different from our own. Fortunately, we now have systematic observational studies for various non-Western societies. These studies recorded the minute details of behavior of substantial numbers of males and females. Any conclusions about female–male differences in aggressiveness, for example, are based on actual counts of the number of times a particular individual tried to hurt or injure another person during a given amount of observation time. Almost all of these

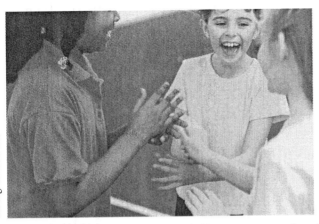 

Cross-culturally, girls more often play in small, intimate groups, boys in larger groups.

differences are subtle and a matter of degree, not a matter of a behavior being present or absent in females or males.

Which differences in personality are suggested by these systematic studies? Most of them have observed children in different cultural settings. The most consistent difference is in the area of aggression; boys try to hurt others more frequently than girls do. In an extensive comparative study of children's behavior, the Six Cultures project, this difference showed up as early as 3 to 6 years of age.[60] In the Six Cultures project, six different research teams observed children's behavior in Kenya (among the Gusii), Mexico, India, the Philippines, Okinawa and the United States. A more recent cross-cultural comparison of four other cultures (the Logoli of Kenya, Nepal, Belize, and American Samoa) supports the sex difference in aggression.[61] Studies in the United States are consistent with the cross-cultural findings: In a large number of observation and experimental studies, boys exhibited more aggression than girls.[62]

Other female–male differences have turned up with considerable consistency, but we have to be cautious in accepting them, either because they have not been documented as well or because there are more exceptions. There seems to be a tendency for girls to exhibit more responsible behavior, including nurturance (trying to help others). Girls seem more likely to conform to adult wishes and commands. Boys try more often to exert dominance over others in order to get their own way. In play, boys and girls show a preference for their own gender. Boys seem to play in large groups, girls in small ones. And boys seem to maintain more distance between each other than girls do.[63]

If we assume that these differences are consistent across cultures, how can we explain them? Many writers and researchers believe that because certain female–male differences are so consistent, they are probably rooted in the biological differences between the two sexes. Aggression is one of the traits talked about most often in this connection, particularly because this male–female difference appears so early in life.[64] But an alternative argument is that societies bring up boys and girls differently because they almost universally require adult males and females to perform different types of roles. If most societies expect adult males to be warriors or to be prepared to be warriors, shouldn't we expect most societies to encourage or idealize aggression in males? And if females are almost always the caretakers of infants, shouldn't we also expect societies generally to encourage nurturant behaviors in females?

Researchers tend to adopt either the biological or the socialization view, but it is possible that both kinds of causes are important in the development of gender differences. For example, parents might turn a slight genetic difference into a large gender difference by maximizing that difference in the way they socialize boys versus girls.

It is difficult for researchers to distinguish the influence of genes and other biological conditions from the influence of socialization. We have research indicating that as early as birth, parents treat boy and girl infants differently.[65] In spite of the fact that objective observers can see no major "personality" differences between girl and boy infants, parents often claim to.[66] But parents may unconsciously want to see differences and may therefore produce them in socialization. So even early differences could be learned rather than genetic. Remember, too, that researchers cannot do experiments with people; for example, parents' behavior cannot be manipulated to find out what would happen if boys and girls were treated in exactly the same ways.

However, there is considerable experimental research on aggression in nonhuman animals. These experiments suggest that the hormone androgen is partly responsible for higher levels of aggression. For example, in some experiments, females injected with androgen at about the time the sexual organs develop (before or shortly after birth) behave more aggressively when they are older than do females without the hormone. These results may or may not apply to humans of course, but some researchers have investigated human females who were "androgenized" in the womb because of drugs given to their mothers to prevent miscarriage. By and large the results of these studies are similar to the experimental studies—androgenized human females show similar patterns of higher aggression.[67] Some scholars take these results to indicate that biological differences between males and females are responsible for the male–female difference in aggression[68]; others suggest that even these results are not conclusive, because females who get more androgen show generally disturbed metabolic systems, and general metabolic disturbance may itself increase aggressiveness. Furthermore, androgen-injected females may look more like males because they develop male-like genitals; therefore, they may be treated like males.[69]

Is there any evidence that socialization differences may account for differences in aggression? Although a cross-cultural survey of ethnographers' reports on 101 societies does show that more societies encourage aggression in boys than in girls, most societies show no difference in aggression training.[70] The few societies that do show differences in aggression training can hardly account for the widespread sex differences in actual aggressiveness. But the survey does not necessarily mean that there are no consistent differences in aggression training for boys and girls. All it shows is that there are no *obvious* differences. For all we know, the learning of aggression and other "masculine" traits by boys could be produced by subtle types of socialization.

One possible type of subtle socialization that could create gender differences in behavior is the chores children are assigned. It is possible that little boys and girls learn to behave differently because their parents ask them to do different kinds of work. Beatrice and John Whiting reported from the Six Cultures project that in societies where children were asked to do a great deal of work, they generally showed more responsible and nurturant behavior. Because girls are almost always asked to do more work than boys, they may be more responsible and nurturant for this reason alone.[71] If this reasoning is correct, we should find that if boys are asked to do girls' work, they will learn to behave more like girls.

A study of Luo children in Kenya supports this view.[72] Girls were usually asked to babysit, cook, clean house, and fetch water and firewood. Boys were usually asked to do very little because boys' traditional work was herding cattle, and most families in the community studied had few cattle. But for some reason more boys than girls had been born, and many mothers without girls at home asked their sons to do girls' chores. Systematic behavior observations showed that much of the behavior of the boys who did girls' work was intermediary between the behavior of other boys and the behavior of girls. The boys who did girls' work were more like girls in that they were less aggressive, less domineering, and more responsible than other boys, even when they weren't working. So it is possible that task assignment has an important influence on how boys and girls learn to behave. These and other subtle forms of socialization need to be investigated more thoroughly.

Misconceptions about Differences in Behavior

Before we leave the subject of behavior differences, we should note some widespread beliefs about them that are not supported by research. Some of these mistaken beliefs are that girls are more dependent than boys, that girls are more sociable, and that girls are more passive. The results obtained by the Six Cultures project cast doubt on all these notions.[73] First, if we think of dependency as seeking help and emotional support from others, girls are generally no more likely to behave this way than boys. To be sure, the results do indicate that boys and girls have somewhat different styles of dependency. Girls more often seek help and contact; boys more often seek attention and approval. As for sociability, which means seeking and offering friendship, the Six Cultures results showed no reliable differences between the sexes. Of course, boys and girls may be sociable in different ways because boys generally play in larger groups than girls. As for the supposed passivity of girls, the evidence is also not particularly convincing. Girls in the Six Cultures project did not consistently withdraw from aggressive attacks or comply with unreasonable demands. The only thing that emerged as a female–male difference was that older girls were less likely than boys to respond to aggression with aggression. But this finding may not reflect passivity as much as the fact that girls are less aggressive than boys, which we already knew.

So some of our common ideas about female–male differences are unfounded. Others, such as those dealing with aggression and responsibility, cannot be readily dismissed and should be investigated further.

As we noted, an observed difference in aggression does not mean that males are aggressive and females are not. Perhaps because males are generally more aggressive, aggression in females has been studied less often. For that reason, Victoria Burbank focused on female aggression in an Australian aborigine community she calls Mangrove. During the 18 months that she was there, Burbank observed some act of aggression almost every other day. Consistent with the cross-cultural evidence, men initiated aggression more often than women, but women were initiators about 43 percent of the time. The women of Mangrove engaged in almost all the same kinds of aggression as men did, including fighting, except that it tended not to be as lethal as male violence. Lethal weapons were most often used by men; when women fought with weapons, they mostly used sticks, not spears, guns, or knives. Burbank points out that, in contrast to Western cultures, female aggression is not viewed as unnatural or deviant but rather as a natural expression of anger.[74]

 Sexuality

In view of the way the human species reproduces, it is not surprising that sexuality is part of our nature. But no society we know of leaves sexuality to nature; all have at least some rules governing "proper" conduct. There is much variation from one society to another in the degree of sexual activity permitted or encouraged before marriage, outside marriage, and even within marriage. And societies vary markedly in their tolerance of nonheterosexual sexuality.

Charles Lenars/Corbis/Bettmann

Some cultures are more relaxed about sexuality than others. Does public sculpture reflect that? A park in Oslo, Norway, is dedicated to sculptures by Gustav Vigeland.

Cultural Regulations of Sexuality: Permissiveness Versus Restrictiveness

All societies seek to regulate sexual activity to some degree, and there is a lot of variation cross-culturally. Some societies allow premarital sex; others forbid it. The same is true for extramarital sex. In addition, a society's degree of restrictiveness is not always consistent throughout the life span or for all aspects of sex. For example, a number of societies ease sexual restrictions somewhat for adolescents, and many become more restrictive for adults.[75] Then, too, societies change over time. The United States has traditionally been restrictive, but until recently—before the emergence of the AIDS epidemic—more permissive attitudes were gaining acceptance.

PREMARITAL SEX The degree to which sex before marriage is approved or disapproved of varies greatly from society to society. The Trobriand Islanders, for example, approved of and encouraged premarital sex, seeing it as an important preparation for later marriage roles. Both girls and boys were given complete instruction in all forms of sexual expression at the onset of puberty and were allowed plenty of opportunity for intimacy. Some societies not only allow premarital sex on a casual basis but specifically encourage trial marriages between adolescents. Among the Ila-speaking peoples of central Africa, at harvest time girls were given houses of their own where they could play at being wife with the boys of their choice.[76]

On the other hand, in many societies premarital sex was discouraged. For example, among the Tepoztlan Indians of Mexico, a girl's life became "crabbed, cribbed, confined" from the time of her first menstruation. She was not to speak to or encourage boys in the least way. To do so would be to court disgrace, to show herself to be crazy. The responsibility of guarding the chastity and reputation of one or more daughters of marriageable age was often a burden for the mother. One mother said she wished her 15-year-old daughter would marry soon because it was inconvenient to "spy" on her all the time.[77] In many Muslim societies, a girl's premarital chastity was tested after her marriage. After the wedding night, blood-stained sheets were displayed as proof of the bride's virginity.

Cultures do not remain the same; attitudes and practices can change markedly over time, as in the United States. In the past, sex was generally delayed until after marriage; in the 1990s, most Americans accepted or approved of premarital sex.[78]

SEX IN MARRIAGE There are some commonalities in marital sexual relations, but in many respects there is considerable variation. In most societies some form of face-to-face sexual intercourse or coitus is the usual pattern, most preferring the woman on her back and the man on top. Couples in most cultures prefer privacy. This is easier in societies with single family dwellings or separate rooms, but in societies with unpartitioned dwellings and multiple families living there, privacy is difficult to attain in the house. For example, the Siriono of Bolivia had as many as 50 hammocks 10 feet apart in their houses. Not surprisingly, couples in such societies prefer to have sex outdoors in a secluded location.[79]

Night is often preferred for sex, but some cultures specifically opted for day. For example, the Chenchu of India believed that a child conceived at night might be born blind. In some societies couples engage in sex quickly with little or no foreplay; in others foreplay may take hours.[80] Attitudes toward marital sex and the frequency of it vary widely from culture to culture. In one cross-cultural survey, 70 percent of the surveyed societies believe that frequent marital sex is viewed as a good thing, but in 9 percent frequent sex by married couples is viewed as undesirable, causing weakness, illness, and sometimes death.[81] People in most societies abstain from intercourse during menstruation, during at least part of pregnancy, and for a period after childbirth. Some societies prohibit sexual relations before various activities, such as hunting, fighting, planting, brewing, and iron smelting. Our own society is among the most lenient regarding restrictions on intercourse within marriage, imposing only rather loose restraints during mourning, menstruation, and pregnancy.[82]

EXTRAMARITAL SEX Extramarital sex is not uncommon in many societies. In about 69 percent of the world's societies men have extramarital sex more than occasionally, and in about 57 percent so do women. The frequency of such sexual activity is higher than we might expect, given that only a slight majority of societies (54 percent) say they allow extramarital sex for men, and only a small number (11 percent) say they allow it for women.[83]

In quite a few societies, then, there is quite a difference between the restrictive code and actual practice. The Navajo of the 1940s were said to forbid adultery, but young married men under the age of 30 had 27 percent of their heterosexual contacts with women other than their wives.[84] And although people in the United States in the 1970s almost overwhelmingly rejected extramarital sex, 41 percent of married men and about 18 percent of married women had had extramarital sex. In the 1990s, proportionately more men and women reported that they had been faithful to their spouses.[85] Cross-culturally, most societies have a double standard with regard to men and women, with restrictions considerably greater for women.[86] A substantial number of societies openly accept extramarital relationships. The Chukchee of Siberia, who often traveled long distances, allowed a married man to engage in sex with his host's wife, with the understanding that he would offer the same hospitality when the host visited him.[87]

Although a society may allow extramarital sex, a recent cross-cultural study of individual reactions to extramarital sex finds that men and women try a variety of strategies to curtail such sex. Men are much more likely than women to resort to physical violence against their wives; women are more likely to distance themselves from their husbands. Gossip may be employed to shame the relationship and in more complex societies a higher authority may be asked to intervene. The researchers conclude that married women and men universally consider extramarital sex inappropriate, even in societies that permit it sometimes.[88]

HOMOSEXUALITY When most anthropologists discuss homosexuality they usually refer to sex between males or sex between females. But while the biological male/female dichotomy corresponds to the gender male/female dichotomy in the West, other societies do not have the same gender concepts, so that the meaning of homosexuality may be different in different societies. For example, the Navajo of the American Southwest traditionally recognized four genders. Only relationships between people of the same gender would be considered homosexual and they considered such relationships inappropriate.[89] Biologically speaking, some of the cross-gender relationships would be considered homosexual in the Western view. Most of the research to date has adopted the biological view that homosexuality is between people of the same biological sex.

The range in permissiveness or restrictiveness toward homosexual relations is as great as that for any other kind of sexual activity. Among the Lepcha of the Himalayas, a man was believed to become homosexual if he ate the flesh of an uncastrated pig. But the Lepcha said that homosexual behavior was practically unheard of, and they viewed it with disgust.[90] Perhaps because many societies deny that homosexuality exists, little is known about homosexual practices in the restrictive societies. Among the permissive ones, there

is variation in the type and pervasiveness of homosexuality. In some societies homosexuality is accepted but limited to certain times and certain individuals. For example, among the Papago of the southwestern United States there were "nights of saturnalia" in which homosexual tendencies could be expressed. The Papago also had many male transvestites, who wore women's clothing, did women's chores, and, if not married, could be visited by men.[91] A woman did not have the same freedom of expression. She could participate in the saturnalia feasts but only with her husband's permission, and female transvestites were nonexistent.

Homosexuality occurs even more widely in other societies. The Berber-speaking Siwans of North Africa expected all males to engage in homosexual relations. In fact, fathers made arrangements for their unmarried sons to be given to an older man in a homosexual arrangement. Siwan custom limited a man to one boy. Fear of the Egyptian government made this a secret matter, but before 1909 such arrangements were made openly. Almost all men were reported to have engaged in a homosexual relationship as boys; later, when they were between 16 and 20, they married girls.[92] Such prescribed homosexual relationships between persons of different ages are a common form of homosexuality.[93] Among the most extremely prohomosexual societies, the Etoro of New Guinea preferred homosexuality to heterosexuality. Heterosexuality was prohibited as many as 260 days a year and was forbidden in or near the house and gardens. Male homosexuality, on the other hand, was not prohibited at any time and was believed to make crops flourish and boys become strong.[94] Even among the Etoro, however, men were expected to marry women after a certain age.[95]

It is only recently that researchers have paid much attention to erotic relationships between females. Although early studies found relatively few societies with female–female sexual relationships, Evelyn Blackwood located reports of ninety-five societies with such practices, suggesting that it is more common than previously thought.[96] As with male homosexuality, some societies institutionalize same-sex sexual relationships—the Kaguru of Tanzania have female homosexual relationships between older and younger women as part of their initiation ceremonies, reminiscent of the male–male "mentor" relationships in ancient Greece.

Cross-culturally, it is extremely unusual to find "gays" or exclusive male or female homosexuals. In most societies, males and females are expected to marry, and homosexuality, if tolerated or approved, either occurs as a phase in one's life or occurs along with heterosexuality.[97]

Reasons for Restrictiveness

Before we deal with the question of why some societies are more restrictive than others, we must first ask whether all forms of restrictiveness go together. The research to date suggests that societies that are restrictive with regard to one aspect of heterosexual sex tend to be restrictive with regard to other aspects. Thus, societies that frown on sexual expression by young children also punish premarital and extramarital sex.[98] Furthermore, such societies tend to insist on modesty in clothing and are constrained in their talk about sex.[99] But societies that are generally restrictive about heterosexuality are not necessarily restrictive about homosexuality. Societies restrictive about premarital sex are neither more nor less likely to restrict homosexuality. In the case of extramarital sex, the situation is somewhat different. Societies that have a considerable amount of male homosexuality tend to disapprove of males having extramarital heterosexual relationships.[100] If we are going to explain restrictiveness, then, it appears we have to consider heterosexual and homosexual restrictiveness separately.

Let us consider homosexual restrictiveness first. Why do homosexual relationships occur more frequently in some societies, and why are some societies intolerant of such relationships? There are many psychological interpretations of why some people become interested in homosexual relationships, and many of these interpretations relate the phenomenon to early parent–child relationships. So far, the research has not yielded any clear-cut predictions, although several cross-cultural predictors about male homosexuality are intriguing.

One such finding is that societies that forbid abortion and infanticide for married women (most societies permit these practices for illegitimate births) are likely to be intolerant of male homosexuality.[101] This and other findings are consistent with the point of view that homosexuality is less tolerated in societies that would like to increase population. Such societies may be intolerant of all kinds of behaviors that minimize population growth. Homosexuality would have this effect, if we assume that a higher frequency of homosexual relations is associated with a lower frequency of heterosexual relations. The less frequently heterosexual relations occur, the lower the number of conceptions there might be. Another indication that intolerance may be related to a desire for population growth is that societies with famines and severe food shortages are more likely to allow homosexuality. Famines and food shortages suggest population pressure on resources; under these conditions, homosexuality and other practices that minimize population growth may be tolerated or even encouraged.[102]

The history of the Soviet Union may provide some other relevant evidence. In 1917, in the turmoil of revolution, laws prohibiting abortion and homosexuality were revoked and reproduction was discouraged. But in the period 1934 to 1936 the policy was reversed. Abortion and homosexuality were again declared illegal, and homosexuals were arrested. At the same time, awards were given to mothers who had more children.[103] Population pressure may also explain why our own society has become somewhat more tolerant of homosexuality recently. Of course, population pressure does not explain why certain individuals become homosexual or why most individuals in some societies engage in such behavior, but it might explain why some societies view such behavior more or less permissively.

Let us now turn to heterosexual behavior. What kinds of societies are more permissive than others? Although we do not yet understand the reasons, we do know that greater restrictiveness toward premarital sex tends to occur in more complex societies—societies that have hierarchies of political officials, part-time or full-time craft specialists, cities and towns, and class stratification.[104] It may be that as social inequality increases and various groups come to have differential wealth, parents become more concerned with preventing their children from marrying "beneath them." Permissiveness toward premarital sexual relationships might lead a person to become attached to someone not considered a desirable marriage partner. Even worse, from the family's point of view, such "unsuitable" sexual liaisons might result in a pregnancy that could make it impossible for a girl to marry "well." Controlling mating, then, may be a way of trying to control property. Consistent with this view is the finding that virginity is emphasized in rank and stratified societies, in which families are likely to exchange goods and money in the course of arranging marriages.[105]

The biological fact that humans depend on sexual reproduction does not by itself help explain why females and males differ in so many ways across cultures, or why societies vary in the way they handle male and female roles. We are only beginning to investigate these questions. When we eventually understand more about how and why females and males are different or the same in roles, personality, and sexuality, we may be better able to decide how much we want the biology of sex to shape our lives.

Summary

1. That humans reproduce sexually does not explain why males and females tend to differ in appearance and behavior, and to be treated differently, in all societies.

2. All or nearly all societies assign certain activities to females and other activities to males. These worldwide gender patterns of division of labor may be explained by male–female differences in strength, by differences in compatibility of tasks with child care, or by economy-of-effort considerations and/or the expendability of men.

3. Perhaps because women almost always have infant- and child-care responsibilities, men in most societies contribute more to primary subsistence activities, in terms of calories. But women contribute substantially to primary subsistence activities in societies that depend heavily on gathering and horticulture and in which warfare occurs while primary subsistence work has to be done. When primary and secondary subsistence work are counted, women typically work more hours than men. In most societies men are the leaders in the political arena, and warfare is almost exclusively a male activity.

4. The relative status of women compared with that of men seems to vary from one area of life to another. Whether women have relatively high status in one area does not necessarily indicate that they will have high status in another. Less complex societies, however, seem to approach more equal status for males and females in a variety of areas of life.

5. Recent field studies have suggested some consistent female–male differences in personality: Boys tend to be

more aggressive than girls, and girls seem to be more responsible and helpful than boys.

6. Although all societies regulate sexual activity to some extent, societies vary considerably in the degree to which various kinds of sexuality are permitted. Some societies allow both masturbation and sex play among children, whereas others forbid such acts. Some societies allow premarital sex; others do not. Some allow extramarital sex in certain situations; others forbid it generally.

7. Societies that are restrictive toward one aspect of heterosexual sex tend to be restrictive with regard to other aspects. And more complex societies tend to be more restrictive toward premarital heterosexual sex than less complex societies.

8. Societal attitudes toward homosexuality are not completely consistent with attitudes toward sexual relationships between the sexes. Societal tolerance of homosexuality is associated with tolerance of abortion and infanticide and with famines and food shortages.

Glossary Terms

compatibility-with child-care theory	primary subsistence activities
economy-of-effort theory	secondary subsistence activities
expendability theory	sex differences
gender differences	sexually dimorphic
gender roles	strength theory
gender stratification	

Critical Questions

1. Would you expect female–male differences in personality to disappear in a society with complete gender equality in the workplace?

2. Under what circumstances would you expect male–female differences in athletic performance to disappear?

3. What conditions make the election of a female head of state most likely?

Research Navigator

1. To access the full resources of Research Navigator, please find the access code printed on the inside cover of the *Prentice Hall Guide to Research Navigator*. You may have received this booklet if your instructor recommended this guide be packaged with new textbooks. (If your book did not come with this printed guide, you can purchase one through your college bookstore.) Visit our Research Navigator site at www.researchnavigator.com. Once at this site click on REGISTER under New Users

and enter your access code to create a personal LOGIN NAME and PASSWORD. (When revisiting the site, use the same Login Name and Password.) Browse the features of the Research Navigator Web site and search the databases of academic journals, newspapers, magazines, and Web links.

2. In the early days of anthropology the focus of ethnography tended to be on men. With the emergence of the feminist movement an increasing number of studies of gender focused on women. Using Link Library/Anthropology look for sites related to "gender" and see how many of those sites focus on women's versus men's issues. What kinds of men's issues are discussed?

3. Using ContentSelect/Anthropology look for two articles on aspects of sexuality that have not been discussed much in this chapter. Possibilities include female homosexuality, transgenders, bisexuality, transvestites, or contraception.

Notes

1. Leibowitz 1978: 43–44.
2. Schlegel 1989: 266; Epstein 1988: 5–6; Chafetz 1990: 28.
3. Jacobs and Roberts 1989.
4. Segal 2004; Segal also cites the work of W. Williams 1992.
5. Lang 1999: 93–94; Blackwood 1984b.
6. Wikan 1982: 168–186.
7. Stini 1971.
8. Frayer and Wolpoff 1985: 431–32.
9. For reviews of theories and research on sexual dimorphism and possible genetic and cultural determinants of variation in degree of dimorphism over time and place, see Frayer and Wolpoff 1985 and Gray 1985: 201–209, 217–25.
10. J. K. Brown 1970b: 1074.
11. Among the Aché hunter-gatherers of Paraguay, women collect the type of honey produced by stingless bees (men collect other honey); this division of labor is consistent with the compatibility theory. See Hurtado et al. 1985: 23.
12. Murdock and Provost 1973: 213; Byrne 1994.
13. R. O'Brian 1999.
14. D. R. White, Burton, and Brudner 1977: 1–24.
15. Mukhopadhyay and Higgins 1988: 473.
16. J. K. Brown 1970b: 1073–78; and D. R. White, Burton, and Brudner 1977.
17. Nerlove 1974.
18. N. E. Levine 1988.
19. M. J. Goodman et al. 1985.
20. Noss and Hewlett 2001.
21. C. R. Ember 1983: 288–89.
22. Mead 1950 [originally published 1935]: 180–84.
23. Rivers 1967 [originally published 1906]: 567.
24. M. Ember and Ember 1971: 573, table 1.
25. Schlegel and Barry 1986.

26. Boserup 1970: 22–25; see also Schlegel and Barry 1986: 144–45.
27. Boserup 1970: 22–25.
28. Ibid., pp. 31–34.
29. C. R. Ember 1983: 286–87; data from Murdock and Provost 1973: 212; Bradley 1995.
30. C. R. Ember 1983.
31. Ibid.
32. Ibid., pp. 287–93.
33. M. Ember and Ember 1971: 579–80.
34. Ibid., p. 581; see also Sanday 1973: 1684.
35. Nerlove 1974.
36. Schlegel and Barry 1986.
37. Whyte 1978a: 217.
38. Nussbaum 1995: 2, based on data from Human Development Report 1993.
39. Whyte 1978a; D. B. Adams 1983.
40. J. K. Brown 1970a.
41. Sanday 1974; and Divale and Harris 1976.
42. Quinn 1977: 189–90.
43. Graham 1979.
44. D. Werner 1982; and Stogdill 1974, cited in ibid.; see also Handwerker and Crosbie 1982.
45. Draper 1975: 103.
46. D. Werner 1984.
47. M. H. Ross 1986.
48. This description is based on the fieldwork of Elizabeth and Robert Fearnea (1956–1958), as reported in M. K. Martin and Voorhies 1975: 304–31.
49. Begler 1978.
50. Ibid. See also Whyte 1978a: 229–32.
51. Whyte 1978b: 95–120; see also Quinn 1977.
52. Whyte 1978b: 124–29, 145; see also Sanday 1973.
53. Whyte 1978b: 129–30.
54. J. K. Brown 1970.
55. Whyte 1978b: 135–36.
56. Ibid., p. 135.
57. Doyle 2005.
58. Quinn 1977: 85; see also Etienne and Leacock 1980: 19–20.
59. Chafetz 1990: 11–19.
60. B. B. Whiting and Edwards 1973.
61. R. L. Munroe et al. 2000: 8–9.
62. Maccoby and Jacklin 1974.
63. For a more extensive discussion of behavior differences and possible explanations of them, see C. R. Ember 1981.
64. B. B. Whiting and Edwards 1973.
65. For references to this research, see C. R. Ember 1981: 559.
66. Rubin, Provenzano, and Haskett 1974.
67. For a discussion of this evidence, see Ellis 1986: 525–27; C. R. Ember 1981.
68. For example, Ellis 1986 considers the evidence for the biological view of aggression "beyond reasonable dispute."
69. For a discussion of other possibilities, see C. R. Ember 1981.
70. Rohner 1976.
71. B. B. Whiting and Whiting 1975; see also B. B. Whiting and Edwards 1988: 273.
72. C. R. Ember 1973: 424–39.
73. B. B. Whiting and Edwards 1973: 175–79; see also Maccoby and Jacklin 1974.
74. Burbank 1994.
75. Heise 1967.
76. C. S. Ford and Beach 1951: 191.
77. O. Lewis 1951: 397.
78. Farley 1996: 60.
79. C. S. Ford and Beach 1951: 23–25, 68–71.
80. Ibid., pp. 40–41, 73.
81. Broude 2004b.
82. C. S. Ford and Beach 1951: 82–83.
83. Broude and Greene 1976.
84. Kluckhohn 1948: 101.
85. M. Hunt 1974: 254–57; Lewin 1994.
86. Broude 1980: 184.
87. C. S. Ford and Beach 1951: 114.
88. Jankowiak, Nell, and Buckmaster 2002.
89. Lang 1999: 97, citing Thomas 1993.
90. J. Morris 1938: 191.
91. Underhill 1938: 117, 186.
92. 'Abd Allah 1917: 7, 20.
93. Cardoso and Werner 2004.
94. R. C. Kelly 1974.
95. Cardoso and Werner 2004.
96. Blackwood and Wieringa 1999: 49; Blackwood 1984a.
97. Cardoso and Werner 2004: 207.
98. Data from Textor 1967.
99. W. N. Stephens 1972: 1–28.
100. Broude 1976: 243.
101. D. Werner 1979; D. Werner 1975.
102. D. Werner 1979: 345–62; see also D. Werner 1975, p. 36.
103. D. Werner 1979: 358.
104. Data from Textor 1967.
105. Schlegel 1991.

CHAPTER 9

POLITICS AND LEADERSHIP

From Chapter 10 of *Cultural Anthropology*, 5/e. Barbara Miller. Copyright © 2009 by Pearson Prentice Hall. All rights reserved.

A political leader of the Ashanti people, Ghana. British colonialists referred to such leaders with the English term "chief" although the English word "king" might have been more appropriate.

POLITICS AND LEADERSHIP

the BIG questions

- ◆ What does political anthropology cover?

- ◆ What are the major cross-cultural forms of political organization and leadership?

- ◆ How are politics and political organization changing?

217

Anthropologists in all four fields address political and legal topics. Archaeologists study the evolution of centralized forms of political organization and the physical manifestations of power in monumental architecture, housing, and material possessions. Primatologists do research on dominant relationships, coalitions, and aggression among nonhuman primates. Linguistic anthropologists analyze power differences in interpersonal speech, the media, political propaganda, and more.

Political anthropology is the subfield of cultural anthropology that focuses on human behavior and thought related to power: who has it and who does not, degrees of power, bases of power, abuses of power, political organization and government, and relationships between political and religious power.

◆◆◆
Politics and Culture

Is politics a human universal? Some anthropologists would say no. They point to instances of cultures with scarcely any institutions that can be called political, with no durable ranking systems, and with very little aggression. Foraging lifestyles, as a model for early human evolution, suggest that nonhierarchical social systems characterized human life for 90 percent of its existence. They point out that only with the emergence of private property, surpluses, and other changes did formal government emerge.

Many studies show how dominance seeking is a learned behavior, emphasized in some cultures and among some segments of the population, such as the military, and deemphasized among others, such as religious leaders, healers, and child-care providers. Being a good politician or a five-star general, therefore, is a matter of socialization rather than reflecting some innate drive (see Everyday Anthropology). Other anthropologists would argue that all societies, no matter how small and egalitarian, require some way to organize decision making and maintain social control. Thus in such societies, something like "politics" exists.

---

power   the capacity to take action in the face of resistance, through force if necessary.

authority   the ability to take action based on a person's achieved or ascribed status or moral reputation.

influence   the ability to achieve a desired end by exerting social or moral pressure on someone or some group.

political organization   the existence of groups for purposes of public decision making and leadership, maintaining social cohesion and order, protecting group rights, and ensuring safety from external threats.

Compared to political scientists, cultural anthropologists take a broader view of politics that includes many kinds of behavior and thought beyond formal party politics, voting, and state governments. Cultural anthropologists offer examples of political systems and behavior that might not look "political" to people who have grown up in modern states. This section explores basic political concepts from an anthropological perspective.

British anthropologists, especially Bronislaw Malinowski and A. R. Radcliffe-Brown, long dominated theory making in political anthropology. Their approach, referred to as functionalism, emphasized how institutions such as political organization and law promote social cohesion. Later, the students of these two teachers moved in new directions and began to look at aspects of political organization that pull societies apart. More recently, anthropologists have studied topics such as the politics of resistance of oppressed groups and how globalization and new media are changing power and politics everywhere. The history of political anthropology in the twentieth century and into the twenty-first century illustrates the theoretical tensions between the individual-as-agent approach and the structurist perspective that sees people as constrained in their choices by larger forces. Examples in this chapter show that power and politics are a double-edged sword: They can be both individually liberating and controlling.

POLITICS: THE USE OF POWER, AUTHORITY, AND INFLUENCE

This book uses the term *politics* to refer to the organized use of public power, not the more private micropolitics of family and domestic groups. **Power** is the ability to bring about results, often through the possession or use of forceful means. Closely related to power are authority and influence. **Authority** is the right to take certain forms of action. It is based on a person's achieved or ascribed status or moral reputation. Authority differs from power in that power is backed up by the potential use of force, and power can be wielded by individuals without their having authority in the moral sense. **Influence** is the ability to achieve a desired end by exerting social or moral pressure on someone or some group. Unlike authority, influence may be exerted from a low-status and marginal position.

All three terms are relational. A person's power, authority, or influence exists in relation to other people. Power implies the greatest likelihood of a coercive and hierarchical relationship, and authority and influence offer the most scope for consensual, cooperative decision making. Power, authority, and influence are all related to politics, power being the strongest basis for action and decision making—and potentially the least moral.

everyday ANTHROPOLOGY

Socialization and Women Politicians in Korea

Parental attitudes and child-rearing practices affect children's involvement as adults in public political roles. Chunghee Sarah Soh's (1993) research in the Republic of Korea reveals how variation in paternal roles affects daughters' political leadership roles. Korean female members of the National Assembly can be divided into two categories: elected members (active seekers) and appointed members (passive recipients). Korea is a strongly patrilineal and male-dominated society, so female political leaders represent "a notable deviance from the usual gender-role expectations" (1993:54). This "deviance" is not stigmatized in Korean culture; rather, it is admired within the category of *yŏgŏl*. A *yŏgŏl* is a woman with "manly" accomplishments. Her personality traits include extraordinary bravery, strength, integrity, generosity, and charisma. Physically, a *yŏgŏl* is likely to be taller, larger, and stronger than most women and to have a stronger voice than other women. Why do some girls grow up to be *yŏgŏl*s?

Analysis of the life histories of elected and appointed female legislators offers clues about differences in their socialization. Elected female legislators were likely to have had atypical paternal experiences of two types: either an absent father or an atypically nurturant father. Both of these experiences facilitated a girl's socialization into *yŏgŏl* qualities, or,

Chunghee Sarah Soh

Representative Kim Ok-son greets some of her constituents who are members of a local Confucian club in Seoul, Republic of Korea. She is wearing a men's-style suit and has a masculine haircut.

in the words of Soh, into developing an androgynous personality that combines both masculine and feminine traits. In contrast, the presence of a "typical" father results in a girl developing a more "traditional" female personality that is submissive and passive.

An intriguing question follows from Soh's findings: What explains the socialization of different types of fathers—those who help daughters develop leadership qualities and those who socialize daughters for passivity?

◆ FOOD FOR THOUGHT

* Given your microcultural experience, what socialization factors do you think might influence boys or girls to become politicians?

◆◆◆ Political Organization and Leadership

Political organization is the existence of groups for purposes such as public decision making and leadership, maintaining social cohesion and order, protecting group rights, and ensuring safety from external threats. Power relationships situated in the private domain—within the household, for example—may be considered "political" and may be related to wider political

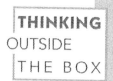

THINKING OUTSIDE THE BOX

Consider the concepts of power, authority, and influence as defined here in the context of campus politics or in some other context with which you are familiar.

realities, but they are not forms of political organization. Political organizations have several features (Tiffany 1979: 71–72):

- Recruitment principles: criteria for determining admission.
- Perpetuity: assumption that the group will continue to exist indefinitely.
- Identity markers: characteristics that distinguish it from others, such as costume, membership card, or title.
- Internal organization: orderly arrangement of members in relation to each other.
- Procedures: rules for behavior of group members.
- Cultural anthropologists cluster the many forms of political organization that occur cross-culturally into four major types (see Figure 1). These four types correspond, roughly, to the major livelihood modes. As with livelihood categories, overlap also exists between types of political organization.

BANDS

A **band**, the form of political organization associated with foraging groups, involves flexible membership and the lack of formal leaders. Because foraging has been the predominant mode of production for almost all of human history, the band has been the most long-standing form of political organization. A band comprises between 20 people and a few hundred people at most, all related through kinship. These units come together at certain times of the year, depending on their foraging patterns and ritual schedule.

Band membership is flexible: If a person has a serious disagreement with another person or a spouse, one option is to leave that band and join another. Leadership is informal, with no one person named as a permanent leader. Depending on events, such as organizing the group to relocate or to send people out to hunt, a particular person may come to the fore as a leader for that time. This is usually someone whose advice and knowledge about the task are especially respected.

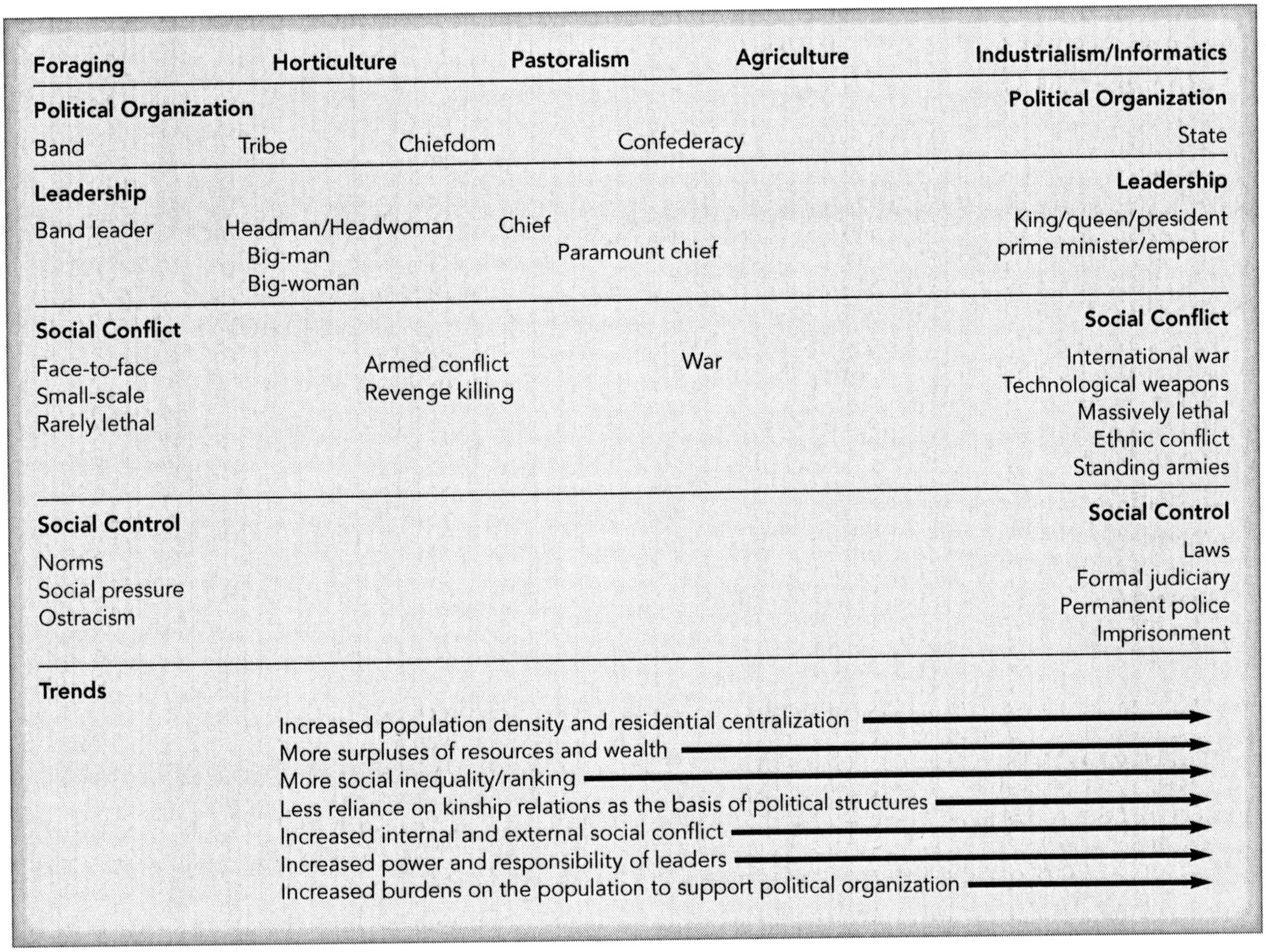

Foraging	Horticulture	Pastoralism	Agriculture	Industrialism/Informatics
Political Organization				**Political Organization**
Band	Tribe	Chiefdom	Confederacy	State
Leadership				**Leadership**
Band leader	Headman/Headwoman Big-man Big-woman	Chief Paramount chief		King/queen/president prime minister/emperor
Social Conflict				**Social Conflict**
Face-to-face Small-scale Rarely lethal	Armed conflict Revenge killing	War		International war Technological weapons Massively lethal Ethnic conflict Standing armies
Social Control				**Social Control**
Norms Social pressure Ostracism				Laws Formal judiciary Permanent police Imprisonment
Trends				

Increased population density and residential centralization ⟶
More surpluses of resources and wealth ⟶
More social inequality/ranking ⟶
Less reliance on kinship relations as the basis of political structures ⟶
Increased internal and external social conflict ⟶
Increased power and responsibility of leaders ⟶
Increased burdens on the population to support political organization ⟶

FIGURE 1 Modes of Political Organization, Conflict, and Social Control

San hunters examining animal tracks near Kalahari Gemsbok National Park, a transnational park spanning Botswana and Namibia that is advertised as a natural area free from human influence. The San, like many indigenous peoples worldwide, are excluded from living and foraging in their traditional territories which are protected by law for the use of tourists as "natural" places.

▶ *Go to the Web and learn about tourist accommodations in the park and transportation access to the park for tourists. How might the presence of tourists affect the "natural" aspects of the park?*

All members of the group are social equals, and a band leader has no special status. He has a certain degree of authority or influence, as perhaps a respected hunter or storyteller, but he does not have power, nor can he enforce his opinions on others. Social leveling mechanisms prevent anyone from accumulating much authority or influence. Political activity in bands involves mainly decision making about migration, food distribution, and resolution of interpersonal conflicts. External conflict between groups is rare because territories of different bands are widely separated and the population density is low.

The band level of organization barely qualifies as a form of political organization because groups are flexible, leadership is ephemeral, and there are no signs or emblems of political affiliation. Some anthropologists argue that true "politics" did not exist in undisturbed band societies because political organization, as defined above, did not exist.

TRIBES

A **tribe** is a more formal type of political organization than the band. Typically associated with horticulture and pastoralism, tribal organization emerged between 10,000 to 12,000 years ago, with the emergence of these modes of production. A tribe is a political group that comprises several bands or lineage groups, each with similar language and lifestyle and each occupying a distinct territory. Tribal groups may be connected through a *clan* structure in which most people claim descent from a common ancestor, although they may be unable to trace the exact relationship. Kinship is the primary basis of membership. Tribal groupings contain from 100 to several thousand people. Tribes are found in the Middle East, South Asia, Southeast Asia, the Pacific, and Africa, as well as among Native Americans.

A tribal headman (most tribal leaders are male) is a more formal leader than a band leader. Key qualifications for this position are being hardworking and generous and possessing good personal skills. A headman is a political leader on a part-time basis only, yet this role is more demanding than that of a band leader. Depending on the mode of production, a headman will be in charge of determining the times for moving herds, planting and harvesting, and setting the time for seasonal feasts and celebrations. Internal and external conflict resolution is also his responsibility. A headman relies mainly on authority and persuasion rather than on power. These strategies are effective because tribal members are all kin and have loyalty to each other.

Among many horticultural groups of the Amazonian rainforest, such as the Kayapo (see Map 1), tribal organization is the dominant political pattern. Each local tribal unit, which is itself a lineage, has a headman (or perhaps two or three). Each tribal group is autonomous, but recently many have united temporarily into larger groups, in reaction to threats to their environment and lifestyle from outside forces.

Pastoralist tribal formations are often linked into a *confederacy*, a loose umbrella organization linking several local tribal units or segments that maintain substantial autonomy. Normally, the local segments meet together rarely, perhaps only at an annual festival. In case of an external threat, however, the confederacy gathers together under one leader to deal with the problem. Once the threat is removed, local units resume their autonomy. This equality and autonomy of tribal units having the ability to unite and then disunite, is referred to as a **segmentary model** of political organization. It exists among pastoralists worldwide (Eickelman 1981). For example, the Qashqa'i (kash-kai), pastoralists of Iran have three levels of political organization: subtribe, tribe, and confederacy (Beck 1986). Leaders at each level deal with higher-level authorities and external forces on behalf of the

band the political organization of foraging groups, with minimal leadership and flexible membership.

tribe a political group that comprises several bands or lineage groups, each with similar language and lifestyle and occupying a distinct territory.

segmentary model type of political organization in which smaller units unite in the face of external threats and then disunite when the external threat is absent.

MAP 1 Kayapo Region in Brazil.
The Kayapo live in several rainforest villages in the Matto Grosso plains region. Their population is around 7000. The Kayapo use their traditional political organizing skills to help them deal with outsiders who seek to pursue commercial logging, mining, and hydroelectric development in the area.

Chief Paul Payakan, leader of the Kayapo. Payakan was instrumental in mobilizing widespread resistance among the Kayapo and several other tribes to the construction of a large hydroelectric dam at Altamira on the Xingu River.

▶ *Find updated information on the Kayapo and the proposed Altamira dam project on the Web.*

tribespeople. They also help group members who are in economic need.

Leadership among the Qashqa'i combines both ascribed and achieved features. Subtribe headmen's positions are based mainly on achievement. Both *khans* (tribe leaders) and *ilkhanis* (confederacy leaders) are members of noble lineages. They gain their positions through patrilineal descent, with the eldest son favored. The role of the Qashqa'i ilkhani is similar in many ways to that of a chief (described in the next section). The increased power of the Iranian state in recent decades has undermined the role of tribal leaders (Beck 1991). The state government formulated new policies regulating migratory schedules, pasture use, and prices of animal products. These rules constrain the power of tribal leaders who then lose significance to their followers who in turn withdraw their support from them and turn increasingly to state-level leaders.

BIG-MAN AND BIG-WOMAN LEADERSHIP In between tribal and chiefdom organizations is the **big-man**

---

big-man or **big-woman system** a form of political organization midway between tribe and chiefdom involving reliance on the leadership of key individuals who develop a political following through personal ties and redistributive feasts.

moka a strategy for developing political leadership in highland Papua New Guinea that involves exchanging gifts and favors with individuals and sponsoring large feasts where further gift giving occurs.

---

system or **big-woman system**, a form of political organization in which individuals build a political base and gain prestige, influence, and authority through a system of redistribution based on personal ties and grand feasts. Anthropological research in Melanesia (see Map 2), a large region in the South Pacific, established the existence of big-man politics (Sahlins 1963). Personalistic, favor-based political systems are, however, found elsewhere.

Political ties of a successful big-man or big-woman include people in several villages. A big-man tends to have greater wealth than his followers, although people continue to expect him to be generous. The core supporters of a big-man tend to be kin, with extended networks including nonkin. A big-man has heavy responsibilities. He is responsible for regulating internal affairs, such as the timing of crop planting, and external affairs, such as intergroup feasts, trade, and war. In some instances, a big-man is assisted in carrying out his responsibilities by a group of other respected men. These councils include people from the big-man's different constituencies.

In several tribes in the Mount Hagen area of the Papua New Guinea highlands, an aspiring big-man develops a leadership position through a process called *moka* (Strathern 1971). **Moka** is a strategy for developing political leadership that involves exchanging favors and gifts, such as pigs, and sponsoring large feasts where further gift giving occurs. A crucial factor in big-manship in the Mount

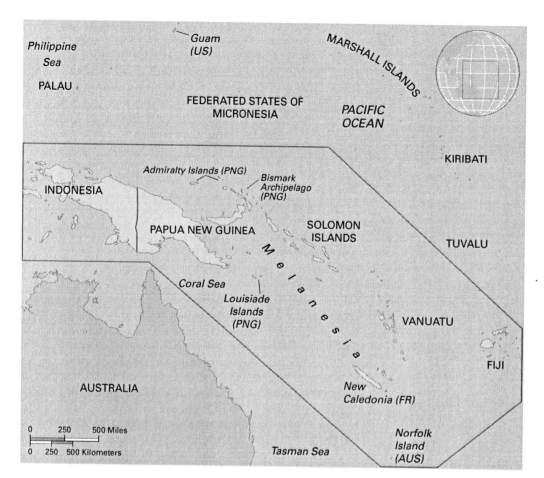

MAP 2 Melanesia. Melanesia is a region in the South Pacific that includes the independent states of Papua New Guinea, the Republic of Vanuatu, the Solomon Islands, and Fiji as well as many islands that are controlled by other countries. It also encompasses the western part of the island of New Guinea, which is controlled by Indonesia, and islands to the west of it, though the people there do not self-identify as Melanesians.

Hagen area is having at least one wife. An aspiring big-man urges his wife or wives to work harder than ordinary women in order to grow more food to feed more pigs. The number of pigs a man has is an important measure of his status and worth. Given the importance of a wife or wives in maintaining a large collection of pigs, a man whose parents die when he is young is at an extreme disadvantage because he lacks financial support for the bridewealth required for marriage. Without parents, he has no bridewealth, no wife, no one to feed and care for pigs, no resource base for moka, and no chance of becoming a big-man.

A married man uses his wife's or wives' production as a basis for developing and expanding exchange ties with contacts throughout the region. An aspiring big-man builds moka relationships first with kin and then beyond. By giving goods to people, he gains prestige over them. The recipient is under pressure to make a return gift of equal or greater value. The exchanges go back and forth, over the years. The more the aspiring big-man gives, and the more people he can maintain in his exchange network, the greater prestige he develops.

Although big-manship is an achieved position, most big-men in the Mt. Hagen area are the sons of big-men, meaning that ascription is also involved (see Figure 2). Ascription plays a role especially for major big-men, of whom over three-quarters were sons of former big-men. It is unclear whether this pattern results from the greater wealth and prestige of big-man families, from socialization into big-manship through paternal example, or from both.

	Father Was a Big-Man	Father Was Not a Big-Man	Totals
Major Big-Men	27	9	36
Minor Big-Men	31	30	61
Total	58	39	97

Source: *The Rope of Moka: Big Men and Ceremonial Exchange of Big-Men in Mount Hagen, Papua New Guinea* by Andrew Starthern. Copyright © Cambridge University Press 1971. Reprinted with permission of Cambridge University Press.

FIGURE 2 Family Background of Big-Men in Mt. Hagen, Papua New Guinea

With few exceptions, the early anthropological literature about tribal politics among indigenous peoples of Melanesia portrays men as dominating public exchange networks and the public political arenas. Women as wives are mentioned as important in providing the material basis for men's political careers. A study on the island of Vanatinai, an island in the Louisiade group (see Map 2), reveals the existence of big-women and big-men (Lepowsky 1990). In this gender-egalitarian culture, both men and women can gain power and prestige by sponsoring feasts at which valuables are distributed, especially *mortuary feasts* (feasts for the dead). Although more Vanatinai men than women are involved in political exchange and leadership, some women are extremely active as political leaders. These women lead sailing expeditions to neighboring islands to visit their exchange partners, who are both male and female, and they sponsor lavish feasts attended by many people. Big-women are also powerful sorcerers, famous healers, and successful gardeners.

CHIEFDOMS

A **chiefdom** is a form of political organization that includes permanently allied tribes and villages under one chief, a leader who possesses power. Compared to most tribes, chiefdoms have large populations, often numbering in the thousands. They are more centralized and socially complex. Hereditary systems of social ranking and economic stratification emerge in chiefdoms. Social divisions exist between the chiefly lineage(s) and nonchiefly groups. Chiefs and their descendants have higher status than commoners, and intermarriage between the two strata is forbidden. Chiefs are expected to be generous, but they may have a more luxurious lifestyle than the rest of the people.

The chiefship is an "office" that must be filled at all times. When a chief dies or retires, he or she must be replaced. In contrast, the death of a band leader or big-man or big-woman does not require that someone else be chosen as a replacement. A chief has more responsibilities than a band or tribal leader. He or she regulates production and redistribution, solves internal conflicts, and plans and leads raids and warring expeditions. Criteria for becoming a chief are clearly defined. Besides ascribed criteria (birth in a chiefly lineage or being the first son or daughter of the chief), achievement is also important. Achievement is measured in terms of personal leadership skills, charisma, and accumulated wealth. Chiefdoms have existed throughout the world.

Anthropologists and archaeologists are interested in how and why chiefdom systems evolved as an intermediary unit between tribes and states and in what the political implications of this evolution are (Earle 1993). Several political strategies support the expansion of power in chiefdoms: improving local production systems and increasing wealth, distributive feasting and gift exchanges, controlling ideological legitimacy applying force internally, and forging stronger

(TOP) Throughout much of the South Pacific, big-man and big-woman politics has long involved the demonstration of political leaders' generosity. Leaders are expected to be able to mobilize resources for impressive feasts such as this one on Tanna Island, one of the many islands of the Republic of Vanuatu in the region of Melanesia. (BOTTOM) A sea turtle off the coast of Fiji, where local people consider them sacred and important as a feasting item.

▶ *How does public feasting play a role in politics in a context with which you are familiar?*

and wider external ties. Depending on local conditions, different strategies were employed. For example, internal control of irrigation systems was the most important factor in the emergence of chiefdoms in prehistoric southeastern Spain, whereas control of external trade was more important in the prehistoric Aegean region (Gilman 1991).

GENDER AND LEADERSHIP IN CHIEFDOMS Much evidence about leadership patterns in chiefdoms comes from historical examples. Prominent chiefs—men and women—are documented in colonial archives and missionary records. Many historical examples of women chiefs and women rulers come from West Africa, including the Queen Mother of the Ashanti of Ghana and of the Edo of Nigeria (Awe 1977).

Oral histories and archival records show that Yoruba women had the institution of the *iyalode,* chief of the women.

The last queen of Hawai'i, Queen Lili'uokalani. Inheriting the throne from her brother, Queen Lili'uokalani reigned for only two years, from 1891 to 1893. She attempted to establish constitutional rights for Hawai'ans and Asians living in the islands. In 1893 she was deposed by a group of European and American businessmen who took political control of the islands. The status of Hawai'i is still contested today by local groups who seek autonomy from the United States.

▶ *What did you learn about Hawai'i in your high school history or government classes? Did you learn about Queen Lili'uokalani and her attempt to assert native rights?*

Christie's Images/CORBIS

Chief Joseph, or Hin-mah-too-yah-lat-kekt (Thunder Rolling Down the Mountain), of the Nez Perce, was born in northern Oregon in 1840. His father, Joseph the Elder, had been an active supporter of peace with the Whites and signed an agreement establishing the Nez Perce Reservation. In 1863, following the discovery of gold, the government took back 6 million acres of land. After Joseph the Elder died, Joseph the Younger was elected Chief. He favored peace, but continued White encroachments on Nez Perce land and government attempts to forcibly relocate his people prompted him to lead a war of resistance.

▶ *Go the Internet and read Chief Joseph's famous speech of surrender delivered in 1877.*

The *iyalode* was the women's political spokes person in the "council of king makers," the highest level of government. She was a chief in her own right, with chiefly insignia, including the necklace of special beads, a wide-brimmed straw hat, a shawl, personal servants, special drummers, and bell ringers.

---

chiefdom a political unit of permanently allied tribes and villages under one recognized leader.

(LEFT) A Ugandan soldier guarding the President's car. (CENTER) President George W. Bush arrives in Airforce One at the Daytona Beach International Airport, Florida, to watch the NASCAR races in 2004. (RIGHT) Queen Elizabeth in her royal carriage in London following her coronation in 1953.

▶ Think of other political contexts in which a leader would avoid signaling his or her high status through a special mode of transportation.

She also had her own council of subordinate chiefs. The position of iyalode was based on achievement. The most important qualifications were her proven ability as a leader, economic resources to maintain her new status as chief, and popularity. Tasks included settling disputes via her court and meeting with women to formulate women's stand on such policy issues as the declaration of war and the opening of new markets. Although she represented all women in the group and had widespread support among women, she was outnumbered at the council of king makers because she was the only female and the only representative of all women.

The Iroquois provide a case of women's indirect political importance (J. K. Brown 1975). Men were chiefs, but women and men councilors were the appointing body. Most men were gone for extended periods, waging war as far away as Delaware and Virginia. Women controlled production and distribution of the staple crop, maize. If the women did not want warriors to leave for a particular campaign, they would refuse to provide them with maize, thereby vetoing the plan. Some anthropologists and others argue that the prehistoric Iroquois are an example of a **matriarchy**, or a society in which women are dominant in terms of economics, politics, and ideology. Most anthropologists, however, characterize the Iroquois as an egalitarian society, because women did not control the society to the exclusion of men nor did they oppress men as a group. Men and women participated equally on the councils.

Why do women play greater political roles in some chiefdoms than in others? The most satisfactory answers point to women's economic roles as the basis for their political power, as among the Iroquois and in many African horticultural societies. In societies where women's economic entitlements are limited, women are unlikely to have public political roles.

The effects of European and North American colonial and missionary influences on nonstate societies have resulted in the decline of women's political status (Etienne and Leacock 1980). For example, British colonialists redefined the institution of iyalode in Nigeria. Now "she is no longer a member of any of the important councils of government. Even the market, and therefore the market women, have been removed from her jurisdiction, and have been placed under the control of the new local government councils in each town" (1980:146). Ethnohistorical research on chiefdoms in Hawai'i documents the existence of powerful women chiefs in precolonial times (Linnekan 1990). Following Captain Cook's arrival in 1778, the colonialists established a Western-model monarchy. By the time the United States annexed the islands in 1898, foreign men had completely displaced indigenous Hawai'ian leaders.

CONFEDERACIES Parallel to the situation discussed in the section on tribes, an expanded version of the chiefdom occurs when several chiefdoms are joined in a confederacy. Such a group is headed by a chief of chiefs, "big chief," or paramount chief. Many prominent confederacies existed, for example, in Hawai'i in the late 1700s, the Iroquois league of five nations, the Cherokee of Tennessee, and the Algonquins of the Chesapeake region in present-day Virginia and Maryland. In the Algonquin confederacy, each village had a chief, and the regional council was composed of local chiefs and headed by the paramount chief. Powhatan, father of Pocahontas, was paramount chief of the Algonquins when the British arrived in the early 1600s.

Chiefdom confederacies of the New World were supported financially by contributions of grain from each local unit. Kept in a central storage area where the paramount

matriarchy   a society in which women are dominant in terms of economics, politics, and ideology.

Water, Pollution, and International Politics

Like air, water can move across state boundaries, carrying environmental pollution. Such movements can cause serious international political conflict and extended negotiations about reparations and planning to prevent future damages. One case is that of mining-related pollution of the Tisza (TEET-zuh) River that flows from Romania to Hungary and beyond, within the Danube River basin.

In January 2000, a dam in Romania holding *tailings* (metal-processing byproducts) from a gold mine breached and released water containing high levels of cyanide, copper, zinc, and other heavy metals into nearby streams (Harper 2005). Three days later, the *plume*, or water carrying the byproducts, had reached Hungary's Tisza River. Within the month, it moved on to Serbia and Bulgaria and eventually reached the Black Sea.

In Hungary, the cyanide killed thousands of tons of fish and waterfowl and raised alarms about people's drinking water. Farmers in the affected region reported the death of cows, and they were unable to sell their farm produce due to negative public perceptions about polluted products. Although cyanide is lethal in the short run, it soon dissipates from the environment as opposed to the heavy metals, which remain in the river's sediments and continue to affect riverine life for a long time.

In spite of the severity of the disaster, the Hungarian state was slow to file claims against the offending corporation or for compensation from Romania. Although postsocialist Hungarian political leaders took up the cause of environmental activism in their rhetoric, they did not follow through with action. This lack of action may be related to the heritage of state

MAP 3   The Danube and Tisza Rivers in Eastern Europe.
The Danube River and its major tributary, the Tisza. Europe's largest remaining natural wetland is in the Danube delta. The core of the Danube delta, which lies mainly in Romania but crosses into Ukraine, was declared a UNESCO World Natural Heritage Site in 1991.

socialism, which did not take environmental problems seriously. Another explanatory factor is that a large number of Hungarians live in Romania, and Hungary's leaders may have wished to avoid an international confrontation that would put Hungarians in Romania at risk.

One positive development is that the European Union offered a wider political framework in which to address the issue of the Tisza River pollution. The Tisza disaster was the first environmental disaster in which the EU took a prominent role. In the end, Hungary decided to sue the mining company for damages in a civil lawsuit rather than taking on an international lawsuit with its neighbor.

◆ FOOD FOR THOUGHT

* The exact reasons for the Hungarian government's inaction are not clear. How can one learn the true reasons behind politicians' actions or inactions?

Rescue workers remove dead fish from the Tisza River in the year 2000 following an accident at a gold mine in northwestern Romania that deposited cyanide and other toxic substances into the Tisza that also flowed into the Danube River and the Black Sea. The accident caused environmental damage in a vast area involving several countries.

(LEFT) Afghanistan President Hamed Karzai wears a carefully assembled collection of regional political symbols. The striped cape is associated with northern tribes. The Persian-lamb hat is an Uzbek style popular in the capital city, Kabul. He also wears a tunic and loose trousers, which are associated with villagers, and sometimes adds a Western-style jacket as well. His clothing implies a statement of unity and diversity about his country. (RIGHT) Secretary of State Condoleeza Rice arrived at the Weisbaden Army Airfield in February 2005 to introduce U.S. President George W. Bush and First Lady Laura Bush to American troops based in Germany.

▶ *Study clothing styles of other state leaders and see if you can "read" their symbolic messages.*

chief lived, the grain was used to feed warriors during external warfare that maintained and expanded the confederacy's borders. A council building existed in the central location, where local chiefs came together to meet with the paramount chief to deliberate on questions of internal and external policy.

STATES

A *state* is a centralized political unit encompassing many communities, a bureaucratic structure, and leaders who possess coercive power.

THE POWERS AND ROLES OF THE STATE States have much more power over their members compared to bands, tribes, and chiefdoms. and state leaders have more responsibilities:

- States engage in international relations in order to deal with other states about mutual concerns (see Eye on the Environment). The state may use force defensively to maintain its borders and offensively to extend its territory.

- States monopolize the use of force and the maintenance of law and order internally through laws, courts, and the police.

- States maintain standing armies and police (as opposed to part-time forces).

- States define citizenship and its rights and responsibilities. In complex societies, since early times, not all residents were granted equal rights as citizens.

- States keep track of the number, age, gender, location, and wealth of their citizens through census systems that are regularly updated.

- States have the power to extract resources from citizens through taxation. Public finance in states is based on formal taxation that takes many forms. **In-kind taxation** is a system of mandatory, noncash contributions to the state. Cash taxes, such as the income tax that takes a percentage of wages, emerged only in the past few hundred years.

- States manipulate information. Control of information to protect the state and its leaders can be done directly

---

in-kind taxation   a system of mandatory noncash contributions to the state.

(through censorship, restricting access to certain information by the public, and promotion of favorable images via propaganda) and indirectly (through pressure on journalists, television networks, and other media to selectively present information or to present information in certain ways).

SYMBOLS AND STATE POWER Religious beliefs and symbols are often closely tied to the power of state leadership: The ruler may be considered to be a deity or part deity, or may be a high priest of the state religion, or perhaps be closely linked with the high priest, who serves as advisor. Architecture and urban planning remind the populace of the greatness of the state. In pre-Columbian Mexico, the central plaza of city-states, such as Tenochtitlan (founded in 1345), was symbolically equivalent to the center of the cosmos and was thus the locale of greatest significance (Low 1995). The most important temples and the residence of the head of state were located around the plaza. Other houses and structures, in decreasing order of status, were located on avenues in decreasing proximity to the center. The grandness and individual character of the leader's residence indicate power, as do monuments—especially tombs to past leaders or heroes or heroines. Egypt's pyramids, China's Great Wall, and India's Taj Mahal are a few of the world's great architectural monuments of state power.

In democratic states where leaders are elected by popular vote and in socialist states where political rhetoric emphasizes social equality, expense and elegance are muted by the adoption of more egalitarian ways of dress (even though in private, these leaders may live relatively opulent lives in terms of housing, food, and entertainment). The earlier practice of all Chinese leaders wearing a "Mao jacket," regardless of their rank, was a symbolic statement of their antihierarchical philosophy. A quick glance at a crowd of people, including the Prime Minister of Canada or Britain or the President of the United States, would not reveal who was the leader because dress differences are avoided. Even members of British royalty wear "street clothes" on public occasions where regalia are not required.

Beyond clothing, other commodities associated with top leadership position include housing quality, food, and modes of transportation. State leaders live in grand mansions and often have more than one residence. The King of Morocco, for example, has several official palaces around the country, and he regularly travels from one to another. President George W. Bush was considered "one of the people" because he liked to eat hamburgers. State leaders do not travel the way ordinary citizens do. For security reasons, their ground vehicles may have bulletproof windows, and a cavalcade of security vehicles protects the leader's vehicle. In many African countries, the most important new symbol of political power is an expensive imported car (Chalfin 2008).

LOCAL POWER AND POLITICS IN DEMOCRATIC STATES

The degree to which states influence the lives of their citizens varies, as does the ability of citizens to influence the political policies and actions of their governments. Some anthropologists, as citizens, use their knowledge of culture at home or abroad to influence politics in their own countries.

In highly centralized states, the central government controls public finance and legal institutions, leaving little power or autonomy in these matters to local governments. In decentralized systems, local governments are granted some forms of revenue generation (taxation) and the responsibility of providing certain services.

Local politics in Japan, Belize, and France illustrate three patterns of local political dynamics. The Japanese case illustrates a community-focused system. The Belize case shows how local politics vary even within the same region. Local politics in both Japan and Belize involve the exchange of gifts and favors. The case of rural France demonstrates the importance of ascription in achieving a leadership position.

In Japan, egalitarian systems of local power structures exist in villages and hamlets. Families subtly vie for status and leadership roles through gift giving, as is common in local politics worldwide (Marshall 1985). Egalitarianism prevails as a community value, but people strive to be "more than equal" by making public donations to the *buraku*, or hamlet. The custom of giving a gift to the community is a way that hamlet families can improve their positions in the local ranking system. In one hamlet, all 35 households recently gave gifts to the community on specified occasions: the 42nd birthday of male family members, the 61st birthday of male family members, the 77th birthday of male family members, the marriage of male family members, the marriage of a female family member whose husband will be the household successor, the birth of the household head or successor couple's first child, and the construction of a new house. These occasions for public gift giving always include a meal to which members of all hamlet households are invited. Since the 1960s, it has also become common to give an item that is useful for the hamlet, such as a set of fluorescent light fixtures for the hamlet hall, folding tables, space heaters, and vacuum cleaners.

Local politics within a democratic framework may involve another type of gift giving and exchange in the interest of maintaining or gaining power. People in elected positions of power give favors in expectation of political loyalty in return. In these cases, various factions vie with each other.

THINKING OUTSIDE THE BOX

What are some key symbols of state power in your home country?

A **faction** is a politically oriented group whose members are mobilized and maintained by a leader to whom the ties of loyalty are lateral—from leader to follower (Brumfiel 1994). Factions tend to lack formal rules and formal succession in their leadership.

Two villages in Belize show a contrast in the development and role of factional politics (Moberg 1991) (see Map 4). One village, Mt. Hope, is faction free; the other village, Charleston, has divisive factionalism. Economic differences between the two villages are important. In Mt. Hope, the government provided residents with land and established a marketing board to purchase villagers' crops. Farmers grow rice for the domestic market and citrus crops for export. Citrus growers account for about half of Mt. Hope's households, receive more than three-fourths of its total income, and control about 87 percent of the land. In Charleston, most men work in small-scale fishing augmented by part-time farming. Lack of a road that would allow export of agricultural crops has inhibited the development of commercial agriculture. Start-up costs for citrus cultivation (fertilizer, insecticide, tractors) are prohibitive for most Charleston households. Charleston is "racked by intense intergroup conflict," and that includes factional conflict that divides kin groups: "One of the village's most acrimonious political conflicts exists between two brothers whose relationship deteriorated when the allies of one brother were excluded from a cooperative that the other had organized" (1991:221). Intense factionalism in Charleston is sustained by outside political party patronage and favor giving. Local faction leaders vie with one another to obtain grants and other benefits from the state. In return, national political parties look to Charleston as a base for developing political loyalties. The national parties have bypassed Mt. Hope because economic development created less dependence on state favors for projects such as a cooperative or a road. Charleston was ripe for political manipulation; Mt. Hope was not.

In rural France, family ties and family reputation influence who becomes an elected local leader (Abélès 1991). The department of Yonne, located in the Burgundy region (see Map 5) southeast of Paris, is the provincial heartland of France. Fieldwork sought to understand how individuals gained access to local political office; it involved interviewing local politicians, attending town council meetings, and following local elections.

France is divided into 36,000 communes that are grouped in 96 departments. Communes and departments are the major arenas for local politics. At the commune level, elected officials are the mayor and town councilors. Several political parties contest the elections—the Socialist party, the Union for French Democracy, and others, including scattered support for

---

faction   a politically oriented group with strong lateral ties to a leader.

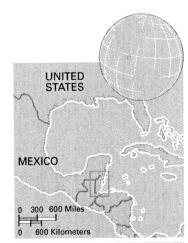

MAP 4   Belize.
The only English-speaking country in Central America, Belize was a British colony known as British Honduras until 1973. Agriculture and international tourism are the most important parts of the economy. The population is 300,000 and growing rapidly. Belize's fertility rate is among the highest in the world. The dominant religion is Christianity in various forms, especially Roman Catholicism. English is the official language, but the most commonly used language is Belizean Kriol, spoken by 70 percent of the population as a first language. Mayan languages are spoken in the west and north.

the Communist party. In France, the only legal requirements for office are French citizenship and age. Other than that, elected positions are, in principle, open to anyone interested in contesting them. According to the perspective that emphasizes human agency in shaping behavior and events, one would hypothesize nearly complete openness in elections and low predictive value of "name" or "family" in determining electoral success. But such "openness" does not seem to be the case in rural Burgundy (Bourgogne) and may not exist elsewhere.

MAP 5 France.
The French Republic comprises a wide variety of landscapes throughout its many departments, both on the mainland (Metropolitan France) and in its overseas departments and territories. France possesses the second largest Exclusive Economic Zone (EEZ) in the world, after the United States. The population of metropolitan France is 61 million people. France is one of the most ethnically diverse countries of the world, with over half of its population claiming a foreign background. The official language is French, although several regional languages are spoken throughout metropolitan France, along with immigrant communities' languages that include many African languages, several varieties of Chinese, Khmer, and Turkish.

In terms of local culture in France, a successful candidate for either commune or department positions should have local roots and come from a distinguished family. Typically, the same family names recur again and again. In one town, the Truchots and the Rostains dominated public life for over a half century. Both families were grain and wine merchants. Another factor influencing electoral choice is a bias toward incumbents. The monopoly of political office by a certain family is perceived by local people to contribute to order and peace. Thus, local roots, reputation, and networks combine with a value placed on continuity as the ingredients for electoral success in rural France. This combination is summed up in the concept of legitimacy. "To enjoy legitimacy is to belong to a world of eligible individuals, those to whom responsibilities can be entrusted. Legitimacy is an elusive quality at first glance: certain individuals canvassing the votes of their fellow-citizens are immediately recognized as legitimate, while others, despite repeated efforts, are doomed to failure. . . . It is

as though a candidate's legitimacy is something people instinctively recognize" (1991:265).

GENDER AND LEADERSHIP IN STATES Most contemporary states are hierarchical and patriarchal, excluding members of lower classes and women from equal participation. Some states are less male dominated than others, but none is female dominated. One view of gender inequality in states suggests that increasing male dominance with the evolution of the state is based on men's control of the technology of production and warfare (Harris 1993). Women in most cultures have limited access to these areas of power. In more peaceful states, such as Finland, Norway, Sweden, and Denmark, women's political roles are more prominent.

Strongly patriarchal contemporary states preserve male dominance through ideologies that restrict women's political power. In much of the Muslim Middle East, Central Asia, Pakistan, and northern India, the practice of *purdah,* female seclusion and segregation from the public world, limits women's public roles. In China, scientific beliefs that categorize women as less strong and dependable than men have long been used to rationalize the exclusion of women from politics (Dikötter 1998). Socialist states typically attempt to increase women's political roles, and the proportion of female members of legislative bodies is higher in socialist states than in capitalist democracies. But it is still not equal to that of men. Although women account for roughly half of the world's population, they form only, on average, 16 percent of the world's parliamentary members (Lederer 2006). Regional differences range from an average of 40 percent female parliamentarians in the Nordic states to 8 percent in Arab states.

A few contemporary states have or have recently had women as prime ministers or presidents. Powerful women heads of state in recent times include Indira Gandhi in India, Golda Meir in Israel, Margaret Thatcher in the United Kingdom, Benazir Bhutto in Pakistan, Michele Bachelet in Chile, Angela Merkel in Germany, Ellen Johnson-Sirleaf in Liberia, and Tarja Halonen in Finland. Some female heads of state are related by kinship, as wife or daughter, to male heads of state. Indira Gandhi, for example, was the daughter of the popular first prime minister of independent India, Jawaharlal Nehru (she was not related to Mahatma Gandhi). It is unclear whether these women inherited the role or achieved it indirectly through their socialization as a result of being born into political families.

Women's political roles can also be indirect, as mothers or wives of male rulers, such as Eva Peron in Argentina as wife of the president and Hillary Clinton in the United States when she was First Lady. Women may wield indirect political power through their children, especially sons. In Turkey, most parents consider politics an undesirable career for their children but more women than men are favorable toward their sons' political ambitions (Günes-Ayata 1995:238–239).

Mothers of male political leaders use their maternal position to influence politics in a context in which direct political roles are largely closed to them.

♦♦♦
Changing Politics

In the early days of political anthropology, researchers examined the varieties of political organization and leadership and created the categories of bands, tribes, chiefdoms, and states. Political anthropologists are now more interested in political dynamics and change, especially in how the state affects local people's lives.

EMERGING NATIONS AND TRANSNATIONAL NATIONS

Many different definitions exist for a nation, and some of them overlap with definitions given for a state (Maybury-Lewis 1997b:125–132). One definition says that a **nation** is a group of people who share a language, culture, territorial base, political organization, and history (Clay 1990). In this sense, a nation is culturally homogeneous, and the United States would be considered not a nation but rather a political unit composed of many nations. According to this definition, groups that lack a territorial base cannot be termed nations. A related term is the *nation-state,* which some say refers to a state that comprises only one nation, whereas others think it refers to a state that comprises many nations. An example is the Iroquois nation.

Depending on their resources and power, nations and other groups may constitute a political threat to state stability and control. Examples include the Kurds in the Middle East (see Culturama, this chapter), the Maya of Mexico and Central America, Tamils in Sri Lanka, Tibetans in China, and Palestinians in the Middle East. In response to this real or perceived threat, states seek to create and maintain a sense of unified identity. Political scientist Benedict Anderson, in his book *Imagined Communities* (1991 [1983]) writes about the symbolic efforts that state builders employ to create a sense of belonging—"imagined community"—among diverse peoples. State symbolic strategies include:

• The imposition of one language as the national language.

• The construction of monuments and museums that emphasize unity.

• The use of songs, dress, poetry, and media messages.

Some states, such as China, control religious expression in the interest of promoting loyalty to and identity with the state. Another strategy is to draw on symbols of

---

nation a group of people who share a language, culture, territorial base, political organization, and history.

Republic of South Africa

The Coat of Arms of South Africa, adopted in 2000, is meant to highlight democratic change and multicultural unity.

▶ *For a research project, study the coat of arms of several countries and analyze the meaning of their symbols and slogans in terms of Benedict Anderson's concept of "imagined community."*

minority or ancestral groups and bring them into the center, thus creating a sense of belonging through recognition. Such recognition may also be interpreted as a form of co-optation, depending on the context. When South Africa launched its new Coat of Arms in 2000, (then) President Mbeke pointed out that the inclusion of a rock art drawing and a slogan in an extinct San language were intended to evoke both South Africa's distant past and its emerging identity as a socially complex and peaceful country (Barnard 2004).

Inspired by Anderson's writings, many anthropologists study state laws, policies, and other practices that seek to create a sense of unity out of diversity. Their work shows that attempts by states to force homogenization of nations and ethnic groups will inevitably prompt resistance of varying degrees from those groups that wish to retain or regain autonomy. Mexico, for example, is promoting a unified identity centered in mestizaje, defined as people of mixed Spanish and Indian ancestry, culture, and heritage in Central and South America (Alonso 2004). Monuments and museums in Mexico City, for example, give prominence to mestizaje symbols and emphasize links to Aztec ancestors while muting connections with highland Indians and the Spanish colonialists. The goal is to forge a new sense of political nationalism and consciousness that values hybridity and mixture. Emphasizing the Aztecs as the cultural roots of Mexican heritage frames out living indigenous groups, further marginalizing their position in the imagined nation-state of Mexico.

For the past few centuries, leading global powers have promoted the notion of the strong state as the best option for

CULTURAMA

The Kurds of the Middle East

The Kurds are an ethnic group of between 20 to 30 million people, most of whom speak some dialect of the Kurdish language, which is related to Persian (Major 1996). The majority are Sunni Muslims. Kurdish kinship is strongly patrilineal, and Kurdish family and social relations are male dominated.

Their home region, called Kurdistan ("Place of the Kurds"), extends from Turkey into Iran, Iraq, and Syria. This area is grasslands, interspersed with mountains, with no coastline. Before World War I, many Kurds were full-time pastoralists, herding sheep and goats. Following the war and the creation of Iraq, Syria, and Kuwait, many Kurdish herders were unable to follow their traditional grazing because they crossed the new country borders. Herders no longer live in tents year-round, though some do for part of the year. Others are farmers. In towns and cities, Kurds own shops, are professionals, and are employed in many different occupations.

Reliable population data for the Kurds in the Middle East do not exist, and estimates vary widely. About half of all Kurds, numbering between 10 and 15 million, live in Turkey, where they constitute 20 percent or perhaps more of the total population. Approximately 6 million live in Iran, 4 to 5 million in Iraq, and 1.5 million in Syria. Others live in Armenia, Germany, France, and the United States.

The Kurds have attempted to establish an independent state for decades, with no success and often facing harsh treatment from government forces. In Turkey, the state used to refer to them as "Mountain Turks," and in many ways still refuses to recognize them as a legitimate minority group. Use of the Kurdish language is restricted in Turkey. The Kurds have faced similar repression in Iraq, especially following their support of Iran in the 1980–1988 Iran–Iraq war. Sadam Hussein razed villages and used chemical weapons against the Kurds. After the Persian Gulf War, 2 million Kurds fled to Iran. Many others have emigrated to Europe and the United States. Iraqi Kurds gained political autonomy from Baghdad in 1991 following a successful uprising aided by Western forces.

Many Kurds feel united by the shared goal of statehood, but several strong internal political factions and a guerrilla movement in Turkey also exist among the Kurds. Kurds in Turkey seek the right to have Kurdish-language schooling and television and radio broadcasts, and they would like to have their folklore recognized as well. The Kurds are fond of music and dancing, and Kurdish villages are known for their distinct performance styles.

Thanks to Diane E. King, University of Kentucky, for reviewing this material.

Ed Kashi/CORBIS

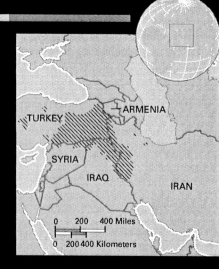

ARMENIA
TURKEY
SYRIA
IRAQ
IRAN

0   200   400 Miles
0   200 400 Kilometers

(LEFT) Herding goats and sheep is a major part of the economy throughout Kurdistan.
(CENTER) In Dohuk, Iraq, the Mazi Supermarket and Dream City are a combination shopping and amusement park. The goods in the market come mainly from Dubai and Turkey.

MAP 6 Kurdish Region in the Middle East. Kurdistan includes parts of Iran, Iraq, Syria, Turkey, and Armenia. About half of all Kurds live in Turkey.

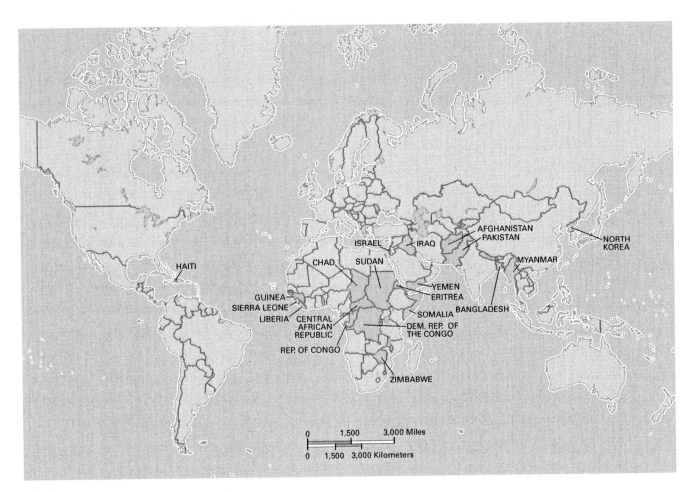

MAP 7 Least Stable States of the World, 2008.
The index for unstable and failed states includes criteria such as these: the government does not have effective control over its territory, is not seen as legitimate by a significant proportion of its population, does not provide services and domestic security to its citizens, and lacks a monopoly on the use of force.

promoting world peace. To that end, minority group movements for autonomy have been suppressed, sometimes brutally, or they lead to long-term internal conflicts. Political theorists and world leaders fear that weak and unstable states are easy targets for outside intervention and provide havens for terrorists. Thus, much international aid and military support goes to programs that aim at strengthening weak states. *Failed states* share features of a breakdown in law and order, economic deterioration, the collapse of service delivery such as education and health, a sharp decline in living standards, and loss of people's loyalty to the government (Foreign Policy 2008). The 2008 index of failed and least stable states included many countries of Africa (see Map 7). Between 2007 and 2008, Nepal dropped from the list of least stable states, but Israel was added.

With so many examples of failed and unstable states, some anthropologists ask if perhaps the idea of the state should be reconsidered (Graeber 2004). Options include the development of more, smaller states that correspond more closely to national/ethnic identities, or, on the other hand, the abandoning of country borders and creation of a

global state within which all people could move freely. If the point of a state is to prevent human suffering by providing a benevolent structure that provides for people's welfare and human rights, and given the evidence that many states are unable to accomplish this goal, then perhaps other options for governance should be explored.

Globalization and increased international migration also prompt anthropologists to rethink the concept of the state (Trouillot 2001). The case of Puerto Rico (see Map 8) is illuminating because of its continuing status as a quasi-colony of the United States (Duany 2000). Puerto Rico is neither fully a state of the United States nor an autonomous political unit with its own national identity. Furthermore, Puerto Rican people do not coexist in a bounded spatial territory. By the late 1990s, nearly as many Puerto Ricans lived in the United States mainland as on the island of Puerto Rico. Migration to Puerto Rico also occurs, creating cultural diversity there. Migrants include returning Puerto Ricans and others from the United States, such as Dominicans and Cubans.

These migration streams—outgoing and incoming—complicate in two ways the sense of Puerto Rico as constituting

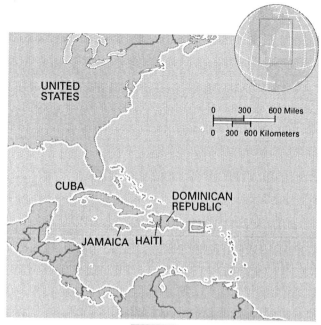

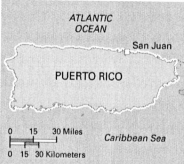

MAP 8 Puerto Rico.
The Commonwealth of Puerto Rico is a U.S. territory with commonwealth status. The indigenous population of the island, the Tainos, is extinct. Analysis of DNA of current inhabitants of Puerto Rico reveals a mixed ancestry, including the Taino, Spanish colonialists, and Africans who came to the island as slaves. The economy is based on agriculture, and sugarcane is the main crop. Tourism is also important, as are remittances. Official languages are Spanish and English. Roman Catholicism is the dominant religion, although Protestantism is increasing.

a nation. First, half of the "nation" lives outside the home territory. Second, within the home territory, ethnic homogeneity does not exist because of the diversity of people who migrate there. The Puerto Ricans who are return migrants are different from the islanders because many have adopted English as their primary language. All of these processes foster the emergence of a transnational identity, which differs from a national identity centered in either the United States or Puerto Rico.

DEMOCRATIZATION

Democratization is the process of transformation from an authoritarian regime to a democratic regime. This process includes several features: the end of torture, the liberation of political prisoners, the lifting of censorship, and the toleration

of some opposition (Pasquino 1996). In some cases, what is achieved is more a relaxation of authoritarianism than a true transition to democracy, which would occur when the authoritarian regime is no longer in control. Political parties emerge, some presenting traditional interests and others oppositional.

The transition to democracy appears to be most difficult when the change is from highly authoritarian socialist regimes. This pattern is partly explained by the fact that democratization implies a transition from a planned economy to one based on market capitalism (Lempert 1996). The spotty record of democratization efforts also has to do with the nonfit of many principles of democracy with local political traditions that are based solely on kinship and patronage.

WOMEN IN POLITICS: NEW DIRECTIONS?

Two questions arise in the area of changing patterns of women in contemporary politics: Is the overall participation of women at varying political levels increasing? Do women in politics bring more attention to women's issues such as the division of labor and wages, access to health care, and violence? The answer to the first question is yes, as noted earlier, although the increase is modest. In terms of the second question, the answer is mainly no, perhaps because women political leaders become "like men" or have to avoid "feminist issues" in order to maintain their position. In all countries, women lack political status equal to that of men. In general, women are marginalized from formal politics and must seek to achieve their goals either indirectly, as wives or mothers of male politicians, or through channels other than formal politics, such as grassroots movements. Nonetheless, some signs of progress exist.

In contrast, in some Native American groups, recovery of women's former political power is occurring (B. G. Miller 1994). In several communities, female participation in formal politics is increasing dramatically, and it is bringing more attention to issues that face women. This change is taking place within the context of colonialism's effects, which resulted in women's greatly decreased political roles compared to the pre-colonial era. One explanation for the recent improvement is that women are obtaining newly available managerial positions on reservations. These positions give women experience in dealing with the outside world and authority for assuming public office. In addition, they face less resistance from men than women in more patriarchal contexts do. Most Native Americans do not view women's roles as contradictory to public authority roles.

THINKING OUTSIDE THE BOX

What is your position on states: Are they the best option for a peaceful world and for providing internal security and services for citizens? What are some examples of successful states?

(LEFT) Aung San Suu Kyi is the leader of the Burmese democracy and human rights movement. The daughter of Burma's national hero, Aung San, who was assassinated just before Burma gained its independence from the British, has frequently been placed under house arrest since 1989. Aung San Suu Kyi was awarded the Nobel Peace Prize, the eighth woman to receive the award.
(RIGHT) An Iraqi Shi'ite woman in the city of Najaf, south of Baghdad, casts her ballot in the 2005 parliamentary elections. Promoting women's participation in democratic processes is challenging in contexts where women's role in the public domain is constrained.

Barack Obama, an African American, was elected the 44th President of the United States in November, 2008.

▶ *Should the proportion of various ethnic groups in a country be accurately reflected in state-level political bodies such as the United States Senate and House of Representatives? If no, why not. If yes, why, and how could it be achieved?*

The resurgence in women's political roles among the Seneca of New York State and Pennsylvania echoes these themes (Bilharz 1995). From women's precolonial position of at least equal political power with men, Seneca women's political status had declined in many ways. Notably, when the constitution of the Seneca Nation was drawn up on a European model in 1848, only men were granted the right to vote. In 1964, Seneca women finally gained the right to vote. Even before enfranchisement, women were politically active and worked on committees formed to stop the building of Kinzua Dam in Pennsylvania. For Seneca women, job creation through the Seneca Nation of Indians (SNI) brought new employment opportunities. Although no woman has run for president of the Seneca Nation as yet and only a few women have been head of a reservation, many women hold elective offices of clerk and judge, and many women head important service departments of the SNI, such as in the areas of education and health. Women of the Seneca Nation still retain complete control over the "clearing" (the cropland), and "their primacy in the home has never been challenged" (1995:112). According to Bilharz, Seneca women have regained a position of equality.

POLITICAL LEADERSHIP IN NEW SOCIAL MOVEMENTS

The Rural Landless Workers' Movement (NSM) in Brazil is one of the most dynamic social movements in Central and South America today (Veltmeyer and Petras 2002). The NSM is a movement of small farmers united in a political struggle for social change through pro-poor programs of land redistribution and limitations on state power. Brazil's NSM is characterized by especially successful leaders who are able to mobilize and sustain popular support. Analysis of NSM leaders' characteristics finds the following features of successful leaders:

- Deep and continuing roots in the countryside
- Relatively more education and strong commitment to education
- Ability to solve problems and take practical action
- Shared vision of alternative social system
- Personality with style and mystique to sustain popular loyalty in difficult times
- Optimism

The opposite of these characteristics define an unsuccessful political leader: origin in a distant social class from the constituency, from the same class but poorly educated, inspired by theory and ideology rather than being pragmatic, lacking in style and charisma, and with little sense of positive alternatives for the future.

GLOBALIZATION AND POLITICS

Since the seventeenth century, the world's nations have been increasingly linked in a hierarchical structure that is largely regulated through international trade. In the seventeenth century, Holland was the one core nation dominating world trade. It was then surpassed by England and France, which remained the two most powerful nations up to around 1900. In the early part of the twentieth century, challenges for world dominance were made by the United States and later Germany and Japan. The outcome of World War II placed the United States as

A flight operation specialist of the European Space Agency (ESA) waits for the launch of Cryosat satellite in Darmstadt, near Frankfurt, Germany, in 2005. Cryosat will circuit on a polar orbit with the primary mission of testing the prediction that polar ice is thinning due to global warming.

leader of the "core." Recently, Japan, the European Union, and China have been playing larger roles.

Cultural anthropology's traditional strength has been the study of small, bounded local groups, so anthropologists have come late to the study of international affairs (Wilson 2000). Now, more anthropologists have enlarged their focus to the international level, studying both how global changes affect local politics and how local politics affect international affairs. Worldwide communication networks facilitate global politics. Ethnic politics, although locally initiated, increasingly has international repercussions. Migrant populations promote interconnected interests across state boundaries.

A pioneering study in the anthropology of international affairs is Stacia Zabusky's (1995) research on patterns of cooperation among international scientists at the European Space Agency (ESA). The ESA involves people from different European nations seeking to cooperate in joint ventures in space and, more indirectly, to promote peaceful relations in Europe. Zabusky attended meetings and interviewed people at the European Space Research and Technology Centre, ESA's primary production site, in the Netherlands. Focusing on people's work roles, their styles of reaching consensus at meetings, and the role of national differences in this cooperative effort, she found that language plays a key part in affecting cooperation. The official languages of the ESA are English and French, but most interactions take place in English. Some nonnative English speakers felt that this gave the British an automatic advantage, especially in meetings where skill in speech can win an argument. A major divisive factor is the sheer geographic dispersal of the participants throughout Europe. This means that travel is a constant, as scientists and engineers convene for important meetings. Despite logistical problems, meetings are an important part of the "glue" that promotes cooperation above and beyond just "working together." Conversations and discussions at meetings allow people to air their differences and work toward agreement.

Zabusky concludes that the ESA represents an ongoing struggle for cooperation that is motivated by more than just the urge to do "big" science. "In working together, participants were dreaming about finding something other than space satellites, other than a unified Europe, or even a functioning organization at the end of their travails. Cooperation indeed appeared to participants not only as an achievement but as an aspiration" (1995:197).

Culture exists at all levels of human interaction—local, national, international, and transnational, and even in cyberspace—and power relations are embedded in culture at all these levels. Anthropologists must "study up," as Laura Nader urged them to do several decades ago (1972), because people, power, and culture are "up" there just as much as they are out in remote villages. As one anthropologist urges, anthropologists should move into research on institutions with lethal powers (Feldman 2003).

the BIG questions REVISITED

◆ What does political anthropology cover?

Political anthropology is the study of power relationships in the public domain and how they vary and change cross-culturally. Political anthropology has moved from a mainly functional perspective about local political systems, characteristic of the first half of the twentieth century, to looking at more macro and global issues related to inequality and conflict and to the role of individual agency in contesting political structures.

Political anthropologists study the concept of power, as well as related concepts such as authority and influence. They have discovered differences between politics and political organization in small-scale societies and large-scale societies by examining issues such as leadership roles and responsibilities, the social distribution of power, and the emergence of the state. Although politics in some form or another is a cultural universal, cross-cultural studies show wide variation in the bases and extent of political leadership and the informality or formality of political organization.

◆ What are the major cross-cultural forms of political organization and leadership?

Patterns of political organization and leadership vary according to mode of production and global economic relationships. Foragers have a minimal form of leadership and political organization in the band. Band membership is flexible. If a band member has a serious disagreement with another person or a spouse, one option is to leave that band and join another. Leadership in bands is informal. A tribe is a more formal type of political organization than the band. A tribe comprises several bands or lineage groups, with a headman or headwoman as leader. Big-man and big-woman political systems are an expanded form of tribe, with leaders having influence over people in several different villages. Chiefdoms may include several thousand people. Rank is inherited, and social divisions exist between the chiefly lineage(s) and nonchiefly groups.

A state is a form of political organization with a bureaucracy and diversified governmental institutions designed to administer large and complex societies. States conduct international relations in their dealings with other states. They control power within state borders and define citizenship and citizens' rights. They maintain records of citizens and have the power to levy indirect and direct taxes. State leaders employ a variety of symbols to bolster their image, including dress, housing, food, and modes of transportation. Strategies for building a sense of unity in culturally plural states may include imposition of one language as the national language; construction of monuments and museums; and promotion of songs, poetry, and other media-relayed messages about the homeland. Ethnic/national politics has emerged within and across states as groups compete for either increased rights within the state or autonomy from it.

States are differentiated in terms of their strength and ability to carry out their responsibilities to their citizens. The concept of a failed or unstable state refers to a government that is unable to maintain order and provide services. In recent decades, several states, especially in Africa, are considered to be failed states. Globalization, increased transnational migration, and the development of international organizations such as the United Nations and the World Trade Organization are major contemporary forces that have certain powers that transcend states.

◆ How are politics and political organization changing?

The anthropological study of change in leadership and political organization has documented several trends, most of which are related to the influences of European colonialism or contemporary capitalist globalization. Postcolonial nations struggle with internal ethnic divisions and pressures to democratize. Women as leaders of states are still a tiny minority. In some groups, however, women leaders are gaining ground, as among the Seneca. Globalized communication networks promote the growth of global politics.

Cultural anthropologists have rarely addressed the topic of international political affairs and the role of international organizations such as the United Nations. They are, however, increasingly interested in demonstrating the usefulness of cultural anthropology in global peacekeeping and conflict resolution.

KEY CONCEPTS

authority
band
big-man or big-woman system
chiefdom
faction

influence
in-kind taxation
matriarchy
moka
nation

political organization
power
segmentary model
tribe

SUGGESTED READINGS

Stanley R. Barrett. *Culture Meets Power*. Westport, CT: Praeger, 2002. The author argues that the two concepts, culture and power, should be considered in understanding contemporary affairs, including events such as the September 11, 2001, attacks on the United States.

Kimberley Coles. *Democratic Designs: International Intervention and Electoral Practices in Postwar Bosnia-Herzegovina*. Ann Arbor: University of Michigan Press, 2008. This book provides an ethnographic analysis of the interaction between international humanitarian aid workers and the postwar political process.

Elizabeth F. Drexler. *Aceh, Indonesia: Securing the Insecure State*. Philadelphia: University of Pennsylvania Press, 2008. The author examines corruption, political violence, and the failure of international humanitarian interventions in the Indonesian province of Aceh.

Mona Etienne and Eleanor Leacock, eds. *Women and Colonization: Anthropological Perspectives*. New York: Praeger, 1980. This classic collection examines the impact of Western colonialism and missionary intervention on women of several indigenous groups of North America and South America, Africa, and the Pacific.

Magnus Fiskesjö. *The Thanksgiving Turkey Pardon, The Death of Teddy's Bear, and the Sovereign Exception of Guantáno*. Chicago: Prickly Paradigm Press, 2003. This interpretation of the U.S. presidential ritual of "pardoning" a turkey every Thanksgiving sheds light on notions of the presidency and its power in the United States.

David Graeber. *Fragments of an Anarchist Anthropology*. Chicago: Prickly Paradigm Press, 2004. The author presents examples of nonstate societies as evidence that alternatives to the state exist and can function. He discusses the tendency of cultural anthropologists to favor small-scale, nonstate political organization as more peaceful and egalitarian than contemporary mega-states.

David H. Lempert. *Daily Life in a Crumbling Empire*. New York: Columbia University Press, 1996. This two-volume ethnography is based on fieldwork conducted in Moscow before perestroika. It is the first comprehensive ethnography of urban Russia and its economic, political, and legal systems and reforms.

Mark Moberg. *Citrus, Strategy, and Class: The Politics of Development in Southern Belize*. Iowa City: University of Iowa Press, 1992. The theoretical debate of structure versus agency frames this ethnography of household and village economies within the world economy and the transformation from factional politics to class formation. The author provides quantitative data and insights from five individuals' lives.

Dan Rabinowitz. *Overlooking Nazareth: The Politics of Exclusion in Galilee*. New York: Cambridge University Press, 1997. This study of Palestinian citizens in an Israeli new town examines conflict and cooperation and provides theoretical insights into nationalism and ethnicity. Biographical accounts of three Palestinians—a medical doctor, a basketball coach, and a local politician—are included.

David Sneath. *The Headless State: Aristocratic Orders, Kinship Society, and Misrepresentations of Inner Asia*. New York: Columbia University Press, 2008. The author describes how anthropologists, since the nineteenth century, have misrepresented Inner Asian nomadic political culture. His analysis continues through to the Soviet and post-Soviet periods and then offers a less essentialized interpretation.

Joan Vincent, ed. *The Anthropology of Politics: A Reader in Ethnography, Theory, and Critique*. Malden, MA: Blackwell Publishers, 2002. Over 40 essays are arranged in four sections: classics of the Enlightenment through the nineteenth century, early ethnographies paired with contemporary updates on the same culture, colonialism and imperialism, and political cosmopolitanism.

Jack M. Weatherford. *Tribes on the Hill*. New York: Rawson, Wade Publishers, 1981. This analysis of politics and political culture within the United States Congress examines the effects of male privilege and seniority on ranking, lobbying tactics, and ritual aspects of the legislation process.

CHAPTER 10

RELIGION

In Nepal, Hindus and Buddhists worship select girls thought to be the living embodiment of a goddess. This girl, who is 6 years old, lives in a special residence in Kathmandu, the capital of Nepal, with other girl goddesses, or kumaris. Kumaris appear at religious events and bless people. When a kumari reaches puberty, she returns to ordinary life and receives a monthly stipend.

RELIGION

the BIG questions

♦ What is religion and what are the basic features of religions?

♦ How do world religions illustrate globalization and localization?

♦ What are some important aspects of religious change in contemporary times?

243

When studying the religious life of people of rural Greece, anthropologist Loring Danforth observed rituals in which participants walk across several yards of burning coals (1989). They do not get burned, they say, because their faith in a saint protects them. Back in the United States, Danforth met an American who regularly walks on fire as part of his New Age faith and organizes training workshops for people who want to learn how to do it. Danforth himself firewalked in a ceremony in rural Maine.

Not every anthropologist who studies religion undertakes such challenges, but they all share an interest in questions about humanity's understanding of the supernatural realm and relationships with it: Why do some religions have many gods and others just one? Why do some religions practice sacrifice? Why do some religions have more participation by women? How do religions respond to changing conditions in the political economy?

Religion has been a cornerstone topic in cultural anthropology since the beginnings of the discipline. The early focus, in the nineteenth century, was on religions of indigenous peoples living in places far from Europe. Now, anthropologists also study the religions of state-level societies and the effects of globalization on religious change.

Christian firewalkers in northern Greece by walking on hot coals. They reaffirm God's protection by not getting burned.

▶ *If you have a religious faith, are pain or other physical discomforts involved in any of the rituals?*

◆ ◆ ◆

Religion in Comparative Perspective

This section sets the stage for the chapter by discussing basic areas in the anthropology of religion, including how to define religion, theories about the origin of religion, and types of religious beliefs, rituals, and religious specialists.

WHAT IS RELIGION?

Since the earliest days of anthropology, scholars have proposed various definitions of religion. In the late 1800s, British anthropologist Sir Edward Tylor defined religion as the belief in spirits. A more comprehensive, current definition says that **religion** is beliefs and behavior related to supernatural beings and forces, parallel to our definition of culture. This definition specifically avoids linking religion with belief in a supreme deity because some religions have no concept of a supreme deity, whereas others have multiple deities.

Religion is related to, but not the same as, a people's *worldview*, or way of understanding how the world came to be, its design, and their place in it. Worldview is a broader concept and does not include the criterion of concern with a supernatural realm. An atheist has a worldview, but not a religious one.

MAGIC VERSUS RELIGION Sir Edward Tylor wrote that magic, religion, and science are alike in that they are different ways in which people have tried to explain the physical world and events in it. He considered science to be the superior, most rational of the three. Sir James Frazer, writing at about the same time as Tylor, defined **magic** as people's attempt to compel supernatural forces and beings to act in certain ways (1978 [1890]). He contrasted magic with religion, which he said is the attempt to please supernatural forces or beings. Frazer differentiated two general principles of magic:

- *The law of similarity,* the basis of imitative magic, is founded on the assumption that if person or item X is like person or item Y, then actions done to person or item X will affect person or item Y. A familiar example is a voodoo doll. If someone sticks pins into a doll X that represents person Y, then person Y will experience pain or suffering.

- *The law of contagion,* the basis of contagious magic, says that persons or things once in contact with a person can still have an effect on that person. Common items for working contagious magic include a person's hair trimmings, nail clippings, teeth, saliva, blood, fecal matter, and the placenta of a baby. In cultures where contagious magic is practiced, people are careful about disposing of their personal wastes so that no one else can get hold of them.

---

religion beliefs and behavior related to supernatural beings and forces.

magic the attempt to compel supernatural forces and beings to act in certain ways.

animism the belief in souls or "doubles."

Tylor, Frazer, and other early anthropologists supported an evolutionary model, with magic preceding religion. They evaluated magic as being less spiritual and ethical than religion and therefore more "primitive." They assumed that, in time, magic would be completely replaced by the "higher" system of religion, which would eventually be replaced by science as the most rational way of thinking. They would be surprised to see the widespread presence of magical religions in the modern world, such as the so-called Wicca, or Neo-Pagan, religion that centers on respect for the Earth, nature, and the seasonal cycle. An anthropologist who studied Wicca in the San Francisco Bay area learned about beliefs, rituals, and magical practices through participant observation (Magliocco 2004). The pentacle is an important Wicca symbol (see Figure 1). As of 2007, the U.S. Veterans Administration added the pentacle to its list of approved religious symbols that can be placed on the headstones of the graves of deceased veterans and their family members.

Many people turn to magical behavior in situations of uncertainty. Magic, for example, is prominent in sports (Gmelch 1997 [1971]). Some baseball players in the United States repeat actions or use charms, including a special shirt or hat, to help them win. This practice is based on the assumption that if it worked before, it may work again. In baseball, pitching and hitting involve more uncertainty than fielding, and pitchers and hitters are more likely to use magic. Magical practices are also common in farming, fishing, the military, and love.

THEORIES OF THE ORIGIN AND FUNCTIONS OF RELIGION

Many theorists adopt a functionalist approach in explaining why religion is such a pervasive aspect of human culture. According to this view, religion provides ways of explaining and coping with universal human problems such as life and death, illness, and misfortune.

Tylor's theory was based on his assumption that early human ancestors needed to explain the difference between the living and the dead (1871). They therefore developed the concept of a soul that exists in all living things and departs from the body after death. Tylor named this way of thinking **animism**, the belief in souls or "doubles." Tylor speculated that the concept of the soul eventually became personified, and human-like deities were conceived. For Tylor, religion evolved from animism to *polytheism* (the belief in many deities) to *monotheism* (the belief in one supreme deity). Once again, this evolutionary model is proved wrong. Animistic beliefs exist in many religions, including, for example, some Christians' beliefs about visitations of the dead (Stringer 1999), and many contemporary religions are polytheistic.

Throughout the nineteenth and twentieth centuries, functionalist theories about religion continued to emerge. Karl Marx emphasized religion's role as an "opiate of the masses." He thought that religion provides a superficial form of comfort to the poor, masking the harsh realities of class inequality and thereby preventing lower-class uprisings against the rich. In contrast, French scholar Emile Durkheim, in his book *The Elementary Forms of the Religious Life* (1965 [1915]), speculated that early humans understood the benefits of social contact, and therefore they developed group symbols and rituals to maintain social continuity over time. Bronislaw Malinowski suggested that rituals reduce individual anxiety and uncertainty. For Sigmund Freud, religion is a *projective system* that expresses people's unconscious thoughts, wishes, and worries.

More recently, noted cultural anthropologist Clifford Geertz combines Durkheimian functionalism with symbolic analysis (1966). In his view, religions are primarily systems of meaning that provide people with a *model of life* (how to understand the world) and a *model for life* (how to behave in the world). Given the local orientation of early anthropologists, they did not address international questions about religion in terms of how it contributes to world peace and world conflict.

VARIETIES OF RELIGIOUS BELIEFS

Religions comprise beliefs and behavior. Scholars of religion generally address belief systems first because they appear to

FIGURE 1 A Pentacle. Sometimes called a pentagram, it is a five-pointed star surrounded by a circle. An important symbol in Neo-Pagan and Wiccan religions, the pentacle is also a magical tool used for summoning energies and commanding spirits.

THINKING OUTSIDE THE BOX

Take careful note of your daily activities and events for a week and assess them in terms of how magic, religion, or science are involved. What did you find?

Religion provides an important source of social cohesion and psychological support for many immigrant groups, whose places of worship attract both worshippers and cultural anthropologists interested in learning how religion fits into migrants' adaptation. This is a scene at a Lao Buddhist temple in Virginia.

▶ Learn about Buddhism in North America from the Internet.

inform patterns of religious behavior. Religious beliefs are shared by a group, sometimes by millions of people, and are passed on through the generations. Elders teach children through songs and narratives, artists paint the stories on rocks and walls, and sculptors create images in wood and stone that depict aspects of religious belief.

HOW BELIEFS ARE EXPRESSED Beliefs are expressed and transferred over the generations in two main forms:

- **Myth**, stories about supernatural forces or beings
- **Doctrine**, direct statements about religious beliefs

A myth is a narrative that has a plot with a beginning, middle, and end. The plot may involve recurrent motifs, the smallest units of narrative. Myths convey messages about the supernaturals indirectly, through the story itself, rather than by using logic or formal argument. Greek and Roman myths, such as the stories of Zeus, Athena, Orpheus, and Persephone, are world famous. Some people would say that the Bible is a collection of myths; others would object to that categorization

as suggesting that the stories are not "real" or "sacred." Myths have long been part of people's oral tradition, and many are still unwritten.

Anthropologists ask why myths exist. Malinowski said that a myth is a charter for society in that it expresses core beliefs and teaches morality. Claude Lévi-Strauss, the most famous mythologist, saw myths as functional in a philosophical and psychological way. In his view, myths help people deal with the deep conceptual contradictions between, for example, life and death and good and evil, by providing stories in which these dualities find a solution in a mediating third factor. These mythological solutions are buried within a variety of surface details in the myth. For example, many myths of the Pueblo Indians of the U.S. Southwest juxtapose grass-eating animals (vegetarians) with predators (carnivores). The mediating third character is the raven, who is a carnivore but, unlike other creatures, does not have to kill to eat meat because it is a scavenger.

A cultural materialist perspective, also functionalist, says that myths store and transmit information related to making a living and managing economic crises (Sobel and Bettles 2000). Analysis of 28 myths of the Klamath and Modoc Indians (see Map 1) reveals that subsistence risk is a consistent theme. The myths also describe ways to cope with hunger, such as skill in hunting and fishing, food storage, resource diversification, resource conservation, spatial mobility, reciprocity, and the role of supernatural forces. Thus, myths are repositories of knowledge related to economic survival, crisis management, and environmental conservation.

Doctrine, the other major form in which beliefs are expressed, explicitly defines the supernaturals, the world and

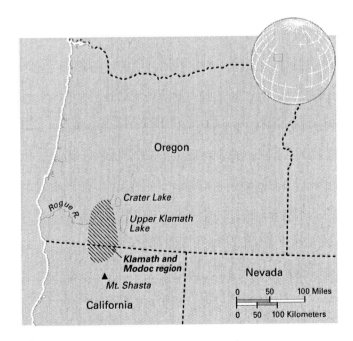

MAP 1 Klamath and Modoc Indian Region in Oregon and California.

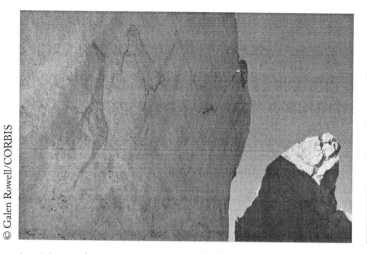

(LEFT) San rock paintings in the Tsodillo Hills, northwestern Botswana. Some of the paintings date back to 800 CE. The site is sacred to the San people because important spirits come to the hills to rest. (RIGHT) A stone sculpture at Mamallapuram, southern India, dating from the eighth or ninth century, depicts the triumph of the goddess Durga (riding the lion) over the bull-headed demon Mahishasura. This site is now more popular among tourists than among Hindu devotees.

how it came to be, and people's roles in relation to the supernaturals and to other humans. Doctrine is written and formal. It is close to law because it links incorrect beliefs and behaviors with punishments. Doctrine is associated with institutionalized, large-scale religions rather with than small-scale "folk" religions.

Doctrine can and does change (Bowen 1998:38–40). Over the centuries, various popes have pronounced new doctrine for the Catholic Church. A papal declaration of 1854, made with the intent of reinvigorating European Catholicism, bestowed authenticity on the concept of the Immaculate Conception, an idea with substantial popular support.

Muslim doctrine is expressed in the Qu'ran, the basic holy text of the Islamic faith, which consists of revelations made to the prophet Muhammad in the seventh century, and in collections of Muhammad's statements and deeds (Bowen 1998:38). In Kuala Lumpur, Malaysia, a small group of highly educated women called the Sisters in Islam regularly debate with members of the local *ulama*, religious authorities who are responsible for interpreting Islamic doctrine especially concerning families, education, and commercial affairs (Ong 1995). Debates concern such issues as polygamy, divorce, women's work roles, and women's clothing.

BELIEFS ABOUT SUPERNATURAL FORCES AND BEINGS

Supernaturals range from impersonal forces to those who look just like humans. Supernaturals can be supreme and all-powerful creators or smaller-scale, annoying spirits that take up residence in people through possession.

The term **animatism** refers to a belief system in which the supernatural is conceived of as an impersonal power. An important example is *mana*, a concept widespread throughout the South Pacific region, including Melanesia, Polynesia, and Micronesia. Mana is a force outside nature that works automatically; it is neither spirit nor deity. It manifests itself in objects and people and is associated with personal status and power, because some people accumulate more of it than others.

Some supernaturals are *zoomorphic*, deities in the shape, or partial shape, of animals. No satisfactory theory has appeared to explain why some religions develop zoomorphic deities, and for what purposes, and why others do not. Religions of classical Greece and Rome and ancient and contemporary Hinduism are especially rich in zoomorphic supernaturals. *Anthropomorphic* supernaturals, deities in the form of humans, are common but not universal. The human tendency to perceive of supernaturals in their own form was noted 2500 years ago by the Greek philosopher Xenophanes, who lived sometime between 570 and 470 BCE. He said,

> But if horses or oxen or lions had hands and could draw with their hands and accomplish such works as men, horses would draw the figures of their gods as similar to horses and the oxen as similar to oxen, and they would make the bodies of the sort which each of them had (Lesher 2001:25).

The question, though, of why some religions have anthropomorphic deities and others do not is impossible to answer.

Anthropomorphic supernaturals, like humans, can be moved by praise, flattery, and gifts. They have emotions. They

---

myth   a narrative with a plot that involves the supernaturals.

doctrine   direct and formalized statements about religious beliefs.

animatism   a belief system in which the supernatural is conceived of as an impersonal power.

Eagle Protection, National Parks, and the Preservation of Hopi Indian Culture

For many generations, young men of the Hopi Indian tribe have searched each spring for golden eaglets in the cliffs of Arizona's Wupatki National Park and other parts of northeastern Arizona (Fenstemaker 2007). They bring the young eagles to the reservation and care for them until the summer when, as mature birds, they are smothered in a ceremony that the Hopi believe frees the spirits of the birds, which convey messages to their ancestors who reside in the spiritual world. This ceremony is the most important Hopi ritual, but they use golden eagle feathers in all their rituals. For the Hopi, golden eagles are their link to the spiritual world, and their ritual use is essential to the continuity of their culture.

In 1783, the Continental Congress adopted the bald eagle as the national symbol of the newly independent country. By 1940, numbers of bald eagles had dropped so low that the U.S. Congress passed the Bald Eagle Protection Act to preserve the species that had become established as the symbol of American ideals of freedom. In 1962, Congress amended the act to include golden eagles, because the young of each species are nearly indistinguishable.

In 1994, President Clinton promoted some official accommodation to Hopi beliefs about golden eagles. His administration established a repository for golden eagle feathers and other remains in Colorado. The demand is, however, higher than the supply.

The Hopi have a permit for an annual take of 40 golden eagles in northeastern Arizona, but they are excluded from Wupatki because of its status as a national park. The United States policy toward national parks follows the *Yellowstone model,* which aims to preserve the physical environment and species but excludes indigenous peoples and their cultures. This model has been applied widely throughout the world to the detriment of peoples who have, for long, successfully lived in regions that are now off limits to them for hunting, fishing, and gathering. In addition, many of these lands are sacred to them, but they are prevented from using them in traditional ways for the sake of "conservation" as defined by the government.

Anthropologists and others support environmental and species preservation, but not to the exclusion of heritage populations and cultures. They suggest that a case-by-case approach should be followed in considering exemptions to national laws. In terms of the golden eagles of Arizona, they point out that golden eagles are abundant, and the Hopi requests for the spring take are small and present no threat to the survival of the species.

Environmentalists are concerned, however, that granting exemptions will establish dangerous precedents that will, over time, destroy pristine environments and precious species. Other environmentalists counter that more eagles are killed every year by airplanes or contact with electrical wires, or they die from eating prey that contain lead bullets.

get annoyed if neglected. They can be loving and caring, or they can be distant and nonresponsive. Most anthropomorphic supernaturals are adults, though some are children. Supernaturals tend to have similar marital and sexual relationships as the humans who worship them do. Divine marriages are heterosexual, and in some societies male gods have multiple wives. Although many supernaturals have children, grandchildren are not prominent. In *pantheons* (collectivities of deities), a division of labor reflects specializations in human society. There may be deities of forests, rivers, the sky, wind and rain, agriculture, childbirth, disease, warfare, and marital happiness. The supernaturals have political roles and hierarchies. High gods, such as Jupiter and Juno of classical Roman religion, are all-powerful, with a range of less powerful deities and spirits below them.

In some cultures, deceased ancestors can be supernaturals. Many African, Asian, and Native American religions have a cult of the ancestors in which the living must do certain things to please the dead ancestors and may also ask for their help in time of need (see Eye on the Environment). In contemporary Japan, ancestor worship is the principal religious activity of many families. Three national holidays recognize the importance of the ancestors: the annual summer visit of the dead to their homes and the visits by the living to graves during the two equinoxes.

BELIEFS ABOUT SACRED SPACE Beliefs about sacred space probably exist in all religions, but such beliefs are more prominent in some religions than others. Sacred spaces, such as rock formations or rapids in a river, may or may not be permanently marked (Bradley 2000). Among the Saami, traditional religious beliefs were closely tied to sacred natural sites (Mulk 1994). The sites, often unmarked, included rock formations resembling humans, animals, or birds. The Saami sacrificed animals and fish at these sites until strong pressures from Christian missionaries forced them to repress their practices and beliefs. Many Saami today know where the sacred sites are, but they will not reveal them to outsiders.

A Kachina doll. Among the Hopi, the word "Kachina" (kuh-CHEE-nuh) refers to a spirit or "life-bringer." Uncles carve Kachina dolls for their nieces to help them learn about the many spirits that exist in the Hopi religion. Kachina dolls, especially older ones, are highly sought after by non-Indians who collect Indian artifacts.

MAP 2 **Hopi Indian Reservation in Arizona.**
The Hopi and Navajo tribes once shared the area known as Big Mountain. U.S. Acts of Congress in 1974 and 1996 divided the area into two reservations, leaving the Hopi completely surrounded by the much larger Navajo reservation. About 7000 people live on the Hopi Reservation.

In contrast to the Yellowstone model, anthropologists advocate for a *parks and people approach*, which builds on community-based conservation that does not exclude heritage populations from continuing to enjoy the economic and religious benefits of their territory while also sharing with the wider population.

◆ FOOD FOR THOUGHT

* Consider how you would feel if you were told that you could no longer practice the most important annual ritual in your religion but that other people could have a touristic experience at the place where you would normally practice the ritual. For secular students, consider a secular ritual, for example, watching the Super Bowl.

Uluru, Kata Tjuta National Park, Australia. Located roughly in the center of Australia in the Northern Territory and 280 miles south of Alice Springs, Uluru is an Aboriginal sacred site and a World Heritage Site. Tourists often want to make the arduous climb to the top, though the Anangu people who are the custodians urge people to consider other ways to enjoy the region.

Another important form of sacred space that has no permanent mark occurs in a domestic ritual conducted by Muslim women throughout the world called the *khatam quran* (kuh-RAHN), the "sealing" or reading of the holy book of the Qu'ran (Werbner 1988). Among Pakistani migrants living in the city of Manchester, northern England (see Map 3), the ritual involves a gathering of women who read the Qu'ran and then share a ritual meal. The reason for gathering is to give thanks or seek divine blessing. During the ritual, the otherwise nonsacred space of the house becomes sacred. A "portable" ritual such as this one is especially helpful in migrant adaptation because it can be conducted without a formally consecrated ritual space. All that is required is a place, a supportive group of kin and friends, and the Qu'ran.

Religions of the Aboriginal people of Australia are closely tied to sacred space. During a mythological past called the *Dream Time*, the ancestors walked the earth and marked out the territory belonging to a particular group. People's knowledge of where the ancestors roamed is secret. In several

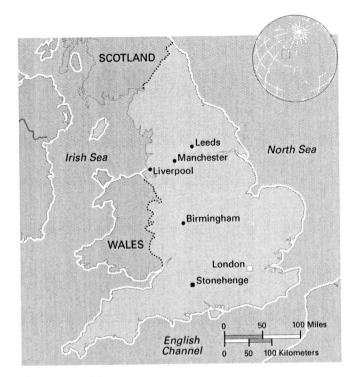

MAP 3   England.

England is the largest of the constituent countries of the United Kingdom, and its population of 50 million accounts for 84 percent of the total. DNA analysis reveals that a majority of the English are of Germanic descent, as is their language. The terrain is mainly rolling hills, with some mountains in the north and east. London is by far the largest city, with Manchester and Birmingham competing for second place. English is the dominant language, with its diverse regional accents. Many other languages brought into the country by immigrant communities are spoken as first languages, including several South Asian languages, Polish, Greek, and Cantonese. An estimated 250,000 people speak British Sign Language. Although the Church of England is the state religion, everyone in England has the right to religious freedom.

cases that have recently been brought to the courts, Aboriginal peoples have claimed title to land that is being sought by commercial developers. Some anthropologists have provided expert testimony documenting the validity of the Aboriginal claims to their sacred space. In one such case, secret Aboriginal knowledge about a sacred place and its associated beliefs was gender specific: It belonged to women and could not be told to men. The anthropologist who was hired to support the women's claims was a woman, so the women could tell her about the sacred places, but she could not convey that knowledge in court to the male judge, a situation

---

ritual   a patterned behavior that has to do with the supernatural realm.

life-cycle ritual   a ritual that marks a change in status from one life stage to another; also called rite of passage.

that demanded considerable ingenuity on the part of the anthropological consultant (see Lessons Applied).

RITUAL PRACTICES

A **ritual** is patterned behavior that is focused on the supernatural realm. Many rituals are the enactment of beliefs expressed in myth and doctrine, such as the Christian ritual of communion. Rituals are distinct from *secular rituals,* such as a sorority or fraternity initiation or a common-law wedding, which are patterned forms of behavior with no connection to the supernatural realm. Some ritual events combine sacred and secular elements. The U.S. holiday of Thanksgiving originated as a Christian sacred meal with the primary purpose of giving thanks to God for the survival of the pilgrims (Siskind 1992). Its original Christian meaning is not maintained by everyone who celebrates the holiday today. Secular features of the holiday, such as watching football, may be of greater importance than the ritual aspect of thanking God for plentiful food.

Anthropologists categorize rituals in many ways. One division is based on their timing. Regularly performed rituals are called *periodic rituals.* Many periodic rituals are performed annually to mark a seasonal milestone such as planting or harvesting or to commemorate some important event. For example, an important periodic ritual in Buddhism, or Buddha's Day, commemorates the birth, enlightenment, and death of the Buddha all on one day. On this day, Buddhists gather at monasteries, hear sermons about the Buddha, and perform rituals such as pouring water over images of the Buddha. Calendrical events such as the shortest day of the year, the longest day, the new moon, and the full moon often

© Adam Wolfitt/CORBIS

A gathering of contemporary Druids at Stonehenge, England. The Druids, who claim that Stonehenge is important to their religion, are one of several groups with interests in the preservation of this World Heritage Site and access to it. Public debates concern possible changes in the location of nearby roads, the planting or removing of trees, and how close the public can get to the stones.

▷ *As a research project, learn about the various groups and preservation issues related to Stonehenge.*

RELIGION

Aboriginal Australian Women's Culture, Sacred Site Protection, and the Anthropologist as Expert Witness

A group of Ngarrindjeri (nar-en-jeer-ee) women and their lawyer hired cultural anthropologist Diane Bell to serve as a consultant to them in supporting their claims to a sacred site in southern Australia (Bell 1998). The area on Hindmarsh Island was threatened by the proposed construction of a bridge that would cross sacred waters between the mainland and the island.

The women claimed protection for the area and sought prevention of the bridge project on the basis of their secret knowledge of its sacredness, knowledge passed down in trust from mother to daughter over generations. The High Commission formed by the government to investigate their claim considered it to be a hoax perpetrated to block a project important to the country.

Helping the women prove their case to a White, male-dominated court system was a challenging task for Diane Bell, a White Australian with extensive fieldwork experience among Aboriginal women. Bell conducted research over many months to marshal evidence for the validity of the women's claims. She examined newspaper archives, early recordings of ritual songs, and oral histories of Ngarrindjeri women. She prepared reports for the courtroom about women's sacred knowledge that were general enough to avoid violating the secrecy rule that applies to women-only knowledge but

detailed enough to convince the High Court judge that the women's sacred knowledge was authentic. In the end, the judge was convinced, and the bridge project was canceled in 1999.

◆ FOOD FOR THOUGHT

• Learn more about this case and other disputes in Australia over sacred sites, from the Internet.

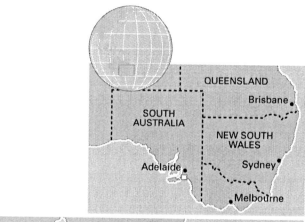

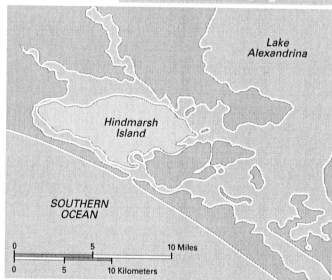

MAP 4   Hindmarsh Island in Southeast Australia.
The Ngarrindjeri name for Hindmarsh Island is Kumarangk.

---

shape ritual cycles. *Nonperiodic rituals,* in contrast, occur irregularly, at unpredictable times, in response to unscheduled events such as a drought or flood, or to mark events in a person's life such as illness, infertility, birth, marriage, or death. The following material presents highlights of various ritual types.

LIFE-CYCLE RITUALS   A **life-cycle ritual**, or rite of passage, marks a change in status from one life stage to another of an individual or group. Victor Turner's (1969) fieldwork

among the Ndembu (en-dem-boo), horticulturalists of northwestern Zambia, provides insights about the phases of life-cycle rituals. Turner found that among the Ndembu, and cross-culturally, life-cycle rituals have three phases: *separation, transition,* and *reintegration.*

• In the first phase, the initiate (the person undergoing the ritual) is separated physically, socially, or symbolically from normal life. Special dress may mark the separation. In many cultures of the Amazon and in East and

West Africa, adolescents are secluded for several years in separate huts or areas away from the village.

- The transition, or *liminal,* phase, is when the person is no longer in the previous status but is not yet a member of the next stage. Liminality often involves the learning of specialized skills that will equip the person for the new status.

- Reintegration, the last stage, occurs when the initiate emerges and is welcomed by the community in the new status.

Differences in the cross-cultural distribution of puberty rituals for boys and girls reflect the economic value and status of males and females. Most societies have some form of puberty ceremony for boys, but puberty ceremonies for girls are less common. In societies where female labor is important and valued, girls have elaborate, and sometimes painful, puberty rites (Brown 1978). Where their labor is not important, menarche is unmarked and there is no puberty ceremony. Puberty rites function to socialize future members of the labor force, among other things. For example, among the Bemba of northern Zambia, during her initiation a girl learns to distinguish 40 kinds of mushrooms and to know which are edible and which are poisonous.

PILGRIMAGE **Pilgrimage** is round-trip travel to a sacred place or places for purposes of religious devotion or ritual. Prominent pilgrimage places are Varanasi (var-uh-NAS-ee) in India (formerly called Banaras) for Hindus; Mecca in Saudi Arabia for Muslims; Bodh Gaya in India for Buddhists; Jerusalem in Israel for Jews, Christians, and Muslims; and Lourdes in France for Christians. Pilgrimage often involves hardship, with the implication that the more suffering that is involved, the more merit the pilgrim accumulates. Compared to a weekly trip to church or synagogue, pilgrimage removes a person further from everyday life, is more demanding, and therefore is potentially more transformative.

Victor Turner applied the three sequences of life-cycle rituals to pilgrimage: The pilgrim first separates from everyday life, then enters the liminal stage during the actual pilgrimage, and then returns to be reintegrated into society in a transformed state. A person who has gone on a pilgrimage often gains enhanced public status as well as spiritual benefits.

RITUALS OF INVERSION In **rituals of inversion**, normal social roles and relations are temporarily inverted. A functionalist perspective says that these rituals allow for social pressure

---

pilgrimage   round-trip travel to a sacred place or places for purposes of religious devotion or ritual.

ritual of inversion   a ritual in which normal social roles and order are temporarily reversed.

sacrifice   a ritual in which something is offered to the supernaturals.

© CORBIS

An Apache girl's puberty ceremony. Cross-cultural research indicates that the celebration of girls' puberty is more likely to occur in cultures in which adult women have valued productive and reproductive roles.

▶ *How does this theory apply to your microcultural experience?*

to be released. They also provide a reminder about the propriety of normal, everyday roles and practices to which people must return once the ritual is over.

Carnival (or *carnaval* in Portuguese-speaking Brazil) is a ritual of inversion with roots in the northern Mediterranean region. It is celebrated widely throughout southern Europe and the Western Hemisphere. Carnival is a period of riotous celebration before the Christian fast of Lent. It begins at different times in different places, but always ends on Mardi Gras (or Shrove Tuesday), the day before the fasting period of Lent begins. The word "carnival," from Latin, means "flesh farewell," referring to the fact that believers give up eating meat during Lent .

In Bosa, a town in Sardegna (Sardinia), Italy (see Map 5), carnival involves social-role reversal and relaxing of usual social norms. Discotheques extend their hours, mothers allow their daughters to stay out late, and men and women flirt with each other in public in ways that are forbidden during the rest of the year (Counihan 1985). Carnival in Bosa has three major phases. The first is impromptu street theater and masquerades that take place over several weeks, usually on Sundays. The skits are social critiques of current events and local happenings. In the masquerades, men dress up as exaggerated women:

> Young boys thrust their padded breasts forward with their hands while brassily hiking up their skirts to reveal their thighs. . . . A youth stuffs his shirt front with melons and holds them proudly out. . . . The high school gym teacher dresses as a nun and lifts up his habit to reveal suggestive red underwear. Two men wearing nothing but bikinis, wigs, and high heels feign a stripper's dance on a table top. (1985:15)

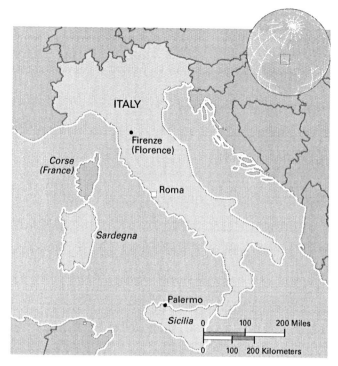

MAP 5 Italy.

Officially the Italian Republic, the country includes the mainland and two large islands. In 2006, Italy had the seventh highest GDP in the world. A mountain system forms the backbone of the peninsula, and the climate varies according to altitude. Its population of nearly 60 million people makes it one of the most densely populated countries in Europe. Roman Catholicism is the dominant religion. Recent waves of immigration, especially from northern Africa, have increased the number of Muslims to perhaps 1 million. The official language is standard Italian, descended from the Tuscan dialect of Firenze (Florence). Many cherished dialects of Italian exist throughout the country; people in northern border provinces speak dialects of German and French. Italy has the largest number of UNESCO World Heritage Sites of any country.

The second phase occurs on the morning of Mardi Gras, when hundreds of Bosans, mostly men, dress in black, like widows, and flood the streets. They accost passersby, shaking in their faces dolls and other objects that are maimed in some way or bloodied. They shriek at the top of their lungs as if mourning, and they say, "Give us milk, milk for our babies. . . . They are dying, they are neglected, their mothers have been gallivanting since St. Anthony's Day and have abandoned their poor children" (1985:16).

The third phase, called *Giolzi*, takes place during the evening. Men and women dress in white, wearing sheets for cloaks and pillow cases for hoods. They blacken their faces. Rushing into the street, they hold hands and chant the word "Giolzi." They storm at people, pretending to search their bodies for Giolzi and then say, "Got it!" It is not clear what Giolzi is, but whatever it is, it represents something that makes everyone happy.

SACRIFICE Many rituals involve **sacrifice**, or the offering of something for transfer to the supernaturals. Sacrifice has a long history throughout the world and is probably one of the oldest forms of ritual. It may involve killing and offering animals; making human offerings (of whole people, parts of a person's body, or bloodletting); or offering vegetables, fruits, grains, flowers, or other products. One interpretation of flowers as sacrificial offerings is that they, like vegetables and fruits, are symbolic replacements for former animal sacrifices (Goody 1993).

Spanish documents from the sixteenth century describe the Aztec practice of public sacrifice of humans and other animals to please the gods. The details are gory and involve marching thousands of human victims up to the top of a temple and then cutting out their hearts so that the blood spurts forth. Debate exists among anthropologists as to how many victims were actually sacrificed and why. Marvin Harris has argued that the numbers were large, up to 100,000 at particular sites, and that the remains of the victims were butchered and eaten by commoners (1977). His argument is that the Aztec state, through such rituals, both demonstrated its power and provided protein to the masses. In opposition to Harris, symbolic anthropologist Peggy Sanday takes an emic perspective and says that the sacrifices were necessary to please the gods and had nothing to do with maintaining the worldly power of leaders or feeding the masses (1986).

RELIGIOUS SPECIALISTS

Not all rituals require the presence of a religious specialist, or someone with extensive, formal training, but all require some level of knowledge on the part of the performer(s) about how to do them correctly. Even the daily, household veneration of an ancestor requires some knowledge gained through informal learning. At the other extreme, many rituals cannot be done without a highly trained specialist.

SHAMANS AND PRIESTS General features of the categories of shaman and priest illustrate key differences between these two types of specialists (many other specialists fit somewhere in between). A *shaman* or *shamanka* is a religious specialist who has a direct relationship with the supernaturals, often by being "called." A potential shaman may be recognized by special signs, such as the ability to go into a trance. Anyone who demonstrates shamanic abilities can become a shaman; in other words, this is an openly available role. Shamans are more often associated with nonstate societies, yet faith healers and evangelists of the United States could fit in this category.

In states, the more complex occupational specialization in religion means that there is a wider variety of types of specialists, especially what anthropologists refer to as *priests* (not the same as the specific modern role of the Catholic priest) and promotes the development of religious hierarchies and power structures. The terms **priest** and **priestess** refer to a category of full-time religious specialists whose position is based mainly on abilities gained through formal training. A priest may receive a divine call, but more often the role is hereditary, passed on through priestly lineages. In terms of ritual performance, shamans are more involved with nonperiodic rituals. Priests perform a wider range of rituals, including periodic state rituals. In contrast to shamans, who rarely have secular power, priests and priestly lineages often do.

OTHER SPECIALISTS Many other specialized religious roles exist cross-culturally. *Diviners* are specialists who are able to discover the will and wishes of the supernaturals through techniques such as reading animal entrails. Palm readers and tarot card readers fit into the category of diviners.

Prophets are specialists who convey divine revelations usually gained through visions or dreams. They often possess charisma, an especially attractive and powerful personality, and may be able to perform miracles. Prophets have founded new religions, some long-lasting and others short-lived.

Witches use psychic powers and affect people through emotion and thought. Mainstream society often condemns witchcraft as negative. Some scholars of ancient and contemporary witchcraft differentiate between positive forms that involve healing and negative forms that seek to harm people.

◆ ◆ ◆

World Religions and Local Variations

The term **world religion** was coined in the nineteenth century to refer to religions that were text-based, with many followers that crossed country borders and had a concern with salvation (the belief that human beings require deliverance from an imperfect world). At that time, the term referred only to Christianity, Islam, and Buddhism. It was later expanded to include Judaism, Hinduism, Confucianism, Taoism, and Shintoism. Because of the global importance of the African diaspora that began with the European colonial slave trade, a sixth category of world religions is included here that describes key elements shared among the diversity of traditional African belief systems.

For many centuries, the world religions have traveled outside their original borders through intentional attempts to expand and gain converts or through migration of believers to new locales. European colonialism was a major force that led to the expansion of Christianity through the missionary work of Protestant sects. Now, the increased rate of population migration and the expansion of television and the Internet give even greater impetus to religious movement and change. The designation of only five world religions is increasingly

inappropriate, because many religions cross state boundaries and have "world" reach.

Cultural anthropologists emphasize that no world religion exists as a single, homogeneous entity. Each comprises many local variants, raising a "predicament" for centrally organized religions in terms of how to maintain a balance between standardization based on core beliefs and the local variations (Hefner 1998).

The following material first discusses the five traditional world religions in terms of their history, distribution, and basic teachings (see Figure 2). The world religions are presented in order by age, largely based on scriptural dates, starting with Hinduism. It then provides examples of variations in local cultural contexts. When a world religion moves into a new cultural region, it encounters local religious traditions. In many cases, the incoming religion and local religions coexist as separate traditions, either as complements or competitors, in what is called **religious pluralism**. In **religious syncretism**, elements of two or more religions blend together. It is most likely to occur when aspects of two religions form a close match with each other. For example, if a local myth involves a hero who has something to do with snakes, there may be a syncretistic link with the Catholic belief in St. Patrick, who is believed to have driven snakes out of Ireland.

Many situations of nonfit also exist. For example, Christian missionaries have had difficulty translating the Bible into some indigenous languages because of lack of matching words or concepts, and because of differing kinship and social structures. Some Amazonian groups, such as the Pirahã have no word that corresponds with the Christian concept of "heaven" (Everett 1995, personal communication). In other cases, matrilineal

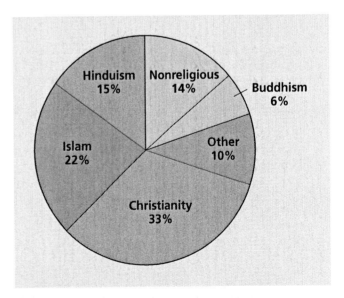

FIGURE 2 Population Distribution of Major World Religions

peoples have found it difficult to understand the significance of the Christian construct of "god the father."

The two world religions that emphasize proselytizing, or seeking converts, are Christianity and Islam. Their encounters with local religions have sometimes been violent, involving physical destruction of sacred places and objects (Corbey 2003). Common methods include burning, overturning, dismantling, or cutting up sacred objects, dumping them into rivers, and hiding them in caves. European Christian missionaries in the 1800s often confiscated sacred goods and shipped them to Europe for sale to private owners or museums. Both Christian and Islamic conversion efforts frequently involved the construction of their own places of worship on top of the original sacred site. Conflict between these two religions is, unfortunately, not a matter of the past only.

HINDUISM

Around 920 million people in the world are Hindus. (*Note:* Population statistics for the world religions are rough averages derived from several Internet sources.) About 97 percent of all Hindus live in India, where Hinduism accounts for 80 percent of the population. The rest live throughout the world in countries such as Bangladesh, Myanmar, Pakistan, Sri Lanka, the United States, Canada, the United Kingdom, Malaysia, Fiji, Trinidad, Guyana, and Hong Kong. A Hindu is born a Hindu, and Hinduism does not actively seek converts. The core texts of Hinduism are the four Vedas, which were composed in Sanskrit in northern India between 1200 and 900 BCE. Many other scholarly texts, epics and stories, and oral traditions enrich the Hindu tradition. The two most widely-known stories are the *Mahabharata* (muh-huh-BHAR-uh-tuh), the story of a war between two patrilineages in which Krishna plays an important role, and the *Ramayana* (ruh-MY-uh-nuh), the story of King Rama and his devoted wife, Sita. Throughout India, many local stories also exist, some containing elements from pre-Vedic times.

Hinduism offers a rich polytheism and at the same time a philosophical tradition that reduces the multiplicity of deities into oneness. Deities range from being a simple stone placed at the foot of a tree to elegantly carved and painted icons of gods such as Shiva and Vishnu and the goddesses Durga and Saraswati. Everyday worship of a deity involves lighting a lamp in front of the god, chanting hymns and mantras (sacred phrases), and taking *darshan* (DAR-shun), which means seeing the deity, usually in the form of an icon (Eck 1985). These acts bring blessings to the worshipper. Local variations of worship often involve deities and rituals unknown elsewhere. For example, firewalking is an important part of goddess worship in southern and eastern India (Freeman 1981) and among some Hindu groups living outside India, notably Fiji (Brown 1984).

© Brooklyn Museum of Art/CORBIS

An early nineteenth-century painting of the Virgin of Guadalupe by Isidro Escamilla, a Mexican artist. The Virgin of Guadalupe, or Our Lady of Guadalupe, is Mexico's most popular image. Her depiction may involve syncretism with the indigenous Aztec goddess Tonantzin, part of a conscious strategy of Christian clergy to convert the Indians. Today, the Virgin of Guadalupe conveys messages of sacrifice and nurturance as well as strength and hope. She appeals to Mexican mothers, nationalists, and feminists alike.

priest/priestess male or female full-time religious specialist whose position is based mainly on abilities gained through formal training.

world religion a term coined in the nineteenth century to refer to a religion that is text-based, has many followers, is regionally widespread, and is concerned with salvation.

religious pluralism when one or more religions coexist as either complementary to each other or as competitive systems.

religious syncretism the blending of features of two or more cultures, especially used in discussion of religious change.

Caste differences in beliefs and practices are also marked, even within the same village. Lower-caste deities prefer offerings of meat sacrifices and alcohol, whereas upper-caste deities prefer flowers, rice, and fruit. Yet the "unity in diversity" of Hinduism has long been recognized as real, mainly because of the shared acceptance of at least some elements of Vedic thought.

A NAYAR FERTILITY RITUAL The matrilineal Nayars (nai-ers) of Kerala, South India, perform a nonperiodic ritual as a remedy for the curse of the serpent deities who cause infertility in women (Neff 1994). This ritual illustrates the unity of Hinduism in several ritual elements: the use of a camphor flame and incense, the importance of serpent deities, and offering flowers to the deity. Locally specific elements are related to the matrilineal cultural context of Kerala.

The all-night ritual includes, first, women painting a sacred design of intertwined serpents on the floor. Several hours of worshipping the deity follow, with the camphor flame, incense, and flowers. Music comes from drumming, cymbals, and singing. The presence of the deity is fully achieved when one of the women goes into a trance. Through her, matrilineal family members may speak to the deity and be blessed.

Among the Nayars, a woman's mother, mother's brothers, and brothers are responsible for ensuring that her desires for motherhood are fulfilled. They share her interest in continuing the matrilineage. What the women say during the trance is important. They typically draw attention to family disharmonies or neglect of the deities. This message diverts blame from the infertile woman for whom the ritual is being

held. It reminds family and lineage members of their responsibilities for each other.

HINDU WOMEN AND KARMA IN NORTHERN ENGLAND
One of Hinduism's basic concepts is *karma*, translated as "destiny" or "fate." A person's karma is determined at birth on the basis of his or her previous life and how it was conducted. The karma concept has prompted many outsiders to judge Hindus as fatalistic, lacking a sense of agency. But anthropological research on how people actually think about karma in their everyday lives reveals much individual variation from fatalism to a strong sense of being in charge of one's destiny. One study looked at women's perceptions of karma among Hindus living in the city of Leeds, northern England (Knott 1996) (see Map 3). Some of the women are fatalistic in their attitudes and behavior. One woman who had a strongly fatalistic view of karma said,

> When a baby's born . . . we have a ritual on the sixth day. That's when you name the baby, you know. And on that day, we believe the goddess comes and writes your future . . . we leave a blank white paper and a pen and we just leave it [overnight]. . . . So I believe that my future—whatever happens—is what she has written for me. That tells me [that] I have to do what I can do, and if I have a mishap in between I have to accept that. (1996:24)

Another woman said that her sufferings were caused by the irresponsibility of her father and the "bad husband" to whom she had been married. She challenged her karma and left her husband: "I could not accept the karma of being with Nirmal [her husband]. If I had done so, what would have become of my children?" (1996:25). Because Hindu women's karma dictates being married and having children, leaving one's husband is a major act of resistance.

Options for women seeking support when questioning or changing their karmic roles can be religious, such as praying more and fasting, or they can be secular, such as seeking the advice of a psychological counselor or social worker. Some Hindu women in England have become counselors, working in support of other women's independence and self-confidence. They illustrate how human agency can work against traditional religious rules.

BUDDHISM

Buddhism originated in a founding figure, Siddhartha Gautama (ca. 566–486 BCE), revered as the Buddha, or Awakened One (Eckel 1995:135). It began in northern India, where the Buddha grew up. From there, it spread throughout the subcontinent, into inner Asia and China, to Sri Lanka, and on to Southeast Asia. In the past 200 years, Buddhism has spread to Europe and North America. Buddhism's popularity declined in India, and Buddhists now constitute less than 1 percent of India's population. Its global spread is

© AFP/CORBIS

Celebration of Holi, a spring festival popular among Hindus worldwide. In this scene in New Delhi, a young woman sprays colored water on a young man as part of the joyous event. The deeper meaning of Holi is tied to a myth about a demon.

▶ *Is the arrival of spring ritually marked in your culture?*

matched by a great diversity of doctrine and practice, to the extent that it is difficult to point to a single essential feature other than the importance of Gautama Buddha. No single text is accepted as authoritative for all forms of Buddhism. Many Buddhists worship the Buddha as a deity, but others do not. Instead, they honor his teachings and follow the pathway he suggested for reaching *nirvana*, or release from worldly life. The total number of Buddhists worldwide is around 400 million.

Buddhism arose as a protest against Hinduism, especially caste inequality, but it retained and revised several Hindu concepts, such as karma. In Buddhism, everyone has the potential for achieving nirvana (enlightenment and the overcoming of human suffering in this life), the ultimate goal of Buddhism. Good deeds are one way to achieve a better rebirth with each incarnation, until finally, release from *samsara* (the cycle of birth, reincarnation, death, and so on) is achieved. Compassion toward others, including animals, is a key virtue. Branches of Buddhism have different texts that they consider their canon. The major division is between the Theravada Buddhism practiced in Southeast Asia and the Mahayana Buddhism of Tibet, China, Taiwan, Korea, and Japan. Buddhism is associated with a strong tradition of monasticism through which monks and nuns renounce the everyday world and spend their lives meditating and doing good works. Buddhists have many and varied annual festivals and rituals. Some events bring pilgrims from around the world to Sarnath, near Varanasi, North India, where the Buddha gave his first teaching, and to Gaya, where he gained enlightenment.

Jack Heaton

Buddhism gained an established footing in Japan in the eighth century. The city of Nara was an important early center of Buddhism. An emperor sponsored the casting of this huge bronze statue of the Buddha.

▶ *Is there a Buddhist temple where you live? If so, have you visited it? If not, find out where the nearest one is, and visit it if possible.*

LOCAL SPIRITS AND BUDDHISM IN SOUTHEAST ASIA

Wherever Buddhism exists outside India, it is never the exclusive religion of the devotees because it arrived to find established local religions already in place (Spiro 1967). In Myanmar, Buddhism and indigenous traditions coexist without one being dominant. Indigenous beliefs remained strong because they offer a way of dealing with everyday problems. Buddhist beliefs about karma in Myanmar are similar to those in Hinduism: A person's karma is the result of previous births and determines his or her present condition. If something bad happens, the person can do little but suffer through it.

In contrast, indigenous supernaturalism says that the bad things happen because of the actions of capricious spirits called *nats*. Ritual actions, however, can combat the influence of nats. Thus, people can deal with nats but not with karma. The continuity of belief in nats is an example of human agency and creativity. Burmese people kept what was important to them from their traditional beliefs and adopted aspects of the new religion.

Buddhism became an important cultural force and the basis for social integration in Myanmar. A typical village may have one or more Buddhist monasteries and several resident monks. All boys are ordained as temporary members of the monastic order. Almost every villager observes Buddhist holy days. Nonetheless, although Buddhism is held to be the supreme truth, the spirits retain control when it comes to dealing with everyday problems such as a toothache or a monetary loss. In Myanmar, the two traditions exist in a pluralistic situation as two separate options.

Other studies of religion in Southeast Asia provide examples in which there is more thorough blending, or syncretism, of local religions with Buddhism (see Everyday Anthropology).

JUDAISM

The first Judaic religious system was defined around 500 BCE, following the destruction of the Temple in Jerusalem by the Babylonians in 586 BCE (Neusner 1995). The early writings, called the Pentateuch (pen-ta-took), established the theme of exile and return as a paradigm for Judaism that endures today. The Pentateuch is also called the Five Books of Moses, or the Torah. Followers of Judaism share in the belief in the Torah as the revelation of God's truth through Israel, a term for the "holy people." The Torah explains the relationship between the supernatural and human realms and guides people in how to carry out the worldview through appropriate actions. A key feature of all forms of Judaism is the identification of what is wrong with the present and how to escape, overcome, or survive that situation. Jewish life is symbolically interpreted as a tension between exile and return, given its foundational myth in the exile of the Jews from Israel and their period of slavery in Egypt.

everyday ANTHROPOLOGY

Tattoos and Sacred Power

Fieldwork among Shan people in northern Thailand reveals the importance of tattooing, a tradition shared with much of Southeast Asia (Tannenbaum 1987). Shan tattooing blends aspects of Buddhism with local spirit beliefs and even elements of Hinduism as practiced by some groups in neighboring Myanmar.

Among the Shan, three types of tattoos exist:

- Tattoos that act on other people, causing them to like or fear the bearer, and that cause the spirits to be kind

- Tattoos that act on the bearer, increasing the bearer's skill

- Tattoos that create a barrier around the person that prevents animals from biting, knives from cutting, and bullets from entering the body

Tattoos are done in two colors—red and blue/black. The first two types tend to be done in red; the third type tends to be done in blue/black. Different designs are associated with each type. For example, the two-tailed lizard is a common tattoo in the first type.

The first type of tattoo is popular among many people, because it brings health to the bearer. It is the main type among women, used for illness prevention as well as for curing an illness. A person who falls ill may get a tattoo incorporating a letter of the Shan alphabet in the design, either on the calf, around a body joint, around the mouth, or on the top of the tongue. Some of the most powerful designs in this category are placed on the back or over the heart.

The most powerful tattoo in this category, called the Five Buddha tattoo, is not allowed for women. Men who get this tattoo have to follow five Buddhist precepts at all times: refrain from killing, stealing, improper sexual behavior, lying, and intoxication. This tattoo is red, but it also includes exfoliated skin from a Buddhist monk. That makes this tattoo different from all others and makes its bearer like a monk. Whereas most tattoos in the first category cause other people to look favorably on the bearer, the Five Buddha tattoo inspires fear and awe.

Tattoos in the second category, worn by men, are all related to words. Some increase people's memory and help them on exams. Others strengthen a person's speaking ability. The most powerful tattoos in this group give a person such great verbal skills that he or she can intimidate others. They increase courage as well. One tattoo in this category is the Saraswati tattoo, which depicts, among other things, the head of Saraswati, the Hindu goddess of knowledge, on the bearer's right shoulder. To call on Saraswati for help, the person brushes his or her lips on the tattoo.

The third category of tattoos, those that provide a protective barrier, has one subset that prevents bites from insects, snakes, dogs, cats, tigers, and so on. If the person has the tattoo and gets bitten nonetheless, the tattoo helps reduce the pain. A general anti-bite tattoo is a cat on the lower arm. More powerful tattoos in this third category protect people from weapons. They seal off the body. A person should be careful not to get too many of these tattoos, however, because they seal the body off completely and therefore prevent good fortune from entering it. Someone with many of these tattoos is likely to be poor or unlucky.

The Shan people do not question why or how their tattoos work. They simply believe that they do. They blend what anthropologists classify as magic with religious beliefs from Buddhism and Hinduism, in the case of the Saraswati tattoo. Sacred power is the key that links all these beliefs together into a coherent system for the Shan.

◆ FOOD FOR THOUGHT

- What do people in your microculture do to get people to like them, to succeed on exams, and protect the body from harmful intrusions?

Judaism is monotheistic, teaching that God is one, unique, and all powerful. Humans have a moral duty to follow Jewish law, to protect and preserve life and health, and to follow certain duties, such as observing the Sabbath. The high regard for human life is reflected in the general opposition to abortion within Jewish law and in opposition to the death penalty. Words, both spoken and written, are important in Judaism. There is an emphasis on truth telling in life and on the use of established literary formulas at precise times during worship. These formulas are encoded in a *sidur*, or prayer book. Dietary patterns distinguish Judaism from other religions; for example, rules of kosher eating forbid the mixing of milk or milk products with meat.

Contemporary varieties of Judaism range from conservative Hasidism to Reform Judaism, which emerged in the early 1800s. One difference between these two perspectives concerns the question of who is Jewish. Jewish law traditionally defined a Jewish person as someone born of a Jewish mother. In contrast, reform Judaism recognizes as Jewish the offspring of a Jewish father and a non-Jewish mother. Currently, the Jewish population numbers about 15 million worldwide, with about half living in North America, a quarter in Israel, and

20 percent in Europe and Russia. Smaller populations are scattered across the globe.

WHO'S WHO AT THE KOTEL The most sacred place to all Jews is the Kotel (ko-TELL), or Western Wall in Jerusalem (see Map 6). Since the 1967 war, which brought Jerusalem under Israeli rule, the Kotel has been the most important religious shrine and pilgrimage site of Israel. The

The Kotel, or Western Wall, in Jerusalem is a sacred place of pilgrimage, especially for Jews. Men pray at a section marked off on the left, women at the area on the right. Both men and women should cover their heads, and when leaving the wall area, women should take care to keep their faces toward it and avoid turning their backs to it.

▶ *Think of some behavioral rules at another sacred place you know.*

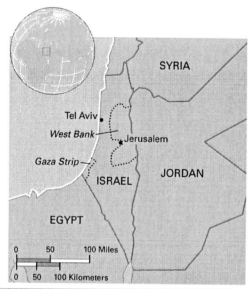

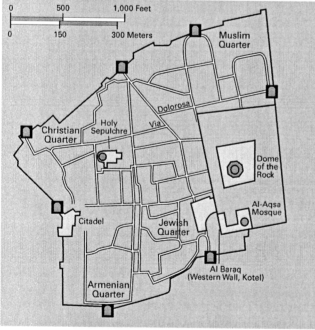

MAP 6   Sacred Sites in the Old City of Jerusalem, Israel. Jerusalem is the holiest city of Judaism, the third holiest city of Islam, and holy to Christians. The section called the Old City is surrounded by walls that have been built, razed, relocated, and rebuilt over several hundred years. The Old City contains four quarters: Armenian, Christian, Jewish, and Muslim, and many sacred sites such as the Kotel and the Via Dolorosa.

Kotel is located at one edge of the Temple Mount (also called Haram Sharif), an area sacred to Jews, Muslims, and Christians. According to Jewish scriptures, God asked Abraham to sacrifice his son Isaac on this hill. Later, King Solomon built the First Temple here in the middle of the tenth century BCE. It was destroyed by Nebuchadnessar (neh-boo-kud-NES-er) in 587 BCE, when the Jews were led into captivity in Babylon. Around 500 BCE, King Herod built the Second Temple on the same site. The Kotel is a remnant of the Second Temple. Jews of all varieties and non-Jews come to the Kotel in vast numbers from around the world. The Kotel plaza is open to everyone, pilgrims and tourists. The wall is made of massive rectangular stones weighing between two and eight tons each. At its base is a synagogue area partitioned into men's and women's sections.

This single site brings together a variety of Jewish worshippers and secular visitors. The great diversity among the visitors is evident in the various styles of dress and gesture:

> The Hasid . . . with a fur shtreimel on his head may enter the synagogue area alongside a man in shorts who utilizes a cardboard skullcap available for "secular" visitors. American youngsters in jeans may ponder Israeli soldiers of their own age, dressed in uniform, and wonder what their lot might have been if they [had been] born in another country. Women from Yemen, wearing embroidered trousers under their dresses, edge close to the Wall as do women accoutred in contemporary styles whose religiosity may have been filtered through a modern education. . . . (Storper-Perez and Goldberg 1994:321)

In spite of plaques that state the prohibition against begging, beggars offer to "sell a blessing" to visitors. They may remind visitors that it was the poor who built the wall in the first place. Another category of people is young Jewish men who, in search of prospective "born again" Jews, "hang around" looking for a "hit" (in their words). Most of the hits are young Americans who are urged to take their Jewishness more seriously and, if male, to be sure to marry a Jewish woman. Other regulars are Hebrew-speaking men who are available to organize a prayer service. One of the most frequent forms of religious expression at the Kotel is the insertion of written prayers into the crevices of the wall.

The social heterogeneity of the Jewish people is thus transcended in a single space, creating some sense of what Victor Turner (1969) called *communitas,* a sense of collective unity that bridges individual difference.

PASSOVER IN KERALA The Jews of the Kochi (ko-chee) area of Kerala, South India, have lived there for about 1000 years (Katz and Goldberg 1989). The Maharaja of Kochi had respect for the Jewish people, who were mainly merchants. He relied on them for external trade and contacts. In recognition of this, he allowed a synagogue, which is still standing, to be built next to his palace. Syncretism is apparent in Kochi Jewish lifestyle, social structure, and rituals. Basic aspects of Judaism are retained, along with adoption of many aspects of Hindu practices.

Three aspects of syncretism with Hinduism are apparent in Passover, one of the most important annual rituals of the Jewish faith. First, the Western/European Passover celebration is typically joyous and a time of feasting. In contrast, the Kochi version has adopted a tone of austerity and is called "the fasting feast." Second, Kochi Passover allows no role for children, whereas at a traditional ritual meal, or *seder* (say-der) children usually ask four questions as a starting point of the narrative. The Kochi Jews chant the questions in unison. (In Hinduism, children do not have solo roles in rituals.) Third, a Kochi seder stresses purity even more than standard Jewish requirements. Standard rules about maintaining the purity of kosher wine usually mean that no gentile (non-Jew) should touch it. But Kochi Jews expand the rule to say that if the shelf or table on which the wine sits is touched by a gentile, the wine is impure. This extra level of "contagion" is influenced by Hindu concepts of pollution.

CHRISTIANITY

Christianity has many ties with Judaism, from which it sprang, especially in terms of the biblical teachings of a coming savior, or *messiah* (anointed one). It began in the eastern Mediterranean in the second quarter of the first century (Cunningham 1995:240–253). Most of the early believers were Jews who took up the belief in Jesus Christ as the messiah who came to earth in fulfillment of prophesies contained in the Hebrew scriptures. Today, Christianity is the largest of the world religions, with about 2 billion adherents, roughly one-third of the world's population. It is the majority religion of Australia, New Zealand, the Philippines, Papua New Guinea, most countries of Europe and of North and South America, and about a dozen southern African countries. Christianity is a minority religion throughout Asia, but Asian Christians constitute 16 percent of the world's total Christians and are thus a significant population.

Christians accept the Bible (Old and New Testaments) as containing the basic teachings of their faith, believe that a supreme God sent His son to earth as a sacrifice for the welfare of humanity, and look to Jesus as the model to follow for moral guidance. The three largest branches of Christianity are Roman Catholic, Protestant, and Eastern Orthodox. Within each of these branches, various denominations exist.

Barbara Miller

Barbara Miller

(LEFT) The Vatican in Rome. The Vatican attracts more pilgrims/visitors each year than any religious site in the world. (RIGHT) In the nearby neighborhood, shops cater to pilgrims/visitors by offering a variety of religious and secular goods.

The greatest growth in Christianity is occurring in sub-Saharan Africa, India, Indonesia, and Eastern Europe.

PROTESTANTISM AMONG WHITE APPALACHIANS

Studies of Protestantism in Appalachia describe local traditions that outsiders who are accustomed to standard, urban versions may view as "deviant." For example, some churches in rural West Virginia and North Carolina, called Old Regulars, practice three obligatory rituals: footwashing, communion (a ritual commemorating the Last Supper that Jesus had with his disciples), and baptism (Dorgan 1989). The footwashing ceremony occurs once a year in conjunction with communion, usually as an extension of the Sunday service. An elder is called to the front of the church, and he preaches for 10 to 20 minutes. A round of handshaking and embracing follows. Two deaconesses then come forward to "prepare the table" by uncovering the sacramental elements placed there earlier under a white tablecloth. The elements are unleavened bread, serving plates for the bread, cups for the wine, and a decanter or quart jar or two of wine. The deacons break the bread into pieces and the moderator pours the wine into the cups. Men and women form separate groups as the deacons serve the bread and wine. The deacons serve each other, and then it is time for the footwashing.

The moderator begins by quoting from the New Testament (John 13:4): "He riseth from supper, and laid aside his garments; and he took a towel and girded himself." The moderator takes a towel and basin from the communion table, puts water in it, and selects a senior elder and removes his shoes and socks. The moderator washes his feet slowly and attentively. Other members come forward and take towels and basins and take turns washing other's feet and having their feet washed. Soon "the church is filled with crying, shouting, and praising as these highly poignant exchanges unleash a flood of emotions" (Dorgan 1989:106). A functional interpretation of the ritual of footwashing is that it helps maintain social cohesion.

Another feature of worship in some small, Protestant churches in Appalachia, especially remote areas of rural West Virginia, involves the handling of poisonous snakes. This practice finds legitimation in the New Testament (Daugherty 1997 [1976]). According to a passage in Mark (16:15–18), "In my name shall they cast out devils; they shall speak with new tongues; they shall take up serpents; and if they drink any deadly thing, it shall not hurt them; they shall lay hands on the sick, and they shall recover." Members of "Holiness-type" churches believe that the handling of poisonous snakes is the supreme act of devotion to God. Biblical literalists, these people choose serpent handling as their way of celebrating life, death, and resurrection and of proving that only Jesus has the power to deliver them from death. Most serpent handlers have been bitten many times, but few have died.

One interpretation says that the risks of handling poisonous snakes mirror the risks of the environment. Rates of

A celebration of the Christian holy day of Palm Sunday in Port-au-Prince, Haiti. European colonialism brought African slaves to the New World and Christianity through missionary efforts. Many forms of Christianity are now firmly established in the Caribbean region.

▶ *Discover through a website or other source what the major Christian denominations in Haiti are.*

unemployment are high and many people are economically poor. The structurist view points to the fact that serpent handling increased when local people lost their land rights to big mining and forestry companies (Tidball and Toumey 2003:4). As their lives became more economically insecure, they turned to a way of increasing their sense of stability through a dramatic religious ritual. Outsiders might ask whether such dangerous ritual practices indicate that the people are psychologically disturbed. Psychological tests indicate that members of Holiness churches are more emotionally healthy, on average, than members of mainline Protestant churches.

Recent U.S. newspaper and television coverage of serpent handling sensationalizes these religious practices. In doing so, it adds a secular avenue to economic success for some of the most famous serpent handlers. One pastor, for example, got a better job offer from a coal mining company, which allowed him and his family to purchase a new house and car (Tidball and Toumey 2003:10).

THE LAST SUPPER IN FIJI   Among Christians in Fiji, the image of the Last Supper is a dominant motif (Toren 1988). This scene, depicted on tapestry hangings, adorns most churches and many houses. People say, "Christ is the head of

THINKING OUTSIDE THE BOX

Visit the Vatican website and explore the Vatican's position on the "Da Vinci code" phenomenon.

this household, he eats with us and overhears us" (1988:697). The image's popularity is the result of its fit with Fijian notions of communal eating and kava drinking. Seating rules at such events place the people of highest status, such as the chief and others close to him, at the "above" side of the room, away from the entrance. Others sit at the "lower" end, facing the highly ranked people. Intermediate positions are located on either side of the person of honor, in ranked order.

Leonardo Da Vinci's fifteenth century painting of the Last Supper places Jesus Christ in the position of a Fijian chief, with the disciples in an ordered arrangement around him. The disciples and the viewers "face" the chief and eat and drink together, as is appropriate in Fijian society. This positioning parallels the orderly placement of Fijian people around the kava as encountered "virtually every day in the village" (1988:706). This kind of cultural fit is a clear example of religious syncretism.

ISLAM

Islam is based on the teachings of the prophet Muhammad (570–632 CE) and is thus the youngest of the world religions (Martin 1995:498–513). The Arabic word *Islam* means "submission" to the will of the one god, Allah, through which peace will be achieved. Followers of Islam, known as Muslims, believe that Muhammad was God's final prophet. Islam has several denominations with essentially similar beliefs but also distinct theological and legal approaches. The two major schools of thought are Sunni and Shi'a. About 85 percent of the total Muslim population worldwide are Sunnis, and about 15 percent are Shi'as. Sufism is a more mystical variant, with much smaller numbers of adherents. Many other subgroups exist.

The Five Pillars of Islam are profession of faith in Allah, daily prayer, fasting, contributing alms for the poor, and the *Hajj* (pilgrimage to Mecca). The five pillars are central to Sunni Islam but less so to other branches of Islam such as the Shi'as and the Sufis.

The total number of Muslims worldwide is about 1.4 billion, making it the second largest religion. Muslim-majority nations are located in northern Africa; the Middle East, including Afghanistan, Pakistan, and Bangladesh in South Asia; and several nations in Central Asia and Southeast Asia. Most of the world's Muslims (60 percent) live in South Asia or Southeast Asia. Muslims live as minorities in many other countries, including China, where they seek to maintain their religious practices (see Culturama). Although Islam originally flourished among pastoralists, only 2 percent of its adherents now are in that category.

A common and inaccurate stereotype of Islam prevalent among many non-Muslims is that it is the same no matter where it exists. This erroneously monolithic model tends to be based on an image of conservative Wahhabist Islam as practiced in Saudi Arabia. But Wahhabist Islam is only one of many varieties of Islam.

A comparison of Islam in highland Sumatra, Indonesia, and Morocco, North Africa, reveals differences that are the result of local cultural adaptations (Bowen 1992). Eid-ul-Adha (eed-ull-ah-dah), or the Feast of Sacrifice, is celebrated annually by Muslims around the world. It commemorates Ibrahim's willingness to sacrifice his son Ishmael (Isaac in Christian and Jewish traditions) to Allah. It occurs on the tenth of the last month of the year, called Pilgrimage Month, and marks the end of the Hajj. The ritual reminds Muslims of their global unity within the Islamic faith.

An important aspect of this ritual in Morocco involves the king publicly plunging a dagger into a ram's throat, a reenactment of Muhammad's performance of the sacrifice on the same day in the seventh century. Each male head of household follows the pattern and sacrifices a ram. The size and virility of the ram are a measure of the man's power and virility. Other men of the household stand to witness the sacrifice, while women and children are

Jack Heaton

The Hassan II Mosque was built for the sixtieth birthday of Morocco's previous king, Hassan II. It is the largest religious monument in the world, after Mecca, with space for 25,000 worshippers inside and another 80,000 outside. The minaret, 210 meters in height, is the tallest in the world.

Hui Muslims of Xi'an, China

The Hui, one of China's largest designated minorities, number around 10 million people. Most live in the northwestern part of the country. The state classifies the Hui as "backward" and "feudal" in comparison to China's majority Han population. Hui residents of Xi'an (shee-ahn), however, reject the official characterization of them as less civilized and less modern than the Han majority (Gillette 2000).

About 60,000 Hui live in Xi'an, mainly in the so-called Old Muslim Area, which is dominated by small shops, restaurants, and mosques. The quality of housing and public services is inferior to that found elsewhere in the city. Parents worry that their children are not getting the best education and feel that the state is not providing adequate schooling in their neighborhood. Many Hui have taken steps to improve their houses themselves and to send their children to schools outside the district.

The Hui of Xi'an construct what they consider to be a modern and civilized lifestyle by choosing aspects of Muslim culture and Western culture. Their form of "progress" is visible in many aspects of their daily life, such as eating habits, dress styles, housing, religious practices, education, and family organization.

Being Muslim in China poses several challenges in relation to the dominant Han culture. Diet is one prominent example. The Qu'ran forbids four types of food to Muslims: animals that have not been consecrated to God and properly slaughtered, blood, pork, and alcohol (Gillette 2000:116). Three of the four rules apply to meat, and meat is the central part of a proper meal for Muslims. The Hui say that pork is especially impure. This belief differentiates the Hui clearly from other Chinese people, for whom pork is a major food item. Given the Hui belief that the kinds of food one eats affect a person's essence and behavior, they view pork eaters with disdain.

Hui residents consider alcohol even more impure than pork (Gillette 2000:167). Hui of Xi'an do not drink alcohol. They avoid using utensils that have touched alcohol and people who are drinking it. Many Hui of Xi'an, however, make a living in the restaurant business, which caters to Chinese Han and foreign tourists. Although selling alcohol boosts business, many Hui object to it. Several Hui formed the Anti-Alcohol Committee to advocate for banning the sale of alcohol in restaurants in the Hui quarter and preventing customers from bringing their own alcohol. Some areas of the market section are alcohol-free zones. Committee members say that restricting alcohol has improved the quality of life by making the neighborhood more peaceful and orderly.

In 2003, an urban development project in the Old Muslim Quarter was launched with financial support from the Norwegian government (*People's Daily* 2003). The project will widen the main street, replace "shabby" housing and infrastructure, and restore crumbling buildings of historic interest. A commercial area will be dedicated to restaurants serving Hui food in recognition of the touristic appeal of traditional Hui specialties such as baked beef and mutton, buns with beef, mutton pancake, and mutton soup. It is unclear where alcohol consumption will fit into this plan.

Thanks to Maris Boyd Gillette, Haverford College, for reviewing this material.

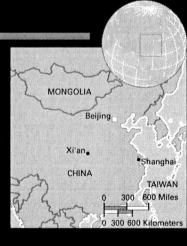

MONGOLIA

Beijing

Xi'an

CHINA

Shanghai

TAIWAN

0   300   600 Miles

0 300 600 Kilometers

Eddie Gerald/Alamy

Maris Boyd Gillette

(LEFT) At a street stand in Xi'an, Hui men prepare and sell a noodle dish. Like Muslim men in many parts of the world, they wear a white cap.
(CENTER) Hui women in Xi'an participate in a ritual that commemorates Hui people who died in a massive conflict that spread across in northwestern China from 1862 to 1874.

MAP 7 The City of Xi'an in China. Xi'an, the capital of Shaanxi province, is one of the most economically developed cities in the northwestern part of China.

absent or in the background. After the ram is killed, the men come forward and dab its blood on their faces. In some villages, women play a more prominent role before the sacrifice by daubing the ram with henna (red dye), thus sanctifying it, and using its blood afterward in rituals to protect the household. These state and household rituals are symbolic of male power in the public and private domains—the power of the monarchy and the power of patriarchy.

In Isak (EE-suk), Sumatra, the cultural context is less patriarchal and the political structure does not emphasize monarchy. Isak is a traditionalist Muslim village where people have been Muslims since the seventeenth century. They sacrifice many kinds of animals: chickens, ducks, sheep, goats, and water buffalo. The people believe that so long as the animal's throat is cut and the meat is eaten, the sacrifice satisfies God. Most sacrifices are family affairs and receive little public notice. They are done in the back of the house. Both women and men of the household refer to it as "their" sacrifice, and there are no signs of male dominance. Women may sponsor a sacrifice, as did one wealthy woman trader who sacrificed a buffalo (the cutting was done by a man).

The Moroccan ritual emphasizes fathers and sons, whereas the Isak ritual includes attention to a wider range of kin on both the husband's and wife's side, daughters as well as sons, and even dead relatives. In Isak, the ritual carries no centralized political meanings. The differences are not due to the fact that Moroccans know the scriptures better than Sumatrans do. The Isak area has many Islamic scholars who are familiar with the scriptures and regularly discuss them with each other. Rather, the two cultural contexts, including kinship and politics, shape the ritual to local realities.

AFRICAN RELIGIONS

Many African religions are now global. In earlier centuries, they spread outside Africa through the coerced movement of people as slaves. African diaspora religions are especially prominent in the United States, the Caribbean region, and Central and South America. This section summarizes some key features of African religions and then offers two examples of African religions in the Western Hemisphere.

FEATURES OF AFRICAN RELIGIONS With its diverse geography, cultural variation, and history, Africa encompasses a wide range of religious affiliations, including many Muslims, Christians, Jews, Hindus, practitioners of indigenous religions, and people who follow some combination of these.

revitalization movement   a socioreligious movement, usually organized by a prophetic leader, that seeks to construct a more satisfying situation by reviving all or parts of a religion that has been threatened by outside forces or by adopting new practices and beliefs.

© Gerd Ludwig/Woodfin Camp & Associates

A sacred altar in a local African religion in Togo, West Africa.
▶ *Can you distinguish some of the ritual elements displayed here? Are some incomprehensible to you? How would an anthropologist begin to learn about the beliefs involved in this religion?*

Indigenous African religions are difficult to typify, but some of their shared features are:

- Myths about a rupture that once occurred between the creator deity and humans
- A pantheon that includes a high god and many secondary supernaturals ranging from powerful gods to lesser spirits
- Elaborate initiation rituals
- Rituals involving animal sacrifices and other offerings, meals, and dances
- Altars within shrines as focal places where humans and deities meet
- Close links with healing

Although these features are fairly constant, African religions are rethought and reshaped locally and over time with complex and variable results (Gable 1995). In their home locations, they have been influenced by foreign religions, notably Islam and various types of Christianity. The out-migration of African peoples has brought African religions to new locations where they have been localized in their new contexts and also revitalized (Clarke 2004). Kamari Clarke's research on the Yorùbá (YOR-uh-buh) revivalist religion in the United States took her from New York City to South Carolina and Nigeria. The focal point of her fieldwork was in Òyòtúnjí Village near Beaufort, South Carolina. African American Yorùbá revivalists have created a place that reconstructs royal Yorùbá spiritual leadership and worship that helps some African Americans reconnect with their lost identity. In the words of Kamari Clarke, "Ritual initiations and rhythmic drumming echo in the endless hours of the night as residents remake their ancestral homeland outside the territory of Africa" (2004:51). The place, the rituals, and the music tie the people to Africa. Many Yorùbá-descent Americans, like other African Americans, go even further in their attempt to reconnect with their heritage. "Roots tourism" is a growing industry that provides culturally informed travel for African Americans to their places of ancestral origin in Africa.

Many religious syncretisms in North and South America combine African traditions with aspects of Christianity, indigenous Indian religions, and other traditions. Widely popular in Brazil are Afro-Brazilian religions such as *umbanda*, *santería*, and *condomblé* that appeal to people of all social classes, urban and rural, especially for providing social support and alleviation of stress (Burdick 2004).

RAS TAFARI Also called Rastafarianism, Ras Tafari is an Afro-Caribbean religion with its original roots in Jamaica. It is not known how many Rastafarians there are because they refuse to be counted (Smith 1995:23). Ras Tafari is a protest religion that shares only a few of the features of African religions just mentioned. It traces its history to several preachers of the early twentieth century who taught that Ras ("Prince") Tafari, then the Ethiopian emperor Haile Selassie, was the "Lion of Judah" who would lead Blacks to the African promised land.

Rastafarianism does not have an organized set of doctrines or written texts. Shared beliefs of the many diffuse groups in the Caribbean, the United States, and Europe include the belief that Ethiopia is heaven on earth, that Haile Selassie is a living god, and that all Blacks will be able to return to the homeland through his help. Since the death of Haile Selassie in 1975, more emphasis has been placed on pan-African unity and Black power, and less on Ethiopia.

Rastafarianism is particularly strong in Jamaica, where it is associated with reggae music, dreadlocks, and *ganja* (marijuana) smoking. Variations within the Rastafarian movement in Jamaica range from beliefs that one must fight oppression to the position that living a peaceful life brings victory against evil.

◆◆◆
Directions of Religious Change

All religions have mythologies and doctrines that provide for continuity in beliefs and practices. Yet no religion is frozen and unchanging. Cultural anthropologists have traced the resurgence of religions that seemed to be headed toward extinction through colonial forces, and they have documented the emergence of new religions. Likewise, they are observing the contemporary struggle of once-suppressed religions in socialist states to find a new position in the postsocialist world. Religious *icons* (images, pictures, or other forms of

Bob Marley, legendary reggae artist and Rastafarian, performing at the Roxy Theater in Hollywood, California, in 1979. Marley died in 1981 at the age of 36, but he is still the most revered reggae musician. He launched the global spread of Jamaican music. Reggae is a genre of Jamaican music associated with Rastafarianism. Its songs address poverty, social injustice, love, and sexuality.

representations), once a prominent feature in Russian Orthodox churches, had been removed and placed in museums. The churches want them back.

Indigenous people's beliefs about the sacredness of their land are an important part of their attempts to protect their territory from encroachment and development by outside commercial interests. The world of religious change offers these examples, and far more, as windows into wider cultural change.

REVITALIZATION MOVEMENTS

Revitalization movements are socioreligious movements that seek to bring about positive change through reestablishing a religion that has been threatened by outside forces or through adopting new practices and beliefs. Such movements often arise in the context of rapid cultural change and appear to represent a way for people to try to make sense of their changing world and their place in it. One such movement that emerged as a response of Native Americans to the invasion of their land by Europeans and Euro-Americans was the Ghost Dance movement (Kehoe 1989). In the early 1870s, a shaman named Wodziwob of the Paiute (pie-yoot) tribe in California declared that the world would soon be destroyed and then renewed: Native Americans, plants, and animals

THINKING
OUTSIDE
THE BOX

Learn about Ọ̀yọ́túnjí Village from the Web. What goes on there? Do people live there? If you went to visit, where would you stay, what would you eat, and what would you do?

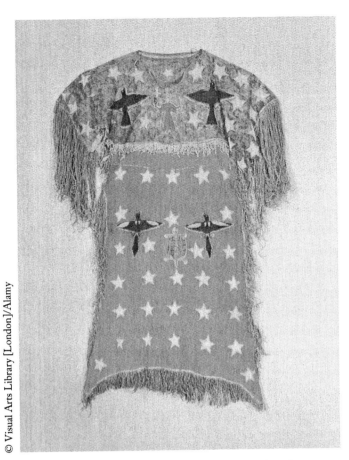

A Ghost Dance shirt of the Arapaho Indians of the Plains region, with painted designs of birds, turtle, and stars. These specially decorated garments were believed to protect the wearer from the White man's bullets.

© Visual Arts Library [London]/Alamy

would come back to life. He instructed people to perform a circle dance, known as the Ghost Dance, at night.

The movement spread to other tribes in California, Oregon, and Idaho but ended when the prophet died and his prophecy was unfulfilled. A similar movement emerged in 1890, led by another Paiute prophet, Wovoka, who had a vision during a total eclipse. His message was the same: destruction, renewal, and the need to perform circle dances in anticipation of the impending event. The dance spread widely and had various effects. Among the Pawnee, it provided the basis for a cultural revival of old ceremonies that had fallen into disuse. The Sioux altered Wovoka's message and adopted a more overtly hostile stance toward the government and White people. Newspapers began to carry stories about the "messiah craze," referring to Wovoka. Ultimately, the government took action against the Sioux, killing Chief Sitting Bull and Chief Big Foot and about 300 Sioux at Wounded Knee. In the 1970s, the Ghost Dance was revived again by the

cargo cult   a form of revitalization movement that emerged in Melanesia and New Zealand following World War II in response to Western and Japanese influences.

American Indian Movement, an activist organization that seeks to advance Native American rights.

Cargo cults are a type of revitalization movement that emerged in much of Melanesia and in New Zealand among the Māori people in response to Western influences. Most prominent in the first half of the nineteenth century, cargo cults emphasize the acquisition of Western trade goods, or cargo in local terms. Typically, a prophetic leader emerges with a vision of how the cargo will arrive. In one instance, the leader predicted that a ship would come, bringing not only cargo but also the people's dead ancestors. Followers set up tables for the expected guests, complete with flower arrangements.

Later, after World War II and the islanders' experiences of aircraft arrivals bringing cargo, the mode of anticipated arrival changed to planes. Once again, people would wait expectantly for the arrival of the plane. Cargo cults emerged as a response to the disruptive effects of new goods being suddenly introduced into indigenous settings. The outsiders imposed a new form of exchange system that emphasized the importance of Western goods and suppressed the importance of indigenous valuables such as shells and pigs. This transformation undermined traditional patterns of gaining status through the exchange of indigenous goods. Cargo cult leaders sought help, in the only way they knew, in obtaining Western goods so that they could acquire social status in the new system.

CONTESTED SACRED SITES

Religious conflict often becomes focused on sacred sites. One place of recurrent conflict is Jerusalem, where many religions and sects within religions compete for control of sacred terrain. Three major religions claim they have primary rights: Islam,

Lamont Lindstrom

John Frum Movement supporters stand guard around one of the cult's flag poles at Sulphur Bay village, on Tanna Island, Vanuatu, in the region of Melanesia.

▶ *Does this scene remind you of anything from your culture?*

After the Chinese takeover of Tibet, many Tibetans became refugees, including the revered head of Tibetan Buddhism, the Dalai Lama. Buddhism, founded in India as a protest against Hinduism, is a minority religion in its homeland. It has millions of followers elsewhere, from Scotland to San Francisco.

Judaism, and Christianity. Among the Christians, several different sects vie for control of the Church of the Holy Sepulchre (see Map 6). In India, frequent conflicts over sacred sites occur between Hindus and Muslims. Hindus claim that Muslim mosques have been built on sites sacred to Hindus. On some occasions, the Hindus have destroyed the mosques. Many conflicts that involve secular issues surrounding sacred sites also exist worldwide. In the United States, White racists have burned African American churches. In Israel, some Jewish leaders object to archaeological research because the ancient Jewish burial places should remain undisturbed.

A similar situation exists among indigenous populations in the Western Hemisphere. Their sacred sites and burial grounds have often been destroyed for the sake of urban growth, petroleum and mineral extraction, and recreational sports. Resistance to such destruction is growing, with indigenous people finding creative ways to protect, restore, and manage their heritage.

RELIGIOUS FREEDOM AS A HUMAN RIGHT

According to a United Nations Declaration, freedom from religious persecution is a universal human right. Yet violations of this right by countries and by competing religions are common. Sometimes people who are persecuted on religious grounds can seek and obtain sanctuary in other places or nations. Thousands of Tibetan Buddhist refugees, including their leader the Dalai Lama, fled Tibet after it was taken over by the Chinese. Several Tibetan communities have been established in exile in India, the United States, and Canada, where the Tibetan people attempt to keep their religion, language, and heritage alive.

The post-9/11 policy enactments in the United States related to its campaign against terrorism are seen by many as dangerous steps against constitutional principles of personal liberty—specifically, as infringements on the religious rights of practicing Muslims. The prevalent mentality in the U.S. government, and in much of the general populace, links the whole of Islam with terrorism and thereby stigmatizes all Muslims as potential terrorists. Many anthropologists (for example, Mamdani 2002) have spoken out against the inaccuracy and indecency of labeling an entire religion dangerous and putting all its members under the shadow of suspicion.

Religions are often the focal point of conflict and dissension and the source of conflict resolution. As an integral part of the heritage of humanity, they can be better understood from a cross-cultural and contextualized perspective. Such understanding is essential for building a more secure and peaceful future.

the BIG questions REVISITED

◆ What is religion and what are the basic features of religions?

Early cultural anthropologists defined religion in contrast to magic and suggested that religion was a more evolved form of thinking about the supernatural realm. They collected information on religions of non-Western cultures and constructed theories about the origin and functions of religion. Since then, ethnographers have described many religious systems and documented a rich variety of beliefs, forms of ritual behavior, and types of religious specialists. Beliefs are expressed in either myth or doctrine and often are concerned with defining the roles and characteristics of supernatural beings and how humans should relate to them.

Religious beliefs are enacted in rituals that are periodic or nonperiodic. Some common rituals worldwide are life-cycle rites, pilgrimage, rituals of inversion, and sacrifice. Rituals are transformative for the participants.

Many rituals require the involvement of a trained religious specialist such as a shaman/shamanka or priest/priestess. Compared to the situation in states, religious specialist roles in nonstate contexts are fewer, less than full-time, less formalized and carry less secular power. In states, religious specialists are often organized into hierarchies, and many specialists gain substantial secular power.

◆ How do world religions illustrate globalization and localization?

The five so-called world religions are based on texts and generally agreed-on teachings and beliefs shared by many people around the world. In order of historic age, they are Hinduism, Buddhism, Judaism, Christianity, and Islam. Christianity has the largest number of adherents, with Islam second and Hinduism third. Due to accelerated global population migration in the past few centuries, many formerly local religions now have a worldwide membership. African diaspora religions are particularly prominent in the Western Hemisphere, with a variety of syncretistic religions attracting many adherents.

As members of the world religions have moved around the world, religious beliefs and practices have become contextualized into localized variants. When a new religion moves into a culture, it may be blended with local systems (syncretism), may coexist with indigenous religions in a pluralistic fashion, or may take over and obliterate the original beliefs.

◆ What are some important aspects of religious change in contemporary times?

Religious movements of the past two centuries have often been prompted by colonialism and other forms of social contact. In some instances, indigenous religious leaders and cults have arisen in the attempt to resist unwanted outside forces of change. In other cases, they evolve as ways of incorporating selected outside elements. Revitalization movements, such as the Ghost Dance movement in the United States Plains region, look to the past and attempt to recover lost and suppressed religious beliefs and practices.

Issues of contemporary importance include the increasing amount of conflict surrounding sacred sites, hostilities related to the effects of secular power interests on religious institutions and spaces, and religious freedom as a human right.

KEY CONCEPTS

animatism

animism

cargo cult

doctrine

life-cycle ritual

magic

myth

pilgrimage

priest/priestess

religion

religious pluralism

religious syncretism

revitalization movement

ritual

ritual of inversion

sacrifice

world religion

SUGGESTED READINGS

Paulo Apolito. *The Internet and the Madonna: Religious Visionary Experience on the Web.* Antony Shugaar, trans. Chicago: University of Chicago Press, 2003. This book traces the Christian cult of Mary as it has developed and grown through the medium of the World Wide Web.

Diane Bell. *Ngarrindjeri Wurruwarrin: A World That Is, Was, and Will Be.* North Melbourne, Australia: Spinifex, 1998. This ethnography describes Ngarrindjeri women's struggles to protect their sacred land from encroachment by developers. It includes the women's voices, the perspective of the Australian government, the media, and disputes among anthropologists.

Janet Bennion. *Desert Patriarchy: Mormon and Mennonite Communities in the Chihuahua Valley.* Tucson: University of Arizona Press, 2004. The ethnographer, raised in a Mormon family, reports on her fieldwork among Mormons in a desert region in Mexico.

Karen McCarthy Brown. *Mama Lola: A Vodou Priestess in Brooklyn.* Berkeley: University of California Press, 1991. This life story of Mama Lola, a voodoo practitioner, is set within an ethnographic study of a Haitian community in New York City.

Sondra L. Hausner. *Wandering with Sadhus: Ascetics in the Hindu Himalayas.* Bloomington: Indiana University Press, 2008. This ethnographic study explores the interactions of Hindu ascetics in northern India with ordinary households and considers how they are part of the public community in spite of their commitment to solitary religious practices.

Klara Bonsack Kelley and Harris Francis. *Navajo Sacred Places.* Bloomington: Indiana University Press, 1994. The authors report on the results of a research project undertaken to learn about Navajo cultural resources, especially sacred sites, and the stories associated with them in order to help protect these places.

Melvin Konner. *Unsettled: An Anthropology of the Jews.* New York: Penguin Compass, 2003. A biological anthropologist is the author of this cultural history of the Jewish people and their religion. It extends from the origins of Judaism among pastoralists in the Middle East through enslavement in the Roman Empire, to the Holocaust and the creation of Israel.

J. David Lewis-Williams and D. G. Pearce. *San Spirituality: Roots, Expression, and Social Consequences.* New York: AltaMira Press, 2004. This book examines the interplay of cosmology, myth, ritual, and art among the San people of southern Africa.

Charlene Makley. *The Violence of Liberation: Gender and Tibetan Buddhist Revival in Post-Mao China.* Berkeley: University of California Press, 2007. Makley combines archival research with fieldwork in a Buddhist monastery in Tibet. She describes the incorporation of the region of Labrang into China.

Fatima Mernissi. *Beyond the Veil: Male–Female Dynamics in Modern Muslim Society.* Bloomington: Indiana University Press, revised edition, 1987. The author considers how Islam perceives female sexuality and regulates it on behalf of the social order.

Todd Sanders. *Beyond Bodies: Rainmaking and Sense Making in Tanzania.* Toronto: University of Toronto Press, 2008. This study of rainmaking rituals among the Inhanzu of central Tanzania reveals ideas about gender roles and relations.

Maureen Trudelle Schwarz. *Blood and Voice: Navajo Women Ceremonial Practitioners.* Tucson: University of Arizona Press, 2003. Contemporary Navajo women are increasingly taking on the ritual role of ceremonial Singer, formerly the domain of men. This book describes how women gain sacred knowledge and explains how they overcome the tradition that only men can be Singers.

Stephen Selka. *Religion and the Politics of Ethnic Identity in Bahia, Brazil.* Gainesville: University Press of Florida, 2008. This study shows how Catholicism, evangelical Protestantism, and the traditional Brazilian religion of Candomblé shape the discourse of race and identity in northeastern Brazil.

Katharine L. Wiegele. *Investing in Miracles: El Shaddai and the Transformation of Popular Catholicism in the Philippines.* Honolulu: University of Hawai'i Press, 2005. This book examines the widespread popularity in the Philippines of a charismatic businessman who became a preacher, Brother Mike. He appears at huge outdoor rallies and uses mass media to spread his message of economic prosperity within a Catholic framework.

CHAPTER 11

COMMUNICATION

COMMUNICATION

the BIG questions

- How do humans communicate?

- How does communication relate to cultural diversity and inequality?

- How does language change?

273

This chapter is about human communication and language, drawing on work in both linguistic anthropology and cultural anthropology. It looks at communication with a wide-angle lens to include topics from word choice to language extinction. The chapter first discusses how humans communicate and what distinguishes human communication from that of other animals. The second section offers examples of language, microcultures, and inequality. The third section discusses language change from its origins in the distant past to contemporary concerns about language loss.

◆ ◆ ◆

The Varieties of Human Communication

Humans can communicate with words, either spoken or signed, with gestures and other forms of body language such as clothing and hairstyle, and through methods such as telephone calls, postal mail, and e-mail.

LANGUAGE AND VERBAL COMMUNICATION

Most people are in almost constant communication—with other people, with supernaturals, or with pets. We communicate in face-to-face situations or indirectly through mail or email. **Communication** is the process of sending and receiving messages. Among humans, it involves some form of **language**, a systematic set of symbols and signs with learned and shared meanings. Language may be spoken, hand-signed, written, or conveyed through body movements, body markings and modifications, hairstyle, dress, and accessories.

TWO FEATURES OF HUMAN LANGUAGE Scholars of language, over many years, have proposed characteristics of human language that distinguish it from communication

among other living beings. This section presents the two most robust of these.

First, human language has **productivity**, or the ability to create an infinite range of understandable expressions from a finite set of rules. This characteristic is a result of the rich variety of symbols and signs that humans use in their communication. In contrast, nonhuman primates have a more limited set of communicative resources. They rely on a **call system**, or a form of oral communication among nonhuman primates with a set repertoire of meaningful sounds generated in response to environmental factors. Nonhuman primates do not have the physiological capacity for speech that humans do. In captivity, however, some bonobos and chimpanzees have learned to communicate effectively with humans through sign language and by pointing to symbols on a chart. The world's most famous bonobo is Kanzi, who lives at the Great Ape Trust in Des Moines, Iowa. He can understand much of what humans say to him, and he can respond by combining symbols on a printed board. He can also play simple video games, such as Ms. Pac-Man (http://www.greatapetrust.org).

Second, human language emphasizes the feature of **displacement**, the ability to refer to events and issues beyond the immediate present. The past and the future, in this view, are considered to be *displaced domains*. They include reference to people and events that may never exist at all, as in fantasy and fiction. Some bonobos who have been raised by and live in a close relationship with humans exhibit some aspects of displacement (http://www.pbs.org). But, especially in the wild, they are far less likely to use it than humans do.

communication   the conveying of meaningful messages from one person, animal, or insect to another.

language   a form of communication that is a systematic set of learned symbols and signs shared among a group and passed on from generation to generation.

productivity   a feature of human language that offers the ability to communicate many messages efficiently.

call system   a form of oral communication among nonhuman primates with a set repertoire of meaningful sounds generated in response to environmental factors.

displacement   a feature of human language that allows people to talk about events in the past and future.

phoneme   a sound that makes a difference for meaning in a language.

© Frans Lanting/Minden Pictures

Primatologist Sue Savage-Rumbaugh, working with Kanzi, an adult male bonobo. Kanzi is involved in a long-term project about ape language. He has learned to communicate with researchers using several symbols. Some chimpanzees, bonobos, orangutans, and gorillas are also able to communicate using American Sign Language and symbols on computer keyboards.

Daniel Everett

A Pirahã shelter. According to Daniel Everett, who has spent many years learning about their culture and language, the Pirahã do not lead a culturally deprived life. The Pirahã are content with their lifestyle that includes leisure activities such as playing tag and other games. In spite of their wish to remain living as they are, their reservation is not secure from outside encroachment.

MAP 1 **Pirahã Reservation in Brazil.**
Linguistic anthropologist Daniel Everett helped to define the boundaries of the Pirahã reservation in the 1980s. With support from Cultural Survival and other sources, the demarcation was legally declared in 1994.

In respect to productivity and displacement in human language, the case of language among the Pirahã (Pee-duh-hah) of Brazil raises many questions (Everett 2005, 2008) (see Map 1). Their language does not emphasize either productivity or displacement, though both exist to some degree. The Pirahã are a group of about 350 foragers living on a reservation in the Amazonian rainforest near the Maici River. Their language contains only three pronouns, few words associated with time, no past-tense verbs, no color terms, and no numbers other than a word that translates into English roughly as "about one." Grammar is simple, with no subordinate clauses. Kinship terms are simple and few. The Pirahã have no myths or stories and no art other than necklaces and a few rudimentary stick figures. In spite of over 200 years of regular contact with Brazilians and neighboring Indians who speak a different language, the Pirahã remain monolingual.

Since 1977, linguist Daniel Everett has lived with the Pirahã and learned their language, so it is unlikely that he has overlooked major aspects of their language. He insists that their language is in no way "primitive" or inadequate. It has extremely complex verbs and rich and varied uses of stress and intonation, referred to in linguistics as *prosody*. The Pirahã especially enjoy verbal joking and teasing, both among themselves and with researchers.

FORMAL PROPERTIES OF VERBAL LANGUAGE Human language can be analyzed in terms of its formal properties: sounds, vocabulary, and syntax (sometimes called grammar),

which are the formal building blocks of all languages. But languages differ widely in which sounds are important, what words are important in the vocabulary, and how people put words together to form meaningful sentences. Learning a new language usually involves learning different sets of sounds. The sounds that make a difference for meaning in a language are called **phonemes**. The study of phonemes is called *phonetics*.

A native English-speaker learning to speak Hindi, the major language of North India, must learn to produce and recognize several new sounds. Four different "d" sounds exist. None is the same as an English "d," which is usually pronounced with the tongue placed on the ridge behind the upper front teeth (try it). One "d" in Hindi, which linguists refer to as a "dental" sound, is pronounced with the tongue pressed firmly behind the upper front teeth (try it) (see Figure 1). Next is a dental "d" that is also aspirated (pronounced "with air"); making this sound involves the tongue being in the same position and a puff of air expelled during pronunciation (try it, and try the regular dental "d" again with no puff of air at all). Next is what is referred to as a "retroflex" sound, made by flipping the tongue back to the central dome of the roof of the mouth (try it, with no puff of air). Finally, there is the aspirated retroflex "d" with the tongue in the center of the roof of the mouth and a puff of air. Once you can do this, try the whole series again with a "t," because Hindi follows the same pattern with this letter as with the "d." Several other sounds in Hindi require careful use of aspiration and placement of the tongue for communicating the right word. A puff of air at the wrong time can produce a serious error, such as

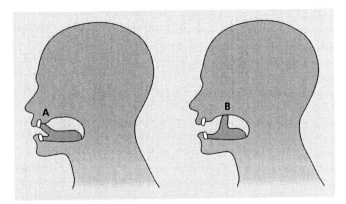

FIGURE 1 DENTAL AND RETROFLEX TONGUE POSITIONS. When making a dental sound, the speaker places the tongue against the upper front teeth (position A in the diagram). When making a retroflex sound, the speaker places the tongue up against the roof of the mouth (position B in the diagram).

- Firm, even snow that falls in mild weather
- Thickly packed snow caused by intermittent freezing/thawing and high winds
- Hard-packed snow formed by strong wind
- Dry, large-grained, water-holding snow at the deepest layers, closest to the ground, found in late winter and spring
- Snow that forms a hard layer after rain
- Ice sheet on pastures formed by rain on open ground that freezes
- A layer of frozen snow between other snow layers that acts as an ice sheet

Source: Jernsletten 1997.

FIGURE 2 Kinds of "Snow" the Saami Recognize Related to Reindeer Herding.

saying the word for "breast" when you want to say the word for "letter."

All languages have a vocabulary, or *lexicon,* which consists of all its meaningful words. Speakers combine words into phrases and sentences to create meaning. *Semantics* refers to the study of the meaning of words, phrases, and sentences. Anthropologists add the concept of **ethnosemantics**, the study of the meaning of words, phrases, and sentences in particular cultural contexts. They find that different languages classify the world in different ways and categorize even such seemingly natural things as color and disease in different ways. Ethnosemantic research reveals much about how people define the world and their place in it, how they organize their social lives, and what is of value to them. *Focal vocabularies* are clusters of words that refer to important features of a particular culture. For example, many circumpolar languages have rich focal vocabularies related to snow (see Figure 2). In mountainous areas of Afghanistan, plentiful terms for kinds of rocks exist.

Syntax, or grammar, consists of the patterns and rules by which words are organized to make sense in a string. All languages have rules for syntax, although they vary in form. Even within the languages of contemporary Europe, syntactical variation exists. German, for example, places verbs at the end of the sentence (try composing an English sentence with its main verb at the end).

---

ethnosemantics the study of the meaning of words, phrases, and sentences in particular cultural contexts.

sign language a form of communication that uses mainly hand movements to convey messages.

NONVERBAL LANGUAGE AND EMBODIED COMMUNICATION

Many forms of language and communication do not rely on verbal speech. Like verbal language, though, they are based on symbols and signs and have rules for their proper combination and meaning.

SIGN LANGUAGE **Sign language** is a form of communication that uses mainly hand movements to convey messages. A sign language provides a fully competent communication system for its users just as spoken language does (Baker 1999). Around the world, many varieties of sign language exist, including American Sign Language, British Sign Language, Japanese Sign Language, Russian Sign Language, and many varieties of indigenous Australian sign languages. Most sign languages are used by people who are hearing impaired as their main form of communication. Indigenous Australian sign languages, in contrast, are used by people who have the capacity for verbal communication. They switch to sign language in situations in which verbal speech is forbidden or undesirable (Kendon 1988). Verbal speech is forbidden in some sacred contexts and for widows during mourning. It is also undesirable when hunting.

Although sign languages are complete and complex languages in their own right, they are often treated as second-class. A breakthrough in recognition of the validity and communicative competence of sign languages came in 1983 when the government of Sweden recognized Swedish Sign Language as a native language. Such recognition is especially important in contexts where a person's sense of identity, and even citizenship itself, is based on the ability to speak an officially accepted language. Anthropologists work with people who are deaf to help promote public understanding of the

Anthropology and Public Understanding of the Language and Culture of People Who Are Deaf

Ethnographic studies of the communication practices and wider culture of people who are deaf have great importance and practical application (Senghas and Monaghan 2002). This research demonstrates the limitations and inaccuracy of the *medical model* that construes deafness as a pathology or deficit and sees the goal as curing it. Instead, anthropologists propose the "cultural model," which views deafness simply as one possibility in the wide spectrum of cultural variation. In this view, a capital D is often used: Deaf culture.

Deafness in fact allows plenty of room for human agency. The strongest evidence of agency among people who are deaf is sign language itself, which exhibits adaptiveness, creativity, and change. This view helps to promote a nonvictim, nonpathological identity for people who are deaf and to reduce social stigma related to deafness.

Anthropologists involved in Deaf culture studies are examining topics such as how people who are deaf become bilingual—for example, fluent in both English and Japanese sign languages. Their findings are being

© Penny Tweedie/CORBIS

In Uganda, James Mwadha, a deaf attendee at a meeting for Action on Disability and Development (ADD), signs to others in the group. ADD seeks to promote the rights of disabled people.

incorporated in improved ways of teaching sign language.

◆ **FOOD FOR THOUGHT**

* Choose five words and learn the signs for them in American Sign Language and in another culture's sign language. Are they the same or different, and how might one explain the similarity or difference?

---

legitimacy of their language and to advocate for improved teaching of sign language (see Lessons Applied).

Gestures are movements, usually of the hands, that convey meanings. Some gestures may be universally meaningful, but most are culturally specific and often completely arbitrary. Some cultures have more highly developed gesture systems than others. Black urban youths in Pretoria and Johannesburg, South Africa, use a rich repertoire of gestures (Brookes 2004). Some of the gestures are widely used and recognized, but many vary by age, gender, and situation (see Figure 3). Men use more gestures than women do; the reason for this difference is not clear.

Greetings, an important part of communication in every known culture, often involve gestures (Duranti 1997b). They are typically among the first communicative routines that children learn, as well as tourists and anyone trying to learn a foreign language. Greetings establish a social encounter. They typically involve both verbal and nonverbal language.

Depending on the context and the social relationship, many variations exist for both the verbal and the nonverbal component. Contextual factors include the degree of formality or informality. Social factors include gender, ethnicity, class, and age.

SILENCE Silence is another form of nonverbal communication. Its use is often related to social status, but in unpredictable ways. In rural Siberia, an in-marrying daughter-in-law has the lowest status in the household, and she rarely speaks (Humphrey 1978). In other contexts, silence is associated with power. In U.S. courts, lawyers speak more than anyone else, the judge speaks rarely but has more power than a lawyer, while the silent jury holds the most power (Lakoff 1990).

Silence is an important component of communication among many Native American cultures. White outsiders, including social workers, have sometimes misinterpreted

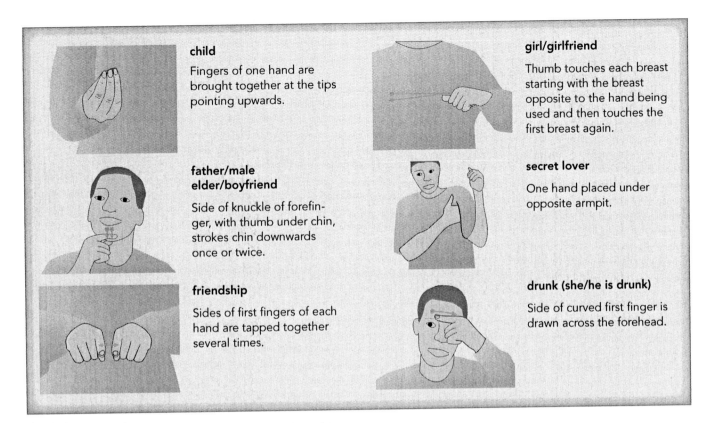

FIGURE 3 Some South African Gestures Used by a Man.

this silence as a reflection of dignity or a lack of emotion or intelligence. How ethnocentric such judgments are is revealed by a study of silence among the Western Apache of Arizona (Basso 1972 [1970]) (see Map 2). The Western Apache use silence in four contexts:

- When meeting a stranger, especially at fairs, rodeos, or other public events. Speaking with a stranger immediately indicates interest in something such as money, work, or transportation, all possible reasons for exhibiting such bad manners.

- In the early stages of courting. Sitting in silence and holding hands for several hours is appropriate. Speaking "too soon" would indicate sexual willingness or interest.

- When parents and children meet after the child has been away at boarding school. They should be silent for about 15 minutes. It may be two or three days before sustained conversations are initiated.

- When "getting cussed out," especially at drinking parties.

An underlying similarity of all these contexts is the uncertainty, ambiguity, and unpredictability of the social relationships involved.

BODY LANGUAGE Human communication, in one way or another, often involves the body in sending and receiving messages. Beyond the mechanics of speaking, hearing, gesturing, and seeing, the body itself can function as a "text" that conveys messages. The full range of *body language* includes eye movements, posture, walking style, the way of standing and sitting, cultural *inscriptions* on the body such as tattoos and hairstyles, and accessories such as dress, shoes, and jewelry. Body language follows patterns and rules just as verbal language does. Like verbal language, the rules and meanings are learned, often unconsciously. Without learning the rules and meanings, one will commit communication errors, which are sometimes funny and sometimes serious.

Different cultures emphasize different body language channels more than others. Some are more touch oriented than others, and some use facial expressions more. Eye contact is valued during Euro-American conversations, but in many Asian contexts, direct eye contact is considered rude or perhaps a sexual invitation.

Modification of and marks on the body, clothing, and hairstyles convey messages about age, gender, sexual interest or availability, profession, wealth, and emotions. Color of clothing can send messages about a person's identity, class, gender, and more. In the United States, gender differentiation begins in the hospital nursery with the color coding of blue

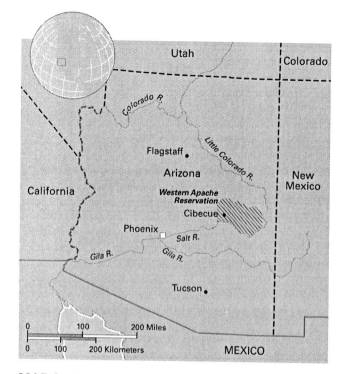

MAP 2 Western Apache Reservation in Arizona.
Before European colonialism, the Apache lived in a wide area extending from present day Arizona to northwestern Texas. Originally foragers, they starting planting some food crops in the 1600s. After the arrival of the Spanish, the Apache gained horses from them and became skilled equestrian warriors. In the second half of the nineteenth century, the U.S. government was active in exterminating many Apache groups and forced those who survived to live on reservations in order to make way for White settlements.

A horse race at Ascot, England, attended by members of the elite.

▶ *If you were going to the races at Ascot and wanted to be dressed properly, what should you wear?*

for boys and pink for girls. In parts of the Middle East, public dress is black for women and white for men.

Covering or not covering various parts of the body with clothing is another culturally coded matter. Consider the different meanings of veiling/head covering in Egypt and Kuwait (MacLeod 1992). Kuwaiti women's head covering distinguishes them as relatively wealthy, leisured, and honorable, in contrast to the immigrant women workers from Asia who do not cover their heads. In contrast, the head covering in Egypt is done mainly by women from the lower and middle economic levels. For them, it is a way to accommodate conservative Islamic values while preserving their right to work outside the home. In Egypt, the head covering says, "I am a good Muslim and a good wife/daughter." In Kuwait, the headscarf says, "I am a wealthy Kuwaiti citizen." In many conservative Muslim contexts, it is important for a woman in public to cover more than her head by wearing a full-length loose garment. These rules, along with other patriarchal values, make it difficult for women in some Muslim contexts to participate in sports while in school and public domains such as the international Olympics.

In Japan, the kimono provides an elaborate coding system for gender and life-cycle stage (Dalby 2001). The higher one's status, the shorter the sleeve of one's kimono. Men's kimono sleeves come in one length: short. Unmarried women's sleeve length is nearly to the ground, whereas a married woman's sleeve is nearly as short as that of a man's.

Lanita Jacobs-Huey's research on African American women's hair culture reveals the links among women's hair, their talk about hair, and their identity (2006). She also learned about the complex linguistic terminology that Black hairstylists use to refer to various hair styling procedures. Stylists use specialized language and language correction to affirm their identities as hair-care specialists.

COMMUNICATING WITH MEDIA AND INFORMATION TECHNOLOGY

Media anthropology is the cross-cultural study of communication through electronic media such as radio, television, film, recorded music, the Internet, and print media, including newspapers, magazines, and popular literature (Spitulnik 1993). Media anthropology is an important emerging area that links linguistic and cultural anthropology (Allen 1994). Media anthropologists study the media process and content, the audience response, and the social effects of media presentations. **Critical media anthropology** asks to what degree access to media messages is liberating or controlling, and whose interests the media serve. It is especially active in examining journalism, television, advertising, and new information technology, as the following examples illustrate.

---

critical media anthropology an approach within the cross-cultural study of media that examines how power interests shape people's access to media and the contents of its messages.

(TOP) Japanese business men meet each other, bow, and exchange business cards. Bowing is an important part of non-verbal communication in Japan. (BOTTOM) The *furisode* kimono is distinguished by its fine silk material, long sleeves, elaborate colors and designs. A girl's twentieth birthday gift is typically a furisode, marking her transition to young adulthood. Only unmarried women wear furisode, so wearing one is a statement of marital availability. Fluttering the long, wide sleeves at a man is a way to express love for him.

▶ *What meanings do the styles and lengths of sleeves convey in your cultural world?*

THE POLITICS OF JOURNALISM   Mark Pedelty studied war correspondents in El Salvador to learn about journalists and journalistic practices during war (1995). He found that the lives and identities of war correspondents are highly charged with violence and terror: "War correspondents have a unique relationship to terror . . . that combines voyeurism and direct participation. . . . They need terror to . . . maintain their cultural identity as 'war correspondents'" (1995:2). The primary job of journalists, including war correspondents, is communication of a specific sort. They gather information that is time sensitive and often brutal. Their job is to provide brief stories for the public.

A critical media anthropology perspective reveals the important role of the news agency that pays their salary or, if they are freelancers or "stringers," that buys their story. War correspondents in El Salvador, Pedelty found, write a story about the same event differently, depending on whether they are sending it to a U.S. newspaper or a European newspaper. How "accurate," then, is "the news"?

GENDER AND JAPANESE TELEVISION PROGRAMMING
Most television programming in Japan presents women as housewives, performing traditional domestic roles (Painter 1996). Many Japanese women now reject such shows. In response, producers are experimenting with new sorts of dramas in which women are shown as active workers and aggressive lovers. One such show is a 10-part serial that first aired in 1992 called *Selfish Women.* The story concerns three women: an aggressive single businesswoman who faces discrimination at work, a young mother who is raising her daughter alone while her photographer husband lives with another woman, and an ex-housewife who divorced her husband because she found home life empty and unrewarding. There are several male characters, but, except for one, they are depicted as less interesting than the women.

The show's title is ironic. In Japan, men often label women who assert themselves as "selfish." The lead women in the drama use the term in a positive way to encourage each other: "Let's become even more selfish!" Although dramas like *Selfish Women* may not be revolutionary, they indicate that telerepresentations of gender in Japan are changing, largely through the agency of Japanese women.

ADVERTISING FOR LATINOS IN THE UNITED STATES
Within the U.S. advertising market, one of the most sought-after segments is the Latino population, also called "the Hispanic market" in the advertising industry (Dávila 2002). Interviews with staff of 16 Latino advertising agencies and content analysis of their advertisements reveal their approach of treating Latinos as a unified, culturally specific market. The dominant theme, or trope, is that of "the family" as being the most important feature of Latino culture, in contrast to the stereotype of the Anglo population as more individualistic.

Recent milk-promotion advertisements for the Anglo population show a celebrity with a milk moustache. The Latino version shows a grandmother cooking a traditional milk-based dessert with the caption "Have you given your loved ones enough milk today?" (2002:270). In Spanish-language television and radio networks, a kind of "standard" Spanish is used, a generic form with no hint of regionalism or accent.

Latinos are, however, a highly heterogeneous population. By promoting a monolithic image of Latino culture, media messages may be contributing to identity change toward a more monolithic pattern. At the same time, they are certainly missing opportunities to tap into more specialized markets within the Latino population.

CROSSING THE DIGITAL DIVIDE IN RURAL HUNGARY

The term **digital divide** refers to social inequality in access to new and emerging information technology, especially access

Barbara Miller

A satellite dish dominates the view of a village in Niger, West Africa. Throughout the world, the spread of electronic forms of communication have many and diverse social effects.

▶ *Pretend you are a cultural anthropologist doing research on communication in this village. What do you want to study in order to assess the effects of satellite communication on the people and their culture?*

MAP 3 Hungary.
The Republic of Hungary has a population of around 10 million. The Roma population, variously estimated at between 450,000, and 600,000, has increased rapidly in recent years. Hungary's landscape is mainly plains with hills and low mountains to the north. One of the newest members of the European Union, Hungary has a growing economy. The main religion is Christianity, with Catholicism accounting for about half of the total; about 30 percent, however, are atheists. Magyar, the Hungarian language, is one of the few European languages that does not belong to the Indo-European language family but belongs instead to the Finno-Ugric family.

to up-to-date computers, the Internet, and training related to their use. Local attempts to overcome the digital divide between Hungary and countries in the European Union involve the development of the Hungarian Telecottage Association (HTA) (Wormald 2005) (see Map 3). The idea of the telecottage, which started in Sweden and Scotland, involves dedicating some space, such as an unused workshop or part of a house, for public use in which a computer with Internet access is provided.

The HTA, centered in Bucharest, promotes village-based Internet access in order to improve the lives of rural people through enhanced communication. Most telecottages in Hungary are located in rural communities of fewer than 5000 people. The HTA website provides announcements about funding opportunities and relevant news. Although these innovations sound highly positive, some emerging interpersonal problems exist related to who gets access first to

digital divide   social inequality in access to new and emerging information technology, notably access to up-to-date computers, the Internet, and training related to their use.

information for posting on the website and to information hoarding by some managers.

Like the Hungarian villagers, many marginalized people around the world, including indigenous people, women, and youth, realize the importance of having access to the Internet and other information and communication technologies (ICT). These technologies can help people preserve and learn their ancestral languages, record traditional agricultural and medical knowledge, and otherwise protect their culture and improve their lives (Lutz 2005, Turner 2002).

◆◆◆

Communication and Cultural Diversity and Inequality

This section presents material about the links between language and microcultures and social inequality. It begins by presenting two models of the relationship between language and culture. Examples follow about class, gender and sexuality, "race" and ethnicity, and age.

LANGUAGE AND CULTURE: TWO THEORIES

During the twentieth century, two theoretical perspectives were influential in the study of the relationship between language and culture. They are presented here as two distinct models, even though they actually overlap in real life and anthropologists tend to draw on both of them (Hill and Mannheim 1992).

The first was formulated by two early founding figures in linguistic anthropology, Edward Sapir and Benjamin Whorf. In the mid-twentieth century, they formulated an influential model called the **Sapir-Whorf hypothesis**, which says that people's language affects how they think. If a language has many words for different kinds of snow, for example, then someone who speaks that language can "think" about snow in more ways than someone can whose language has fewer "snow" terms. Among the Saami, whose traditional occupation was reindeer herding (see Culturama), a rich set of terms exist for "snow" (review Figure 2). If a language has no word for "snow," then someone who speaks that language

---

Sapir-Whorf hypothesis   a theory in linguistic anthropology that says language determines thought.

sociolinguistics   a theory in linguistic anthropology that says that culture and society and a person's social position determine language.

critical discourse analysis   the study of the relations of power and inequality in language.

tag question   a question seeking affirmation, placed at the end of a sentence.   ◀

cannot think of "snow." Thus, a language constitutes a *thought world*, and people who speak different languages inhabit different thought worlds. This catchy phrase became the basis for *linguistic determinism*, a theory stating that language determines consciousness of the world and behavior. Extreme linguistic determinism implies that the frames and definitions of a person's primary language are so strong that it is impossible to learn another language fully or, therefore, to understand another culture fully. Most anthropologists see value in the Sapir-Whorf hypothesis, but not in its extreme form.

A second model for understanding the relationship between language and culture is proposed by scholars working in the area of **sociolinguistics**, the study of how cultural and social context shapes language. These theorists support a *cultural constructionist* argument that a person's context and social position shape the content, form, and meaning of their language. Most anthropologists see value in this model and agree that language and culture are interactive: Language shapes culture and culture shapes language.

CRITICAL DISCOURSE ANALYSIS: CLASS, GENDER, INDIGENEITY, AND "RACE"

Critical discourse analysis is an emerging area that focuses on the relations of power and inequality in language (Blommaert and Bulcaen 2000). This part of the chapter looks at distinctive communication styles, or *registers*, that include variation in vocabulary, grammar, and intonation. Critical discourse analysis reveals links between language and social inequality, power, and stigma as well as agency and resistance through language.

CLASS AND ACCENT IN NEW YORK CITY   William Labov launched the subfield of sociolinguistics with his classic study of accents among mainly Euro-American people of different socioeconomic classes in New York City (1966). For example, pronunciation of the consonant "r" in words such as car, card, floor, and fourth tends to be associated with upper-class people, whereas its absence ("caw," "cawd," "flaw," "fawth") is associated with lower-class people. In order to avoid the observer's paradox, Labov used informal observations of sales clerks' speech in three Manhattan department stores of different "class" levels: Saks (the highest), Macy's, and S. Klein (the lowest). Labov wanted to find out whether the clerks in the different stores spoke with different class accents. He would approach a clerk and inquire about the location of an item that he knew was on the fourth floor. The clerk would respond, and then Labov would say, "Excuse me?" in order to prompt a more emphatic repeat of the word fourth. He found that the higher-status "r" was pronounced both the first and second times by 44 percent of the employees in Saks, by 16 percent of the employees in Macy's, and by 6 percent of the employees in S. Klein.

GENDER IN EURO-AMERICAN CONVERSATIONS

Most languages contain gender differences in word choice, grammar, intonation, content, and style. Early studies of language and gender among white Euro-Americans revealed three general characteristics of female speech (Lakoff 1973):

- Politeness
- Rising intonation at the end of sentences
- Frequent use of **tag questions** (questions seeking affirmation placed at the end of sentences, such as, "It's a nice day, isn't it?")

In English, male speech, in general, is less polite, maintains a flat and assertive tone in a sentence, and does not use tag questions. Related to politeness is the fact that, during cross-gender conversations, men tend to interrupt women more than women interrupt men.

Deborah Tannen's popular book *You Just Don't Understand* (1990) shows how differences in conversational styles between white Euro-American men and women lead to miscommunication. She says that "women speak and hear a language of connection and intimacy, whereas men speak and hear a language of status and independence" (1990:42). Although both men and women use indirect response (not really answering the question), their different motivations, create different meanings embedded in their speech:

Michele: What time is the concert?
Gary: We have to be ready by seven-thirty. (1990:289)

Gary sees his role as one of protector in using an indirect response to Michele's question. He feels that he is simply "watching out for her" by getting to the real point of her question. Michele feels that Gary is withholding information by not answering her directly and is maintaining a power position. A wife's indirect response to a question from her husband is prompted by her goal of being helpful in anticipating her husband's underlying interest:

Ned: Are you just about finished?
Valerie: Do you want to have supper now? (1990:289)

Women's speech cross-culturally is not universally accommodating, subservient, and polite. In cultural contexts in which women's roles are prominent and valued, their language reflects and reinforces their position.

GENDER AND POLITENESS IN JAPANESE, AND THOSE NAUGHTY TEENAGE GIRLS

Gender registers in spoken Japanese reflect gender differences (Shibamoto 1987). Certain words and sentence structures convey femininity, humbleness, and politeness. One important contrast between male and female speech is the attachment, by female speakers, of the honorific prefix "o-" to nouns (see Figure 4). This addition gives women's speech a more refined and polite tone.

	Male	Female
Box lunch	bentoo	obentoo
Money	kane	okane
Chopsticks	hasi	ohasi
Book	hon	ohon

Source: *Language, Gender, and Sex in Comparative Perspective*, by Susan U. Philips, Susan Steele, Chrisitne Tanz. Copyright © Cambridge University Press 1987. Reprinted with permission of Cambridge University Press.

FIGURE 4 Male-Unmarked and Female-Marked Nouns in Japanese

A contrasting pattern of gendered language comes from the *Kogals*, young Japanese women between 14 and 22 years of age, known for their female-centered coolness (Miller 2004). The Kogals have distinctive language, clothing, hairstyles, make-up, attitude, and activities, all of which challenge prescriptive norms for young women. Their overall style is flashy and exuberant, combining global and local elements. Heavy users of cell phones, Kogals have created an extensive set of emoticons, or "face characters," far more complex than the American smiley face. Read vertically, they include icons for "wow," "ouch," "applause," and "I can't hear you." They have also invented a unique text message code for their cell phones that uses mixed scripts such as mathematical symbols and Cyrillic (Russian) letters.

The spoken language of Kogals is a rich and quickly changing mixture of slang, some classic but much newly created. They create new words through compounds and by adding the Japanese suffix "-ru," which turns a noun into a vowel, such as *maku-ru* ("go to McDonald's). They intentionally use strongly masculine language forms, openly talk about sex, and rework taboo sexual terms into new meanings. Reactions from mainstream society to Kogals are mixed, ranging from horror to fascination. No matter what, they have cultural influence and are shaking up the gender order.

"FAT TALK" AMONG EURO-AMERICAN ADOLESCENT GIRLS

In the United States, Euro-American adolescent girls' conversations exhibit a high level of concern with their body weight and image (Nichter 2000). A study of 253 girls in the eighth and ninth grades in two urban high schools of

THINKING OUTSIDE THE BOX

These broad generalizations about Euro-American conversational styles do not apply to all situations. What are your microcultural rules?

A Kogal in Tokyo's trendy Shibuyu district displays her cell phone that is covered with stickers. Her facial make-up and dress are characteristic of some, but not all, Kogals. Various Kogal make-up and dress styles, like their language, exist and keep changing.

the Southwest reveals the contexts and meanings of fat talk. Fat talk usually starts with a girl commenting, "I'm so fat." The immediate response from her friends is "No, you're not." Girls who use fat talk are typically not overweight and are not dieting. The weight of the girls in the study was within "normal" range, and none suffered from a serious eating disorder. Fat talk occurs frequently throughout a day. Sometimes it appears to function as a call for reinforcement from friends that the initiator is an accepted group member. In other cases, it occurs at the beginning of a meal. In this context, fat talk may function to absolve the girl from guilty feelings and to give her a sense of agency.

GAY LANGUAGE AND BELONGING IN INDONESIA

The national language of Indonesia is referred to as *bahasa Indonesia*. Many homosexual men in Indonesia speak *bahasa gay*, or "gay language" (Boellstorff 2004). Indonesia is the world's fourth largest country in terms of population, with nearly 250 million citizens living in over 6000 islands and speaking nearly 700 local languages. In spite of this cultural and linguistic diversity, bahasa gay is highly standardized.

Bahasa gay has a distinct vocabulary that plays humorously on mainstream language and provides a political commentary on mainstream life. Some of the vocabulary changes involve sound-alikes; others add a suffix to a standard word. In terms of the state's strongly heterosexual image, Indonesian gays would seem to be a clearly excluded group. Nonetheless, bahasa gay is moving into mainstream linguistic culture, where it conveys agency and freedom from official control.

CUING AMONG THE AKWESASNE MOHAWKS

Linguistic *cues* are words or phrases that preface a remark to indicate the speaker's attitude toward what is being said. Standard English cues include *maybe* and *in my opinion* (Woolfson et al. 1995). Three functions of cuing exist in Mohawk English, a version of English spoken by the Akwesasne people of the St. Lawrence River area (see Map 4). They are:

- The speaker's unwillingness or inability to verify the certainty of a statement
- Respect for the listener
- The inability to make statements that have to do with matters that are in the domain of religion

Frequent miscommunication occurs between the Akwesasne people and Anglo medical professionals. Analysis of doctor–patient conversations reveals the role that Akwesasne cuing plays and how it is misinterpreted by the professionals. Here is a response to a question posed by an anthropologist about the kinds of diseases Akwesasne people had in the past, with the cues italicized:

> Hmm . . . That [tuberculosis] . . . was mostly, it well . . . they always said cirrhosis. . . . *It seems* like no matter what anybody died from . . . if they drank, it was cirrhosis. *I don't know* if anybody *really* knew a long time ago what anybody really died from. Even if the doctor requested an autopsy, the people would just say no . . . you know . . . it won't be done. So *I don't think* it was . . . you know . . . it was just what the doctor thought that would go down on the death certificate. (1995:506)

The White medical practitioners misinterpret such clues as indications of indecisiveness or noncooperation. The Akwesasne speakers are following linguistic rules about truthfulness, humility, and the sacred.

AFRICAN AMERICAN ENGLISH: PREJUDICE AND PRIDE

The topic of African American English (AAE), or African American Vernacular English (AAVE), is complicated by racism of the past and present (Jacobs-Huey 2006). Scholars debate whether AAE/AAVE is a language in its own right or a dialect of English. "Linguistic conservatives" who champion standard American Mainstream English (AME) view AAE as an ungrammatical form of English that needs to be "corrected." In the current linguistic hierarchy in the United States, with

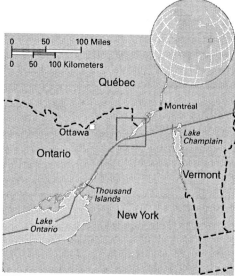

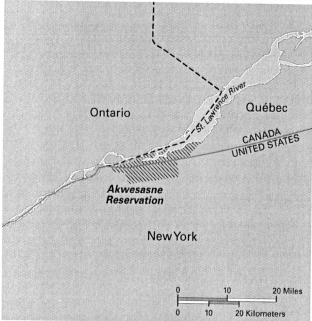

MAP 4 Akwesasne Territory in New York State and Ontario, Canada.
The Akwesasne Territory has an international border running through it with New York State on one side and two provinces of Canada on the other: Ontario and Québec. The Mohawk Council of Akwesasne comprises 12 District Chiefs and a Grand Chief. Since the 1960s, the Akwesasne Territory has been negatively affected by environmental pollution of the water, soil, and food supply from industries along the St. Lawrence River. In 1987, the Akwesasne formed a Task Force to restore and protect the environment and the survival of their culture.

AME at the top, speakers of AAE may be both proud of their language and feel stigmatized by those who judge AAE negatively and treat its speakers unfairly (Lanehart 1999).

African American English is a relatively new language, emerging out of slavery to develop a degree of standardization across the United States, along with many local variants. Some of its characteristic grammar results from its African roots.

One of the most prominent is the use, or nonuse, of forms of the English verb "to be" (Lanehart 1999:217). In AAE, one says, "She married," which in AME means "she is married." Viewed incorrectly by outsiders as "bad" English, the sentence "She married" follows a grammatical rule in AAE. The fact that AME has its own grammar and usage rules is evident in the fact that when non-AME speakers attempt to speak it or imitate it, they often make mistakes (Jacobs-Huey 1997).

Ethnographic research among African American school-age children in a working-class neighborhood of southwest Philadelphia examined within-gender and cross-gender conversations, including *directives* (getting someone to do something), argument, he-said-she-said accusations, and storytelling (Goodman 1990). All of these speech activities involve complex verbal strategies that are culturally embedded. In arguments, the children may bring in imaginary events as a "put-on," preceded by the cue term "psych," or use words of a song to create and maintain playfulness within an argument. Much of their arguments involve highly ritualized insults that work quickly to return an insult to the original giver. When a group of girls were practicing some dance steps and singing, a boy said, "You sound terrible." A girl responded, "We sound just like you look" (1990:183). The study revealed the importance of verbal play and art among the children. It also showed that girls often excel at verbal competitions in mixed gender settings.

Children who grow up speaking a version of AAE at home and with peer groups face a challenge in schools where they are expected to perform in AME. Just like native Spanish speakers or any non–English-speaking new immigrants, African American children are implicitly expected to become bilingual in AAE and AME. More than vocabulary and grammar are involved. Teachers should understand that African American children may have culturally distinct styles of expression that should be recognized and valued. For example, in narrative style, African American children tend to use a spiral pattern, skipping around to different topics before addressing the theme, instead of a linear style. Rather than being considered a deficiency, having AAE speakers in a classroom adds cultural diversity to those whose linguistic worlds are limited to AME.

Inspired by such findings, the Oakland School Board in California approved a resolution in 1996 to recognize *Ebonics*, or AAE, as the primary language, or vernacular, of African American students. The school developed a special teaching program, called the Bridge Program, in which AAE speakers were encouraged to learn Standard American English through a process of translation between AAE and SAE (Rickford 1997). After several months, students in the Bridge Program had progressed in their SAE reading ability much faster than African American students who were not in the program. Nevertheless, the program received so much negative publicity and raised such sensitive questions about the best way to enhance minority student learning that it was cancelled within the year.

The underlying issues of the so-called *Ebonics controversy* are still unresolved. One of the thorniest questions debated is whether AAE/AAVE/Ebonics is sufficiently distinct (either as a separate language from SAE or a vernacular form) that schools should address it in their curriculum with special programs. If so, can it be dealt with in a positive way as a rich part of Black cultural heritage? Or should it be suppressed in public schools in favor of promoting SAE? No easy answers exist. According to John Rickford, a sociolinguist at Stanford University and an expert on AAE, the Bridge Program of using AAE to teach SAE was well intentioned and demonstrated persuasively that the approach works (1997).

◆ ◆ ◆

Language Change

Languages, like the cultures of which they are a part, experience both continuity and change, and for similar reasons. Human creativity and contact lead to linguistic innovation and linguistic borrowing. War, imperialism, genocide, and other disasters may destroy languages. This section looks first at what is known about the origins of human language and provides a brief history of writing. Later sections discuss the role of European colonialism on languages, nationalism and language, world languages, and contemporary language loss and revitalization.

THE ORIGINS AND HISTORY OF LANGUAGE

No one knows how verbal language began. Current evidence of other aspects of human cultural evolution suggests that verbal language began to develop between 100,000 and 50,000 years ago when early modern humans had both the physical and mental capacity for symbolic thinking and verbal communication. Facial expressions, gestures, and body postures were likely important features of hominin communication as they are among many nonhuman primate species today.

Early scholars of language were often misled by ethnocentric assumptions that the structure of European languages was normative and that languages with different structures were less developed and deficient. For example, they considered the Chinese language "primitive" because it lacks the kinds of verbs that European languages have. As discussed at the beginning of this chapter, the Pirahã language appears "simpler" in many ways when compared to English, as does the Pirahã culture, but both Pirahã and English have to be examined within their cultural contexts. Pirahã is a language that works for a rainforest foraging population. English works for a globalizing, technology-driven, consumerist culture. Languages of foraging cultures today can, with caution, provide insights about what foragers' language may have been like thousands of years ago. But they are not "frozen in time" examples of "stone age" language.

Eriko Sugita/Reuters/CORBIS

© Gallo Images/CORBIS

(LEFT) An African bonobo male waves branches in a display of power. (RIGHT) In the United States, women lacrosse players use sticks in a competitive sport invented by American Indians.

▶ *Threat is clearly conveyed by the bonobo's behavior. In lacrosse, are sticks also used to communicate threats?*

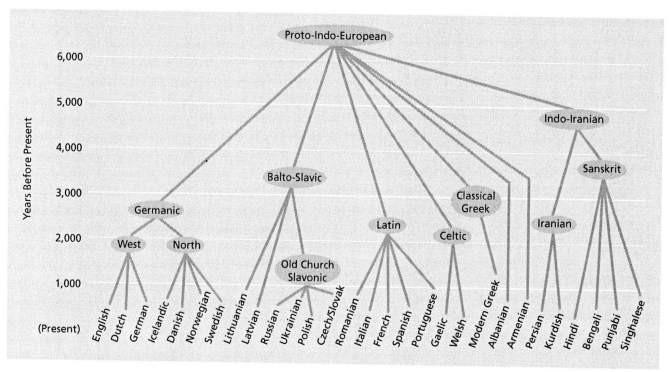

FIGURE 5 The Indo-European Language Family.

HISTORICAL LINGUISTICS

Historical linguistics is the study of language change through history. It relies on many specialized methods that compare shifts over time and across space in aspects of language such as phonetics, syntax, and meaning. It originated in the eighteenth century with a discovery made by Sir William Jones, a British colonial administrator working in India. During his spare time, he studied Sanskrit, a classical language of India. He noticed strong similarities among Sanskrit, Greek, and Latin in vocabulary and syntax. For example, the Sanskrit word for "father" is *pitr;* in Greek it is *patér,* and in Latin it is *pater.* This was an astounding discovery for the time, given the prevailing European mentality that placed its cultural heritage firmly in the classical Graeco-Roman world and depicted the "Orient" as completely separate from "Europe" (Bernal 1987).

Following Jones's discovery, other scholars began comparing lists of words and grammatical forms in different languages: the French *père,* the German *Vater,* the Italian *padre,* the Old English *faeder,* the Old Norse *fadhir,* the Swedish *far.* These lists allowed scholars to determine degrees of closeness and distance in their relationships. Later scholars contributed the concept of **language families,** or languages descended from a parent language (see Figure 5). Descendant languages that are part of the same language are referred to as *sister languages,* such as French and Spanish.

Using comparative evidence from historical and contemporary Eurasian languages, historical linguists developed a hypothetical model of the original parent language, or

proto-language, of most Eurasian languages. It is called *Proto-Indo-European* (PIE). Linguistic evidence suggests that PIE was located in Eurasia, either north or south of the Black Sea (see Map 5). From its area of origin, between 6000 and 8000 years ago, PIE spread into Europe, central and eastern Asia, and South Asia, where local variants developed over the centuries.

Similar linguistic methods reveal the existence of the original parent form of the Bantu language family, Proto-Bantu (Afolayan 2000). Scholars can trace the *Bantu expansion* in Africa starting around 5000 years ago (see Map 6). Today, some form of Bantu language is spoken by over 100 million people in Africa, not to mention the number of people in the African diaspora worldwide. Over 600 African languages are derived from Proto-Bantu. According to linguistic analysis, the homeland of Proto-Bantu is the present-day countries of Cameroon and Nigeria, West Africa. It is likely that Proto-Bantu spread through population migration as the farming population expanded and moved, over hundreds of years, into areas occupied by indigenous foragers. Bantu cultural imperialism may have wiped out some local languages, although it is impossible to document possible extinctions. Substantial linguistic evidence, however, suggests some

---

historical linguistics the study of language change using formal methods that compare shifts over time and across space in aspects of language such as phonetics, syntax, and semantics.

language family languages descended from a parent language.

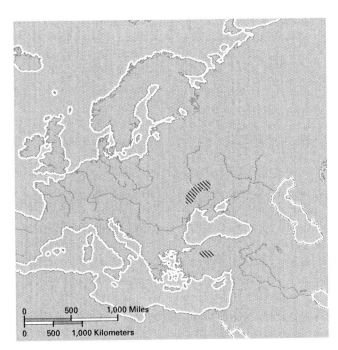

MAP 5 Two Sites of Proto-Indo-European Origins.
Two major theories about the location of PIE exist, with
the site south of the Black Sea considered to be earlier.

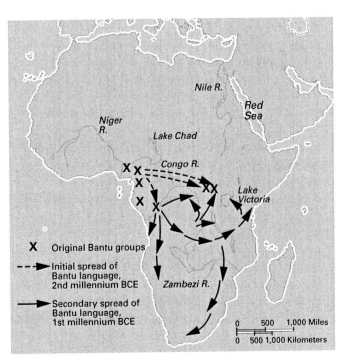

MAP 6 The Bantu Migrations in Africa.
Linguistic evidence for the migrations of Bantu-speaking
people relies on similarities between languages in parts of
eastern, central, and southern Africa and languages of the
original Bantu homeland in West Africa. Over 600 African
languages are derived from Proto-Bantu.

interactions between the farmers and the foragers through
which standard Bantu absorbed elements from local languages.

WRITING SYSTEMS

Evidence of the earliest written languages comes from
Mesopotamia, Egypt, and China. The oldest writing system
was in use in the fourth millennium BCE in Mesopotamia
(Postgate, Wang, and Wilkinson 1995). All early writing
systems used **logographs**, signs that indicate a word, syllable,
or sound. Over time, some logographs retained their original
meaning; others were kept but given more abstract meaning,
and nonlogographic symbols were added (see Figure 6).

The emergence of writing is associated with the development of the state. Some scholars take writing as a key diag-
nostic feature that distinguishes the state from nonstate
political forms because recordkeeping was such an essential
task of the state. The Inca empire, centered in the Peruvian
Andes, is a notable exception to this generalization. It used
khipu (KEE-poo), or cords of knotted strings of different
colors, for keeping accounts and recording events. Scholars
are not quite sure how khipu worked in the past because their
coding system is so complicated. Debates are ongoing as to
whether khipu served as an actual language or more simply as
an accounting system. Whatever is the answer, the world's
largest empire in the fourteenth century relied on khipu.

Two interpretations of the function of early writing
systems exist. The first says that early writing was mainly for
ceremonial purposes because of its prevalence on tombs, bone
inscriptions, or temple carvings. The second says that early

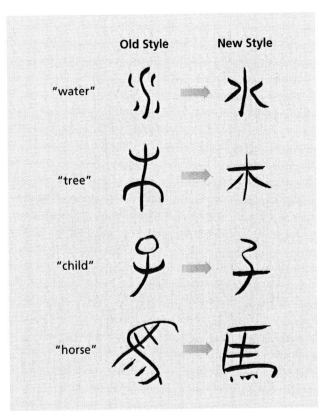

FIGURE 6 Logographic and Current Writing Styles in China

writing was mainly for secular use in government record-keeping and trade. The archaeological record is biased toward durable substances such as stone. Because ceremonial writing was intended to last, it was more likely to be inscribed on stone. Utilitarian writing, in contrast, was more likely to have been done on perishable materials because people would be less concerned with permanence (consider the way you treat shopping lists). Compared to what has been preserved, more utilitarian writing and other forms of nonceremonial writing must have existed.

The scripts of much of South and Southeast Asia originated in the Aramaic system of the Middle East (Kuipers and McDermott 1996). It spread eastward to India, where it took on new forms, and continued to move into much of Southeast Asia, including Indonesia and the Philippines but excluding Vietnam. The functions of the scripts vary from context to context. Writing for recordkeeping and taxation exists but is subordinate to, and carries less status than, writing for communication with the spirits, to record medical knowledge, and for love poetry. Writing love poetry is exalted and esteemed, and sometimes done in secret. Some love songs in the Philippine highlands have strict rules regulating such matters as how many syllables may be used per line. All adolescents seek to learn the rules of writing love poetry and to be able to write it well.

COLONIALISM, NATIONALISM, AND GLOBALIZATION

European colonialism was a major force of language change. Not only did colonial powers declare their own language as the language of government, business, and education, but they often took direct steps to suppress indigenous languages and literatures. Widespread bilingualism, or competence in a language other than one's birth language, is one prominent effect of colonialism. Globalization is also having substantial and complex effects on language.

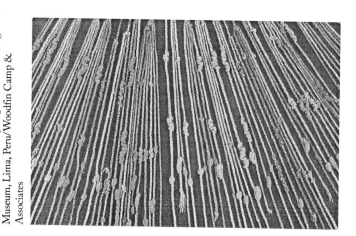

Khipu, or knotted strings, were the basis of state-level accounting in the Incan empire. The knots convey substantial information for those who could interpret their meaning.

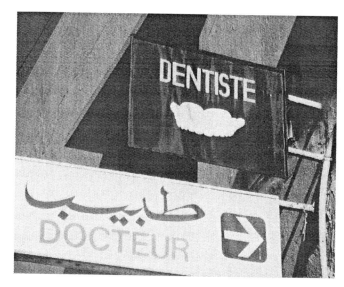

French colonialism added another cultural layer to Arabic influences in Morocco, resulting in many bilingual and trilingual shop signs.

▶ *Where have you seen multilingualism in public use? What languages were used and why?*

EUROPEAN COLONIALISM AND CONTACT LANGUAGES Beginning in the fifteenth century, European colonialism had dramatic effects on the people with whom it came into contact, as discussed elsewhere in this book. Language change is an important part of the story of colonialism and indigenous cultures. Depending on the type and duration of contact, it resulted in the development of new languages, the decline of others, and the extinction of many, along with the people who spoke them (Silverstein 1997). Two forms of new languages prompted by European colonialism are pidgins and creoles.

A **pidgin** is a language that blends elements of at least two parent languages and that emerges when two different cultures with different languages come in contact and must communicate (Baptista 2005). All speakers have their own native language(s) but learn to speak pidgin as a second, rudimentary language. Pidgins are typically limited to specific functional domains, such as trade and basic social interactions. Many pidgins of the Western Hemisphere were the result of the Atlantic slave trade and plantation slavery. Owners needed to communicate with their slaves, and slaves from various parts of Africa needed to communicate with each other.

---

logograph a symbol that conveys meaning through a form or picture resembling that to which it refers.

khipu cords of knotted strings used during the Inca empire for keeping accounts and recording events.

pidgin a contact language that blends elements of at least two languages and that emerges when people with different languages need to communicate.

A pidgin often evolves into a **creole**, which is a language descended from a pidgin with its own native speakers, richer vocabularies, and more developed grammar. Throughout the Western Hemisphere, many localized creoles have developed in areas such as Louisiana, Haiti, Ecuador, and Suriname. Though a living reminder of the heritage of slavery, Creole languages and associated literature and music are also evidence of resilience and creativity in the African diaspora.

Pidgins are common throughout the South Pacific. Tok Pisin, the pidgin language of Papua New Guinea, consists of a mixture of English, Samoan, Chinese, and Malayan. Tok Pisin is now a creole language and recognized as one of the official languages of Papua New Guinea.

NATIONALISM AND LINGUISTIC ASSIMILATION

Nationalist policies of cultural assimilation of minorities have led to suppression and loss of local dialects and the extinction of many indigenous and minority languages throughout the world. Direct policies of linguistic assimilation include declaration of a lingua franca, or standard language and rules about the language of instruction in public schools. Indirect mechanisms include discrimination in hiring on the basis of language and social stigma.

The Soviet attempt to build a USSR-wide commitment to the state after the 1930s included mass migration of Russian speakers into remote areas, where they eventually outnumbered indigenous peoples (Belikov 1994). Russian officials burned books in local languages. Many children were forcibly sent away to boarding schools, where they were taught in Russian. The indigenous Komi traditionally formed the majority population in an area around the Pechora River (see Map 7). Russian immigration brought in so many outsiders that the Komi were outnumbered. The Russians initiated the use of the Russian language in schools, and the Komi people became bilingual. Eventually, the Komi language was so heavily influenced by Russian that it may be extinct.

This story can be repeated for many indigenous languages of the former Soviet Union. Enforced attendance at boarding schools was also a strategy of the United States, Canada, and Australia in their attempts to assimilate indigenous peoples. Often, Christian missionaries worked to suppress indigenous languages as part of their attempts to "civilize" "pagan" peoples (see Culturama).

GLOBAL LANGUAGES Ninety-six percent of the world's population speaks 4 percent of the world's languages

---

creole a language directly descended from a pidgin but possessing its own native speakers and involving linguistic expansion and elaboration.

global language or **world language** a language spoken widely throughout the world and in diverse cultural contexts, often replacing indigenous languages.

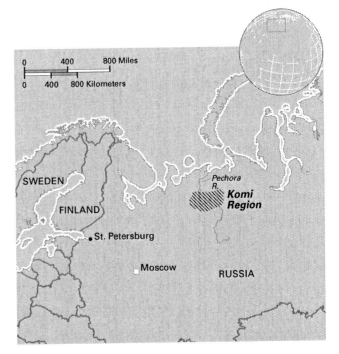

MAP 7 Komi Region in Russia.
The Komi were traditionally reindeer hunters. The Komi language belongs to the Finno-Ugric language family and is closer to Finnish and Estonian than to Russian.

(Crystal 2000:14). The eight most-spoken languages are Mandarin, Spanish, English, Bengali, Hindi, Portuguese, Russian, and Japanese. Languages that are gaining widespread currency are called **global languages,** or **world languages**. Global languages are spoken worldwide in diverse cultural contexts. As they spread to areas and cultures beyond their home area and culture, they take on new, localized identities. At the same time, the "mother language" picks up words and phrases from local languages (see Figure 7). Global languages may act as both a form of linguistic and economic opportunity and a form of cultural imperialism.

English is the most globalized language in history (Bhatt 2001; Crystal 2003). British English was first transplanted through colonial expansion to the present-day United States, Canada, Australia, New Zealand, South Asia, Africa, Hong Kong, and the Caribbean. English was the dominant language in the colonies, used in government and commerce and taught in schools. Over time, regional and subregional varieties of English have developed, often leading to a "New English" that a native speaker from England cannot understand at all. So many varieties of English now exist that scholars are beginning to talk of the English language family that includes American English, Spanglish, Japlish, and Tex-Mex.

ENDANGERED LANGUAGES AND LANGUAGE REVITALIZATION

The emergence of linguistic anthropology was prompted by the need to document disappearing indigenous languages in the United States. Today, anthropologists and other scholars,

CULTURAMA

The Saami of Lapland, or Sapmi

The Saami (SAH-mee) are indigenous, "fourth world" people who live in the northernmost stretches of Norway, Sweden, Finland, and western Russia (Gaski 1993). The area is called Lapland or Sapmi, the land of the Saami. The total Saami population is around 100,000 people, with the majority in Norway (Magga and Skutnabb-Kangas 2001).

At the time of the earliest written records of 1000 years ago, all Saami hunted wild reindeer, among other land and sea species, and may have kept some tamed reindeer for transport (Paine 2004). Over time, herding domesticated reindeer developed and became the economic mainstay. In the past few hundred years, though, reindeer pastoralism declined to being a specialization of about 10 percent of the population. Settled Saami are farmers or work in trade,

small-scale industry, handicrafts, services, and the professions.

Traditional Saami reindeer herding has been a family-based system. Men and women cared for the herd, and sons and daughters inherited equally the rights to the herd (Paine 2004). The value of social equality was strong, entailing both rights and privileges.

In their relationships with the modern state, the Saami have experienced discrimination, exclusion, loss of territorial rights, and cultural and linguistic repression. Specific risks to Saami cultural survival include being downwind of the prevailing winds after the 1986 Chernobyl disaster, being near the earlier Soviet atomic testing grounds in Siberia, having their ancestral territory and sacred spaces suffer environmental degradation from hydroelectric dam construction, and having grazing lands

taken over for use as military training grounds (Anderson 2004).

State policies of cultural assimilation and forced Christianization in the twentieth century marginalized the Saami language and led to language loss (Magga and Skutnabb-Kangas 2001). Several Saami languages and dialects still exist, however, and spatially distant versions are mutually unintelligible (Gaski 1993:116).

Language is of central cultural value to the Saami, and efforts to maintain it have been under way since the 1960s. Besides the Saami language, a traditional song form, the *yoik*, is of particular importance (Anderson 2005). Yoik lyrics allow a subtle system of double meanings that can camouflage political content (Gaski 1997).

Thanks to Myrdene Anderson, Purdue University, for reviewing this material.

Barbara Miller

© Anders Ryman/Alamy

(LEFT) The well-known Saami singer-songwriter Marie Boine performs at the Easter Festival in Kautokeino, Sapmi, northern Norway.
(CENTER) A Saami herder with his reindeer in Kautokeino, the northern most municipality in Norway and the first municipality to be given a Saami name.

MAP 8 Saami Region in Lapland, or Sapmi. Sapmi spreads across Norway, Sweden, Finland, and Russia's Kola Peninsula.

Alcohol	Arabic, Middle East
Avocado	Nahuatl, Mexico/Central America
Banana	Mandingo, West Africa
Bogus	Hausa, West Africa
Candy	Arabic, Middle East
Caucus	Algonquin, Virginia/Delaware, North America
Chimpanzee	Bantu, West and Central Africa
Chocolate	Aztec Nahuatl, Mexico/Central America
Dungaree	Hindi, North India, South Asia
Gong	Malaysia, Southeast Asia
Hammock	Arawakan, South America
Hip/hep	Wolof, West Africa
Hurricane	Taino, Caribbean
Lime	Inca Quechua, South America
Moose	Algonquin, Virginia/Delaware, North America
Panda	Nepali, South Asia
Savannah	Taino, Caribbean
Shampoo	Hindi, North India, South Asia
Sugar	Sanskrit, South Asia
Tepee	Sioux, Dakotas, North America
Thug	Hindi, North India, South Asia
Tobacco	Arawak, South America
Tomato	Nahuatl, Mexico/Central America
Tundra	Saami, Lapland, Northern Europe
Tycoon	Japanese
Typhoon	Mandarin Chinese, East Asia
Zombie	Congo and Angola, Central and West Africa

FIGURE 7 Loan Words in North American English

as well as descendant language communities themselves, are still concerned about the rapid loss of languages (Fishman 1991; Maffi 2005). The task of documenting declining languages is urgent. It is often accompanied by applied work to preserve and revive endangered and dying languages (see Critical Thinking).

---

language shift or **language decay** condition of a language in which speakers adopt a new language for most situations, begin to use their native language only in certain contexts, and may be only semi-fluent and have limited vocabulary in their native language.

language endangerment condition of a language when it has fewer than 10,000 speakers.

language extinction condition of a language in which speakers abandon it in favor of a new language to the extent that the native language loses functions and no longer has competent users.

Scholars have proposed ways to assess degrees of language loss or decline (Walsh 2005). The general stages proceed from shift to extinction. **Language shift**, or **language decay**, is a category of language decline when speakers have limited vocabulary in their native language and more often use a new language in which they may be semifluent or fluent (Hill 2001). An intermediary stage, **language endangerment**, is judged to exist when a language has fewer than 10,000 speakers. Near-extinction is a situation in which only a few elderly speakers are still living. **Language extinction**, or language death, occurs when the language no longer has any competent users (Crystal 2000:11).

Keeping track of endangered and dying languages is difficult because no one is sure how many languages have existed in the recent past and even now (Crystal 2000). Estimates of the number of living languages today range between 5000 and 7000. Part of the explanation for the fuzzy numbers is the problem in separating languages from dialects. The largest number of languages of any world region is found on the island of New Guinea, which includes the island of New Guinea (comprising Papua New Guinea and West Papua) and several neighboring small islands (Foley 2000). Some 1000 languages exist in this area, many from completely separate language families.

Language extinction is especially acute in the Australia/Pacific region, where 99.5 percent of the indigenous languages have fewer than 100,000 speakers (Nettle and Romaine 2000:40). The situation of indigenous languages in the Americas, Siberia, Africa, and South and Southeast Asia is increasingly serious. Over half of the world's languages have fewer than 10,000 speakers, and one-fourth have fewer than 1000 speakers.

Linguistic diversity is closely tied to cultural survival and diversity. It is also closely tied to biological diversity. The

© Bryan and Cherry Alexander Photography/Alamy

Indigenous language dictionaries and usage guides are increasingly available on the Web and help indigenous peoples preserve their cultures.

▶ Check out *The Internet Guide to Australian Languages*.

CRITICAL Thinking

Should Dying Languages Be Revived?

The Western media often carry articles about endangered biological species, such as certain frogs or birds, and the need to protect them from extinction. The reasons for concern about loss of biological species are many. One major factor is simply that biological diversity is a good thing to have on the earth. Opponents of taking special measures to protect endangered species find support for their position in a Darwinian view that progress involves competition and fitness as measured in the long-term survival of species that succeed in reproducing over time. Consider this imagined scenario: An economic development project involves building a new shopping center or airport with a massive parking lot that will bring about the extinction of a particular kind of plant. In the Darwinian view, that loss is simply the price of progress as the

stronger drives out the weaker. But is it all so simple? What if that particular plant held a unique cure for cancer, and now it is gone forever? If the cure had been discovered, it would have contributed to the survival of many humans. What looks "weak" may in fact be important and valuable.

Some parallels exist between the survival of endangered biological species and endangered languages. Supporters of language preservation and revitalization point to the sheer fact of diversity on earth as a good thing, a sign of a culturally healthy planet with room for many languages. They also argue that a people's language is an intrinsic part of their culture. Without language, the culture, too, will die. They argue that dying cultures, like dying languages, are treasures lost forever to humanity.

The Darwinian view, in contrast, says that languages, like species, live in a world of competition. Language survival means that the strong and fit carry on while the weak and unfit die out. They are likely to point out that preserving linguistic heritage is useless because dying languages are part of a past that no longer exists. They resist spending public funds on language preservation and regard revitalization programs as wasteful.

◆ CRITICAL THINKING QUESTIONS

- Have you read or heard of an endangered biological species in the media recently? What was the species?
- Have you read or heard of an endangered language in the media lately? What was the language?
- Where do you stand on biological species preservation and on language preservation, and why?

greatest linguistic diversity is found in the same regions as the greatest biodiversity (Maffi 2005). These are areas where indigenous people live, the "keepers" of much of the world's cultural and biological heritage, including the knowledge of how to live a culturally and biologically sustainable life. Yet they are also the people, languages, and biological species most in danger of extinction in the near future.

Efforts to revive or maintain local languages face many challenges (Fishman 2001). Political opposition may come from governments that fear local identity movements. Governments are often averse to devoting financial resources to supporting minority language programs. Deciding which version of an endangered language to preserve may have political consequences at the local level (Nevins 2004). Notable achievements have been made, however, with perhaps one of the most robust examples of language maintenance occurring in French-speaking Québec.

Approaches to language maintenance and revitalization must respond to local circumstances and factors such as how serious the degree of loss is, how many living speakers there are, what version of the language should be maintained or revived, and what resources for maintenance and revitalization programs are available. Major strategies include (Walsh 2005):

- Formal classroom instruction
- Master-apprentice system in which an elder teaches a nonspeaker in a one-on-one situation
- Web-based tools and services to support language learning

Each method has both promise and pitfalls. One thing is key: It takes living communities to activate and keep alive the knowledge of a language (Maffi 2003).

the BIG questions REVISITED

How do humans communicate?

Human communication is the sending of meaningful messages through language. Language is a systematic set of symbols and signs with learned and shared meanings. It may be spoken, hand-signed, written, or conveyed through body movements, marking, or accessories.

Human language has two characteristics that distinguish it from communicative systems of other living beings. It has productivity, or the ability to create an infinite number of novel and understandable messages, and displacement, the ability to communicate about the past, the future, and imaginary things.

Language consists of basic sounds, vocabulary, and syntax. Cross-culturally, however, languages vary substantially in the details of all three features.

Humans use many forms of nonverbal language to communicate with each other. Sign language is a form of communication that uses mainly hand movements to communicate. Silence is a form of nonverbal communication with its own cultural values and meaning. Body language includes body movements and placement in relation to other people, body modifications such as tattoos and piercing, dress, hairstyles, and odors.

Media anthropology sheds light on how culture shapes media messages and the social dynamics in media institutions. Critical media anthropology examines the power relations involved in the media.

How does communication relate to cultural diversity and inequality?

In order to study language in society, anthropologists have to deal with the observer's paradox, or the difficulty of collecting data on language without affecting the object of study in the process. Translation is another challenge.

The Sapir-Whorf hypothesis emphasizes how language shapes culture. A competing model, called sociolinguistics, emphasizes how one's culture and one's position in it shape language. Each position has merit, and many anthropologists draw on both models.

Critical discourse analysis studies the relations of power and inequality in language. Language can reveal social difference and reinforce exclusion. It can also empower oppressed people, depending on the context. In mainstream North America, women's speech is generally more polite and accommodating than that of men. In Japan, gender codes emphasize politeness in women's speech, but many young Japanese women, Kogals, are creating a new linguistic style of resistance. Gay language in Indonesia is entering the mainstream as an expression of freedom from official control. Linguistic cuing among the Akwesasne Mohawks has been frequently misinterpreted by Anglo medical practitioners as a sign of indecisiveness or noncooperation. African American English (AAE) has evolved from the tragic heritage of slavery to become a standard language with many local variants.

How does language change?

The exact origins of human verbal language will never be known. The discovery of language families provides insights about human history and settlement patterns. The emergence of writing can be traced to around 6000 years ago, with the emergence of the state in Mesopotamia. Scripts have spread widely throughout the world, with the Aramaic system the basis of scripts in South and Southeast Asia. The functions of writing vary from context to context. In some situations, official recordkeeping predominates, whereas in others, writing is important for courtship.

The recent history of language change has been influenced by the colonialism of past centuries and by Western globalization of the current era. Nationalist policies of cultural integration often involve the repression of minority languages and promotion of a lingua franca. Colonial contact created the context for the emergence of pidgin languages, many of which evolved into creoles. Western globalization supports the spread of English and the development of localized variants.

In the past 500 years, colonialism and globalization have resulted in the extinction of many indigenous and minority languages. Many others are in danger of dying. Applied linguistic anthropologists seek to preserve the world's linguistic diversity. They document languages and participate in designing programs for teaching dead and dying languages. A key element in language revitalization and survival is having communities use the language.

KEY CONCEPTS

call system

communication

creole

critical discourse analysis

critical media anthropology

digital divide

displacement

ethnosemantics

global language, or world language

historical linguistics

khipu

language

language endangerment

language extinction

language family

language shift or language decay

logograph

phoneme

pidgin

productivity

Sapir-Whorf hypothesis

sign language

sociolinguistics

tag question

SUGGESTED READINGS

Keith H. Basso, *Wisdom Sits in Places: Landscape and Language among the Western Apache.* Albuquerque: University of New Mexico Press, 1996. Fieldwork on the Fort Apache Indian Reservation, Arizona, reveals the importance of natural places in people's everyday life, thought, and language.

David Crystal, *English as a Global Language,* 2nd ed. New York: Cambridge University Press, 2003. This book discusses the history, current status, and future of English as a world language. It covers the role of English in international relations, the media, international travel, education, and "New Englishes."

Joshua A. Fishman, ed. *Can Threatened Languages Be Saved?* Buffalo, NY: Multilingual Matters Ltd., 2001. Seventeen case studies examine language shift and language loss and the attempts to reverse such changes.

Marjorie H. Goodwin. *He-Said-She-Said: Talk as Social Organization among Black Children.* Bloomington: Indiana University Press, 1990. A study of everyday talk among children of an urban African American community in the United States, this book shows how children construct social relationships among themselves through verbal interactions, including disputes, pretend play, and stories.

Niloofar Haeri, *Sacred Language, Ordinary People: Dilemmas of Culture and Politics in Egypt.* New York: Palgrave Macmillan, 2003. Classical Arabic is the official language of all Arab states and the language of the Qur'an, but no Arabs speak it as their mother tongue. This book uses research in Cairo to show how the state maintains its identity in people's everyday lives through classical Arabic.

Lanita Jacobs-Huey. *From the Kitchen to the Parlor: Language and Becoming in African-American Women's Hair Care.* New York: Oxford University Press, 2006. Jacobs-Huey combines childhood experiences as the daughter of a cosmetologist with multisited fieldwork in the United States and England. She finds a complex world centered on hair that relates to race, gender, religion, body esthetics, health, and verbal language.

William L. Leap. *Word's Out: Gay Men's English.* Minneapolis: University of Minnesota Press, 1996. Fieldwork among gay men in the Washington, DC, area produced this ethnography. It addresses gay men's speech as a cooperative mode of discourse, bathroom graffiti, and discourse about HIV/AIDS.

Julie Lindquist. *A Place to Stand: Politics and Persuasion in a Working-Class Bar.* New York: Oxford University Press, 2002. The author did participant observation while working as a bartender in a White, working-class bar in the U.S. Midwest. The book is an ethnography of speaking in which the bar is a site of cultural performance related to White, working-class identity.

Karen Nakamura. *Deaf in Japan: Signing and the Politics of Identity.* Ithaca, NY: Cornell University Press. 2007. This book combines archival and ethnographic data to understand ideas about modernity and Westernization.

Lisa Philips Valentine. *Making It Their Own: Ojibwe Communicative Practices.* Toronto: University of Toronto Press, 1995. This ethnography examines speech events in a small Ojibwe community in northern Ontario, Canada. It considers speech variations among speakers, code switching, multilingualism, and church music.

GLOSSARY

GLOSSARY

acculturation a form of cultural change in which a minority culture becomes more like the dominant culture.

Acheulian tradition a toolkit of *H. erectus*, used from 1.7 million years ago to 300,000 years ago, and characterized by handaxes.

achieved position a person's standing in society based on qualities that the person has gained through action.

adolescence a culturally defined period of maturation from the time of puberty until adulthood that occurs in some but not all cultures.

age set a group of people close in age who go through certain rituals, such as circumcision, at the same time.

agency the ability of humans to make choices and exercise free will even within dominating structures.

agriculture a mode of livelihood that involves growing crops with the use of plowing, irrigation, and fertilizer.

amazon a person who is biologically female but takes on a male gender role.

Anatomically Modern Humans (AMH) or *Homo sapiens* or **modern humans** the species to which modern humans belong and also referred to by that term; first emerged in Africa between 300,000–160,000 years ago and then spread throughout the Old and New Worlds.

animatism a belief system in which the supernatural is conceived of as an impersonal power.

animism the belief in souls or "doubles."

anomie the breakdown of traditional values associated with rapid social change.

anthropogenic caused by humans.

anthropology the study of humanity, including prehistoric origins and contemporary human diversity.

applied anthropology or **practicing anthropology** or **practical anthropology** the use of anthropological knowledge to prevent or solve problems or to shape and achieve policy goals.

applied medical anthropology the application of anthropological knowledge to furthering the goals of health care providers.

archaeology or **prehistory** the study of past human cultures through their material remains.

archaic *Homo* a category of several extinct hominin species that lived from 2.4 million years to 19,000 years ago and is characterized by different stone tool traditions, depending on the species.

art the application of imagination, skill, and style to matter, movement, and sound that goes beyond what is purely practical.

artifact a portable object made or modified by humans.

ascribed position a person's standing in society based on qualities that the person has gained through birth.

assimilation a form of culture change in which a culture is thoroughly acculturated, or decultured, and is no longer distinguishable as having a separate identity.

australopithecines a category of several extinct hominin species found in Africa that lived between 4.5 and 3 million years ago.

authority the ability to take action based on a person's achieved or ascribed status or moral reputation.

balanced exchange a system of transfers in which the goal is either immediate or eventual equality in value.

band the political organization of foraging groups, with minimal leadership and flexible membership.

banditry a form of aggressive conflict that involves socially patterned theft, usually practiced by a person or group of persons who are socially marginal and who may gain a mythic status.

berdache a blurred gender category, usually referring to a person who is biologically male but who takes on a female gender role.

big-man or **big-woman system** a form of political organization midway between tribe and chiefdom involving reliance on the leadership of key individuals who develop a political following through personal ties and redistributive feasts.

bilineal descent a kinship system in which a child is recognized as being related by descent to both parents.

biological anthropology or **physical anthropology** the study of humans as biological organisms, including evolution and contemporary variation.

biological determinism a theory that explains human behavior and ideas mainly as shaped by biological features such as genes and hormones.

bipedalism upright locomotion on two feet.

blood sport a form of competition that explicitly seeks to bring about a flow of blood, or even death, of human–human contestants, human–animal contestants, or animal–animal contestants.

bracero an agricultural laborer who is permitted entry to a country to work for a limited time.

brachiation arboreal travel, using the forelimbs to swing from branch to branch, that is distinct to apes.

brideprice or **bridewealth** the transfer of cash and goods from the groom's family to the bride's family and to the bride.

brideservice a form of marriage exchange in which the groom works for his father-in-law for a certain period of time before returning home with the bride.

call system a form of oral communication among nonhuman primates with a set repertoire of meaningful sounds generated in response to environmental factors.

cargo cult a form of revitalization movement that emerged in Melanesia and New Zealand following World War II in response to Western and Japanese influences.

cash crop a plant grown primarily for sale rather than for one's own use.

caste system a form of social stratification linked with Hinduism and based on a person's birth into a particular group.

chain migration a population movement in which a first wave of migrants comes and then attracts relatives and friends to join them in the destination.

chiefdom a political unit of permanently allied tribes and villages under one recognized leader.

circular migration a regular pattern of population movement between two or more places, either within or between countries.

civil society the collection of interest groups that function outside the government to organize economic and other aspects of life.

class   a way of categorizing people on the basis of their economic position in society, usually measured in terms of income or wealth.

Clovis culture   the New World population characterized by the Clovis point with the earliest site dated to 11,000 years ago in the Southwest United States.

collaborative research   an approach to learning about culture that involves anthropologists working with members of the study population as partners and participants rather than as "subjects."

communication   the conveying of meaningful messages from one person, animal, or insect to another.

community healing   healing that emphasizes the social context as a key component and which is carried out within the public domain.

consumerism   a mode of consumption in which people's demands are many and infinite and the means of satisfying them are insufficient and become depleted in the effort to satisfy these demands.

consumption fund   a category of a personal or household budget used to provide for consumption needs and desires.

couvade   customs applying to the behavior of fathers during and shortly after the birth of their children.

creole   a language directly descended from a pidgin but possessing its own native speakers and involving linguistic expansion and elaboration.

critical development anthropology   an approach to international development in which the anthropologist takes on a critical-thinking role and asks why and to whose benefit particular development policies and programs are pursued.

critical discourse analysis   the study of the relations of power and inequality in language.

critical legal anthropology   an approach within legal anthropology that examines how law and judicial systems serve to maintain and expand dominant power interests rather than protecting marginal and less powerful people.

critical media anthropology   an approach within the cross-cultural study of media that examines how power interests shape people's access to media and the contents of its messages.

critical medical anthropology   approach within medical anthropology involving the analysis of how economic and political structures shape people's health status, their access to health care, and the prevailing medical systems that exist in relation to them.

critical military anthropology   the study of the military as a power structure in terms of its roles and internal social dynamics.

Cro-Magnons   the first modern humans in Europe, dating from 40,000 years ago.

cross-cousin   the offspring of either one's father's sister or one's mother's brother.

cultural anthropology or **social anthropology**   the study of living peoples and their cultures, including variation and change.

cultural constructionism   a theory that explains human behavior and ideas mainly as shaped by learning.

cultural fit   a characteristic of informed and effective project design in which planners take local culture into account; opposite of one-size-fits-all project design.

cultural materialism   a theoretical position that takes material features of life, such as the environment, natural resources, and mode of production, as the bases for explaining social organization and ideology.

cultural relativism   the perspective that each culture must be understood in terms of the values and ideas of that culture and should not be judged by the standards of another.

culture   people's learned and shared behavior and beliefs.

culture shock   the persistent feelings of uneasiness, loneliness, and anxiety that often occur when a person has shifted from one culture to a different one.

culture-specific syndrome   a collection of signs and symptoms that is restricted to a particular culture or a limited number of cultures.

dalit   the preferred name for the socially defined lowest groups in the Indian caste system, meaning "oppressed" or "ground down."

deductive approach (to research)   a research method that involves posing a research question or hypothesis, gathering data related to the question, and then assessing the findings in relation to the original hypothesis.

demographic transition   the change from the agricultural pattern of high fertility and high mortality to the industrial pattern of low fertility and low mortality.

descent   the tracing of kinship relationships through parentage.

development   directed change to achieve improved human welfare.

development aggression   the imposition of development projects and policies without the free, prior, and informed consent of the affected people.

development project   a set of activities designed to put development policies into action.

development-induced displacement (DID)   a forced migration due to development projects, such as dam building.

diaspora population   a dispersed group of people living outside their original homeland.

diffusion   the spread of culture through contact.

digital divide   a social inequality in access to new and emerging information technology, notably access to up-to-date computers, the Internet, and training related to their use.

disease   in the disease/illness dichotomy, a biological health problem that is objective and universal.

disease of development   a health problem caused or increased by economic development activities that affect the environment and people's relationship with it.

displaced person   someone who is forced to leave his or her home and community or country.

displacement   a feature of human language that allows people to talk about events in the past and future.

doctrine   direct and formalized statements about religious beliefs.

domestication   the process by which human selection causes changes in the genetic material of plants and animals.

dowry   the transfer of cash and goods from the bride's family to the newly married couple and to the groom's family.

ecological/epidemiological approach   an approach within medical anthropology that considers how aspects of the natural environment and social environment interact to cause illness.

economic system   the linked processes of livelihood, consumption, and exchange.

emic   insiders' perceptions and categories, and their explanations for why they do what they do.

endogamy   marriage within a particular group or locality.

entitlement   a culturally defined right to life-sustaining resources.

ethnicity   a shared sense of identity among a group based on a heritage, language, or culture.

ethnocentrism   judging other cultures by the standards of one's own culture rather than by the standards of that particular culture.

ethno-esthetics   culturally specific definitions of what art is.

ethno-etiologies   culturally specific causal explanations for health problems and suffering.

ethnography   a firsthand, detailed description of a living culture, based on personal observation.

ethnomedicine the study of cross-cultural health systems.

ethnomusicology the cross-cultural study of music.

ethnosemantics the study of the meaning of words, phrases, and sentences in particular cultural contexts.

etic an analytical framework used by outside analysts in studying culture.

evolution an inherited and cumulative change in the characteristics of a species, population, or culture.

exogamy a marriage outside a particular group or locality.

expected reciprocity an exchange of approximately equally valued goods or services, usually between people roughly equal in social status.

expressive culture the behavior and beliefs related to art, leisure, and play.

extended household a coresidential group that comprises more than one parent–child unit.

extensive strategy a form of livelihood involving temporary use of large areas of land and a high degree of spatial mobility.

extractive industry a business that explores for, removes, processes, and sells minerals, oil, and gas that are found on or beneath the earth's surface and are nonrenewable.

faction a politically oriented group with strong lateral ties to a leader.

family a group of people who consider themselves related through a form of kinship, such as descent, marriage, or sharing.

family farming a form of agriculture in which farmers produce mainly to support themselves and also produce goods for sale in the market system; formerly called *peasant farming.*

female genital cutting a term used for a range of genital cutting procedures, including the excision of part or all of the clitoris, excision of part or all of the labia, and sometimes infibulation, the stitching together of the vaginal entry.

fertility the rate of births in a population, or the rate of population increase in general.

feuding long-term, retributive violence that may be lethal between families, groups of families, or tribes.

fieldwork the research in the field, which is any place where people and culture are found.

foraging obtaining food available in nature through gathering, hunting, or scavenging.

formal sector the salaried or wage-based work registered in official statistics.

fossil the preserved remains of a plant or animal of the past.

functionalism the theory that a culture is similar to a biological organism, in which parts work to support the operation and maintenance of the whole.

gender culturally constructed and learned behaviors and ideas attributed to males, females, or blended genders.

gender pluralism the existence within a culture of multiple categories of femininity, masculinity, and blurred genders that are tolerated and legitimate.

generalized reciprocity an exchange involving the least conscious sense of interest in material gain or thought of what might be received in return.

globalization the increased and intensified international ties related to the spread of Western, especially United States, capitalism that affects all world cultures.

global language or **world language** a language spoken widely throughout the world and in diverse cultural contexts, often replacing indigenous languages.

great apes a category of large and tailless primates that includes orangutans, gorillas, chimpanzees, bonobos, and humans.

groomprice the transfer of cash and goods, often large amounts, from the bride's family to the groom's family.

Hawthorne effect a research bias due to participants changing their behavior to conform to expectations of the researcher.

heterotopia a new situation formed from elements drawn from multiple and diverse contexts.

hijra a term used in India to refer to a blurred gender role in which a person, usually biologically male, takes on female dress and behavior.

historical linguistics the study of language change using formal methods that compare shifts over time and across space in aspects of language such as phonetics, syntax, and semantics.

historical trauma the intergenerational transfer of the negative effects of colonialism from parents to children.

holism the perspective in anthropology that cultures are complex systems that cannot be fully understood without paying attention to their different components, including economics, social organization, and ideology.

hominins a category of primates that includes modern humans and extinct species of early human ancestors that are more closely related to humans than to living chimpanzees and bonobos.

horticulture a mode of livelihood based on growing domesticated crops in gardens, using simple hand tools.

household a group of people, who may or may not be related by kinship, who share living space.

humoral healing the healing that emphasizes balance among natural elements within the body.

illness in the disease/illness dichotomy, culturally shaped perceptions and experiences of a health problem.

incest taboo a strongly held prohibition against marrying or having sex with particular kin.

indigenous knowledge (IK) the local understanding of the environment, climate, plants, and animals.

indigenous people groups who have a long-standing connection with their home territory that predates colonial or outside societies that prevail in that territory.

inductive approach (to research) a research approach that avoids hypothesis formation in advance of the research and instead takes its lead from the culture being studied.

industrial capital agriculture a form of agriculture that is capital-intensive, substituting machinery and purchased inputs for human and animal labor.

industrialism/informatics a mode of livelihood in which goods are produced through mass employment in business and commercial operations and through the creation and movement of information through electronic media.

infanticide the killing of an infant or child.

influence the ability to achieve a desired end by exerting social or moral pressure on someone or some group.

informal sector work that is not officially registered, and sometimes illegal.

informed consent an aspect of fieldwork ethics requiring that the researcher inform the research participants of the intent, scope, and possible effects of the study and seek their consent to be in the study.

in-kind taxation a system of mandatory noncash contributions to the state.

institutional migrant someone who moves into a social institution (such as a school or prison), voluntarily or involuntarily.

intangible cultural heritage UNESCO's view of culture as manifested in oral traditions, languages, performing arts, rituals and festive events, knowledge and practices about nature and the universe, and craftmaking; also called living heritage.

intensive strategy a form of livelihood that involves continuous use of the same land and resources.

internal migration the population movement within country boundaries.

internally displaced person someone who is forced to leave his or her home and community but who remains in the same country.

international migration the population movement across country boundaries.

interpretive anthropology or **interpretivism** the view that cultures can be understood by studying what people think about, their ideas, and the meanings that are important to them.

interview a research technique that involves gathering of verbal data through questions or guided conversation between at least two people.

invention the discovery of something new.

khipu the cords of knotted strings used during the Inca empire for keeping accounts and recording events.

kinship system the predominant form of kin relationships in a culture and the kinds of behavior involved.

knuckle-walking a form of nonhuman primate terrestrial travel that involves walking flat-footed while supporting the upper body on the front of fingers bent beyond the knuckle.

kula a trading network, linking many of the Trobriand Islands, in which men have long-standing partnerships for the exchange of everyday goods such as food as well as highly valued necklaces and armlets.

language a form of communication that is a systematic set of learned symbols and signs shared among a group and passed on from generation to generation.

language endangerment condition of a language when it has fewer than 10,000 speakers.

language extinction condition of a language in which speakers abandon it in favor of a new language to the extent that the native language loses functions and no longer has competent users.

language family languages descended from a parent language.

language shift or **language decay** condition of a language in which speakers adopt a new language for most situations, begin to use their native language only in certain contexts, and may be only semi-fluent and have limited vocabulary in their native language.

law a binding rule created through enactment or custom that defines right and reasonable behavior and is enforceable by threat of punishment.

legal pluralism a situation in which more than one way exists of defining acceptable and unacceptable behavior and ways to deal with the latter.

leveling mechanism an unwritten, culturally embedded rule that prevents an individual from becoming wealthier or more powerful than anyone else.

life project the local people's definition of the direction they want to take in life, informed by their knowledge, history, and context.

lifeboat mentality a view that seeks to limit enlarging a particular group because of perceived resource constraints.

life-cycle ritual a ritual that marks a change in status from one life stage to another; also called rite of passage.

linguistic anthropology the study of human communication, including its origins, history, and contemporary variation and change.

localization the transformation of global culture by local cultures into something new.

logograph a symbol that conveys meaning through a form or picture resembling that to which it refers.

magic the attempt to compel supernatural forces and beings to act in certain ways.

male bias in development the design and implementation of development projects with men as beneficiaries and without regard to their impact on women's roles and status.

market exchange the buying and selling of commodities under competitive conditions in which the forces of supply and demand determine value.

marriage a union between two people (usually), who are likely to be, but are not necessarily, coresident, sexually involved with each other, and procreative.

material cultural heritage the sites, monuments, buildings, and movable objects considered to have outstanding value to humanity; also called cultural heritage.

matrescence motherhood, or the cultural process of becoming a mother.

matriarchy a society in which women are dominant in terms of economics, politics, and ideology.

matrifocality a household pattern in which a female (or females) is the central, stable figure around whom other members cluster.

matrilineal descent a kinship system that highlights the importance of women by tracing descent through the female line, favoring marital residence with or near the bride's family, and providing for property to be inherited through the female line.

mechanical solidarity the social bonding among groups that are similar.

medicalization labeling a particular issue or problem as medical and requiring medical treatment when, in fact, that issue or problem is economic or political.

medical pluralism the existence of more than one health system in a culture, or a government policy to promote the integration of local healing systems into biomedical practice.

menarche the onset of menstruation.

menopause the cessation of menstruation.

mestizaje literally, racial mixture; in Central and South America, indigenous people who are cut off from their Indian roots, or literate and successful indigenous people who retain some traditional cultural practices.

microculture a distinct pattern of learned and shared behavior and thinking found within larger cultures.

migration the movement of a person or people from one place to another.

minimalism a mode of consumption that emphasizes simplicity, is characterized by few and finite consumer demands, and involves an adequate and sustainable means to achieve them.

mode of consumption the dominant pattern, in a culture, of using things up or spending resources in order to satisfy demands.

mode of exchange the dominant pattern, in a culture, of transferring goods, services, and other items between and among people and groups.

mode of livelihood the dominant way of making a living in a culture.

mode of reproduction the predominant pattern of fertility and mortality in a culture.

modernization a model of change based on belief in the inevitable advance of science and Western secularism and processes including industrial growth, consolidation of the state, bureaucratization, market economy, technological innovation, literacy, and options for social mobility.

moka a strategy for developing political leadership in highland Papua New Guinea that involves exchanging gifts and favors with individuals and sponsoring large feasts where further gift giving occurs.

money a medium of exchange that can be used for a variety of goods.

monogamy the marriage between two people.

Mousterian tradition the toolkit of the Neanderthals characterized by the predominance of small, light, and more specialized flake tools such as points, serapers, and awls.

multisited research the fieldwork conducted in more than one location in order to understand the behaviors and ideas of dispersed members of a culture or the relationships among different levels such as state policy and local culture.

museum an institution that collects, preserves, interprets, and displays objects on a regular basis.

myth a narrative with a plot that involves the supernaturals.

nation a group of people who share a language, culture, territorial base, political organization, and history.

natural selection the process by which organisms better adapted to the environment reproduce more effectively compared with less well-adapted forms.

Neolithic Revolution the period of rapid transformation in technology, related to plant and animal domestication, which includes tools such as sickle blades and grinding stones.

new immigrant an international migrant who has moved since the 1960s.

norm a generally agreed-upon standard for how people should behave, usually unwritten and learned unconsciously.

nuclear household a domestic unit containing one adult couple (married or partners), with or without children.

Oldowan tradition the oldest hominin toolkit, characterized by core tools and flake tools.

organic solidarity the social bonding between and among groups with different abilities and resources.

parallel cousin the offspring of either one's father's brother or one's mother's sister.

participant observation the basic fieldwork method in cultural anthropology that involves living in a culture for a long period of time while gathering data.

pastoralism a mode of livelihood based on keeping domesticated animals and using their products, such as meat and milk, for most of the diet.

patrescence fatherhood, or the cultural process of becoming a father.

patrilineal descent a kinship system that highlights the importance of men in tracing descent, determining marital residence with or near the groom's family, and providing for inheritance of property through the male line.

personality an individual's patterned and characteristic way of behaving, thinking, and feeling.

phoneme a sound that makes a difference for meaning in a language.

phytotherapy healing through the use of plants.

pidgin a contact language that blends elements of at least two languages and that emerges when people with different languages need to communicate.

pilgrimage round-trip travel to a sacred place or places for purposes of religious devotion or ritual.

placebo effect or **meaning effect** a positive result from a healing method due to a symbolic or otherwise nonmaterial factor.

policing the exercise of social control through processes of surveillance and the threat of punishment related to maintaining social order.

political organization the existence of groups for purposes of public decision making and leadership, maintaining social cohesion and order, protecting group rights, and ensuring safety from external threats.

polyandry a marriage of one wife with more than one husband.

polygamy a marriage involving multiple spouses.

polygyny a marriage of one husband with more than one wife.

potlatch a grand feast in which guests are invited to eat and to receive gifts from the hosts.

poverty the lack of tangible and intangible assets that contributing to life and the quality of life.

power the capacity to take action in the face of resistance, through force if necessary.

priest/priestess a male or female full-time religious specialist whose position is based mainly on abilities gained through formal training.

primary group a social group in which members meet on a face-to-face basis.

primates an order of mammals that includes modern humans.

productivity a feature of human language that offers the ability to communicate many messages efficiently.

project cycle the steps of a development project from initial planning to completion: project identification, project design, project appraisal, project implementation, and project evaluation.

pronatalism an ideology promoting many children.

puberty a time in the human life cycle that occurs universally and involves a set of biological markers and sexual maturation.

pure gift something given with no expectation or thought of a return.

push–pull theory an explanation for rural-to-urban migration that emphasizes people's incentives to move based on a lack of opportunity in rural areas (the "push") compared to urban areas (the "pull").

qualitative data non-numeric information.

quantitative data numeric information.

questionnaire a formal research instrument containing a pre-set series of questions that the anthropologist asks in a face-to-face setting, by mail, or by email.

"race" a classification of people into groups on the basis of supposedly homogeneous and largely superficial biological traits such as skin color or hair characteristics.

rainforest an environment, found at mid-latitudes, of tall, broadleaf evergreen trees, with annual rainfall of 400 centimeters (or 60 inches) and no dry season.

rapport a trusting relationship between the researcher and the study population.

redistribution a form of exchange that involves one person collecting goods or money from many members of a group, who then, at a later time and at a public event, "returns" the pooled goods to everyone who contributed.

refugee someone who is forced to leave his or her home, community, or country.

religion the beliefs and behavior related to supernatural beings and forces.

religious pluralism when one or more religions coexist as either complementary to each other or as competitive systems.

religious syncretism the blending of features of two or more cultures, especially used in discussion of religious change.

remittance the transfer of money or goods by a migrant to his or her family in the country of origin.

repatriation returning art or other objects from museums to the people with whom they originated.

revitalization movement a socioreligious movement, usually organized by a prophetic leader, that seeks to construct a more satisfying situation by reviving all or parts of a religion that has been threatened by outside forces or by adopting new practices and beliefs.

revolution a political crisis prompted by illegal and often violent actions of subordinate groups that seek to change the political institutions or social structure of a society.

right of return the United Nations guaranteed right of a refugee to return to his or her home country to live.

ritual a patterned behavior that has to do with the supernatural realm.

ritual of inversion a ritual in which normal social roles and order are temporarily reversed.

sacrifice a ritual in which something is offered to the supernaturals.

Sapir-Whorf hypothesis a theory in linguistic anthropology that says language determines thought.

savanna an environment that consists of open plains with tall grasses and patches of trees.

secondary group people who identify with each other on some basis but may never meet with one another personally.

sedentism a lifestyle associated with residence in permanent villages, towns, and cities, generally linked with the emergence of farming.

segmentary model a type of political organization in which smaller units unite in the face of external threats and then disunite when the external threat is absent.

sex ratio the number of males per 100 females in a population.

shaman/shamanka a male or female healer who have a direct relationship with the supernaturals.

sign language a form of communication that uses mainly hand movements to convey messages.

social capital the intangible resources existing in social ties, trust, and cooperation.

social control the processes that maintain orderly social life, including informal and formal mechanisms.

social group a cluster of people beyond the domestic unit who are usually related on grounds other than kinship.

social impact assessment a study conducted to gauge the potential social costs and benefits of particular innovations before change is undertaken.

social stratification the hierarchical relationships between different groups as though they were arranged in layers, or "strata."

sociality a preference for living in groups and interacting regularly with members of the same species.

sociolinguistics a theory in linguistic anthropology that says that culture and society and a person's social position determine language.

somatization the process through which the body absorbs social stress and manifests symptoms of suffering; also called embodiment.

status a person's position, or standing, in society.

stem household a coresidential group that comprises only two married couples related through males, commonly found in East Asian cultures.

structural suffering the human health problems caused by such economic and political situations as war, famine, terrorism, forced migration, and poverty.

structurism a theoretical position concerning human behavior and ideas that says large forces such as the economy, social and political organization, and the media shape what people do and think.

susto a fright/shock disease; a culture-specific syndrome found in Spain and Portugal and among Latino people wherever they live; symptoms include back pain, fatigue, weakness, and lack of appetite.

symbol an object, word, or action with culturally defined meaning that stands for something else; most symbols are arbitrary.

tag question a question seeking affirmation, placed at the end of a sentence.

tell a human-made mound resulting from the accumulation of successive generations of house construction, reconstruction, and trash.

theater a form of enactment, related to other forms such as dance, music, parades, competitive games and sports, and verbal art, that seeks to entertain through acting, movement, and sound.

toponymy the naming of places.

trade the formalized exchange of one thing for another according to set standards of value.

traditional development anthropology an approach to international development in which the anthropologist accepts the role of helping to make development work better by providing cultural information to planners.

transnational migration a form of population movement in which a person regularly moves between two or more countries and forms a new cultural identity transcending a single geopolitical unit.

trial by ordeal a way of determining innocence or guilt in which the accused person is put to a test that may be painful, stressful, or fatal.

tribe a political group that comprises several bands or lineage groups, each with similar language and lifestyle and occupying a distinct territory.

unbalanced exchange a system of transfers in which one party seeks to make a profit.

unilineal descent a kinship system that traces descent through only one parent, either the mother or the father.

Upper Paleolithic the period of modern human occupation in Europe and Eurasia (including the Middle East) from 45,000–40,000 years ago to 12,000 years ago, characterized by microlithic tools and prolific cave art and portable art.

use rights a system of property relations in which a person or group has socially recognized priority in access to particular resources such as gathering, hunting, and fishing areas and water holes.

wa a Japanese word meaning discipline and self-sacrifice for the good of the group.

war an organized and purposeful group action directed against another group and involving lethal force.

Western biomedicine (WBM) a healing approach based on modern Western science that emphasizes technology for diagnosing and treating health problems related to the human body.

world religion a term coined in the nineteenth century to refer to a religion that is text-based, has many followers, is regionally widespread, and is concerned with salvation.

youth gang a group of young people, found mainly in urban areas, who are often considered a social problem by adults and law enforcement officials.

Page references followed by "f" indicate illustrated figures or photographs; followed by "t" indicates a table.

marriage in, 162
Cash crop, 139, 298
Casino capitalism, 132
Cassava, 95
Caste system
    Buddhism and, 257-258
    in India, 98, 145, 187, 252, 300
    varna categories, 187
Catholicism
    divorce and, 160
Cattle, 25, 51-53, 89, 124, 209
Cave art, 48-49, 303
Center for California Native Nations (CCNN), 133
Central African Republic, 134, 234
Central America
    migrant laborers from, 102
Chain migration, 298
Chauvet, 49
Chenchu
    marital sex and, 210
Child labor, 101, 119
Childbirth, 198
Children
    adoption of, 134, 260
    in agricultural societies, 100, 147
    in foraging societies, 93, 129
    in horticultural societies, 98, 202
    naming, 136, 146, 303
    violence against, 211
Chimpanzees, 4, 35-40, 274, 300
China
    dowry in, 156
    ethnicity in, 103
    Hui Muslims of Xi'an, 243
    logographic and current writing styles in, 288
    women's movement in, 189
Christianity
    branches of, 260
    Jesus Christ, 260
    missionaries, 162, 254-255
    Protestantism, 261
    Protestantism among white Appalachians, 261
    sacred sites and, 267
Chukchee
    extramarital sex, 210-212
Circular migration, 298
Circumpolar regions
    consumerism and, 118
    natural resources in, 92
Civil society
    activist groups, 173
    Chinese women's movement, 189
    CO-MADRES, 189
    new social movements and cyberpower, 191
Clan structure, 221
Clarke, Kamari, 264
Class
    characteristics, 28, 173-174, 237, 294, 300
    consumption and, 116-122, 180
    health problems and, 299
    language and, 90, 276-277
    modernization and, 139
Class struggle, 20
Clinton, Hillary, 231
Closed adoption, 149
Clothing
    complex, 13-15, 34, 74, 102, 124, 163, 211-212, 228, 275
    culturally coded, 279
    simple, 23, 46-47, 74, 94, 123, 162, 274-275
    veiling, 279
    wedding, 66, 163, 210
Clovis point, 48-49, 299
Clubs and fraternities, 175-176
Collaborative research, 82, 299
Collateral extended household, 157
Communication
    critical discourse analysis, 294-295, 299
    definition, 13, 40, 301
    language and verbal communication, 274
    language change, 7, 273-274, 300
    Sapir-Whorf hypothesis, 294-295, 303
    sociolinguistics, 7, 294-295, 303
    with media and information technology, 279
Communitas, 260
Comparative study, 206-208
Complex clothing, 47
Complex households, 157
Condomblé, 265

Confederacy, 220-222
Connecticut, 123-124
Conservation of natural resources
    Yellowstone model, 248-249
Consumerism
    costs of, 157
Consumption
    changing patterns of, 115
    class and, 122, 181
    food taboos and, 138
    gender and, 110, 123
    inequalities in, 123
    modes of, 89-91, 116-117, 144-145
Consumption fund, 118-119, 299
Contemporary human biological variation, 5
Convention on the Protection of Underwater Heritage, 6
Cooking, 200
Cooperatives, 179
Core tool, 44
Councils
    tribal, 203
Countercultural groups, 173
Courts, 164, 228, 250, 277
Couvade, 299
Cows, 24-25, 34, 227
Craft cooperatives in Panama, 179
Creationism, 34
Creole, 290, 299
Creolization, 19
Critical cultural relativism, 23
Critical development anthropology, 299
Critical discourse analysis, 282, 299
Critical legal anthropology, 299
Critical media anthropology, 279-280, 299
Critical medical anthropology, 10, 299
Critical military anthropology, 299
Critique, 10, 111, 239
Cro-Magnon people, 49
Cross-cousin
    marriage of, 156-157, 302
Cross-cultural research, 207
Cátedra, María, 66
Cultivation, 202
Cultural anthropology
    and the future, 274
    areas of specialization, 7
    distinctive features of, 10
    history of, 10-13, 82, 183, 212, 218, 269, 286
    theoretical debates in, 24
Cultural change
    assimilation and, 291
    education and, 28, 123, 193, 234, 263
    invention and, 40
    migration and, 49, 183, 254
    technology and, 93
Cultural constructs
    meaning of, 207
Cultural diversity
    increasing, 213
Cultural fit, 262, 299
Cultural imperialism, 23, 287
Cultural interaction, 19
Cultural materialism
    definition of, 10, 40, 64, 99, 152, 244, 301
    myths and, 12, 80
Cultural relativism
    absolute, 23, 120
    critical, 10, 33, 63, 92, 120, 213, 273, 299
    gaining, 67, 105, 148, 188, 238, 266, 290
Cultural rights, 85
Cultural Survival, 23, 134, 275
Cultural tourism, 110
Culture
    and microcultures, 282
    archaic Homo, 41, 298
    aspects of, 210
    characteristics of, 14, 34-35, 174, 268, 274, 300
    cultural interaction, 19
    definitions of, 244, 282, 299
    expressive, 46, 177, 300
    nonhuman primate, 5, 39-40
    revolution, 212
Culture shock, 72-74, 299
Culture-specific syndrome, 299

D

Dalai Lama, 267
Dalby, Liza, 72-73

Dalit, 187, 299
Dalit Panthers, 188
Dance
    healing, 264, 302-303
Data
    emic, 74-75, 106, 299
    etic, 74-75
    qualitative, 74-75, 302
    quantitative, 74-76, 239, 302
Data analysis
    ethnography, 80-81, 105, 161, 180, 213, 239, 295, 299
Data collection
    archival and historical sources, 77
    combining observation and talking, 75
    field notes, 77
    interviews, 74-75, 189
    life history, 75-76
    multiple research methods, 77
    participant observation, 10, 64-65, 189, 245, 295, 302
    questionnaire, 74-75, 302
    team projects, 77
    texts, 76
    time allocation study, 76
Deaf culture, 277
Death
    infants, 203
Death penalty, 258
Deductive approach (to research), 74, 299
Defiant individualist, 177
Democratization, 235
Demographic transition, 299
Dependency, 209
Depersonalized consumption, 118-119
Descent
    bilineal, 145-147, 298
    marriage, 143, 223, 251, 300
    matrilineal, 143, 301
    modes of livelihood and, 144
    patrilineal, 145-148, 222, 302
    sharing, 124, 143, 249, 300
    unilineal, 145-147, 303
Descriptive linguistics, 7
Design
    interior, 26
Development
    cultural anthropology and, 26
    defining, 301
    development projects, 19, 69, 299
    diffusion, 299
    human, 4-6, 33, 80, 102-105, 189, 221, 253-254, 277-278, 299-300
    invention, 53, 104, 301
    life projects and, 29
    modernization, 301
    sustainable, 103, 293, 301
    women and, 12, 101-102, 148, 189, 226, 262
Development aggression, 299
Development anthropology, 7, 299
Development projects, 19, 69, 299
Diaspora population, 184-185, 299
Difference, 36, 72, 144, 180, 211, 245, 274-275, 302
Diffusion, 51, 299
Digital divide, 185, 281, 299
Disease
    of development, 299
Disease of development, 299
Displaced domains, 274
Displacement, in human language, 275
Distance from necessity, 122
Diviners, 254
Division of labor
    and gender, 204
    economy-of-effort theory, 200
    expendability theory, 200
    foragers, 201
    horticultural societies, 201-202
    in agriculture, 100
    in foraging, 93, 120
    in horticulture, 97-98, 201-202
    strength theory, 199-200
    women, 198-206
    worldwide patterns in, 199-200
Divorce, 16, 155, 247
Dmanisi hominins, 44
Doctrine, 246-247, 299
Dodd, Alice, 151
Dogs, 34, 73, 89, 201, 258

bands, 220-221, 303
big-man or big-woman system, 222, 298
states, 7, 34, 64-65, 91, 117-120, 144, 171-172, 198, 218, 244-245, 283-285, 299-300
tribes, 64, 99, 117, 221-222, 249, 298
Political process, variation in
leadership, 197
political participation, 204
Politics
authority and, 218
democratization, 235
emerging nations and transnational nations, 232
leadership, 82, 147, 179-180, 217-222, 264, 301-302
of journalism, 280
organization, 11-12, 180, 205-206, 217-222, 263, 295, 300
power and, 205, 218, 294
women in contemporary, 235
Polo, Marco, 10
Polyandry, 156-157, 302
Polygyny, 156-157, 302
Polytheism, 245
Postmodernism, 12
Potato, 52-53, 126
Poverty
health and, 122
Power
in the military, 204
of state, 186, 227-229, 244
Powhatan, 226
Prehistoric archaeology, 5
Premarital sex, 210
Priest/priestess, 255, 302
Primary group, 172, 302
Primate infants
play, 207-209
Primate learning
play in, 208-209
Primate social behavior
learning, 209
Prisons, 22, 172-173
Private property, 93, 207, 218
Privatization, 108
Project Camelot, 82
Project cycle, 302
Pronatalism, 302
Property ownership
agricultural societies, 207
Prophets, 254
Proselytizing, 255
Prosody, 275
Prostitution, 105
Protection of human subjects, 67
Protestantism
among white Appalachians, 261
Proto-Bantu, 287-288
Proto-language, 287
Psychological anthropology, 7
Puberty
rituals, 244, 298
Public anthropologist, 12
Public/private dichotomy, 101
Purdah, 231
Pure gift, 130, 302

Q
Qualitative data
analyzing, 80, 90
Queer anthropology, 12
Questionnaire, 74-75, 109, 302

R
"Race"
racial classification, 183
Racial inequality
United States, 207-208
Raffia cloth, 129
Rainforest, 8-9, 89, 134, 221-222, 275, 302
Rapport, 70-73, 302
Reciprocity
expected, 129-130, 300
Redistribution, 54, 130-131, 222, 302
Refugee
right of return, 303
Relationships, 198
Religion
origin and functions of, 245

religious specialists, 244
ritual practices, 250
Sikhism, 185
Tibetan Buddhism, 108, 267
umbanda, 265
Religious pluralism, 254-255, 302
Religious specialists, 244
Remittance, 302
Rent and tax fund, 119-120
Reproductive strategies
female, 200
Research
cross-cultural, 203
explanation, 200
false role assignments, 70
funding for, 9
informed consent, 66-67, 132, 299-300
rapport, 70
Research methods and techniques
archival research, 77, 145, 193, 269
armchair anthropology, 10, 64
collaborative research, 82, 299
data collection, 75-76
fieldwork, 8, 63-68, 90, 132, 149, 172, 230, 251, 295, 300
multisited research, 64-65, 302
war zone anthropology, 83
Research participant, 82, 135
Restudy, 66, 108
retention of "mother tongues"
sibling, 199
Revenue Sharing Trust Fund (RSTF), 133
Reverse culture shock, 74
Revitalization movement, 264, 298
Revolution, 6, 33, 175, 302-303
Rickford, John, 286
Right of return, 303
Ritual
life-cycle, 250-251, 301
Nayar fertility, 256
of inversion, 268-269, 303
pilgrimage, 259, 302
sacrifice, 259-260, 303
Ritual of inversion, 252, 303
Ritually established kinship, 151
Robertson, Jennifer, 68
Rock paintings, 49, 247
Roma
in Hungary, 186, 281
in Slovakia, 186
Roman Catholicism, 160, 230, 253
Ross, Marc, 205
Royal British Columbia Museum (RBCM), 137

S
Sacred space
contested, 225, 266
Sacrifice, 54, 244, 303
Salamandra, Christa, 70
Salt, 108, 128, 279
Salvage anthropology, 64
Same-sex marriage, 151
San Juan fiesta, 127
San peoples of southern Africa
hunters, 117, 221, 290
Sanday, Peggy, 176, 253
Sanskrit, 187, 255, 287
Santería, 265
Saraswati tattoo, 258
Savishinsky, Joel, 90
Scheper-Hughes, Nancy, 10
Scientific explanation, in anthropology
relationships, 198
Scratch notes, 79
Secondary group, 172, 303
Secondary subsistence activities, 201
Secular ritual, 249
Sedentary foragers, 52
Sedentism, 51-53, 303
Segmentary model, 221, 303
Self-help groups, 180
Semantics, 287, 300
Sentumbwe, Nayinda, 154
Sex, 22, 104-106, 151-152, 183, 300
extramarital, 210
premarital, 210
Sex differences, 197
Sex ratio, 303
Sex work, 104

Sexual behavior
intercourse, 14, 40, 152-153, 198
marital satisfaction and, 159
of bonobos, 59
Sexual dimorphism
among nonhuman primates, 35
Sexuality
homosexuality, 211
Shaman/shamanka, 268, 303
Sharing
kinship through food, 148
Sherpas of Nepal
employment, 161
Shifting cultivation, 202
Shostak, Marjorie, 76
Sibling relationships, 159
Sickle blades, 51, 302
Siddhartha Gautama, 256
Silence, 277-278
Silverback gorilla, 37
Simple clothing, 47
Siriono, 210
Sister languages, 287
Site selection, 67
Sites
stratified, 212
Six Cultures project, 208-209
Sleeping nests, 40
Slow Food Movement, 136
Smith, Adam, 189
Social capital, 303
Social class
determinants of, 213
Social conflict
banditry, 298
ethnic conflict, 184, 220
feuding, 300
interpersonal, 151, 218, 281
revolution, 6, 33, 175, 302-303
warfare, 18-19, 54-55, 148, 228
Social control
systems of, 138, 182-183, 224, 245, 294
Social group
clubs and fraternities, 175
cooperatives, 179
countercultural groups, 173
friendship, 174-175, 278
self-help groups, 180
work groups, 107, 160, 173
Social inequality
gender-based, 12, 93, 173
in Russia and Eastern Europe, 66, 135
variation in degree of, 205
Social stratification
achieved position, 180-181, 223, 298
ascribed position, 180-181, 298
civil society, 171-172, 298
status, 18-19, 53, 71-72, 94, 115-117, 148-149, 173, 197-198, 218, 247, 277, 298
Sociality, 35, 303
Societal cohesion, 181
Societies
egalitarian, 197
Somatization, 303
South Africa
Coat of Arms, 232
Taiwanese industrialists in, 109
South Africa, apartheid in, 202
South Baffin Island Place Name Project, 78
South Korea
Seoul, 119, 163, 219
Southeast Asia
local spirits and Buddhism in, 257
tattoos, 258, 278
Souvenirs, 104
Spain
Valencia, 79, 118
Sports
blood, 244
Spouse/partner relationships, 159
Sri Lanka, 20, 85, 111, 153, 172, 232, 255-256
State
failed, 121
gender and leadership in, 231
powers and roles of, 228
State formation
population growth, 212
Status
achieved, 180-181, 218, 262, 298

LALA! LALA!